SAGE was founded in 1965 by Sara Miller McCune to support the dissemination of usable knowledge by publishing innovative and high-quality research and teaching content. Today, we publish over 900 journals, including those of more than 400 learned societies, more than 800 new books per year, and a growing range of library products including archives, data, case studies, reports, and video. SAGE remains majority-owned by our founder, and after Sara's lifetime will become owned by a charitable trust that secures our continued independence.

Los Angeles | London | New Delhi | Singapore | Washington DC | Melbourne

TRANS-PACIFIC PARTNERSHIP AGREEMENT

Thank you for choosing a SAGE product!
If you have any comment, observation or feedback,
I would like to personally hear from you.

Please write to me at **contactceo@sagepub.in**

Vivek Mehra, Managing Director and CEO, SAGE India.

Bulk Sales

SAGE India offers special discounts
for purchase of books in bulk.
We also make available special imprints
and excerpts from our books on demand.

For orders and enquiries, write to us at

Marketing Department
SAGE Publications India Pvt Ltd
B1/I-1, Mohan Cooperative Industrial Area
Mathura Road, Post Bag 7
New Delhi 110044, India

E-mail us at **marketing@sagepub.in**

Get to know more about SAGE

Be invited to SAGE events, get on our mailing list.
Write today to **marketing@sagepub.in**

This book is also available as an e-book.

TRANS-PACIFIC PARTNERSHIP AGREEMENT

A framework for future trade rules?

Edited by
ABHIJIT Das
SHAILJA Singh

Los Angeles | London | New Delhi
Singapore | Washington DC | Melbourne

Copyright © Centre for WTO Studies, Indian Institute of Foreign Trade, 2018

All rights reserved. No part of this book may be reproduced or utilized in any form or by any means, electronic or mechanical, including photocopying, recording, or by any information storage or retrieval system, without permission in writing from the publisher.

First published in 2018 by

SAGE Publications India Pvt Ltd
B1/I-1 Mohan Cooperative Industrial Area
Mathura Road, New Delhi 110 044, India
www.sagepub.in

SAGE Publications Inc
2455 Teller Road
Thousand Oaks, California 91320, USA

SAGE Publications Ltd
1 Oliver's Yard, 55 City Road
London EC1Y 1SP, United Kingdom

SAGE Publications Asia-Pacific Pte Ltd
3 Church Street
#10-04 Samsung Hub
Singapore 049483

Published by Vivek Mehra for SAGE Publications India Pvt Ltd, typeset in 10/12 pts Times New Roman by Zaza Eunice, Hosur, Tamil Nadu, India and printed at Saurabh Printers Pvt Ltd, Greater Noida.

Library of Congress Cataloging-in-Publication Data Available

ISBN: 978-93-528-0011-7 (HB)

SAGE Team: Rajesh Dey, Vandana Gupta and Ritu Chopra

12 Trade Remedies, Trade Facilitation and Regulatory Coherence under the TPP *Mukesh Bhatnagar, Monika and R.V. Anuradha*	**291**
13 Conclusions and Way Forward *Abhijit Das, Shailja Singh and Harimaya Gurung*	**304**
About the Editors and Contributors	331
Index	334

Contents

List of Tables	vii
List of Figures	ix
List of Abbreviations	xi
Preface	xvii

1. **Introduction** — 1
   Abhijit Das and Shailja Singh
2. **TPP and Market Access for Goods** — 38
   Abhijit Das, Prajyna Paramita Barua and Dilfy Ann Philip
3. **Services Coverage in TPP, TiSA and GATS: A Comparative Analysis and Implications for India** — 76
   Pralok Gupta
4. **IPR and New Rule-making** — 112
   Chandni Raina
5. **Conforming India's IPR Laws to the TPP's IPR Standards: Issues and Concerns for India** — 155
   Jayant Raghu Ram
6. **Investment Protection in TPP: Analysis from an Indian Perspective** — 184
   Shailja Singh
7. **Standards under the TPP: Much Ado about Nothing?** — 217
   R.V. Anuradha
8. **Addressing 'Labour' in Trade Agreements: The TPP Approach** — 232
   R.V. Anuradha
9. **Trade and Environment under the TPP** — 247
   R.V. Anuradha
10. **Government Procurement Provisions in the GPA: Ceding Policy Space for Uncertain Gains** — 259
    Monika and Neeraj R.S.
11. **State-owned Enterprises (SOEs)** — 278
    Mukesh Bhatnagar

List of Tables

1.1	TPP countries in a changing economic world	10
2.1	India's exports to the TPP countries	48
2.2	Comparing the results of various studies by Petri, Plummer and Zhai	50
2.3	Impact of increase in costs due to compliance with labour standards in the TPP and TTIP	54
2.4	Summary of tariff reductions under the TPP	59
2.5	Overview of the agricultural safeguard measures available to the USA	61
2.6	Overall tariff profile of India and TPP countries	66
2.7	Assessing the number of products in which India may not be price-competitive	67
4.1	Transition periods for the IPR chapter in the TPP	116
6.1	List of prohibited performance requirements	201
6.2	List of performance requirements under TPP with the exceptions	202
6.3	List of transfers that cannot be prohibited/restricted or delayed by the host country	205
6.4	List of transfers that may be prevented or delayed by the host country	206
7.1	Impact of specific international standards	224
8.1	Status of ratifications of fundamental ILO conventions by developed countries under the TPP (including the USA)	238
10.1	Comparison of public procurement markets and their share in GDP in select TPP countries	262
10.2	Comparison of threshold levels of TPP countries with their GPA threshold levels	274

List of Figures

1.1	Three options for Entry into Force (EIF) of the TPP	6
2.1	India's trade as percentage of its GDP	40
2.2	India's exports of goods: Value and global share	42
2.3	India's imports of goods: Value and global share	43
2.4	India's exports of services: Value and global share	44
2.5	India's imports of services: Value and global share	45
10.1	Internationally committed public procurement market	263
10.2	Procurement market level of openness	263
10.3	Import penetration ratio of public procurement markets	266

List of Abbreviations

ACTA	Anti-Counterfeiting Trade Agreement
AD	anti-dumping
APEC	Asia-Pacific Economic Cooperation
ASCM	Agreement on Subsidies and Countervailing Measures
ASEAN	Association of Southeast Asian Nations
AUSFTA	Australia–US Free Trade Agreement
BATNA	best alternative to a negotiated agreement
BITs	bilateral investment treaties
BoP	balance of payments
Budapest Treaty	Budapest Treaty on International Recognition of the Deposit of Microorganisms for the Purposes of Patent Procedure
CABs	conformity assessment bodies
CAFTA	Central American Free Trade Agreement
CARICOM	Caribbean Community
CBD	Convention on Biological Diversity
CECA	Comprehensive Economic Cooperation Agreement
CEO	chief executive officer
CEPA	Comprehensive Economic Partnership Agreement
CETA	Comprehensive Economic Trade Agreement
CFE	Comisión Federal de Electricidad (The Federal Electricity Commission)
CITES	Convention on International Trade in Endangered Species of Wild Fauna and Flora
Codex	Codex Alimentarius
CPB	Cartagena Protocol on Biosafety
CSR	corporate social responsibility
CSS	contract service supplier
CTD	Common Technical Document
CVD	countervailing duty
DBT	direct bank transfer
DCGI	drug controller general of India

DDR	Doha Development Round
DR	domestic regulation
DUS	distinctness, uniformity and stability
EIF	entry into force
ENT	economic needs test
EU	European Union
EUFTAs	European Union free trade agreements
FBI	Federal Bureau of Investigation
FDA	Food and Drug Authority
FDI	foreign direct investment
FET	fair and equitable treatment
FIPB	Foreign Investment Promotion Board
FTA	free trade agreement
FTAAP	Free Trade Area of Asia-Pacific
G20	Group of Twenty
GATS	General Agreement on Trade in Services
GATT	General Agreement on Tariffs and Trade
GDP	gross domestic product
GHTF	Global Harmonization Task Force
GIs	geographical indications
GMOs	genetically modified organisms
GP	government procurement
GPA	Government Procurement Agreement
GSTP	Global System of Trade Preferences
GTAP	Global Trade Analysis Project
GURT	genetic use restriction technology
GVC	global value chains
ICANN	Internet Corporation for Assigned Names and Numbers
ICH	International Conference on Harmonisation of Technical Requirements for Registration of Pharmaceuticals for Human Use
ICT	intra corporate transferee/information and communications technology
IEC	International Electrotechnical Commission
IIA	international investment agreement
ILO	International Labour Organization
IMDRF	International Medical Device Regulators Forum
IMF	International Monetary Fund
IPRs	intellectual property rights
ISDS	investor–state dispute settlement

ISO	International Organization for Standardization
ISPs	Internet service providers
IT	information technology
ITA	Information Technology Agreement
ITES	information technology enabled services
JD	Jordanian dinar
KORUS FTA	Korea–US Free Trade Agreement
LLP	low level presence
LMOs	living modified organisms
MA	market access
Madrid Protocol	Protocol Relating to the Madrid Agreement Concerning the International Registration of Marks
MAI	Multilateral Agreement on Investment
MBR	multi-brand retail
MEA	multilateral environmental agreement
MERCOSUR	Mercado Común del Sur
MFN	most favoured nation
MNC	multinational corporation
MRA	Mutual Recognition Agreements
MRA-ETR	Mutual Recognition Arrangement for Equivalence of Technical Requirements
MRA-TEL	Mutual Recognition Arrangement for Conformity Assessment of Telecommunications Equipment
NAFTA	North American Free Trade Agreement
NBA	National Biodiversity Authority
NC	net cost
NCMs	non-conforming measures
Nice Classification	Nice Agreement on International Classification of Goods and Services for the Registration of Marks
NME	new molecular entity
NOC	no objection certificate
NRI	non-resident Indian
NTB	non-tariff barrier
OECD	Organisation for Economic Co-operation and Development
OFDI	outward foreign direct investment
PEMEX	Petróleos Mexicanos (Mexican Petroleums)
PhRMA	Pharmaceutical Research and Manufacturers of America
PIO	person of Indian origin
PLT	Patent Law Treaty

PPVFR Act	Protection of Plant Varieties and Farmers' Right Act
PTA	preferential trade agreement
QR	quantitative restriction
RBI	Reserve Bank of India
RCEP	Regional Comprehensive Economic Partnership
RIM	Research in Motion
RM	Malaysian ringgit
RMI	rights management information
SAARC	South Asian Association for Regional Cooperation
SADC	South African Development Community
SAIL	Steel Authority of India Limited
SDG	Sustainable Development Goal
SDR	special drawing right
Singapore Treaty	Singapore Treaty on the Law of Trademarks
SMEs	small and micro enterprises
SMS	short message service
SOE	state-owned enterprise
SPS	sanitary and phytosanitary
STE	state trading enterprise
TBT	technical barriers to trade
TFA	Trade Facilitation Agreement
TiSA	Trade in Services Agreement
TLT	Trademark Law Treaty
TM	trademark
TPM	technology protection measure
TPP or TPP Agreement	Trans-Pacific Partnership Agreement
TRIMs Agreement	Agreement on Trade-Related Investment Measures
TRIPS	Trade-Related Intellectual Property Rights
TRQ	tariff rate quota
TTIP Agreement	Trans-Atlantic Trade and Investment Partnership Agreement
UNCITRAL	United Nations Commission on International Trade Law
UNCTAD	United Nations Conference on Trade and Development
UNFCC	United Nations Framework Convention on Climate Change
UPOV	Union for the Protection of New Plant Varieties
USA	United States of America

US$	United States dollar
USTR	United States Trade Representative
WCO	World Customs Organization
WCT	WIPO Copyright Treaty
WHO	World Health Organization
WIOD	World Input–Output Database
WIPO	World Intellectual Property Organization
WITS	World Integrated Trade Solution
WOS	wholly owned subsidiary
WPPT	WIPO Performances and Phonogram Treaty
WTO	World Trade Organization

Preface

The existing global trade architecture is experiencing a tumultuous time. Long-established institutions and rules are facing a backlash. This is, in part, reflected in the political developments in the United States and the United Kingdom—in the election of Donald Trump as president and Brexit, respectively. It is perhaps, therefore, not surprising to see the uncertain fate that the Trans-Pacific Partnership Agreement (TPP) has met with. Propagated globally as the gold standard for new trade rule-making, it now stands abandoned by its chief proponent—the USA—leaving the other 11 signatories looking for alternatives. Japan, now the biggest economy amongst the existing TPP signatories, appears keen to go ahead with the agreement sans the USA. Whether Japan's efforts will succeed remains unclear at the time of this book going into publication. However, what is evident is the intention of the original 12 TPP signatories, including the USA, to use the TPP's text as a template for future trade agreements at bilateral as well as multilateral levels. This makes the rights and obligations enshrined in the TPP extremely significant for all countries, notwithstanding the future of the agreement itself.

This book is an endeavour to critically understand the rules contained in the TPP. In particular, it highlights the effect such trade rules will have on India, should India decide to join an agreement based on the TPP template at a future date. This book provides one of the most exhaustive analyses of the various chapters of the TPP available till date, covering goods, services, intellectual property rights, standards, investment, government procurement, state-owned enterprises, etc. The authors of the book provide theoretical as well as practical insights into TPP rules and the implications of using them as a blueprint for future.

A project of this magnitude could not have been conceptualized and completed without the active help and valuable contributions from many persons. It is a pleasure to sincerely acknowledge all of them.

We express our profound thanks to the authors for their contributions to this book and the patience they exhibited in the process. This book would not have been possible without their cooperation.

We gratefully acknowledge our debt of gratitude to Bhagirath Lal Das, India's former Ambassador to the General Agreement on Tariffs and Trade (GATT), for his painstaking effort in reading the manuscript, discussing it even at odd hours and being a constant source of inspiration. His constructive suggestions have significantly enriched the text. We owe a huge debt to the following people who have read all or part of the manuscript and came up with many useful suggestions, particularly from the policy perspective: V.S. Seshadri, former Ambassador of India to Myanmar and a veteran trade policy hand; Anu Mathai, Economic Advisor, Department of Commerce (Government of India); and Bipin Menon and Aparna Sinha, Directors, Department of Commerce (Government of India). A special word of thanks to Manoj Pant, Professor at Jawaharlal Nehru University, and James Nedumpara, Associate Professor at Jindal Global Law School, both of whom raised some uncomfortable questions that helped us sharpen the arguments in the book.

Two key personalities from the Department of Commerce, Government of India, deserve our special thanks. Rita Teaotia, Commerce Secretary, Government of India, was a source of constant encouragement and provided unstinted support for our efforts. Rajeev Kher, former Commerce Secretary, provided the initial motivation for analysing the provisions of the TPP as it was evolving.

Not many can match Sanya Smith, from the Third World Network, in her understanding of the legal intricacies of even the most complex provisions of the TPP and their implications for developing countries. We have benefitted immensely from the long hours of discussions with her. Thank you, Sanya, for generously sharing your insights with us. We are also grateful to Harsha Vardhana Singh, who has edited a megavolume on the TPP, for being ever-willing to discuss some aspects of the TPP, and for granting permission to use tables from his book. We thank Kinda Mohamadieh too for permitting us to use tables from South Centre publication.

We appreciate the contribution of Siddhartha Rajagopal, Manab Majumdar, Pranav Kumar and Siddhartha Roy for providing industry perspectives on the TPP.

Vipin Kumar deserves a special appreciation for his efforts in formatting the various versions of the manuscript. Without his dedication, the book would have taken much longer to complete. We are also grateful to two colleagues at the Centre for WTO Studies, Murali Kallummal and

Sachin Sharma, for their words of encouragement and in responding to our request for help.

We are grateful to Trishna Menon, from Gujarat National Law University, for her valuable contribution towards proofreading and copy-editing the manuscript.

One of us (Abhijit Das) would like to specially thank Sucharita and Isha for bearing with the long hours of neglect at home while the book was being written and subsequently during the various stages of publication.

SAGE Publications deserves our profound gratitude for expediting our proposal and for agreeing to publish the book within a compressed time frame, given the topical significance of the book. The SAGE team continued to believe in the book, even at times when we had given up hope. We are also grateful to them for helping us at every step of the publication process.

Abhijit Das and Shailja Singh

1
Introduction

Abhijit Das and Shailja Singh

1.1 Background

In the arena of international trade policy and commercial diplomacy, few issues have created as much controversy in recent years as the Trans-Pacific Partnership Agreement (TPP or 'the Agreement'). The TPP was signed by 12 countries in February 2016 and it would have been implemented after completion of the process of ratification of the Agreement. However, in fulfilment of his election promise, in a presidential memorandum dated 23 January 2017, President Donald Trump of the United States of America directed the United States Trade Representative (USTR) to 'withdraw the United States as a signatory to the Trans-Pacific Partnership (TPP), to permanently withdraw the United States from TPP negotiations, and to begin pursuing, wherever possible, bilateral trade negotiations to promote American industry, protect American workers, and raise American wages'. As of May 2017, the possibility of the TPP being implemented in the form as it was signed in February 2016 was rather low. Despite this development, for three reasons, the rules on international trade and investment as contained in the Agreement continue to remain extremely relevant for many countries. First, on certain issues the provisions in the TPP could serve as a template for negotiations at the World Trade Organisation (WTO) and in free trade agreements (FTAs). Several pointers in this direction already exist.[1] Thus, it will hardly be

---

[1] See, for example, Independent Commission on Trade Policy (2015). One of the recommends of the report is that countries should be encouraged to advance the high standards found in the TPP through unilateral reforms, other trade negotiations and WTO activity.

surprising if some of the provisions in the TPP text provide inspiration to negotiators in different negotiating fora, either at a bilateral or at a multilateral level, even if the TPP itself fails to come into effect. The second ground for continued relevance of the TPP arises from the possibility that the TPP might be implemented, possibly in a slightly modified form, by the 11 remaining signatory countries. Japan is reported to be pushing for such an outcome (WTO Centre VCCI 2017). Third, some key persons in the Trump administration have stated that the USA could use the rules contained in the TPP in its bilateral trade negotiations (see, for example, Mayeda and Gura 2017). What lends some credence to this approach is the fact that implementation by other countries of the TPP provisions would significantly promote the commercial interests of the USA, particularly of its pharmaceutical industry and that of its investors in other countries. It would be extremely unusual for the US industry and trade not to intercede with the Trump administration to implement the TPP provisions in a modified form in bilateral and multilateral fora. Overall, there are substantive grounds for the continued relevance of the provisions of the TPP. As the existing provisions of the TPP could have a profound influence on the evolution of rules of international trade and the negotiations at the WTO forum and in bilateral trade negotiations, it is crucial to understand how its provisions could affect developing countries, particularly India. This book is an attempt at undertaking precisely such an objective examination.

The task of analysing the implications for developing countries, which implement rules created on the basis of the TPP, is extremely complex. The Agreement appears to have polarized opinion in the academic arena, and sharply divided the polity, not only in the signatory countries, but also in other nations. While some studies project the TPP as being unusually productive for emerging markets and developed countries (see, for example, Petri et al. 2012), a few of these studies, particularly by a team of Petri, Plummer and Zhai, have been criticized for 'seriously overstating the size of projected trade benefits that do not appear to have solid analytical foundations' (see, for example, Bertram and Terry 2014). Further, some commentators seem to misinterpret the results of econometric analysis of certain studies, and hence appear to significantly exaggerate the gains from the TPP (see, for example, Bergsten 2015). Though the proponents of the Agreement view it as the gold standard 21st-century trade agreement (see, for example, the statement of USTR Kirk 2009a), many critics are up in arms against many provisions in the TPP. According to the Nobel Laureate Joseph Stiglitz, the TPP is 'a very big mistake' (Stiglitz 2015). In short, the TPP conveys vastly different messages to different groups. Given the diametrically different perspectives on the TPP and the likelihood of it being used as a template for future trade agreements, it is relevant to understand the origins of the Agreement and the broad issues covered by it.

1.2 How Did the Trans-Pacific Partnership Agreement Emerge

Elms (2015) provides an insightful and detailed account of the origin and evolution of the TPP. What started as hesitant steps towards trade and investment integration among Brunei, Chile, New Zealand and Singapore through the Trans-Pacific Strategic Economic Partnership Agreement (commonly referred to as Pacific 4 or P4) in 2006 acquired considerable momentum in February 2008 when the USA joined the discussions on investment and financial services under the P4 umbrella. It gathered further traction in September 2008 when the USA announced that it would seek to join the agreement in its entirety (ibid.). This proved to be the tipping point as some other economies in the Asia-Pacific region—Australia, Peru and Vietnam—decided to join P4, which thereafter morphed into the TPP Agreement. Eventually, Australia, Brunei, Canada, Chile, Japan, Malaysia, Mexico, New Zealand, Peru, Singapore, the USA and Vietnam concluded the negotiations on TPP on 5 October 2015. The text of the Agreement was brought in the public domain in November 2015. Subsequently, in February 2016, the Agreement was formally signed by the 12 countries. The Agreement needs to be ratified by the signatory countries before it can be implemented. However, given the deep differences created by the TPP in the polity of some of the signatory countries, eventual ratification of the Agreement cannot be assumed.

At the initial stage, the TPP was envisaged to 'build on the Trans-Pacific Strategic Economic Partnership Agreement (P4) between Brunei, Chile, New Zealand and Singapore, which entered into force in 2006'.[2] The original intention of the P4 countries was to expand the membership of the agreement through accession of additional countries. However, when

[2] http://dfat.gov.au/fta/tpp/index.html (last visited 18 July 2017).

delegates from the original P4 countries and the new entrants—Australia, Peru, USA, and Vietnam—met in Melbourne in March 2010 to expand the P4, the P4 text was quickly discarded as a negotiating template. Moreover, the delegates decided to start again with a new agreement (ibid.). Given the relative economic weight of the USA and other TPP partners, the US influence in drafting new text for the TPP increased (ibid.). On the basis of interviews with trade negotiators of various TPP countries, Elms has observed that many TPP member officials outside the USA recognized that the USA was likely to rewrite draft texts in its own image. It is, therefore, not surprising that as the TPP negotiations proceeded, the final texts in various chapters continued to closely resemble the existing FTA template of the USA, especially the US–Korea FTA (ibid.).

In less than a decade, the rules for trade liberalization under P4 were transformed into a new template that appears to significantly promote the commercial interests of the USA. To complete the picture of why the TPP would promote the interests of the USA, it is relevant to recall the statement made by Robert Zoellick, the former USTR, about the expectation of the USA from its FTA partners. Speaking at the Institute for International Economics in Washington, Zoellick is reported to have stated that an FTA with the USA is a privilege to be earned by a partner country via the support of US policy goals (Higgott 2006). In this background, some relevant questions arise. What are the issues covered in the TPP? What are the requirements to be met for entry into force of the Agreement? Can countries, other than the 12 signatory countries, become members of the TPP? The next section addresses these questions.

1.3 Contents of the TPP

Brief Description of the TPP Chapters[3]

The Agreement, running into more than 5,000 pages, contains 30 chapters covering tariff and services liberalization and a large number of domestic non-trade issues. Specifically, the Agreement contains the following chapters: 'Preamble', 'Initial Provisions and General

---

[3] We gratefully acknowledge the research assistance provided by Nishant Anurag in this section.

Definitions', 'National Treatment and Market Access for Goods', 'Rules of Origin and Origin Procedures', 'Textiles and Apparel', 'Customs Administration and Trade Facilitation', 'Trade Remedies', 'Sanitary and Phytosanitary Measures', 'Technical Barriers to Trade', 'Investment', 'Cross Border Trade in Services', 'Financial Services', 'Temporary Entry for Business Persons', 'Telecommunications', 'Electronic Commerce', 'Government Procurement', 'Competition Policy', 'State-Owned Enterprises and Designated Monopolies', 'Intellectual Property', 'Labour', 'Environment', 'Cooperation and Capacity Building', 'Competitiveness and Business Facilitation', 'Development', 'Small and Medium-Sized Enterprises', 'Regulatory Coherence', 'Transparency and Anti-Corruption', 'Administrative and Institutional Provisions', 'Dispute Settlement', 'Exceptions' and 'Final Provisions'. The TPP also includes side letters on currency manipulation and labour issues.

Ratification and Entry into Force of the TPP

In the context of international agreements, though a State might have 'signed' an agreement to indicate its intention to bind itself to the obligations thereof, it does not have such effect immediately. As prescribed in the Agreement, a critical mass of countries must ratify the Agreement, before it can enter into force. The TPP provides for three different circumstances for entry into force of the Agreement. These options are explained briefly in Figure 1.1.

According to Article 30.5.1 of the TPP, the Agreement shall enter into force 60 days after the date on which all original signatories have ratified the Agreement. Where all original signatories do not ratify the Agreement within 2 years of the date of the signing of the TPP, Article 30.5.2 provides that it shall enter into force 60 days after the expiry of this period (2 years since signing) if at least 6 out of the 12 original signatories have ratified the TPP. However, the Agreement specifies that these 6 States must together account for at least 85 per cent of the combined GDP of the original signatories in 2013. Under the provision of Article 30.5.2, the TPP would enter into force in April 2018. Article 30.5.3 provides for entry into force where conditions under neither Article 30.5.1 nor Article 30.5.2 are met. In such a situation, the agreement would come into force 60 days after the date on which six or more parties who constitute at least 85 per cent of the

Figure 1.1
Three options for Entry into Force (EIF) of the TPP

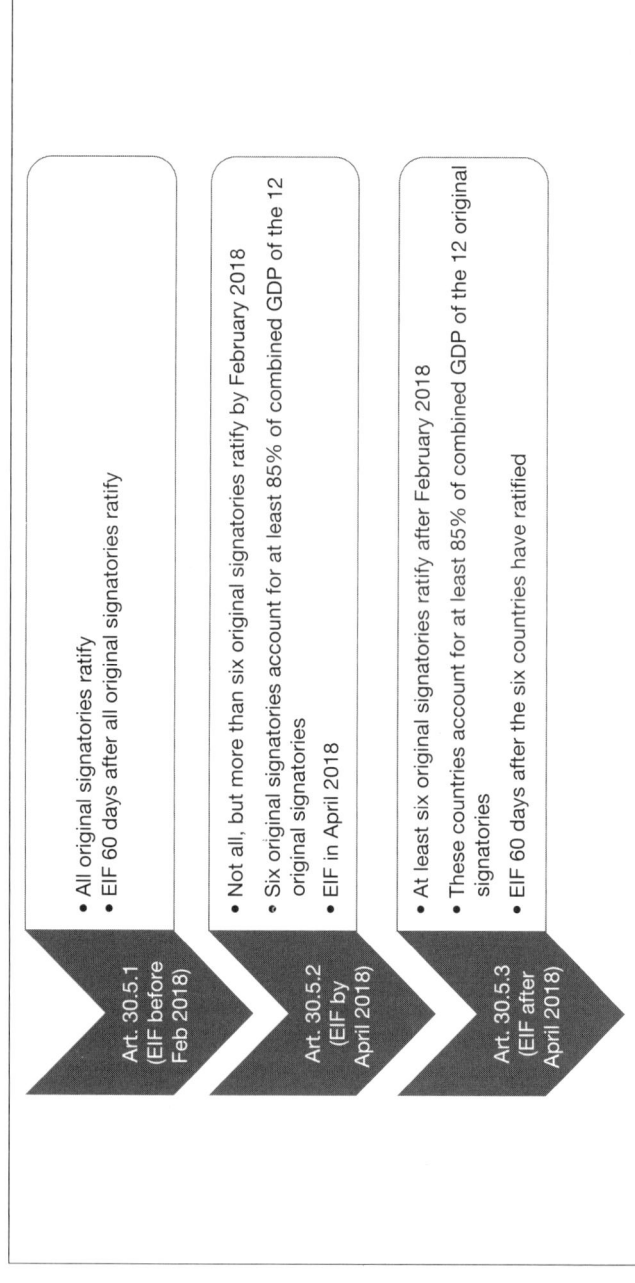

Source: Authors.

combined GDP of the TPP membership notify the depository on the completion of domestic procedures.

The 85 per cent GDP formula may be viewed as offering an advantage to the larger economies among the TPP members. No combination of minimum six members under paragraphs 2 or 3 of Article 30.5 can constitute the threshold for 85 per cent of the GDP, unless it includes the USA. Effectively, the agreement cannot come into force for any of the other TPP members until the USA ratifies the Agreement (Kelsey 2016, 31, 32).

If the TPP comes into force under Article 30.5.2 or 30.5.3, original signatories that were yet to complete the ratification process would be required to notify the parties of the completion of its applicable legal procedures and its intention to become a party to this Agreement (Article 30.5.4). The TPP does not place any restriction on the time within which original signatories that did not ratify the Agreement when it entered into force must subsequently complete their ratification process. The provisions on entry-into-force may need to be amended if the Agreement has to be implemented by the remaining 11 signatory countries, minus the USA.

Accession of New Parties to the TPP

Apart from the original signatories, other countries can accede to the TPP, subject to terms and conditions that may be negotiated between the TPP members and the acceding country. Any State (or customs territory) other than the 12 negotiating/signatory parties can accede to the TPP. Merely having an accession clause does not make an agreement truly open. Accession to the TPP is not automatic. It is in the nature of a 'semi-closed' type of agreement where acceptance of a new member requires the unanimous approval of the existing signatory states.

For the purposes of accession, the TPP makes two categories of States in Article 30.4.1, to whom accession is open: (a) any State or separate customs territory that is a member of the Asia-Pacific Economic Cooperation (APEC), and (b) such other State or separate customs territory as the parties may agree.

In accordance with Article 30.4.2, any State (or customs territory) that wishes to join the TPP must give notice of such intention by submitting a request to the depository (in New Zealand) in writing. On receiving such a request, the TPP Commission is bound to establish a 'working group' to negotiate the terms and conditions for the accession. It needs to be noted that different States under Article 30.4.1 are treated differently in this context. The language of Article 30.4.3 (a) suggests that if the acceding State is a member of the APEC, the request for accession is automatically deemed to have been accepted by the TPP membership for establishment of a working group. However, where the acceding State is not a member of the APEC, existing parties need to agree on the establishment of a working group. Thus, there needs to be consensus among the existing TPP members to even begin the accession process for non-APEC States.

The working group is required to provide a written report to the TPP Commission. When the working group reaches an agreement with the acceding State, the report must contain the terms and conditions of accession, a recommendation to approve those terms and a 'proposed Commission decision inviting the accession candidate to become a Party' to the TPP (Article 30.4.3). In the interest of clarity, the TPP provides in Article 30.4.3*bis* that a commission or working group shall take a decision 'only' when all parties have indicated agreement to establish a working group or all member parties of a working group agree to a request for accession, respectively. This means that any existing TPP member that participates in the accession process must agree on the same. Paragraph (ii) of both Article 30.4.3*bis* (a) and (b) conveys that a single existing member of the TPP can block the establishment of a working group or its decision thereafter. If a party 'does not indicate agreement' when the Commission or a working group considers an issue in relation to accession, such party must submit its objections in writing within 7 days for it to have an effect on the decision of the Commission or the working group. When such objections are not submitted within the prescribed 7 days, the Commission or working group shall be deemed to have taken its decision.

When a decision approving the terms and conditions for accession has been approved by the TPP Commission, it shall invite the acceding State to become a party to the TPP. The Commission shall specify a period, which may be extended, within which the acceding State shall deposit an 'instrument of accession' indicating that it accepts those terms and conditions. All parties must agree if an acceding State requires an extended period of time to deposit an 'instrument of accession' (Article 30.4.4).

Article 30.4.1 requires that an acceding State must be 'prepared to comply with the obligations set out in the Agreement, subject to such terms and conditions as may be agreed between the State or customs territory and the Parties'. Effectively, any country wanting to join the

TPP must be prepared to accept not only all terms of an agreement they had no role in negotiating but also any additional terms that the existing parties may require of them. This denies acceding States an opportunity to represent their own national priorities.

1.4 TPP in the Context of the Emerging Global Trade and Investment Scenario

The relative economic weight of the TPP countries compared to rest of the world is one of the reasons why the Agreement has attracted considerable attention of policymakers and researchers. However, it is also a fact that the salience of the TPP countries in the global economy has generally declined over time. Table 1.1 compares the decadal performance of the TPP countries across the 1970s, 1980s, 1990s and 2000s, as well as the annual performance from 2010 onwards, in respect of GDP, imports and exports of goods, imports and exports of services, foreign direct investment (FDI) inflows and outward FDI (OFDI) outflows.

As shown in Table 1.1, the share of the 12 TPP countries in the global GDP and trade peaked during the 1990s and declined thereafter. However, in respect of investment flows, the decadal share of TPP countries peaked a decade earlier, that is, during the 1980s. Overall, the 1980s and 1990s represent the high noon for the economic might of the TPP countries, before the onset of decline in the 2000s. However, trends in investment suggest that the TPP countries are gradually progressing towards reclaiming the share they had during the peak period of the 1980s. These trends appear to suggest that the TPP could be an attempt by the signatory countries, particularly the USA, to reclaim their gradually eroding economic and commercial salience in a changing world. What are the specific motivations and triggers behind the TPP? How would the Agreement seek to promote the interests of some of the key stakeholders in the USA? The following seeks to provide some answers.

1.5 Motivations and Triggers Behind the TPP

In order to appreciate the continuing relevance of the TPP provisions, it is essential to first understand the motivations and the triggers behind

Table 1.1

TPP countries in a changing economic world

	Average Decadal Share				Annual Share				
	1970s	1980s	1990s	2000s	2010	2011	2012	2013	2014
Share in global GDP	41.74	45.75	47.91	45.47	39.18	37.71	38.26	36.84	36.34
Share in global export of goods	26.68	28.51	30.74	26.47	24.29	23.40	23.53	22.82	23.04
Share in global imports of goods	27.10	30.00	31.98	31.28	27.63	27.17	27.87	27.17	27.61
Share in global services exports		28.88	31.42	27.57	25.55	25.12	25.52	25.18	
Share in global services imports		29.34	30.43	27.15	24.39	23.84	24.14	23.22	
Share in FDI	36.79	51.20	34.69	28.85	29.11	28.45	28.57	35.21	28.09
Share in OFDI	56.28	43.53	35.65	32.76	33.88	39.54	44.07	44.24	42.78

Source: Calculations based on UNCTAD Statistics.

the Agreement. As discussed earlier in this chapter, the origin of the TPP can be traced to the P4, which was an attempt at trade and investment integration among Brunei, Chile, New Zealand and Singapore in 2006. The decision of the USA to join the P4 was an outcome of its growing concern about the discussions in Asia aimed at creating new trade arrangements in the region that might exclude the USA (Elms 2015). In a letter to Congressional leaders notifying the Congress of President Obama's intention to enter into TPP negotiations, USTR Ron Kirk voiced concern that the USA was not a party in the proliferating trade agreements in Asia. Consequently, he observed: 'These agreements, as well as other economic developments, have led to a significant decline in the US share of key Asia-Pacific markets over the past decade.' According to Kirk, the TPP promised to reverse this trend. The objective, at least in the initial phase of the TPP negotiations, appears to have been to include 'additional countries throughout the Asia Pacific region' (Kirk 2009a). It is relevant to note that the US decision to enter into the TPP negotiations was taken in the backdrop of Japan promoting a plan to integrate Asian trade—the grouping later became the Association of Southeast Asian Nations (ASEAN)+6 (Elms 2015). This grouping is now popularly known as the Regional Comprehensive Economic Partnership (RCEP). However, between 2010 and 2015, the stated objective of the TPP from the US perspective appears to have undergone two subtle shifts. First, the TPP was no longer merely about reversing the trend in declining US share in key Asia-Pacific markets, but an imperative not to 'let countries like China write the rules of the global economy' (Obama 2015). Second, it was no longer in response to Japan's attempts at economic integration in Asia, but a reaction to China's increased economic salience in Asia. This aspect is amply clear from an opinion piece by President Obama in the *Washington Post*, in which, in the context of RCEP negotiations, he stated that 'China is negotiating a trade deal that would carve up some of the fastest-growing markets in the world at our expense, putting American jobs, businesses and goods at risk' (Obama 2016).

In a statement issued on 5 October 2015 on the conclusion of the TPP negotiations, President Obama of the USA stated that 'we can't let countries like China write the rules of the global economy. We should write those rules' (Obama 2015). This appears to provide the ostensible reason for the TPP. From the perspective of the USA, this statement suggests a few other objectives of the TPP. These include the following: levelling the playing field for American workers and businesses, increasing exports of products made in the USA, setting high standards for protecting workers and preserving the environment. While these are the officially articulated reasons behind the TPP, there appear to be three crucial triggers for the TPP—progress in the WTO's Doha Round not fully reflecting the interests of the USA and the need to create a suitable 'best alternative to a negotiated agreement' (BATNA); increasing concern among US pharmaceutical companies about attempts by some developing countries to reduce the extent of monopoly protection enjoyed by patented medicines; and growing realisation among developing countries regarding the implications of investment protection provisions in international investment agreements (IIAs). These latent drivers of the TPP are discussed subsequently.

Progress in the WTO's Doha Round of Trade Negotiations: Creating a BATNA and Blocking Outcomes from Heading Against the Commercial and Trade Interests of the USA

The USA was at the forefront of launching the Doha Round of the multilateral trade negotiations under the aegis of the WTO in November 2001. The principal interest of the USA in the Doha Round was to open markets for agriculture, industrial goods and services (Statement of Robert Zoellick, USTR, during the Doha Ministerial Conference of the WTO, WTO document no. WT/MIN(01)/ST/3 dated 10 November 2001). However, by 2007, it was gradually becoming clear that the USA may not be able to succeed in achieving some of its key objectives under the Doha Round. Its attempts at negotiating multilateral rules at the WTO on investment protection, competition and transparency in government procurement had already floundered in August 2004 when the General Council of the WTO decided that 'no work towards negotiations on any of these issues will take place within the WTO during the Doha Round' (Decision adopted by the General Council on 1 August 2004 contained in document WT/L/579 dated 2 August 2004).

By August 2007, the progress in negotiations implied that the USA would not be able to secure effective market access for agriculture and industrial products in some emerging developing countries. On the other hand, a group of developing countries led by Brazil, Argentina and India (popularly called Group of Twenty [G20]) had succeeded in garnering support from almost all the WTO members in seeking significant reduction in domestic farm support by the developed countries, particularly the USA and the European Union (EU). In order to get an idea of the progress in negotiations on agriculture issues, see, for example, WTO document TN/AG/W/4 dated 1 August 2007. Further, on the issue of reduction of cotton subsidies—of considerable commercial salience for African countries—the USA found itself pushed against the wall. This issue has been politically difficult for the USA, which appears to have resorted to different stratagems to avoid detailed discussions on it. Drawing upon the recollection of Arancha Gonzalez, Pascal Lamy's spokeswoman, Blustein (2009, 155), hints that in 2003 the USA allowed the Cancun Ministerial Conference of the WTO to collapse on the so-called Singapore issues. By avoiding a discussion, and hence a breakdown of this important meeting, on cotton subsidies, the EU officials suspected that the USA prevented being blamed for the failure of the Cancun meeting. Subsequently, the USA found itself unable to implement the decision taken at the Hong Kong Ministerial meeting of the WTO in 2005 which would have required it to sharply cut subsidies on cotton over a compressed time frame. Thus, by the closing months of 2007, the USA found itself trapped in a double bind—unable to secure most of its offensive interests, but at the risk of having to concede considerable ground on some issues of its defensive concern. Given this situation, the USA desperately required an alternative to a negotiated outcome at the WTO—commonly referred to in negotiations theory as the BATNA. Creating the TPP provided the USA with its BATNA.

The US response to the difficult situation that it found itself in appears to have been two-pronged—unshackle itself from the mandate and progress achieved under the Doha Round; and seek to create a negotiating template that would be more closely aligned to its economic and commercial interests. In pursuance of the first objective, it dug in its heels and sought to ensure that there would be no meaningful progress on most of the issues under negotiations under the Doha Round after December 2008. While some might contest this conclusion, what is unequivocal is the role of the USA, during the Nairobi Ministerial Conference of the WTO held in December 2015, in ensuring that there would be no consensus on using the Doha mandate as the basis for concluding the Doha Round. Discussions with Geneva-based diplomats, who were involved in negotiating the Nairobi Ministerial Declaration of the WTO, suggest that the USA was not only reluctant but often openly hostile to reaffirming the Doha mandate in the Nairobi Ministerial Declaration.

With the progress in WTO negotiations not proceeding along lines that would enhance its commercial interests, by early 2008 the USA appears to have embarked on the second limb of its trade policy strategy. As stated in Section 1.1 above, in February 2008 the USA joined the discussions on investment and financial services under the P4 umbrella. This was followed up with the announcement in September 2008 that it would join the agreement in its entirety. As the P4 gradually morphed into the final TPP Agreement in October 2015 based essentially on the USA–Korea FTA, the second element for promoting the commercial and trade interests of the USA appears to have been secured.[4]

---

[4] In terms of negotiation theory, this can also be viewed as creating the most advantageous alternative, commonly referred to as the BATNA, in case negotiations at the WTO fail to promote the interest of the USA.

The denouement of the two-pronged strategy seems to have been reached two months later in Nairobi in December 2015, when the Tenth Ministerial Conference of the WTO failed to endorse concluding the Doha Round on the basis of the Doha mandates. As a result, the USA freed itself 'from the strictures of Doha', an objective strongly advocated by the USA.[5] Thus, it appears to have created a pathway for escaping from taking onerous commitments under the Doha Round, particularly in respect of farm support. In parallel, it has also finalized an architecture of trade and investment rules under the TPP that is likely to promote its trade and commercial interests, but without any attendant obligations for reducing farm subsidies. With the Nairobi Ministerial Declaration[6] of the WTO having created a window for launching multilateral negotiations on issues such as investment, labour, environment, etc., the provisions in the TPP could become the template for future rule-making on these issues, either at the WTO or in similar other fora.

Protecting the Financial Interests of Big Pharma in the USA

While the developments at the multilateral forum of the WTO appear to have provided the push for the USA towards the TPP, the interests of its two important stakeholders—pharmaceutical manufacturers and investors in foreign markets—also seem to have been crucial triggers for the US engagement in the TPP. This subsection discusses the role of US pharmaceutical manufacturers in shaping the provisions of the TPP for countering developments in other countries that would have an adverse impact on the profits of the US industry.

Considerable empirical evidence exists to support the view that special interest groups[7] use their campaign contributions to influence the positions of politicians (see, for example, Kau and Rubin 1982, Fremdreis and Waterman 1985, and Tosini and Tower 1987). Grossman

---

[5] See, for example, the statement by Michael Froman, USTR, at the plenary session of the Nairobi Ministerial Meeting of the WTO, available at https://www.wto.org/english/thewto_e/minist_e/mc10_e/mc10_planarysessions_e.htm#USA (last visited 18 July 2017).
[6] WTO document WT/MIN(15)/DEC dated 21 December 2015.
[7] According to Grossman and Helpman (1994) special interest groups are collections of voters who share a common interest in the non-ideological policies and cooperate with one another, so they can influence the parties' positions on the non-ideological issues.

and Helpman (1994) identify two motivations of the special interest groups for making campaign contributions. First, an interest group may gain if its campaign contribution enhances the prospects of the politicians whose position on the non-ideological issues is more similar to its own; and second, an interest group may influence the candidates to support policies that serve the group's own interests. In the specific context of trade policy, Baldwin and Magee (2000) attempt to determine the importance of campaign contributions and other factors affecting voting behaviour in the US House of Representatives on three important trade policy bills that came before the US Congress in 1993–94. They conclude that political contributions to legislators by organized labour and business groups significantly affected the voting outcome on two (North American Free Trade Agreement [NAFTA] and General Agreement on Tariffs and Trade [GATT]) of the three trade bills analysed. It is, therefore, relevant to analyse the role of the US pharmaceutical industry in lobbying for provisions in the TPP that would promote its financial interest.

It is no secret that different industry groups in the USA spend billions of dollars each year in lobbying US Congress and federal agencies for favourable government policies and interventions. Among different industry groups, the pharmaceuticals/health products industry is the highest spender on lobbying. During 1998–2016, pharmaceuticals/health products industry spent US$3.3 billion in lobbying the US Congress and federal agencies.[8] The Pharmaceutical Research and Manufacturers of America (PhRMA), the industry's lead lobbying group, has spent nearly US$132 million on lobbying since 2008, and ranks fifth among the top lobbying spenders in the USA. It even outspends powerful interests such as defence contractors and the oil and gas industry (Ludwig 2014).

An important objective of lobbying by the pharmaceutical industry in the USA appears to be to prevent countries from making rightful use of the flexibilities contained in the Agreement on Trade-Related Aspects of Intellectual Property Rights (TRIPS Agreement) of WTO and influencing the US government to negotiate provisions in FTAs that would promote the interests of US pharmaceutical multinational corporation (MNCs). An investigation by Truthout has revealed that an aggressive lobbying effort by pharmaceutical interests pushed Congress and the White House to put mounting pressure on India to change its patent laws

---

[8] Centre for Responsive Politics; details available at https://www.opensecrets.org/lobby/top.php?showYear=a&indexType=i (last visited 4 June 2016).

(ibid.). While some developing countries have fallen in line with the attempts of the USA to restrict countries from utilising the flexibilities provided under the TRIPS Agreement, there are important exceptions to this overall trend.

India,[9] Philippines[10] and Argentina[11] have strong provisions in their patent law to safeguard against evergreening of patents, a phenomenon whereby the patent holder seeks to extend the period of protection beyond the mandated 20 years for essentially the same product. More recently, Brazil and South Africa have recognized the need to amend their patent provisions for adopting India's approach against evergreening. Brazil introduced Projeto de Lei no. 5.402/2013[12] to reform its Industrial Property Law[13] in 2013. Article 3 of the Bill introduced the test of enhanced efficiency and incorporates the language contained in Section 3 (d) of Indian Patents Act, 2005. South Africa released the Draft National Policy on Intellectual Property in September 2013 which noted that weak patents, when there is no innovation on the original or dependant patent, stifle the possibility of having access to public health. It recommends that 'South African legislation should allow strict rules to apply to patenting as competition principles may be undermined. This should exclude diagnostic, therapeutic and surgical methods from patentability, including new uses of known products' (Department of Trade and Industry 2013, 21).

With Philippines and Argentina having enacted legislative changes to restrict patent evergreening along the lines of Section 3(d), and Brazil and South Africa in the process of undertaking similar legislation, one commentator has observed that the '3(d) wave is spreading to other developing countries' (Guha 2013). Another scholar is of the view that section 3(d) could see widespread adoption outside India (Banerjee 2013). If this process were to gather momentum and spread to other developing countries, it is likely to dent the profits of Big Pharma in the USA. The TPP could perhaps be viewed as an attempt by the pharmaceutical industry in the USA to pre-empt the 3(d) wave from spreading to other developing countries.

---

[9] See, for example, Section 3(d) of the Indian Patents Act, 2005.
[10] See, for example, amendment to Section 22 of RA 8239 in 2008.
[11] Res. Nos. 118/2012, 546/2012, 107/2012, 8 May 2012 (Arg.), available at http://www.moellerip.com/index.php?PN=news_detail&FX=0&EX=1&DX=139 (English translation).
[12] Bill No: H.R. 5402/2013.
[13] Law No. 9.279 of 14 May 1996.

The pharmaceutical lobby in the USA was active in trying to influence the TPP even before the commencement of the first formal meeting held in Melbourne in 2010. In a detailed analysis of trends in lobbying, Drutman (2014) states that during 2009, the pharmaceutical lobby was at the forefront in trying to shape the trade agreement while it was still secret from the public. According to Drutman, during 2009 until mid-2013, drug companies and associations mentioned the TPP in 251 separate lobbying reports—two and a half times more than the next most active industry (as measured by lobbying reports). Among the top 20 organizations, PhRMA, the pharmaceutical industry's trade association, lobbied the most. The lobbying efforts are largely reflective of the interests that are most likely to be affected by the trade agreement. This time period coincided with the negotiating phase when the language of the agreement was still open. He concludes that the early-stage lobbying during the agenda-setting stage has paid off as the TPP is friendly to drug manufacturers. The success of the pharmaceutical lobby in seeking to secure its objectives can be gauged by the fact that the Agreement contains an explicit provision—paragraph 2 of Article 18.37—mandating countries to provide patents for new uses of a known product, new methods of using a known product or new processes of using a known product. This would prevent countries that have signed the TPP from adopting India's approach to restricting evergreening of patents.

Protecting the Interest of US Foreign Investors

The third trigger for the TPP appears to be the developments related to IIAs and the need to protect the interests of US investors in foreign markets. As the IIAs are mainly about protecting the legal rights of foreign investors in the host country, it is relevant to understand the changing perception in some developing countries about these agreements. The share of USA in global outward FDI had declined from 45 per cent in the 1970s to 20 per cent in the 2000s. However, in recent years it has started to pick up. Nevertheless, the past few years have increasingly seen countries questioning the utility of IIAs in promoting inflow of investments. Other concerns voiced against the IIAs include the non-transparent method of resolving investor-to-State disputes, extremely high compensation that countries have had to pay to foreign investors pursuant to losing these disputes and constraints on introducing new policies and measures in pursuit of national development objectives induced by the fear of being sued by foreign investors. Given these concerns, many developing countries have started revisiting their approach to IIAs. Some countries, including Argentina, India, Indonesia and South Africa, have decided not to renew some of their existing bilateral investment treaties (BITs). If this trend gathers momentum, it would severely undermine the protection that investments of US MNCs enjoy in developing countries and also restrict their future profits. It would appear that the TPP is perhaps an attempt by the USA to protect the interests of its MNCs by having strong provisions on investment protection in the mega-FTA.

With implementation of the TPP now in the realm of considerable uncertainty, what is the basis to assume that the provisions of the Agreement continue to remain relevant and could provide a basis for negotiating rules on international trade and investment at the WTO, as well as in bilateral fora? The next section seeks to answer this crucial question.

1.6 TPP Provisions Providing the Blueprint for Multilateral and Bilateral Trade and Investment Negotiations: Reviewing Some Evidence

After the US withdrawal from the TPP, why does the Agreement continue to remain relevant, particularly for non-signatory countries such as India? Is there any evidence to support the premise that despite the uncertainty in implementation of the TPP, its provisions are likely to form an important basis for international trade and investment negotiations at the multilateral forum of the WTO, as well as in various bilateral negotiations? Further, why would developing countries, such as India, agree to bind themselves to legal provisions based on the TPP, when these are likely to be against their stated policies and national interest? In this section, we seek to answer these questions by drawing upon evidence from two sources—first, past developments at multilateral institutions such as the GATT, WTO and the Organisation for Economic Co-operation and Development (OECD); and second, contemporary developments at the WTO and various bilateral and mega-regional trade and investment negotiations.

Continuing Relevance of the TPP

Evidence from Theoretical Considerations and the Developments in the Past

Concepts from international relations theory are useful and relevant for explaining why the developed countries, particularly the USA, would seek to use the provisions of the TPP as a basis for future bilateral and multilateral trade negotiations. Finnemore and Sikkink (1998) use a constructivist approach of international relations and argue that the norms that set standards for appropriate behaviour of States evolve in a three-stage 'life cycle' comprising emergence, 'norm cascades', and internalization. Under their analytical framework, during the emergence phase, norm entrepreneurs[14] seek to convince a critical mass of States to adopt a new norm. The norm is institutionalized after a critical mass of countries accept it. The international norm enters the phase of norm cascades, during which norm entrepreneurs socialize other States to become norm followers. During this phase, more countries adopt the norm that was initially advanced by norm entrepreneurs. This phase is motivated by a combination of pressure for conformity, desire to increase international legitimation and the need of political leaders of norm followers to enhance self-esteem. Finally, during the third stage, through a process of internalization, the norm acquires a taken-for-granted character.

What is the empirical evidence that the three-stage norm life cycle proposed by Finnemore and Sikkink (ibid.) is applicable in the context of international trade agreements? Without referring to the work of these two authors, Cottier (2015) provides some support for the first two phases of the norm life cycle theory. According to the author, the initial multilateral agreements in international economic law[15] were consolidated on the basis of a critical mass of bilateral agreement on patents, trademarks,

---

[14] According to Cass Sunstein (1996), a norm entrepreneur is someone interested in changing social norms.
[15] The Paris Convention on the Protection of Industrial Property (1883) and the Berne Convention on the Protection of Literary and Artistic Works (1886).

and copyright in the decades before 1883 and 1886. Further, the GATT emerged on the basis of the 1934 USA Reciprocal Trade Agreements, which were concluded mainly during the interwar period. In more recent years, the influence of the developments at the APEC forum and those at the OECD on prospects for negotiated outcomes at the WTO provides additional support for the relevance of the three-stage norm life cycle in the context of international trade and investment.

The interlinkages between the discussions and negotiations on certain issues at the APEC and subsequent negotiated outcomes on the same issues at the multilateral forum of the WTO provide further evidence for the first two phases of the norm life cycle. In December 1996, 29 members of the WTO signed the Ministerial Declaration on Trade in Information Technology Products,[16] commonly referred to as the Information Technology Agreement (ITA). The ITA sought to eliminate customs duties on IT products by 1 January 2000. According to Yanai (2000), this agreement at the WTO was possible primarily due to the prior background discussion and negotiations in the APEC, resulting in the ministers and leaders of the APEC endorsing the ITA in November 1996. The author makes two additional points that are extremely relevant to the norm life cycle. First, he is of the view that the APEC can provide interesting insights on the likelihood of reaching an agreement at the global level. Second, he asserts that the USA had in its mind to use the APEC 'as a locus to reach agreements on specific sectors prior to the start of the new WTO negotiations'. In terms of the norm life cycle, on certain issues, the APEC appears to serve as the platform for the emergence phase, with the norm cascades phase unfolding subsequently at the WTO. In this background, is it a mere coincidence that the TPP emerged in the Asia-Pacific region? Perhaps not.

In addition to the APEC, developments at the OECD in respect of the Multilateral Agreement on Investment (MAI) provide further evidence in support of the three-stage norm life cycle being relevant for IIAs. While the WTO's Agreement on Trade-Related Investment Measures contains disciplines on some aspects of investment, some of the developed countries were of the view that further negotiations were needed for widening and deepening the disciplines for providing additional rights to foreign investors regarding establishment, national treatment and profit repatriation. In pursuance of this objective, in May 1995, the OECD members, comprising mainly the developed countries, launched

---

[16] WTO document WT/MIN(96)/16, dated 13 December 1996.

negotiations for a MAI. According to Lawrence and Devereaux (2006), the MAI negotiations were explicitly limited to a set of parties who would generally agree on what investment rules were desirable. After the limited group of countries had negotiated an agreement, representing the emergence phase of the three-stage norm life cycle, they could put forward the MAI as the model to which developing countries would accede in time. According to the authors, the expectation among the proponents was that eventual association with the WTO would come when the momentum towards developing countries joining the MAI became unstoppable. If the expectation of the association between the MAI and the WTO had materialized, then it could have been considered to represent the norm cascades phase. It may, therefore, be concluded that the three-stage norm life cycle proposed by Finnemore and Sikkink (1998) is also applicable to international trade agreements.

Drawing on the work of Finnemore and Sikkink (ibid.), Fleury and Marcoux (2016) posit that in respect of the rules on state-owned enterprises (SOEs) in the TPP, the USA acted as the key norm entrepreneur throughout the TPP negotiations. As the norm life cycle pertaining to SOE disciplines is still at an early stage, many more countries are likely to adopt these disciplines during the emergence phase and the norm cascades phase. While the USA was a norm entrepreneur on the SOEs, is there a basis to assume that it was also a key norm entrepreneur in other areas, including investment, services, intellectual property rights (IPRs), standards, labour issues, environment, included in the TPP? To the best of our knowledge, specific research which seeks to answer this question does not exist. However, as discussed later, considerable evidence exists to support the contention that the USA was the key norm entrepreneur in respect of most of the issues addressed in the TPP.

Recognizing the USA as *the* dominant political, military, and economic power of our day, Hart (1997) is of the view that globalisation involves the extension around the world of American values, assumption and priorities. According to Tita (1998), with the exception of the USA, all other countries are 'finding that their capacity for effective economic intervention is, to say the least, slight'. Coming specifically to the TPP, as mentioned earlier, Elms (2015) has concluded that the TPP was written by the USA in its own image and that the final texts closely resemble the FTA template of the USA. This should leave us in no doubt that the USA was the key norm entrepreneur on most of the issues contained in the TPP. But, what is the evidence to suggest that the norms contained in the TPP will be accepted by other countries, resulting in the norm cascades phase of the three-stage norm life cycle? In this regard, the views of some influential commentators on international trade and erudite scholars of trade law are extremely instructive.

Hufbauer and Cimino-Isaacs (2015) are of the view that even if the TPP is not implemented, its negotiating objectives on several contentious issues could set precedents and translate into new ideas for the WTO, thereby shaping the future of this institution. They caution that the stature of the WTO as an arbiter of commercial relations between nations collectively will get diminished if it fails to be prodded by the mega-regional accords such as the TPP. Based on Cottier (2015), an eminent scholar of trade law, seven reasons can be identified for supporting the possibility that many of the provisions in Preferential Trade Agreements (PTAs) and mega-FTAs, including the TPP, may eventually find their way to the WTO. First, rules on issues such as progressive removal of non-tariff barriers, environment or labour standards, and enhanced standards for protection of intellectual property are inherently origin-neutral. Rules in these areas would result in a single and uniformly applied regime in domestic law, equally applicable across the board to all countries. Thus, the legal nature of trade regulations in these areas is more suitable for a multilateral forum like the WTO than agreements between a few countries. Second, given the economic heft of mega-FTAs, such as the TPP and the TTIP (Trans-Atlantic Trade and Investment Partnership), countries that are not members of these mega-FTAs would have a strong incentive to adjust to the new rules contained in the mega-FTAs *unilaterally*, for securing market access in these countries. This suggests a strong potential for multilateralizing the TPP rules within the WTO. Third, negotiating within the WTO would create a global common law applicable to a larger number of countries than in a mega-FTA like the TPP. Fourth, obligations entered into at the WTO are subject to its dispute settlement mechanism and multilaterally authorized enforcement mechanism. This can provide a strong incentive for norm entrepreneurs to induce other countries to accept the TPP rules at the WTO. Fifth, rules on some of the issues included in the TPP, such as fisheries subsidies, cannot be efficiently addressed in a mega-FTA. In these areas, rules need to be extended to all competitors, particularly those who are not signatories to the mega-FTA. If rules on capping subsidies are implemented only among mega-FTA partners, and not extended to other competitors through rule-making at the WTO, then it would lead to perverse outcomes. While the competitors will not be constrained in providing subsidies, the norm entrepreneurs and others conforming to the norm would not be able to provide subsidies beyond the agreed ceilings. Sixth, rules relating to global infrastructure, such as internet, are best addressed in a global forum so that loopholes are avoided. Seventh, given the proliferation of FTAs, countries could face a conflict between different treaty regimes. Multilateralizing the norms in mega-FTAs, such as the TPP, can eliminate the possibility of conflicting legal regimes.

Overall, based on international relations theory, as well as the influence of developments at forums such as the APEC and OECD on WTO negotiations, and the inherent logic in negotiating rules on certain issues at the global forum instead of undertaking rule-making within a small group of countries, it can be concluded that some of the provisions of the TPP would be used for future rule-making at the WTO and in some mega-regional forums. But is there any evidence from contemporary developments to support this conclusion? The next subsection discusses this aspect.

Continuing Relevance of the TPP

Evidence from Contemporary Developments

There is no denying the fact that the decision of President Trump to withdraw USA from the TPP has created considerable uncertainty regarding implementation of the Agreement. However, recent developments at some international forums, as well as the statements of key officials and ministers from the TPP countries, lend credence to the continuing relevance of the rules under the TPP.

The USA is utilizing key international forums, such as the WTO and the G-20, for pushing its interests on issues related to international trade and investment. As discussed in Section 1.5 earlier, the Nairobi Ministerial Declaration of the WTO has opened a window for discussion and subsequent negotiations on 'other issues' that are not within the negotiating mandate of the Doha Round. This provides the USA a significant opportunity to advance its negotiating interests in areas such as investment, services, protection of IPRs, SOEs, etc. In parallel, the G-20 Leaders Communique that emerged from the Hangzhou Summit (4–5 September 2016) noted the important role that bilateral and regional trade agreements can play 'in the development of trade rules'.[17] This could be a pointer to the TPP provisions providing an important basis for negotiating rules on international trade and investment at the bilateral and multilateral fora. Leaked texts of the Trade in Services Agreement (TiSA) suggest that the architecture of commitments, and the detailed provisions, in TiSA have considerable similarity with the rules on services in the TPP. Further, the imprint of the provisions on electronic commerce and the telecommunications chapter in the TPP is clearly discernible in some of the submissions made on this issue by the USA (WTO 2016a) and Japan (WTO 2016b) at the WTO. It is interesting to note that the former chief TPP negotiator for the office of USTR, Wendy Cutler, is reported to have explicitly suggested that some aspects of the TPP—ecommerce and digital trade issues—were ripe for an outcome at the WTO (*Inside US Trade* 2017).[18] In the area of fisheries subsidies, the proposals made by some countries at the WTO have considerable convergence with corresponding provisions in the TPP.

In the context of bilateral and regional trade agreement negotiations, statements emerging from some of the countries in the Asia-Pacific region clearly recognize the continuing relevance of the provisions in the TPP. To illustrate, Mexico's foreign minister, Luis Videgaray, is reported to have said that the standards and rules negotiated in the TPP could be integrated into other bilateral and regional trade arrangements.[19] This sentiment also appears to have been echoed by Vietnam's ambassador to the USA Pham Quang Vinh and South Korea's ambassador to the USA Ahn Ho-young.[20] During his presidential campaign, Donald Trump had criticized the TPP as a 'potential disaster for our country'. It would, therefore, be a supreme irony if the provisions of the TPP are used by the USA as a starting point for renegotiating the NAFTA—a possibility that has been alluded to by the US Commerce Secretary Wilbur Ross (Mayeda and Gura 2017). Some analysts and experts have conjectured that Australia, Japan and Singapore—signatories to the TPP—may seek to incorporate some of the rules of this Agreement into the RCEP (see, for example, Seshadri [2017]).

---

[17] http://www.g20.org/English/Dynamic/201609/t20160906_3396.html (last visited 18 July 2017).
[18] 'Asia-Pacific Ambassadors: Keep TPP Alive with, or Without the US'. *Inside US Trade* 9 March 2017.
[19] 'USA Not Invited to TPP Meeting in Chile; Ministers to Meet Again at APEC'. *Inside US Trade* 15 March 2017.
[20] 'Asia-Pacific Ambassadors: Keep TPP Alive with, or Without the US'. *Inside US Trade* 9 March 2017.

It is relevant to point out that the Joint Statement from President Donald J. Trump and Prime Minister Shinzo Abe dated 10 February 2017[21] has noted that the USA has withdrawn from the TPP. The Joint Statement recognizes the possibility of Japan continuing to advance regional progress throughout the Asia-Pacific region on the basis of 'existing initiatives'. The reference to 'existing initiatives' could imply that the USA is not averse to Japan taking the initiative to implement the TPP even without the USA. Japan is reported to have contemplated such an initiative during the meeting of APEC countries held in May 2017 (Grammar 2017). Some reports suggest that the eleven countries (minus the US) have agreed to 'launch a process to assess options to bring the comprehensive, high quality Agreement into force expeditiously, including how to facilitate membership for the original signatories.' (Yamazaki and Yasoshima 2017).

The developments mentioned in this subsection strengthen the possibility of the TPP provisions forming the basis for bilateral and multilateral negotiations on trade and investment issues. However, the different chapters in this book suggest that developing countries, such as India, would be adversely impacted if they are required to implement most of the rules contained in the TPP. Given this reality, why would most of the developing countries become norm followers and adopt rules of the TPP in future bilateral and multilateral agreements? The next subsection tries to address this difficult question.

Why Would Developing Countries, Such as India Be Compelled to Use the TPP Provisions as a Basis for Trade Negotiations?

Many authors have highlighted how, despite strongly opposing the initiation of multilateral negotiations on services and IPRs, under the GATT framework, the developing countries ultimately agreed to the inclusion of binding rules in these areas under the Uruguay Round (1986–94) (see, for example, Hrbata [2010] and Winslett [2016]). Hrbata (2010) and Winslett (2016) suggest three reasons to explain why developing

---

[21] Joint Statement from President Donald J. Trump and Prime Minister Shinzo Abe. Available at https://www.whitehouse.gov/the-press-office/2017/02/10/joint-statement-president-donald-j-trump-and-prime-minister-shinzo-abe (last visited 5 May 2017).

countries accepted rules that were perceived to be against their national interest. First, liberalization of trade in agriculture and textiles was viewed as important gains by the developing countries. Hence, they reluctantly agreed to accept onerous obligations in some other areas in order to garner gains in agriculture and textiles. Second, they apprehended that if a multilateral agreement could not be reached, then the USA would 'pursue trade liberalization bilaterally and regionally, thus denying those developing countries the benefits of increased market access'. Third, they hoped that a stronger WTO could curtail the USA, increasing resort to using unilateral trade sanctions.

Analysing GATT/WTO negotiations from the perspective of international institutions, Steinberg (2002) is of the view that different modalities of bargaining have dominated at different stages of international trade negotiations. According to the author, trade rounds were launched through law-based bargaining that yielded equitable contracts identifying the topics to be addressed in the negotiations. In contrast, subsequent agenda setting and determining the outcomes at the conclusion of trade rounds was dominated by power-based bargaining by powerful countries. Salience of the different modalities of bargaining at different stages of trade negotiations provides a useful conceptual framework for explaining why the developing countries accepted negotiated outcomes at the GATT/WTO, despite not wanting to enter into those agreements.

The fundamental tenet of Steinberg (ibid.) is that whether trade bargaining takes the form of reciprocal market opening or threats of market closure, developed markets are better placed than smaller markets in trade negotiations. Consequently, powerful states are able to contract asymmetrically, thereby generating consensus support for outcomes that are skewed in their favour. Further, weaker countries may be coerced by powerful nations into supporting measures skewed in favour of the latter. Sovereign equality in rules of decision-making at the GATT/WTO confers legitimacy on the asymmetrical outcomes of the trade rounds. Even if many weaker countries perceived that some of their preferences were ignored, they had difficulty in sustaining a cooperative strategy of obstructing the final outcome. Overall, the author identifies the legal concept of 'single undertaking' as an important element in the power play for concluding the Uruguay Round that was based on asymmetrical outcomes. Under the single undertaking approach, all the outcomes of the Uruguay Round negotiations formed an integral part and were binding on all member countries.

Introduction 27

Abbott (2007) provides support for power-based orientation of trade negotiations. According to the author, when the developed countries tender a draft PTA to a developing country, they expect the basic template of their proposal to be followed, and in some areas, such as investment rules or strengthening of IPRs protection, 'the possibilities for effective counterproposal are almost non-existent'. The author finds 'the exercise of virtually unconstrained political and economic power by the USA and EU to secure concessions from developing (and developed) countries' to be the most troubling aspect of the PTA phenomenon.

Given the past history of dominance of power play in the GATT/WTO after the launch of trade rounds, the USA may not find it very difficult to use the provisions of the TPP as a basis for negotiating rules in future at the WTO. In the light of this unsettling reality, it becomes important to briefly discuss the reaction to the TPP in some of the signatory countries. The next section seeks to capture how the TPP has evoked sharp criticism even in the signatory countries.

1.7 TPP: Splitting the Polity in Signatory Countries

The Agreement is beset with many ironies. This has provided some of the ground for criticism of the Agreement. Although the Agreement has detailed provisions on transparency, it was negotiated in considerable secrecy. In the USA, many stakeholder groups, including prominent Congressmen, articulated their concern at the lack of openness in the negotiating process.[22] While the TPP aims at bolstering free trade, its provisions on IPR protection would severely limit competition in the pharmaceutical market. Although the TPP negotiations sought to reduce non-tariff barriers, the final agreement imposes new non-tariff barriers in the form of labour standards and environmental compliance requirements. Some US-based think-tanks flash impressive gains for consumer welfare for countries like India if they join the TPP, while remaining silent on the negative impact on consumers on account of sharp rise in medicine prices that might result from the patent protection provisions

---

[22] See, for example, the letter from over 130 members of the House of Representatives to USTR seeking greater transparency in the TPP, available at http://infojustice.org/archives/26456 (last visited 4 June 2016).

in the TPP (see, for example, Petri et al. 2012). While the 'Dispute Settlement' chapter of the TPP requires dispute settlement panels under the TPP to consider relevant interpretations in reports of panels and the WTO Appellate Body adopted by the WTO Dispute Settlement Body, some of the provisions of the TPP go against the grain of WTO jurisprudence (see, for example, the TPP provision on the definition of the SOE and the WTO jurisprudence on 'public body').

The TPP has been severely criticized, not just by civil society organizations but also by important political leaders in some of the signatory countries. Criticism of the Agreement is directed mostly against the secrecy involved in the negotiations, perception that the agreement accords primacy to corporate profit over public interest, spike in medicine prices that is apprehended on account of some of its provisions, restrictions on SOEs, weakening health and environment standards, deepening the ability of corporates to sue governments, etc. It appears to have almost fractured the polity in Canada, Malaysia and the USA. Of course, different groups provide different reasons for opposing the TPP. When the TPP was finalized in October 2015, Thomas Mulcair, the leader of the New Democratic Party of Canada stated that he would not feel compelled to honour the provisions of the TPP if his party came to power (see, for example, Chase 2015). In Malaysia, the former prime minister and strongman of the country, Mahathir Mohamad, has been openly critical of the TPP, voicing concerns that the FTA would pose a threat to the country's sovereignty and is not good for Malaysia (see, for example, Tani 2016, *Today* 2014). In the USA, the TPP has seen intense criticism from across the political spectrum.

While the TPP was championed by Barack Obama, the former president of the USA, most of the candidates in the presidential race in the USA opposed the TPP. Bernie Sanders is on record opposing the TPP. He is of the view that the USA needs 'trade policies that promote the interests of American workers and not just the CEOs of corporations'.[23] Hillary Clinton initially cited currency manipulation enforcement, benefits for pharmaceutical companies and impacts on American workers as the reasons for opposing the trade agreement. However, she also added: 'I don't believe it's going to meet the high bar I have set' (Merica and Bradner 2015). Elizabeth Warren is another stringent opponent of the TPP. Her criticism of the TPP is centred around the investor–state dispute settlement (ISDS) provisions in the Agreement. She has expressed

---

[23] http://learningenglish.voanews.com/content/trade-obama-trump-pacific-partnership-clinton-sanders/3032839.html (last visited 18 July 2017).

the apprehension that the ISDS provisions would severely undermine the ability of the USA to undertake regulatory changes (Warren 2015). In his election campaign, Donald Trump characterized the TPP as a disaster and upon winning the elections, he has withdrawn the USA from the Agreement.

No doubt, an agreement with a comprehensive coverage of issues, such as the TPP, cannot satisfy all constituencies in all the signatory countries. Nevertheless, criticism of the Agreement should also not be dismissed as being representative of views of fringe elements in polity of different countries—a tendency that appears to be creeping into some media reports. Instead, criticism of the Agreement should be viewed as an articulation of deep concerns regarding the adverse economic impacts that might result from the implementation of the TPP. What about the likely impact on countries such as India, which are not signatories to the TPP, but could be affected if the provisions of the Agreement become a basis for negotiations at the WTO or in other fora? This book is an attempt at undertaking such an assessment. Chapter scheme of the book is provided in the next section.

1.8 Chapter Scheme of This Book

Although the TPP has not yet been implemented, some commentators have characterized it as a game changer. A few others perceive it as being a seismic event for international trade. Relying on a few studies by influential US-based think tanks, analysts and media commentators in India have sought to highlight the adverse consequences for India of remaining outside the TPP. While some of these studies focus on export losses on account of India remaining outside the TPP, little or no consideration has been given to the cost for India if it were to join the TPP. A few studies assert that the TPP would result in upward harmonization of product standards, which could impose a higher burden of compliance for India's exports for access to TPP markets. Some experts have also expressed an apprehension that the TPP will result in India being excluded from global value chains. Both these viewpoints suffer from incorrectly attributing to the TPP perceived deficiencies arising on account of other factors that already afflict India's trade. Further, if the provisions of the TPP, or their close variants, get included in the WTO agreements, then India would have to mandatorily comply with these rules. Thus, India would get impacted by the TPP template of rules even if it does not join the Agreement, if and when it is implemented. In this background, it becomes essential to undertake a balanced and objective analysis of the likely impact of the TPP template of rules on India. This book is a modest attempt at providing such an analysis.

Each chapter of the book seeks to address certain key questions, particularly the following: Which are some of the polices, regulatory framework and applicable domestic law in India that would be required to be modified, if it were required to comply with international trade rules based on the TPP provisions? What could be the economic impact of these changes? What would be the impact of these changes on the ability of the government to pursue development priorities? What changes would be required in India's domestic enforcement machinery for complying with some of the obligations contained in the TPP? Are there provisions in the TPP that are in line with India's overall negotiating approach on specific issues? Even if India's existing policy regime and domestic laws on certain issues might not diverge significantly from the requirements under the TPP, what could be the implications of complying with the TPP provisions for addressing development needs that might arise in the future? Even if India has taken commitments on some issues in its FTAs along the lines of those contained in the TPP, what would be the implications of agreeing to similar obligations at the WTO? Even if some of the issues such as labour and environment may be desirable, are trade agreements the appropriate legal instruments for enforcing obligations on these issues? Could there be benefits for India from complying with international trade rules based on the TPP?

Each subsequent chapter of the book provides a brief narrative of some of the key obligations that would arise from a framework of international trade rules based on the TPP provisions. An attempt is made to highlight how the provisions differ from the corresponding provisions in the relevant WTO agreements. This sets the stage for assessing the likely impact on India if it were required to adhere to a framework of rules based on the TPP provisions. A few chapters also briefly discuss the likely impact of such a framework of laws on developing countries that appear to be inclined to seek membership of the TPP.

Chapter 2 provides a brief overview of literature, which estimates the likely impact on India of two scenarios—remaining outside the TPP or joining it. Thereafter, it provides a brief snapshot of the existing tariff profiles of the TPP countries. This provides the context for understanding the commitments made by the TPP countries for market access in goods. Finally, this chapter examines the likely impact on India's manufacturing and agriculture sectors, if the country were to comply with the rules based on the TPP provisions.

The Agreement binds the signatory countries to further opening of market in services, particularly for financial services and tele-communication services. Further, the TPP prohibits countries from implementing measures aimed at restricting data flow over the Internet. Chapter 3 commences with a comparison between GATS provisions on the one hand and the TPP's services chapter and sector-specific obligations relating to financial services, temporary entry of business persons, telecommunication services and electronic commerce on the other. Thereafter, implications for India if it were to adhere to the TPP template of rules are discussed. To illustrate, the market access rules in financial services are examined with a view to assessing the changes that may be required in the existing policy of the RBI pertaining to foreign banks, if India conforms to the TPP.

The most contentious provisions of the TPP relate to protection of IPRs. With the TPP providing more stringent protection for IPRs, this is aimed at limiting, if not totally eliminating, competition faced by patented medicines from cheaper generic drugs. It should surprise no one if national budgets on public health in the TPP countries soar on account of patented medicines enjoying monopoly pricing for longer periods. Of course, for the general public, access to affordable medicine could fast become a receding dream, if the rules in the TPP become the basis for negotiating new rules on the protection of IPRs at the WTO. Civil societies in many TPP countries have been protesting against this negative aspect of the TPP. In this background, Chapter 4 examines the TPP provisions on IPRs and highlights how these provisions seek higher level of minimum commitments for protecting IPRs, reduce or remove safeguards while also substantially enhancing the enforcement provisions. This chapter further identifies specific provisions in the TPP that would adversely affect the manufacture of generic medicines by delaying their entry in the market. Chapter 5 identifies some of the changes that may be required to be made in India's laws and regulations, if it were to adhere to the TPP template of rules on a mandatory basis.

In the TPP context, some commentators have voiced concern that India might experience investment diversion, particularly as countries such as Vietnam would offer more robust investor protection (see, for example, Mehta 2015). However, to project IIAs as the magic wand for countries to attract foreign investment appears to be more a matter of faith, as there is no conclusive empirical evidence establishing that bilateral investment agreements indeed enhance investment flows. On the contrary, based on a rigorous empirical exercise, UNCTAD's Trade and Development Report (2014) has concluded that IIAs 'appear to have no effect on bilateral North–South FDI flows'. The report strikes a cautionary note by exhorting developing-country policymakers not to assume that signing investment agreements will boost FDI. Despite extremely strong provisions for protecting the interests of investors, IIAs have failed to significantly boost FDI flows. On the other hand, regulatory chill that may be induced due to the threat of being sued under ISDS can severely circumscribe the policy space in developing countries. After stiffly resisting this provision for more than a year, Australia eventually acquiesced to it. These provisions are more about protecting the rights of foreign investors and less about attracting foreign investments. Even in the USA, there is strong bipartisan opposition to some of the investment provisions. Chapter 6 of this book describes some of the key provisions relating to investment protection in the TPP and compares them with the corresponding provisions in India's model BIT. The comparison clearly brings out specific details in each element of the rules on investment protection where India's model BIT is at variance with the TPP provisions.

On the likely impact of the provisions on standards in the TPP, analysts have suggested a wide range of outcomes. Some analysts are of the view that the TPP would result in upward harmonization of product standards, which could impose a higher burden of compliance for India's exports for access to TPP markets (see, for example, Palit 2015 and Rajagopalan 2015). Another conjecture is that the TPP will give wider acceptance for including social standards in trade agreements between developed and developing countries. According to this perspective, the TPP will encompass higher-than-present standards, mainly by validating certain private standards by making reference to them or to the criteria, such as labour standards, which today are outside the standards justified under the WTO. Further, as private standards keep on evolving faster than public standards, this will result in dynamic increasing level of standards over time (Singh 2016). On the assumption that one of the objectives of the developed countries is to upgrade their standards, some studies have recommended that India should raise its standards to those of advanced economies (Meltzer 2016).

It is quite possible that many of the effects on standards mentioned above may arise in future, even in the absence of the TPP. Whether some of the effects mentioned above on standards can be attributed specifically to the TPP and similar other mega-FTAs requires a detailed analysis of the provisions on sanitary and phytosanitary (SPS) and technical barriers to trade (TBT) issues in the TPP. This analysis has been undertaken in Chapter 7. In the process, it also examines some of the likely impacts of the TPP, as suggested in many studies. Chapters 8 and 9 analyse the TPP provisions on labour standards and environment issues and seek to identify their likely impact on India if it were required to comply with international rules modelled on the TPP.

Agreeing to non-discriminatory rules on government procurement has been projected as a win-win situation for developing countries. On the one hand, the developing countries are expected to benefit from such rules by having access to goods and services at competitive prices, expanding consumer choices and enhancing transparency in procurement thereby reducing costs; on the other hand, by becoming parties to a non-discriminatory regime on government procurement, developing countries are expected to enhance their exports by securing a share in government procurement markets in developed countries. However, many countries, both developing and developed, have used government procurement as a policy instrument for meeting social and economic objectives by discriminating in favour of their domestic producers and service suppliers, thereby providing stimulus to domestic manufacturing. Thus, accepting to grant non-discriminatory treatment to foreign producers and service suppliers in government procurement would severely restrict the policy space in developing countries. Chapter 10 examines the provisions on government procurement in the TPP and undertakes a brief analysis of implications for India of abiding by rules based on the TPP provisions.

The SOEs are a common feature in many developing countries. Apart from pursuing commercial objectives, many SOEs are expected to achieve other economic and social goals as well. In many cases, governments may need to subsidize SOEs in order to make them commercially viable. Using some of the concepts of the WTO Agreement on Subsidies and Countervailing Measures (ASCM), the TPP seeks to formulate additional rules and disciplines on the SOEs. These rules seek to limit the ability of the TPP member countries to provide financial support to their SOEs. In this background, Chapter 11 undertakes a brief analysis of the TPP provisions for SOEs. It compares concepts, such as non-commercial assistance and adverse effects, used in the TPP with similar concepts in the ASCM and identifies instances of deviation in SOE rules from ASCM disciplines. Thereafter, this brief chapter assesses the impact on India of SOE rules that might be negotiated on the basis of the TPP provisions.

Chapter 12 is a miscellaneous chapter containing analysis of issues related to regulatory coherence, trade facilitation and trade remedies in the TPP. Regulatory coherence appears to be applicable to certain procedural aspects of governance. However, during the initial stages of the TPP negotiations, Australia had pushed its proposal that would have resulted in significant obligations regarding administrative structures, decision-making process and disciplines to be followed by countries seeking to make changes in their regulatory environment. Chapter 12 also makes a comparison between the TPP provisions on trade facilitation and similar provisions in WTO's Trade Facilitation Agreement. Finally, this chapter provides a brief analysis of the provisions on safeguard measures in the TPP. It focuses on two types of these measures. First, textile-specific measures and, second, safeguard measures. Both these measures are time-bound and are linked to the end of the transition period for the product concerned.

Chapter 13 brings together the conclusions emerging from each chapter and suggests a way forward for India's trade policy in a dynamic world of changes in global trade and the legal framework of rules of governance of international trade, which may be induced by the TPP.

References

Abbott, Frederick M. 2007. 'A New Dominant Trade Species Emerges: Is Bilateralism a Threat?' *Journal of International Economic Law* 10 (3): 571–83.

Baldwin, Robert E., and Magee Christopher S. 2000. 'Is Trade Policy for Sale? Congressional Voting on Recent Trade Bills'. *Public Choice* 105 (1/2): 79–101.

Banerjee, Rajarshi. 2013. 'The Success of, and Response to, India's Law Against Patent Layering'. *Harvard International Law Journal* 54 (May): 204–32.

Bergsten, Fred C. 2015. 'India's Rise: A Strategy for Trade-led Growth'. PIIE Briefing 15-4, PIIE, Washington, DC.

Bertram, G., and Simon Terry. 2014. *Economic Gains and Costs from the TPP*. Sustainability Council of New Zealand, Wellington.

Blustein, Paul. 2009. *Misadventures of the Most Favoured Nations*. New York: Public Affairs.

Chase, Steven. 2015, October 2. 'NDP Government Would Not Adhere to a TPP Deal, Mulcair Says in Letter'. *The Globe and Mail*. Retrieved 18 July 2017, from http://www.theglobeandmail.com/news/politics/ndp-government-would-not-adhere-to-a-tpp-deal-mulcair-says-in-letter/article26631467/

Cottier, Thomas. 2015. 'The Common Law of International Trade and the Future of the World Trade Organization'. *Journal of International Economic Law* 18 (March): 3–20.

Department of Trade and Industry. 2013. 'Draft National Policy on Intellectual Property'. Notice No. 918 of 2003, Department of Trade and Industry, Makati.

Drutman, Lee. 2014. 'How Big Pharma (and Others) Began Lobbying on the Trans-Pacific Partnership Before You Ever Heard of It'. Retrieved 6 June 2016, from http://sunlightfoundation.com/blog/2014/03/13/tpp-lobby/

Elms, Deborah. 2015. 'The Origins and Evolution of the Trans-Pacific Partnership (TPP) Trade Negotiations'. Asian Trade Centre Working Paper, Asian Trade Centre, Singapore.

Finnemore, M., and K. Sikkink. 1998. 'International Norm Dynamics and Political Change'. *International Organization* 52 (4): 887–917.

Fleury, Julien S., and J. Marcoux. 2016. 'The US Shaping of State-owned Enterprise Disciplines in The TPP'. *Journal of International Economic Law* 19: 445–65.

Fremdreis, John P. and Richard W. Waterman. 1985. 'PAC Contributors and Legislative Behavior: Senate Voting on Trucking Deregulation'. *Social Science Quarterly* 66: 401–12.

Grammer, Robbie. 2017. 'Japan Wants to Revive the Trans Pacific Partnership Even Without the U.S'. Foreign Policy, 24 April. Retrieved from http://foreignpolicy.com/2017/04/24/japan-wants-to-revive-trans-pacific-partnership-even-without-united-states-asia-trade-agreements/.

Grossman, Gene, and Elhanan Helpman. 1994. 'Electoral Competition and Special Interest Politics'. NBER Working Paper Series, Working Paper no. 4877, NBER, Cambridge, MA.

Guha, Shouvik K. 2013. 'Argentina Goes the 3(d) Way: Creases of Worry for the Pharmaceutical Patent Applicants?' SPICY IP. Retrieved 18 July 2017, from http://spicyipindia.blogspot.com/2012/05/argentina-goes-3d-way-creases-of-worry.html

Hart, Michael. 1997. 'The WTO and the Political Economy of Globalization'. *Journal of World Trade* 31 (5): 75–95.

Higgott, Richard. 2006. 'The Limits to Multilateral Economic Governance'. In *Globalisation and Economic Security in East Asia*, edited by Helen Nesadurai. London and New York: Routledge, 176; original quote in *New Statesman*, 23 June 2003, 17.

Hrbata, Veronika. 2010. 'No International Organization is an Island'. *Journal of World Trade* 44 (1): 1–47.

Hufbauer, Gary C., and Cathleen Cimino-Isaacs. 2015. 'How Will TPP and TTIP Change the WTO System?' *Journal of International Economic Law* 18: 679–96.

Independent Commission on Trade Policy. 2017, March. 'Charting a Course for Trade and Economic Integration in the Asia-Pacific'. *Asia Society Policy Institute Report*. Manhattan, NY: Asia Society Policy Institute.

Kau, James B. and Paul H. Rubin. 1982. *Congressmen, Constituents, and Contributors*. Boston, MA: Martinus Nijhoff Publishing.

Kelsey, Jane. 2016. 'The TPP: Treaty Making, Parliamentary Democracy, Regulatory Sovereignty and the Rule of Law'. Third World Resurgence, No. 303/304. Penang, Malaysia: Third World Network.

Kirk, Ron. 2009a. December 14. 'Text of USTR Letter to Congressional Leaders'. USTR. Retrieved August 29, 2014, from http://www.ustr.gov/webfm_send/1559. (Also available in Barston, R.P. 2014. *Modern Diplomacy*, 314–15. Routledge.)

Kirk, Ron. 2009b. 'Remarks on Trans-Pacific Partnership Negotiations'. USTR. Retrieved 18 July 2017, from https://ustr.gov/about-us/policy-offices/press-office/press-releases/2009/december/ustr-ron-kirk-remarks-trans-pacific-partnership-n

Lawrence, Robert Z., and C. Devereaux. 2006. *Case Studies in US Trade Negotiation, Volume 1: Making the Rules*. Washington, DC: Institute for International Economics.

Ludwig, Mike. 2014. 'Big Pharma Lobbies Hard to End India's Distribution of Affordable Generic Drugs'. *Truthout*. Retrieved 4 June 2016, from http://www.truth-out.org/news/item/26721-big-pharma-lobbies-hard-to-end-india-s-distribution-of-affordable-generic-drugs

Mayeda, Andrew, and David Gura. 2017. 'Wilbur Ross Says TPP Could Form "Starting Point" for U.S. on Revamped NAFTA Talks'. *Bloomberg News*, 3 May.

Mehta, Pratap Bhanu. 2015. 'As India Stays Away'. *The Indian Express*, 9 October.

Meltzer, Joshua P. 2016. 'Standards and Regulations in Trans-Pacific Partnership Negotiations: Implications for India'. In *TPP and India: Implications of Mega-regionals for Developing Economies*, edited by H.V. Singh. New Delhi: Wisdom Tree.

Merica, Dan, and Eric Bradner. 2015. 'Hillary Clinton Comes Out Against TPP Trade Deal'. CNN, 7 October. Retrieved 18 July 2017, from http://edition.cnn.com/2015/10/07/politics/hillary-clinton-opposes-tpp/

Obama, Barack. 2015, October 5. 'Statement by the US President on the TPP'. Office of the Press Secretary, The White House. Retrieved 30 July 2016, from https://www.whitehouse.gov/the-press-office/2015/10/05/statement-president-trans-pacific-partnership

———. 2016. 'President Obama: The TPP Would Let America, Not China, Lead the Way on Global Trade'. *The Washington Post*, 2 May. Retrieved 30 July 2016, from https://www.washingtonpost.com/opinions/president-obama-the-tpp-would-let-america-not-china-lead-the-way-on-global-trade/2016/05/02/680540e4-0fd0-11e6-93ae-50921721165d_story.html

Patil, Amitendu. 2015. 'TPP and India: Lasting Lessons'. *The Financial Express*, October 9. Retrieved 18 July 2017, from http://www.financialexpress.com/article/fe-columnist/tpp-and-india-lasting-lessons/148244/

Rajagopalan, T.N.C. 2015. 'How the Trans-Pacific Partnership Will Affect India's Foreign Trade'. *Business Standard*, 11 October.

Seshadri, V.S. 2017. 'Regional Comprehensive Economic Partnership Agreement: Need for a Strategy'. RIS Discussion Paper No. 209, RIS, New Delhi.

Singh, H.V., ed. 2016. 'Trans-Pacific Partnership Agreement: Impact on India and Other Developing Nations'. In *TPP and India: Implications of Mega-regionals for Developing Economies*. New Delhi: Wisdom Tree.

Steinberg, Richard H. 2002. 'In the Shadow of Law or Power? Consensus-based Bargaining and Outcomes in the GATT/WTO'. *International Organization* 56 (2): 339–74.

Stiglitz, Joseph. 2015. 'Rewriting the Rules of the American Economy'. *Independent Global News*, October 27. Retrieved 8 June 2016, from http://www.democracynow.org/2015/10/27/nobel_laureate_joseph_stiglitz_on_rewriting_the

Sunstein, Cass R. 1996. 'Social Norms and Social Roles'. *Columbia Law Review* 96 (4): 903–68.

Tani, Shotaro. 2016. 'TPP Not Beneficial for Member Nations—Malaysia's Mahathir'. *Nikkei Asian Review* (May 31). Retrieved 7 August 2017, from https://asia.nikkei.com/Politics-Economy/International-Relations/TPP-not-beneficial-for-member-nations-Malaysia-s-Mahathir

Today. 2014, December 6. 'Mahathir Slams UMNO for Ignoring TPP Pact, Education System Issues'. Retrieved 18 July 2017, from http://www.todayonline.com/world/asia/mahathir-slams-umno-ignoring-tpp-pact-education-system-issues

Tita, Alberto. 1998. 'Globalization: A New Political and Economic Space Requiring Supranational Governance'. *Journal of World Trade* 32 (3): 47–55.

Trump, Donald J. 2017, 23 January. 'Presidential Memorandum Regarding Withdrawal of the United States from the Trans-Pacific Partnership Negotiations and Agreement'. Office of the Press Secretary, The White House. Retrieved 13 June 2017, from https://www.whitehouse.gov/the-press-office/2017/01/23/presidential-memorandum-regarding-withdrawal-united-states-trans-pacific

Tosini, Suzanne C., and Edward Tower. 1987. 'The Textile Bill of 1985: The Determinants of Congressional Voting Patterns'. *Public Choice* 54: 19–25.

UNCTAD. 2014. 'Do Bilateral Investment Treaties Attract FDI Flows to Developing Economies?' *Trade and Development Report*. Retrieved 18 July 2017, from http://unctad.org/en/PublicationsLibrary/tdr2014_en.pdf

Warren, Elizabeth. 2015. 'The Trans-Pacific Partnership Clause Everyone Should Oppose'. *The Washington Post*, February 25. Retrieved 18 July 2017, from https://www.washingtonpost.com/opinions/kill-the-dispute-settlement-language-in-the-trans-pacific-partnership/2015/02/25/ec7705a2-bd1e-11e4-b274-e5209a3bc9a9_story.html

Winslett, Gary. 2016. 'How Regulations Became the Crux of Trade Politics'. *Journal of World Trade* 50 (1): 47–70.

WTO. 1996, 13 December. 'WTO Document No. WT/MIN(96)/16'. Geneva: WTO.

———. 2001, 10 November. 'WTO Document No. WT/MIN(01)/ST/3'. Geneva: WTO.

———. 2004, 2 August. 'WTO Document No. WT/L/579'. Geneva: WTO.

———. 2007, 1 August. 'WTO Document No. TN/AG/W/4'. Geneva: WTO.

———. 2015, 21 December. 'WTO Document No. WT/MIN(15)/DEC'. Geneva: WTO.

———. 2016a, 4 July. 'Work Programme on Electronic Commerce Non-paper from the United States'. WTO Document No. JOB/GC/94. Geneva: WTO.

———. 2016b, 25 July. 'Work Programme on Electronic Commerce Non-paper for the Discussions on Electronic Commerce/Digital Trade from Japan'. WTO Document No. JOB/GC/100. Geneva: WTO.

WTO Centre VCCI. 2017, April 25. 'Japan to Push for Implementation of TPP Without U.S'. Retrieved 5 May 2017, from http://wtocenter.vn/news/japan-push-implementation-tpp-without-us. (Citing *The Mainichi Japan* as the source.)

Yamazaki, Yun and Ryohei Yasoshima. 2017. 'TPP 11 Ministers Pledge to Revive Stalled Agreement'. *Nikkei Asian Review*, 21 May. https://asia.nikkei.com/Politics-Economy/International-Relations/TPP-11-ministers-pledge-to-revive-stalled-agreement?page=2 (last visited 7 August 2017).

Yanai, Akiko. 2000. 'APEC and the WTO: Seeking Opportunities for Cooperation'. IDE APEC Study Centre Working Paper Series 99/00 No. 2, Institute of Developing Economies, Chiba.

2
TPP and Market Access for Goods

Abhijit Das, Prajyna Paramita Barua and Dilfy Ann Philip

2.1 Introduction

It is now an accepted fact that the Indian economy has got more integrated with the global economy after the country initiated economic reforms in 1991. Consequently, developments in international markets, as well as in international trade rules, now have a significant impact on India's overall economic development. Over the past decades, two features stand out prominently in the landscape of trade agreements. First, there has been an explosion in the number of preferential trade agreements (PTAs) that have been implemented. Countries that are not parties to a PTA face the prospect of trade diversion—a PTA diverts trade, away from a more efficient supplier outside the PTA, towards a less efficient supplier within the PTA. Second, these agreements increasingly include rules going beyond the traditional area of customs duties and contain disciplines on many behind-the-border measures such as protection of intellectual property rights, competition, labour, environment, standards and regulatory coherence. Consequently, countries are voluntarily ceding some of their sovereignty in order to become a member of a free trade agreement (FTA)/PTA. India has not remained insulated from the impact of both these prominent features in the trade landscape. This chapter analyses the impact of the provisions of the Trans-Pacific Partnership Agreement (TPP, or the Agreement) on trade in goods from both these perspectives—examining the effects on India if the TPP is implemented, with India remaining outside the Agreement; and what would be the impact on India if it were to comply with some of these provisions that might get included in international trade rules in the future.

Section 2.2 analyses the trends in India's trade of goods and services and briefly discusses India's growing integration into the global economy. This provides a larger market for India's exports, thereby offering the possibility of spurring economic growth domestically. However, the dependence on global markets as an important driver of the Indian economy makes India vulnerable to trade diversion arising from its competitor countries entering into PTAs/FTAs and benefitting from facing lower, or no, import duties and reduced barriers to trade. In case the TPP gets implemented, India is likely to face trade diversion. Section 2.3 examines some studies on this issue. One of the main aims of this book is to understand the likely impact on India if the provisions of the TPP become a basis for negotiating international trade rules multilaterally and bilaterally. Section 2.4 provides details of some of the key provisions in the TPP on trade in goods. Section 2.5 assesses the impact on India if it were required to follow the disciplines on trade in goods contained in the TPP. Section 2.6 sums up some of the key points emerging from this chapter.

2.2 Gradual, But Increasing Integration of India into the Global Economy

Over the past decades, Indian economy has gradually got more integrated with the global economy. The trade exposure to the outside world has shown a significant change after the initiation of economic liberalization. During the 1960s–80s, India's total exports as a share of its gross domestic product (GDP) was almost flat, being between 3 per cent and 6 per cent. This ratio started increasing rapidly after the 1990s. During 2010–14, it reached almost 25 per cent, indicating deepening of the integration into the global economy. This point is illustrated more starkly, if we examine the ratio of total trade to GDP. This ratio was between 9 per cent and 13 per cent during the 1960s–80s, but had surged to 52 per cent during 2010–14 (Figure 2.1). Further, according to the Organisation for Economic Co-operation and Development (OECD), the foreign content of India's exports has increased significantly in the last two decades, more than doubling from under 10 per cent in 1995 to 24 per cent in

Figure 2.1
India's trade as percentage of its GDP

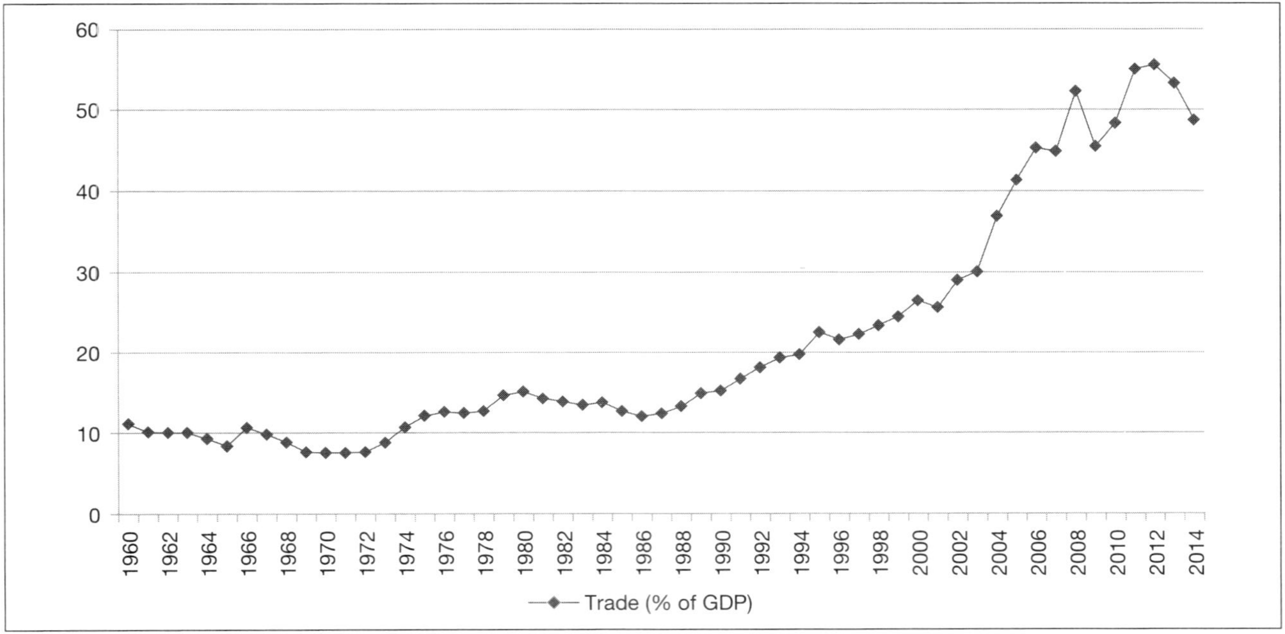

Source: Data based on the World Development Indicators.

2011 (OECD 2015). This provides another indicator of India's growing integration into the global economy.

Although India's integration into the world economy has increased over the years, its share in world trade remains low. Figures 2.2–2.5 graphically represent the trends in India's exports and imports of goods and services.[1] No doubt, India's share in global exports of goods has doubled during 2001–15, yet it reached only a modest level of 1.7 per cent in 2014. In the services sector, India's share in world exports has been higher than that in goods. It stood at 3.2 per cent in 2015. Nevertheless, goods exports were almost 1.5 times higher than services exports in the year 2015. Thus, goods exports continue to remain prominent in India's overall export basket. Given this background of India's trade and its role in the national economy, how would the country be impacted, if the TPP were to be implemented? The next section reviews some studies that have undertaken a quantitative estimate on this aspect.

2.3 Quantifying the Impact of Implementation of the TPP: Reviewing Some Studies

Given the wide coverage of policy measures that would be subjected to the rules under the TPP, understanding the quantitative impact of implementation of the Agreement becomes important. This is relevant not only for the countries that are signatories to the TPP, but also for other countries. The former category of countries has used quantitative assessments, some of them by US-based think tanks, to justify their participation in the TPP negotiations (see, for example, Bertram and Terry 2014 for New Zealand). The latter category of countries might have remained outside the TPP on account of perceived difficulties in complying with some of the provisions under the Agreement. However, a country might be tempted to seek membership of the TPP if losses on account of exclusion from the TPP are high and overall gains are also estimated to be high if it were to join the TPP. Thus, quantifying the impact of the TPP could have crucial implications for trade policies of excluded countries and their overall approach to seeking accession to the TPP. However, such an assessment is rather complex.

---

[1] We gratefully acknowledge Dr Pralok Gupta for preparing these figures.

Figure 2.2
India's exports of goods: Value and global share

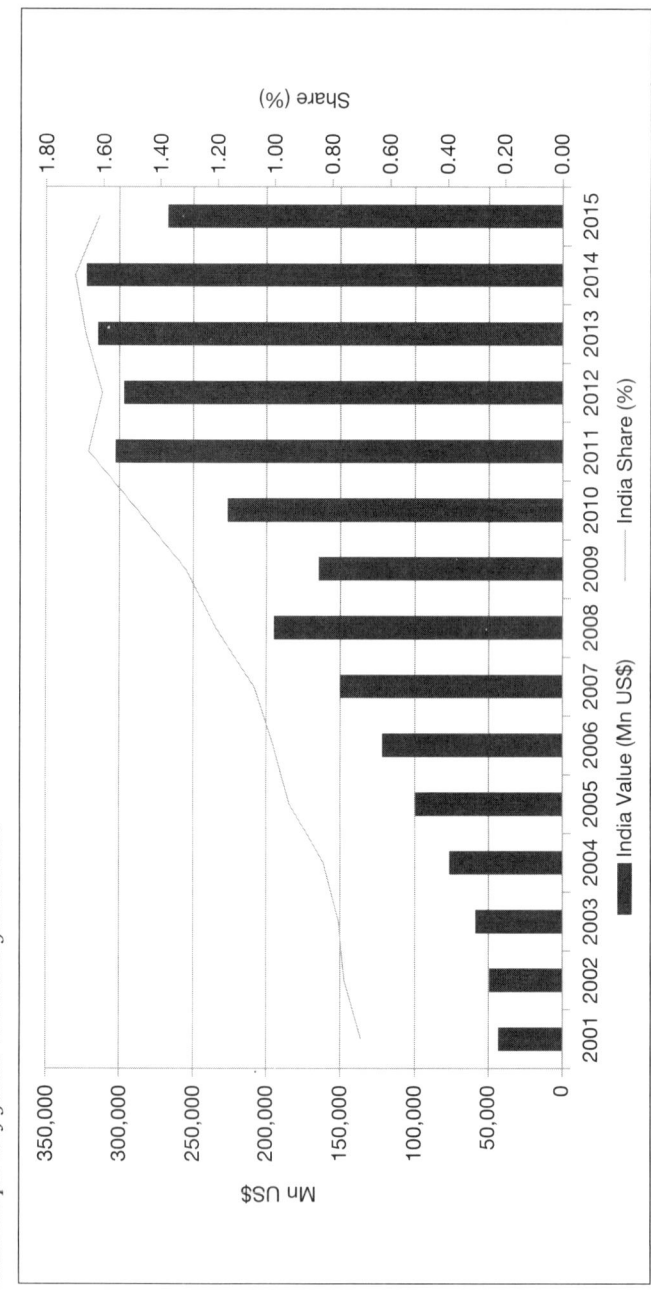

Source: UNCTAD.

Figure 2.3

India's imports of goods: Value and global share

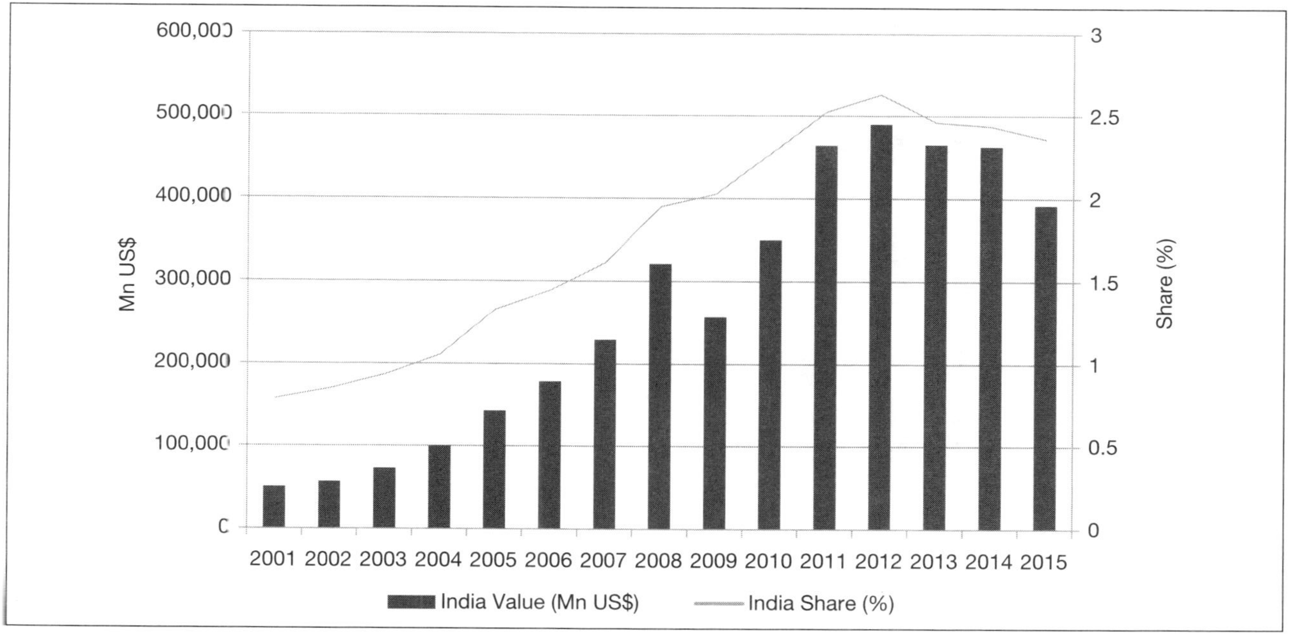

Source: UNCTAD.

Figure 2.4
India's exports of services: Value and global share

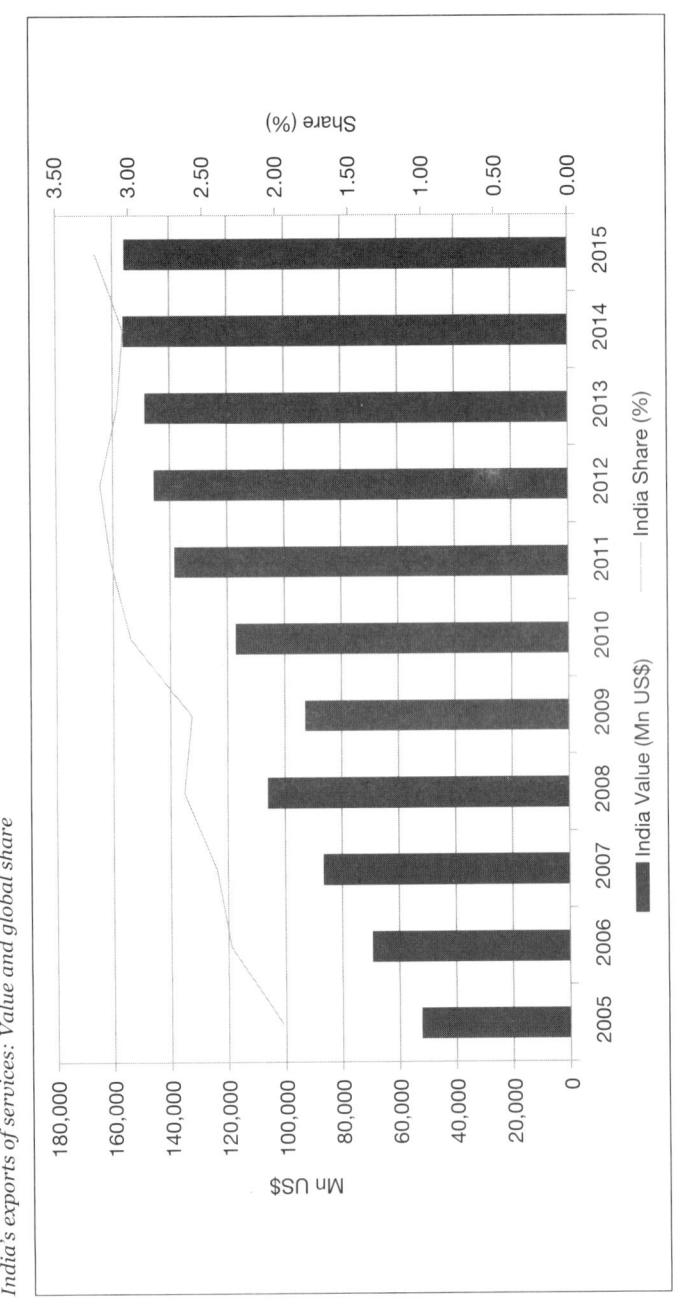

Source: UNCTAD.

Figure 2.5
India's imports of services: Value and global share

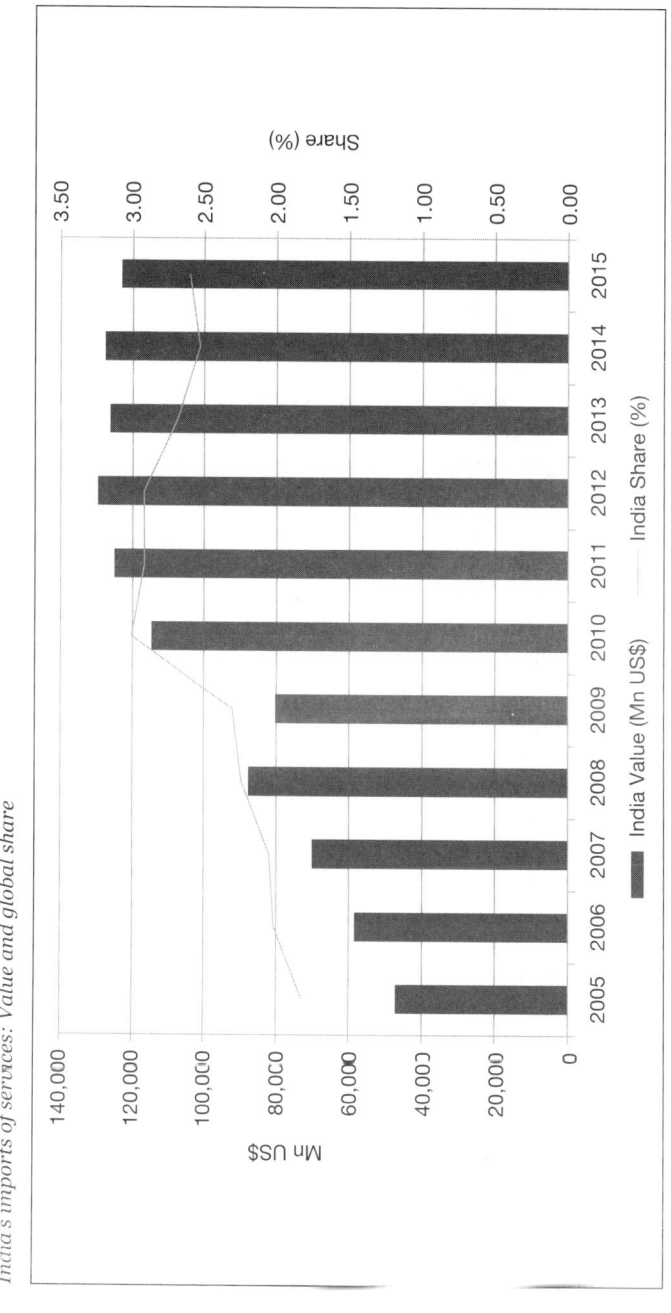

Source: UNCTAD.

Complexities involved in modelling the impact of trade and investment agreements arise mainly from two sources—first, how the policy changes induced by a trade agreement are simulated or measured by the model; and second, what assumptions are made regarding the impact of policy changes on the economy. A model is required to simulate a wide range of policy changes that would arise from implementation of the trade agreement, including tariff liberalization, services liberalization, reduction in non-tariff barriers (NTBs), stronger investment protection regime, changes in standard of protection of intellectual property, non-discriminatory treatment in government procurement, prohibition on export taxes, etc. How to simulate these policy changes poses a significant challenge for a trade economist. While modelling tariff reductions is relatively standardised, there is no widely accepted methodology for modelling the changes in NTBs. A model also has to make assumptions regarding the impact of trade and investment liberalization on the allocation of resources across different sectors of the economy, whether labour markets are flexible to compensate for job losses in one sector by gains in another sector, whether wages would increase—to illustrate a few challenges. Overall, the credibility of a model would, to some extent, depend on whether the assumptions are standard, have a theoretical basis, reflect reality or have been frequently used in past credible models.

The estimates of economic impact of the TPP in some of the frequently cited studies do not appear to be based on strong theoretical and empirical foundations. Not only is there no consensus regarding the overall impact of the TPP on the signatory parties and non-member countries, but also the estimates seem to diverge rather sharply. Further, some of the prominent studies seeking to estimate the impact of the TPP have been criticised for making arbitrary assumptions. In addition, some commentators appear to misinterpret the results of some of the estimations and consequently claim gains from the TPP that appear rather exaggerated. This section examines the contribution of the TPP countries in India's export basket. Thereafter, it discusses some of frequently quoted studies on the TPP and their underlying assumptions. Finally, this section discusses the results of some of the studies from the perspective of the likely impact of the mega-FTA on India.

Declining Significance of TPP Countries as Destinations for India's Exports

Over the past decade and a half, India's exports to the TPP countries has increased significantly from US$14 billion in 2000 to US$79 billion in 2014. However, India's dependence on the TPP countries for its exports has declined, as the share of these countries in India's export basket has reduced from 33.2 per cent in 2000 to 24.8 per cent in 2014 (Table 2.1). Despite the declining trend, some of the TPP countries remain important export destinations for India. With India's competitors from the TPP countries set to enjoy the benefits of zero duty access in the markets of the 12 signatory countries, the possibility of trade diversion from India cannot be ruled out. However, the extent of trade diversion is likely to be relatively small compared to the value of India's total global exports.

As India has FTAs with Japan and ASEAN, it already enjoys preferential access/zero duty access in 5 of the 12 TPP countries—Brunei, Japan, Malaysia, Singapore and Vietnam. India is also at an advanced stage of concluding FTA negotiations with Australia and Canada. Thus, trade diversion is likely to be significant mainly in the United States of America (USA).

Quantifying the Impact of Implementation of the TPP: Optimistic Claims Based on Shaky Foundations

Optimistic claims about the TPP's economic impacts for the member countries are largely based on economic modelling projections in various studies by Petri et al. (2011, 2012, 2014). Some of the signatory countries of the TPP have used the results of these studies to highlight the gains from the Agreement (see, for example, Bertram and Terry 2014 for New Zealand). This underscores the influence of these studies on the public policies of some countries participating in the TPP. It could also have an impact on the decisions of other countries, presently outside the TPP, to seek accession to it. It is, therefore, appropriate to discuss the studies by Petri et al. in some detail.

These studies are based on an advanced 18 sector, 24 region computable general equilibrium model of the world economy. The basic model makes a baseline projection of GDP and exports in 2010, 2015, 2020 and 2025 under the scenario without implementation of the TPP. Thereafter,

Table 2.1

India's exports to the TPP countries

Partner Country	2000		2005		2010		2014	
	India's Exports to Partner Country (Billion US$)	% Share of Partner Country in India's Total Exports	India's Export to Partner Country (Billion US$)	% Share of Partner Country in India's Total Exports	India's Export to Partner Country (Billion US$)	% Share of Partner Country in India's Total Exports	India's Exports to Partner Country (Billion US$)	% Share of Partner Country in India's Total Exports
Australia	0.40	0.94	0.83	0.82	1.65	0.75	2.59	0.82
Brunei	0.00	0.01	0.00	0.00	0.02	0.01	0.04	0.01
Canada	0.64	1.52	0.99	0.99	1.25	0.57	2.17	0.68
Chile	0.10	0.24	0.14	0.14	0.48	0.22	0.62	0.19
Japan	1.83	4.31	2.46	2.45	4.81	2.18	5.76	1.81
Malaysia	0.53	1.25	1.14	1.14	3.56	1.61	4.64	1.46
Mexico	0.18	0.43	0.41	0.40	0.77	0.35	2.92	0.92
New Zealand	0.06	0.14	0.14	0.14	0.19	0.09	0.32	0.10
Peru	0.02	0.05	0.09	0.09	0.40	0.18	0.75	0.24
Singapore	0.79	1.86	5.43	5.41	9.07	4.11	9.68	3.05
USA	9.30	21.97	16.54	16.48	23.59	10.70	42.68	13.44
Vietnam	0.20	0.46	0.63	0.63	2.48	1.12	6.53	2.06
Total (all TPP countries)	14.06	33.19	28.80	28.70	48.25	21.89	78.70	24.79

Source: Authors' calculations based on World Integrated Trade Solution (WITS).

based on certain assumptions for quantifying the impact of different provisions of the TPP, the model estimates welfare/income gains and export increases on account of implementation of the TPP. The model takes into account the utilization rate of tariff preferences, tariff liberalization, removal of NTBs, rules of origin and removal of barriers to foreign direct investment (FDI). The model also makes estimations under other scenarios, including implementation of the expanded Free Trade Area of Asia Pacific (FTAAP). The results of the various studies on the TPP by Petri, Plummer and Zhai are summarized in Table 2.2. The results suggest that the gains from the TPP, in terms of increase in GDP and exports, appear rather modest for the world and for the USA. The most recent study by these authors estimates the overall net income gains, ranging from 0.5 per cent in the USA to 13 per cent in Vietnam over 15 years (Petri et al. 2016).

It is important to note that the changes in exports and world income gains in Petri et al. (2011) are almost double the corresponding values in Petri et al. (2012). This is mainly on account of different assumptions made in the two studies regarding trade costs. Petri et al. (2011) assumes that implementation of the TPP will reduce the variable cost of export sales. On the other hand, Petri et al. (2012) makes the assumption that half of the trade costs represented by tariffs and NTBs are fixed costs. This study further assumes that trade liberalization will reduce both fixed as well as variable costs. As reduction in fixed costs has a stronger effect on the expansion of trade than a commensurate reduction in variable costs, it is not surprising that the gains in income and trade are significantly higher in Petri et al. (ibid.) as compared to Petri et al. (2011). This also highlights the crucial role of assumptions underlying a model in determining the outcome of the modelling exercise.

As the results of modelling can be misinterpreted, it is important to clarify that the changes in welfare/income and exports as shown in Table 2.2 represent a comparison with a baseline scenario in which the TPP is not implemented by 2025. Thus, each figure shown in the table represents a change that would occur by 2025 in the scenario of the TPP being implemented, compared to the value of the variable in the baseline year of 2025 when the TPP is not implemented. It does not represent the annual change in the variable in the year 2025. To elaborate, based on the results of Petri et al. (2014), it would be incorrect to conclude that the exports of the USA would increase by 6.8 per cent in 2025 compared to the previous year. The correct interpretation is that if the scenario of the TPP Plus four countries is implemented, then US exports would be higher than

Table 2.2

Comparing the results of various studies by Petri, Plummer and Zhai

Study	Scenario	Welfare/Income Gains in 2025 (Billion US$)			Welfare/Income Gains % change from Baseline GDP			Export Increase from Baseline (Billion US$)			% Export Increase from Baseline		
		World	USA	India	World	USA	India	World	USA	India	World	USA	India
Petri et al. (2011)	TPP + Korea	104	13.9	−0.6	0.1	0.15	−0	226	55	−3	0.8	2	−0.3
Petri et al. (2012)	TPP + Korea	295	78	−3.8	0.29	0.38	−0.1	444	124	−6.7	1.6	4.4	−0.8
Petri et al. (2014)	TPP + 4	338	69	−6.9	0.3	0.7	−0.1	655	190	−13.2	2.3	6.8	−1.5
Petri et al. (ibid.)	FTAAPX with India	1870	202	213	1.8	1	4.1	4048	625	536	14.2	22.3	62

Sources: Petri et al. (2011, 2012, 2014).

Notes:
1. 2025 has been used as the baseline year in Petri et al. (2011, 2012, 2014).
2. TPP + 4 includes the 12 TPP countries, along with Korea, Indonesia, Philippines and Thailand.
3. FTAAPX includes 21 members of APEC, along with India, Cambodia, Laos and Myanmar.
4. Petri et al. (2011) estimates welfare change, instead of GDP change.
5. The studies assume different scenarios for the date of implementation of the TPP by its various signatory countries.

the baseline exports in 2025 by 6.8 per cent. Some commentators appear to have made the error of interpreting the increase from the baseline as representing annual change or change per year. To illustrate, Bergsten (Preface to Petri et al. [2012, ix]) interprets the modelling results as representing an increase in world income by US$295 billion (and for the US$78 billion) 'per year' (Bergsten 2015). This interpretation is incorrect and is likely to overstate the annual gains from the TPP for its member countries. At the risk of stating the obvious—per year change in exports would require a comparison between export levels in two different years. However, in the studies by Petri et al., the comparison is between export levels in the same year (2025) under different simulation scenarios. The result of this comparison should not be interpreted as the per year change.

At the other end of the spectrum, a working paper of the Tufts University (by Capaldo et al. 2016) finds that the TPP is more likely to lead to net employment losses in many countries (771,000 jobs lost overall, with 448,000 in the USA alone). Declining worker purchasing power would weaken aggregate demand, slowing economic growth. The USA (–0.5 per cent) and Japan (–0.1 per cent) are projected to suffer small net income losses, not gains, from the TPP.

Both these streams of studies have been subject to considerable criticism. Rodrik (2016) provides a concise, yet insightful, account of shortcomings of the studies by Petri et al. and of that by Capaldo (2016). According to Rodrik, Petri et al. assume that labour markets are sufficiently flexible and rule out unemployment. Although their studies predict that most of the economic benefits of the TPP will come from reductions in NTBs and lower obstacles to foreign investment, Rodrik is of the view that modelling these effects is based on assumptions that require many 'arbitrary shortcut'. Turning to Capaldo's framework, Rodrik observes that this study 'lacks sectoral and country detail; its behavioural assumptions remain opaque; and its extreme Keynesian assumptions sit uneasily with its medium-term perspective' (Rodrik 2016).

Bertram and Terry (2014) have closely examined the assumptions underlying the model used by Petri et al. (2012) and have raised several technical questions about the model. They have concluded that 'the resulting gains reported do not appear to have solid analytical foundations' (Bertram and Terry 2014). Based primarily on Bertram and Terry (ibid.), following are some of the points of criticism of the model used by Petri et al.:

1. The wide-ranging TPP provisions have been treated as efficiency-enhancing cost reductions. No attempt has been made to account

for the downsides of the TPP provisions. Thus, welfare and income changes would, ab initio, be positive for signatory countries. Even without undertaking the estimation, based merely on the underlying assumptions, it could have been concluded that the TPP will enhance welfare and incomes in signatory countries.
2. The modelling exercise is almost entirely limited to the anticipated positive effects of the TPP. The model does not provide any rigorous account of the main negative effects of the provisions of the TPP. As costs are not included in the model, the results have a one-sided focus. Thus, they do not provide a cost-benefit assessment of the TPP.
3. The authors use subjective judgement to model NTBs, resulting in significantly overstating the gains from the TPP. While estimating the impact of reduction of NTBs, the authors assume that two-thirds of NTBs consist of barriers that can be eliminated by trade policy changes. No basis has been provided for this assumption.
4. The authors translate measures to enforce intellectual property rights and copyright protection into cost reductions that increase trade in services. However, they do not explain the basis for assuming the extent of cost reductions from these measures. They also appear to ignore the likely increase in medicine prices that could be experienced by developing countries on account of more stringent standards of IP protection.
5. The assumption that half of the trade costs represented by tariffs and NTBs are fixed costs has no theoretical basis. The gains decline sharply if the fixed cost assumption is not made.
6. The authors arbitrarily assume that every dollar of FDI transferred from country to country within the TPP bloc generates a net gain in the annual income of 33 cents, divided evenly between the two countries. There is no economic theory or modelling practice that supports this claim.

Quantifying the Impact of Implementation of the TPP: Segregating the Sources of Adverse Impact on Non-members

So far, in this section, the overall impact of the TPP on GDP and exports has been discussed. This provides an overall assessment of economic and trade impacts of the TPP. The composite picture does not provide granular details of the impact of some of the areas of policy liberalization under the TPP. This subsection seeks to fill this gap.

It is important for a country, which is not a member of the TPP, to understand the sources of adverse impact of remaining outside the Agreement. The adverse impact could arise on account of trade diversion due to tariffs and services liberalization, implementation of labour standards, stronger rules for environment protection, investment diversion—to name a few. If the adverse impact on account of a policy variable is high and the country does not have domestic sensitivities in accepting the rules under the TPP for liberalization in that policy area, the country could give positive consideration to seeking TPP membership. On the other hand, a country may feel justified in staying out of the TPP, if the perceived losses are in respect of policy variables where considerable domestic sensitivities exist. Thus, decomposing, or unpacking, the impact of the TPP can provide useful pointers for countries in trade policy making.

The studies by Petri et al. on the TPP do not discuss the disaggregated impact of different policy areas under the TPP on TPP signatories and non-member countries. An insightful thought experiment by Narayanan et al. (2016) estimates the overall impact, as well as the impact segregated by policy variables, of the TPP and the Trans-Atlantic Trade and Investment Partnership (TTIP)—a mega-FTA being negotiated by the USA and the European Union (EU). This study shows that the combined impact of these two mega-FTAs would cumulatively change the GDP during 2015–30 to the following extent for countries that are part of either of these two trade agreements—EU: 1.97 per cent; USA: 1.52 per cent; Japan: 1.72 per cent; Vietnam: 0.51 per cent; Mexico: –0.02 per cent, etc. In respect of countries that are not members of the TPP or TTIP, Narayanan et al. (ibid.) estimate the following change in the GDP from the base projections in 2030—India: –3.44 per cent; China: –2.47 per cent; Indonesia: –1.68 per cent; Philippines: –1.68 per cent; Thailand: –0.38 per cent. It should be noted that the figures mentioned above are not annual changes in GDP due to the combined impact of the TPP and TTIP. Rather, the percentage changes represent the extent to which the GDP would be higher (or lower) if both the mega-FTAs are implemented, compared to the likely estimate of the GDP in the baseline year of 2030 in the absence of the two mega-FTAs. In other words, by remaining excluded from the TPP and TTIP, from 2015 onwards India's GDP would get progressively reduced and the cumulative impact over 15 years would be that by 2030 the GDP would be lower by 3.44 percentage points, as compared to the scenario without the TPP and TTIP.

An extremely important point made by this study is that the real wages of unskilled labour in developing countries across the world will rise as a result of increase in labour standards due to the provisions in the TPP and TTIP. Thus, even if countries such as India, China, and Indonesia are not part of these mega-FTAs, they would still face adverse impact of provisions related to labour standards contained in these agreements. The results of this study point to the extremely pernicious impact of labour standards on developing countries. To elaborate, the impact on India of remaining outside the TPP and the TTIP is quantified by estimating the overall extent to which India's GDP will decline from the base value in 2030. Further, the overall impact on the GDP is disaggregated in terms of the impacts on GDP that is attributable to different underlying reasons, including trade diversion due to tariff and NTB liberalization, labour standards, services, etc. Table 2.3 provides details of the percentage increase in costs arising from compliance with labour standards in different countries, overall impact of the TPP and TTIP on the GDP of the countries by 2030 and impact on the GDP in 2030 that

Table 2.3

Impact of increase in costs due to compliance with labour standards in the TPP and TTIP

Country (a)	% Increase in Costs Arising from Compliance with Labour Standards (b)	Overall GDP Change (%) (c)	GDP Change due to Tariffs and NTB Liberalization on Goods (%) (d)	GDP Change Due to Labour Standards (%) (e)	Contribution of Labour Standards in Overall GDP Change (%) $(f) = e \times 100/c$
	2015–30				
EU 28	0	1.97	0.40	0.28	14.21
USA	0	1.52	0.42	0.34	22.37
Japan	0	1.72	0.53	0.38	22.09
India	14.66	–3.44	–0.96	–2.00	58.14
China	5.75	–2.47	–0.96	–1.01	40.89
Indonesia	8.36	–1.68	–0.61	–0.73	43.45
Philippines	9.9	–1.68	–0.60	–0.74	44.05
Thailand	4.36	–0.38	–0.33	–0.27	71.05

Source: Narayanan et al. (2016, Tables 4.1 and A4).

can be attributed to labour standards in the two mega-FTA. In order to obtain a deeper understanding, the impact of labour standards is compared with the impact of liberalization of tariffs and NTBs on goods. For some of the countries excluded from the TPP and TTIP, the adverse impact on account of labour standards exceeds the impact of trade diversion that would arise due to tariff and NTB liberalization by the member countries of the two mega-FTAs.

To elaborate, out of the 3.44 percentage points decline in India's GDP on account of remaining outside the TPP and TTIP, 2 percentage points decline is attributable to labour standards. This is more than a twofold decline in GDP, as compared to the adverse impact of trade diversion due to tariff and NTB liberalization under the two mega-FTAs. Carrying this analysis further, the increase in wages due to labour standard provisions in the TPP and TTIP accounts for 58 per cent of India's GDP loss due to these two mega-FTAs. The situation in some of the other developing countries is not starkly different from that in India. In China, Indonesia and Philippines, labour standards account for 40–45 per cent of the total decline in GDP due to exclusion from the mega-FTAs. As is the projection for India, these three countries would lose more from labour provisions under the TPP and TTIP than from tariff and NTB liberalization by the member countries of the two mega-FTAs. While the estimates of the impact of labour standards have been made if China, India, Indonesia and Philippines are not parties to the two mega-FTAs, it is apprehended that the impact of labour standards may get further accentuated if these countries were to join the TPP/TTIP. In the scenario of these developing countries joining the mega-FTAs, the labour standards would need to be implemented on economy-wide basis and not remain confined merely to exporters to TPP/TTIP markets. This would make the adverse impact of labour standards even more acute. While increase in wages as a consequence of market forces is desirable, inducing changes in wages through trade agreements may be questionable. Raising the cost of labour above its level of productivity by way of mandatory standards does not improve wages and working conditions of workers in poor countries. In fact, many researchers have argued that workers may suffer negative consequences when their wages are raised above the market value of their productivity (Stern and Turrell 2003).[2] Further, there is no

---

[2] Stern and Turrell refer to numerous empirical studies which have measured the degree to which workers were displaced when mandated minimum wages were raised by different amounts.

evidence to show that adoption of international labour standards has led to rise in productivity (Flanagan 2002).

Quantifying the Impact of Implementation of the TPP on India

Limited literature exists that seeks to quantify the impact on India of remaining outside the TPP. As shown in Table 2.2, Petri et al. (2011) have estimated that India would suffer trade diversion to the extent of 0.3 per cent of its global exports in 2025. This translates into export loss to the extent of US$3 billion in 2025. Petri et al. (2012) make slightly different assumptions and estimate that India would suffer trade diversion to the extent of 0.8 per cent of the baseline exports in 2025. More controversial is the interpretation of the results of Petri et al. (2014). According to the study, if India joins an expanded Free Trade Area of Asia Pacific (FTAAPX) comprising Asia-Pacific Economic Cooperation (APEC) members along with Cambodia, Laos and Myanmar, its exports in 2025 would be higher than the baseline exports by US$536 billion. Bergsten (2015) appears to misinterpret, and significantly overstate, the estimates of Petri et al. (2014) as he claims that 'India could experience export expansion of more than US$500 billion per year'. As clarified earlier in this section, US$536 billion does not represent the amount of annual increase in India's exports in 2025. Instead, it represents the likely increase in exports of India by 2025 if it joins the FTAAPX, above the baseline projection of exports in the absence of the TPP and FTAAPX. While this figure of export gains is being widely cited by commentators and analysts to argue for India joining the TPP, it should be noted that Bertram and Terry (2014) have raised serious questions about the assumptions underlying the model.

Narayanan and Sharma (2013) use the standard Global Trade Analysis Project (GTAP) model for tariff elimination and conclude that India would suffer trade diversion to the extent of US$177 million. According to the authors, India's exports would increase by $22.6 billion and imports by $21.8 billion if India were to join the TPP. A more recent study by Banga and Sahu (2015) uses SMART simulation and estimates India's loss on account of trade diversion to be limited to $191 million. Exports would increase by $5.3 billion and imports by $10.4 billion if India joins the TPP. It should be noted that both these studies model the more limited, yet conventional and non-controversial, aspect of trade agreements—tariff reduction. Neither of these two studies ventures to estimate the impact of liberalization of services or reduction in NTBs.

This section has reviewed some of the studies that seek to quantify the adverse impact on India if it remains outside the Agreement and the Agreement gets implemented. What about the situation in which the TPP is not implemented, but its provisions form the basis of future trade rules at the multilateral and bilateral level? To answer this question, the next section discusses some of the provisions on trade in goods in the TPP.

2.4 TPP and Market Access for Goods: Some Key Provisions

Rules in the TPP on market access for goods are mainly found in the chapters on national treatment and market access for goods, rules of origin and origin procedures, and textiles and apparel. In addition, the chapters on sanitary and phytosanitary (SPS) measures and technical barriers to trade (TBT) are also relevant in the context of market access for goods. In this section we discuss some of the key provisions in the TPP governing market access for goods. These include the provisions on tariff concessions, remanufacturing, export duties and taxes, Information Technology Agreement (ITA), export restrictions on foodstuffs and genetically modified organisms. The provisions on SPS and TBT measures are discussed in detail in Chapter 7.

Provisions on Tariff Concessions in the TPP

Provisions of Article XXIV(8)(b) of General Agreement on Tariffs and Trade (GATT) 1994 requires countries that enter into an agreement for establishing a free trade area to eliminate duties and other restrictive regulations of commerce on 'substantially all trade' between constituent territories in products originating in such territories. However, what constitutes 'substantially all trade' has not been defined or further elaborated. Pursuant to the requirement of eliminating tariffs on substantially all trade between the signatory countries, Article 2.4.2 of the TPP mandates each party to the Agreement to progressively eliminate its customs duties on originating goods in accordance with its schedule of tariff elimination. As will be discussed in the next subsection, tariffs on a large percentage of products would be eliminated on the date of entry into force (EIF) of the Agreement. In respect of most of the residual products, tariffs would be progressively eliminated over a negotiated transition period indicated in the schedule of tariff elimination. Some of the parties to the TPP have negotiated to retain tariffs on a low fraction of products. Overall, the requirement of eliminating customs duties on substantially all trade between the constituent parties of the FTA appears to have been met by the TPP.

Summary of Tariff Concessions

The TPP has followed a flexible architecture of tariff reduction whereby some countries have a common schedule of tariff concessions for other 11 countries, while a few of the TPP members have country-specific schedules. Chile, Japan, Mexico and USA fall in the latter category. This is reflective of two concerns—a TPP signatory country may have a different degree of sensitivity in respect of imports from certain TPP countries; and country-specific schedules may also reflect the extent of reciprocal market access being granted by partner countries. Table 2.4 provides the country-level summary of the tariff concessions to be extended under the TPP. Four key conclusions can be drawn from the table.

First, the TPP does not mandate a uniform transition period for eliminating tariffs. Countries have negotiated transition periods that are as short as 3 years for Australia and as long as 29 years for the USA. It is ironical that the largest economy among the 12 countries has the longest transition period. Normally, under the GATT and the World Trade Organization (WTO) rules, developed countries get relatively shorter transition periods for implementing their obligations, as compared to developing countries. The TPP architecture for tariff elimination turns the WTO framework on its head. Second, Singapore will provide the most liberal tariff concession to other TPP countries, as tariffs will be eliminated on all the products on the date of EIF of the agreement. However, it should be noted that even outside the TPP framework, Singapore has already eliminated tariffs on virtually all products on the most favoured nation (MFN) basis. Thus, Singapore would not be providing any additional market access under the TPP.

Table 2.4

Summary of tariff reductions under the TPP

Country	% of Tariff Lines Duty Free on EIF	% of Additional Tariff Lines Duty Free After Transition Period	% of Tariff Lines not Zero at End of Transition Period	% of Tariff Lines with a TRQ	Duration of Transition Period
Australia	93.0	6.8	0.1		2–3
Brunei	91.7	8.3			2–10
Canada	94.9	3.9		1.1	3–11
Chile	95.1–93.8	4.8–5.5	0–0.6		3–7
Japan	86.1–85.9	10.6–11.1	0.8–1.1	2.0–2.4	3–20
Malaysia	84.7	15.1		0.1	2–15
Mexico	77.7–77.4	22.2	0.2–0.6	0–0.3	2–15
New Zealand	94.6	5.0			1–6
Peru	80.7	18.6	0.6		5–15
Singapore	100	0.0			
USA	95.6–78.6	4.3–21.1		0–1.6	2–29
Vietnam	64.6	33.3	0.2	1.9	1–15

Source: Tariff schedules of TPP countries.

Third, Vietnam has the most restrictive schedule of tariff concessions, as only 64.2 per cent of the tariff lines will witness tariff elimination on EIF of the Agreement. Despite a restrictive schedule of tariff concessions, Vietnam would provide significant additional market access to other TPP countries for non-agriculture products, as it has the highest average tariffs (8.4 per cent) amongst the 12 signatory countries. Fourth, even at the end of the transition period, with the exception of Brunei and Singapore, tariffs on all products would not be eliminated by the remaining 10 TPP countries.

In addition to the statistical details highlighted above, the schedule of tariff concessions of some of the TPP member countries provides certain interesting features. Mexico has committed to provide a tariff rate quota (TRQ) for the following products: milk and cream; milk powder; evaporated milk; condensed milk; butter; products consisting of natural milk constituents; cheese; dairy-based preparations; and palm oil and palm kernel oil.

Mexico has also negotiated a special dispensation for sugar, under which all sugar imports into Mexico would be subject to MFN tariffs. However, Mexico shall grant tariff concession for sugar under the TPP only when it requires to import sugar to address its domestic demand through unilateral MFN TRQs. In such situations, Mexico has committed to grant Australia 7 per cent of any unilateral MFN TRQ that Mexico may open.

The USA has committed to provide country-specific TRQs for the following: Australia (raw sugar; sugar and sugar-containing products; creams and ice cream; condensed milk; butter; milk powders; other dairy products; American and Cheddar cheese; and Swiss, European and other cheeses), Canada (cheese; skim milk powder; whole milk powder; dried yogurt, sour cream, whey, etc.; concentrated milk; cream, sour cream, ice cream and milk beverages; butter and butter substitutes; other dairy products; sugar; and sugar-containing products), Chile (sugar and sugar-containing products), Japan (beef; and sugar and sugar-containing products), Malaysia (sugar and sugar-containing products), New Zealand (cheese; skim milk powder; whole milk powder; concentrated milk; creams; butter and butter substitutes; organic butter; and other dairy products), Peru (cheese; condensed and evaporated milk; processed dairy products; and sugar and sugar-containing products) and Vietnam (sugar and sugar-containing products) (TPP Annex 2-D: Appendix A—USA).

It is relevant to note that the USA has negotiated the right to impose country-specific safeguard measures to counter surges in import quantities (TPP Annex 2-D: Appendix B—USA). These safeguard measures are available for specific products imported from specific countries. If, in a particular year, the import quantity of the product from the specified country exceeds the prescribed threshold, then the USA would have the right to impose a safeguard duty. There is no overarching formula to determine the trigger threshold or the amount of safeguard duty that can be imposed on the relevant agriculture products. Instead, each of these measures has a distinct quantity trigger and a distinct schedule of the safeguard duty. Further, for each product, the maximum number of years for which the right to impose country-specific safeguard duty would be available to the USA has been prescribed in the US schedule. To illustrate, the USA has secured the right to impose an agriculture safeguard measure on imports of Swiss cheese from Australia. The trigger quantity of imports has been specified to be 800 Mt. during the first year of implementation of the Agreement. In the subsequent years, the trigger quantity would increase at a compound annual growth rate of 3 per cent. During the first seven years of implementation of the Agreement, the safeguard

Table 2.5

Overview of the agricultural safeguard measures available to the USA

Source of Imports	Product	No. of Tariff Lines at 9 Digit HS	No. of Tariff Lines at 9 Digit HS	No. of Years for which the Right to Impose Agricultural Safeguard Available
Australia	Swiss cheese	1	1	24
	Milk powders	8	5	34
New Zealand	Other cheese	1	1	24
	Whole milk powder	6	4	34
Peru	Condensed and evaporated milk	4	2	Until the year 2024
	Cheese	52	6	Until the year 2024

Source: Tariff schedules of TPP countries.

duty would be the MFN rate. During the 8th–14th year, the safeguard duty would be 75 per cent of the prevailing MFN rate. The extent of safeguard duty would be reduced to 50 per cent of the MFN rate during the 15th–20th year. During the 21st–24th year the duty would be 25 per cent of the prevailing MFN duty. The USA shall not have the right to apply safeguard duty on imports of Swiss cheese from Australia beyond the 24th year of implementation of the Agreement. Table 2.5 provides an overview of the agricultural safeguard measures available to the USA.

Remanufactured Goods

Business enterprises are remanufacturing goods across a wide range of sectors including earth-moving equipment, automotive parts, medical devices, information and communication technology products, industrial machinery, precision instruments and office equipment. However, what constitutes a remanufactured good has not been defined. Further, there is no specific provision related to trade in remanufactured goods in GATT 1994 or the WTO agreements. Some countries have argued that Article XI of GATT 1994 prohibits countries from imposing restrictions on imports of remanufactured products. The provision on remanufacturing contained in the TPP is aimed at curtailing the elbow room, if any, available to countries for regulating trade in remanufactured goods.

According to Article 2.12 of the TPP, 'If a Party adopts or maintains measures prohibiting or restricting the importation of used goods, it shall not apply those measures to remanufactured goods.' Effectively, this provision prohibits TPP countries from restricting imports of used goods that meet the definition of remanufactured goods. Remanufactured goods have been defined as goods that are entirely or partially composed of recovered materials and meet the following requirements: (a) have a similar life expectancy and perform the same as or similar function to new goods; and (b) have a factory warranty similar to that applicable to new goods. The scope of remanufactured good is limited to products classified in Chapters 84–90 (under the Harmonised System of tariff nomenclature), with the exception of goods classified under 84.18.[3]

Export Duties and Taxes

At the end of the Uruguay Round, while countries bound import tariffs, in most countries export duties and taxes remained unbound. During the Doha Round of multilateral trade negotiations, the EU made a proposal for restricting the use of export duties and taxes for non-agricultural goods (WTO 2006). However, this proposal could not garner much support. In parallel development, China imposed export restrictions on various raw materials (Bauxite, Coke, Fluorspar, Magnesium, Manganese, Silicon Carbide, Silicon Metal, Yellow Phosphorus, Zinc, etc.) and rare earth metals. These export restrictions have triggered considerable concern in Japan and the USA. The TPP provision on export duties and taxes should be viewed in the background of these two developments.

Article 2.16 of the TPP prohibits countries from imposing export duties and taxes, unless the tax is also imposed on goods destined for domestic consumption. Malaysia and Vietnam have negotiated a list of products on which export duties and taxes can be maintained for a period not exceeding 15 years. Thus, the prohibition on export duties and taxes are perhaps aimed at ensuring that TPP countries do not follow China's

---

[3] Harmonised System (HS) of tariff nomenclature is an internationally standardized system of names and numbers to classify traded products. It came into effect in 1988 and has since been developed and maintained by the World Customs Organization (WCO). The HS nomenclature is widely used for categorizing goods for the purpose imposing import duty and export taxes. Each good or a category of goods can be identified based on the number assigned under the Harmonised System of tariff nomenclature.

example and impose restrictions on exports of raw materials. Further, if China becomes a TPP member in future, the provisions on export restrictions and export duties would be used against it.

Trade in Information Technology Products

Pursuant to WTO's ITA, 81 WTO members, which account for approximately 97 per cent of the world trade in information technology (IT) products, have eliminated and bound customs duties at zero for all products specified in the Agreement.[4] The products covered by the ITA include computers, telecommunication equipment, semiconductors, semiconductor manufacturing and testing equipment, software, scientific instruments, as well as most of the parts and accessories of these products. However, not all TPP signatory countries are participants in the ITA. Article 2.20 of the TPP mandates the signatory countries to be a participant in the ITA. While Brunei will get a 1-year transition period to comply with this obligation, Mexico and Chile (who are not members of the ITA) will merely 'endeavour' to join the ITA.

Export Restrictions in the Context of Food Security

Article XI.1 of the GATT prohibits countries from imposing restrictions, other than duties, on imports or exports of products. However, Article XI.2(a) provides a narrow exception, whereby countries can restrict or prohibit exports temporarily. However, the restrictions are required to be applied to relieve or prevent critical shortages of foodstuffs essential to the exporting country. During the time of global food crisis in 2008, many countries imposed restrictions on exports of foodstuff. For some of the TPP countries, particularly Japan, export restrictions on food items have been a matter of considerable concern. Article 2.26 of the TPP builds on Article XI.2(a) of GATT 1994 by imposing the following

---

[4] The original Information Technology Agreement (ITA) was reached on 13 December 1996, through a 'Ministerial Declaration on Trade in Information Technology Products,' at the first WTO Ministerial Conference, held in Singapore.

additional requirements that countries have to comply with if they resort to temporary restriction on foodstuffs:

1. The country imposing the measure would need to notify alternate measures that it considered before imposing export restrictions.
2. Upon request of another party, the country imposing the measure would need to provide relevant economic indicators for establishing that a critical shortage of foodstuff exists or is likely to occur in the absence of the measure and how the measure will prevent or relieve the critical shortage.
3. A party imposing export restrictions would ordinarily terminate the measure within 6 months after its imposition.
4. Export restrictions shall not continue beyond 1 month, unless the member imposing the measure has consulted with all other TPP parties who are net importers of the foodstuff that is the subject matter of export restriction.

Trade of Products of Modern Biotechnology

Article 2.29 of the TPP's chapter on market access contains provisions regarding trade of products of modern biotechnology, the scope of which includes living modified organisms (LMO). This term refers to genetically modified organisms (GMO) as well. A major component of Article 2.29 concerns low level presence (LLP) occurrences. According to footnote 13 of Article 2.29, an LLP is the occurrence of the inadvertent LLP in a shipment of plants or plant products of an rDNA plant material that is authorized for use in at least one country, but not in the importing country (TPP member or not). This meaning is narrower than the meaning given to an LLP under the Cartagena Protocol on Biosafety (CPB). Provisions regarding LLP in the CPB are contained in Article 17 of the CPB. Even though the CPB does not specifically define an LLP, a meaning that can be extracted from paragraph 1 of Article 17 of the CPB is an occurrence under the jurisdiction of a CPB party resulting in a release that leads to unintentional trans-boundary movement of an LMO.

With regard to importing countries, the TPP contains provisions which are more in the nature of obligations than rights. Article 2.29 of the TPP requires an importing TPP Party to inform the importer or its agents of the LLP occurrence and of any additional information which the importer will be required to submit to allow the importing TPP Party to make a decision on the disposition of the shipment in which the LLP occurrence has been found. Another obligation under Article 2.29 is that it requires the importing TPP Party to ensure that the measures applied to address the LLP occurrence are 'appropriate' to achieve compliance with its domestic laws, regulations and policies. This is an odious provision as, in the absence of a definition, it is unclear what the standard for 'appropriate' measure is. The danger with such a provision is that it exposes a TPP Party to litigation before a panel under the TPP's dispute settlement mechanism.

2.5 Assessing the Impact on Manufacturing and Agriculture in India If It Complies with the TPP Provisions on Market Access for Goods

In this section, we examine the impact on India if it were required to comply with the template of rules on market access for goods contained in the TPP. At certain places, a comparison has also been attempted with relevant developments in the negotiations under the Doha Round.

India Eliminating Tariffs: Severe Adverse Impact on Industrialization

Under the GATT/WTO the main policy instrument available to WTO member countries for regulating imports is tariffs. However, this flexibility is not unfettered. In respect of various products, many WTO members have taken a commitment not to raise the import tariffs beyond the negotiated limits—commonly referred to as the bound rate for the product. As shown in Table 2.6, India's average bound rates are significantly higher than those of the TPP signatory countries. Will the Indian domestic industry be able to face import competition if India were to eliminate tariffs on most of the products—a requirement under the TPP? We answer this important question in the next few paragraphs.

We use a non-rigorous, but useful, methodology for assessing whether India's domestic industry will be able to face import competition under

Table 2.6

Overall tariff profile of India and TPP countries

Country	Final Bound Tariffs		
	Total	Agriculture	Non-agriculture
Australia	9.9	3.4	11
Brunei	25.4	32.1	24.4
Canada	6.8	16.3	5.3
Chile	25.1	26.1	25
India	48.5	113.5	34.5
Japan	4.4	16.6	2.5
Malaysia	22.3	62.1	14.9
Mexico	36.2	45	34.8
New Zealand	10.2	5.9	10.9
Peru	29.5	30.9	29.3
Singapore	9.6	23.3	6.5
USA	3.5	4.8	3.3
Vietnam	11.5	19.1	10.4

Source: World tariff profiles.

a zero-tariff regime. We make an extreme assumption that the unit value of India's export of a product is a proxy for domestic price of that product. Next, we compare India's unit value of exports with that of some of the TPP countries including the USA, Malaysia, Vietnam and Japan. This exercise is undertaken for industrial products. If India's export unit value for a particular product is higher than that of any of these four TPP countries, then it can be concluded that the Indian domestic industry is not competitive in that product. It may be noted that the domestic prices are generally higher than the export prices. In the absence of tariff protection, if the export unit value of any of the four TPP countries is lower than India's export unit value for the product, India's domestic price will be higher than the export unit value of the concerned TPP country. Thus, our extreme assumption will identify products where India is almost certainly uncompetitive. This sets the lower limit of the number of products in which India is not competitive. Table 2.7 provides details of the number of products in which the Indian domestic industry may not be competitive with respect to the TPP countries.

Table 2.7

Assessing the number of products in which India may not be price-competitive

Chapter	Chapter Description	Total No. of TLs at 6 Digit	No. of TL in which India is less Competitive than at Least one TPP Country	No. of TL (Tariff Line) in which India is more Competitive than other TPP Countries
25	Salt; sulphur; earths and stone; plastering materials, lime and cement	68	9	11
26	Ores, slag and ash.	37	2	1
27	Mineral fuels. mineral oils and products of their distillation; bituminous substances; mineral, etc.	43	14	5
28	Inorganic chemicals; organic or inorganic compounds of precious metals, of rare-earth metals, etc.	166	32	21
29	Organic chemicals	332	60	12
30	Pharmaceutical products	31	3	4
31	Fertilizers	23	11	2
32	Tanning or dyeing extracts; tannins and their derivatives; dyes, pigments and other colouring, etc.	44	12	22
33	Essential oils and resinoids; perfumery, cosmetic or toilet preparations	29	10	14
34	Soap, organic surface-active agents, washing preparations, lubricating preparations, artificial, etc.	23	10	12
35	Albuminoidal substances; modified starches; glues; enzymes	15	3	6
36	Explosives; pyrotechnic products; matches; pyrophoric alloys; certain combustible preparations	8	3	2

(*Continued*)

Table 2.7
Continued

Chapter	Chapter Description	Total No. of TLs at 6 Digit	No. of TL in which India is Less Competitive than at Least One TPP Country	No. of TL (Tariff Line) in which India is more Competitive than Other TPP Countries
37	Photographic or cinematographic goods	31	1	1
38	Miscellaneous chemical products	81	24	17
39	Plastics and articles thereof	126	71	41
40	Rubber and articles thereof	85	46	22
41	Raw hides and skins (other than furskins) and leather	37	7	3
42	Articles of leather; saddlery and harness; travel goods, handbags and similar containers; articles, etc.	20	7	1
43	Furskins and artificial fur; manufactures thereof	12	3	
44	Wood and articles of wood; wood charcoal	76	31	12
45	Cork and articles of cork	7		1
46	Manufactures of straw, of esparto or of other plaiting materials; basketware and wickerwork	11	4	4
47	Pulp of wood or of other fibrous cellulosic material; recovered (waste and scrap) paper, etc.	21	2	
48	Paper and paperboard; articles of paper pulp, of paper or of paperboard	101	46	38
49	Printed books, newspapers, pictures and other products of the printing industry; manuscripts,	19	4	6

50	Silk	9	5	
51	Wool, fine or coarse animal hair; horsehair yarn and woven fabric	38	2	1
52	Cotton	124	56	7
53	Other vegetable textile fibres; paper yarn and woven fabrics of paper yarn	23	2	
54	Man-made filaments; strip and the like of man-made textile materials	70	27	10
55	Man-made staple fibres	106	36	10
56	Wadding, felt and nonwovens; special yarns; twine, cordage, ropes and cables and articles thereof	30	14	11
57	Carpets and other textile floor coverings	21	4	5
58	Special woven fabrics; tufted textile fabrics; lace; tapestries; trimmings; embroidery	38	12	5
59	Impregnated, coated, covered or laminated textile fabrics; textile articles of a kind suitable, etc.	24	14	1
60	Knitted or crocheted fabrics	43	9	11
61	Articles of apparel and clothing accessories, knitted or crocheted	106	48	35
62	Articles of apparel and clothing accessories, not knitted or crocheted	112	68	20
63	Other made-up textile articles; sets; worn clothing and worn textile articles; rags	51	18	22
64	Footwear, gaiters and the like; parts of such articles	25	10	14
65	Headgear and parts thereof	8	2	3

(Continued)

Table 2.7
Continued

Chapter	Chapter Description	Total No. of TLs at 6 Digit	No. of TL in which India is Less Competitive than at Least One TPP Country	No. of TL (Tariff Line) in which India is more Competitive than Other TPP Countries
66	Umbrellas, sun umbrellas, walking sticks, seat-sticks, whips, riding-crops and parts thereof	6	2	1
67	Prepared feathers and down and articles made of feathers or of down; artificial flowers; articles, etc.	8	2	2
68	Articles of stone, plaster, cement, asbestos, mica or similar materials	49	12	15
69	Ceramic products	29	4	13
70	Glass and glassware	64	10	12
71	Natural or cultured pearls, precious or semi-precious stones, precious metals, metals clad, etc.	51	13	7
72	Iron and steel	167	98	40
73	Articles of iron or steel	124	48	46
74	Copper and articles thereof	50	27	9
75	Nickel and articles thereof	17	2	
76	Aluminium and articles thereof	35	14	15
78	Lead and articles thereof	8	6	
79	Zinc and articles thereof	9	5	1
80	Tin and articles thereof	5	2	1

81	Other base metals; cermets; articles thereof	48	10	1
82	Tools, implements, cutlery, spoons and forks, of base metal; parts thereof of base metal	64	15	26
83	Miscellaneous articles of base metal	36	9	24
84	Machinery; mechanical appliances, nuclear reactors, boilers; parts thereof	507	80	112
85	Electrical machinery and equipment and parts thereof; sound recorders and reproducers, television, etc.	264	38	49
86	Railway or tramway locomotives, rolling stock and parts thereof; railway or tramway track fixtures, etc.	22		1
87	Vehicles other than railway or tramway rolling stock, and parts and accessories thereof	74	14	29
88	Aircraft, spacecraft, and parts thereof	15	2	
89	Ships, boats and floating structures	18		
90	Optical, photographic, cinematographic, measuring, checking, precision, medical or surgical, etc.	145	19	22
91	Clocks and watches and parts thereof	49	5	3
92	Musical instruments; parts and accessories of such articles	17	1	6
93	Arms and ammunition; parts and accessories thereof	18		
94	Furniture; bedding, mattresses, mattress supports, cushions and similar stuffed furnishings, etc.	39	16	17
95	Toys, games and sports requisites; parts and accessories thereof	31	9	5
96	Miscellaneous manufactured articles	48	11	22
Total		4291	1213	892

Source: Authors' calculations based on WITS data.

Given the fact that around 20 per cent of the products may be price competitive and about 28 per cent of the products are definitely not price competitive, prospects of the Indian industry being able to face import competition at zero tariffs appear bleak. While some experts have expressed optimism about the ability of the domestic industry to adapt to changing realities, the past experience does not provide any such reassurance. To illustrate, after becoming a participant of the WTO ITA, India progressively eliminated tariffs on IT products. As evidenced in discussions with the domestic hardware manufacturers, this had a severe adverse impact on hardware manufacturers in India. Thus, there may be little reason to be confident that the Indian producers will successfully face the challenge of zero duty imports if India were to join an agreement based on the TPP template requiring countries to eliminate tariffs.

Continued viability of Indian agriculture would be at a serious risk if India were to join the TPP template. Not only would India lose the right to impose customs tariffs to protect its agriculture sector, but there would also be a persistent threat of surge in subsidized imports from the USA, Canada, Australia and other TPP countries that would continue to provide tens of billions of subsidies to their agriculture.

Prohibiting Restrictions on Remanufactured Goods: Threat to Industrialization in Developing Countries

At the WTO, some countries including Japan, Switzerland and the USA have been pushing for a specific provision to restrict the ability of countries to impose restrictions on imports of remanufactured goods. The stated objectives for this include protecting and preserving the environment, promoting sustainable development by preventing unnecessary waste and conserving energy and raw materials. On the other hand, there is a growing concern among many developing countries that trade in remanufactured goods can be detrimental to the interests of the importing countries from at least three perspectives. First, the extended producer liability would be shifted from manufacturers in the developed countries to importers and consumers in developing countries. This will relieve the producers in developed countries from considerable financial costs, particularly from costs related to disposal of the goods concerned. Second, as the remanufactured goods may not be as energy efficient as new products, the benefits related to energy conservation may be somewhat overstated. Third, the price of a remanufactured good may be significantly lower than that of a new good manufactured in developing countries. Thus, imports of remanufactured goods could have an adverse impact on domestic industry in the importing country. If India were to join an agreement requiring it to adhere to TPP-type rules on remanufacturing, it would significantly undermine industrialization efforts in the country.

Prohibiting Export Duties and Taxes: Disincentive for Promoting Domestic Value Addition in Raw Materials

Article 2.16 of the TPP prohibits countries from imposing export duties and taxes, unless the tax is also imposed on any such good destined for domestic consumption. Many developing countries, particularly those rich in natural resources, use this policy instrument to make indigenous raw materials available to domestic processing industries at a price lower than what would be available in international market. Thus, export taxes have been used as an important policy instrument for stimulating processing and value-added industry in developing countries. India, too, has occasionally resorted to export taxes, in order to prevent exports of raw materials—including raw hides and skin and chrome—thereby making it available to domestic processors at lower prices. Overall, if India were to adhere to the prohibition on export duties and taxes, its leather and steel industry would be deprived of access to critical inputs at competitive prices. This would have a negative impact on downstream processing industries in the country.

LLP

Indian laws do not specifically deal with LLP but contain provisions that can apply to an LLP occurrence. Provisions regarding LMOs in the applicable Indian laws are rather strict and prohibitive in nature; seemingly in line with the precautionary principle. The applicable Indian laws absolutely prohibit, inter alia, the 'import' of LMOs without the approval of the Genetic Engineering Advisory Committee. The implication for LLPs under Indian laws is that trans-boundary shipments into

India inadvertently having a LLP of an LMO are liable to enforcement action such as confiscation and imposition of penalties by the customs authorities.

The provisions of Article 2.29 are at odds with the applicable Indian law on inadvertent trans-boundary shipments. If India decides to conform its provisions regarding trans-boundary shipments of LMO to the provisions of paragraph 7 of Article 2.29, it may lose the right to confiscate the LMO products. On the other hand, it will have to deal with the inadvertent LMO shipment in a positive manner.

2.6 Conclusions

If India were to conform to the template of rules on market access in goods as contained in the TPP, it would pose severe challenges to India's manufacturing sector. The domestic industry may not be able to face import competition in a duty-free regime. Further, provisions on remanufacturing would undermine domestic manufacturing. The provision on export duty and taxes would eliminate the possibility of India using these policy measures for supporting the establishment of the downstream processing industry. On the agriculture front, the farmers will be continuously exposed to the risk of being knocked out of the market by cheap and subsidized exports, particularly from the USA, Australia and New Zealand. Tariff as a policy instrument would not be available to the government to regulate such imports. The consequences of such a situation can be extremely alarming.

References

Banga, R., and Pritish Kumar Sahu. 2015, October. 'Trans Pacific Partnership Agreement (TPPA): Implications for India's Trade and Investments'. Working Paper No. 24, Centre for WTO Studies, New Delhi Implications for Indian Economy.

Bergsten, Fred C. 2015. 'India's Rise: A Strategy for Trade-led Growth'. PIIE Briefing No. 15–4, PIIE, Washington, DC.

Bertram, G., and Simon Terry. 2014. *Economic Gains and Costs from the TPP*. Wellington: Sustainability Council of New Zealand.

Capaldo, Jeronim and Alex Izurieta with Jomo Kwame Sundaram. 2016, January. 'Trading Down: Unemployment, Inequity and Other Risks of the Trans-Pacific Partnership

Agreement', Global Development and Environment Institute Working Paper No. 16–01', Tufts University, Medford, USA.

Narayanan, Badri G., Harsha Vardhana Singh and Dan Ciuriak. 2016. 'Quantifying Trans-Pacific Partnership and Transatlantic Trade and Investment Partnership Spillovers on India', in *TPP and India: Implications of Mega-regionals for Developing Economies*, edited by Harsha V. Singh. New Delhi: Wisdom Tree.

Narayanan, Badri G., and Sachin Kumar Sharma. 2014. 'An Analysis of Trans-Pacific Partnership (TPP): Implications for Indian Economy'. Working Paper No. 14, Centre for WTO Studies, New Delhi.

OECD. 2015. 'Trade in Value-Added: India'. *OECD Document*. Paris: OECD.

Petri, Peter A., and Michael G. Plummer. 2016, January 1. 'The Economic Effects of the Trans-Pacific Partnership: New Estimates'. Peterson Institute for International Economics Working Paper No. 16–2; East-West Center Workshop on Mega-Regionalism—New Challenges for Trade and Innovation. Retrieved 25 August 2017, from https://ssrn.com/abstract=2723413

Petri, A. Peter, Michael G. Plummer, and Fan Zhai. 2011, October 24. 'The Trans-Pacific Partnership and the Asia-Pacific Integration: A Quantitative Assessment'. Working Paper, Economic Series No. 119, East-West Centre, Honolulu, HI.

———. 2012. *The Trans-Pacific Partnership and Asia-Pacific Integration: A Quantitative Assessment*. Washington, DC: Peterson Institute for International Economics.

———. 2014. 'The Effects of a China-US Free Trade and Investment Agreement'. Social Science Research Network. Retrieved 29 October 2015, from http://ssrn.com/abstract=2513839

Robert J. Flanagan, Labour Standards and International Competitive Advantage 36 (International Labour Standards Conference, Stanford Law School, May 20, 2002) available at www.iza.org/iza/en/papers/transatlantic/1_flanagan.pdf

Robert Stern and Katherine Turrell. 2003. Labour Standards and the World Trade Organization. Retrieved from www.wto.org/english/forums_e/ngo_e/labour_standards_e.doc

Rodrik, Dani. 2016. 'The Trade Numbers Game'. Project Syndicate. Retrieved July 18, from https://www.project-syndicate.org/commentary/tpp-debate-economic-benefits-by-dani-rodrik-2016-02?barrier=true

WTO. 2006, 27 April. 'Annex: WTO Agreement on Export Taxes—Core Disciplines'. Negotiating Group on Market Access, Market Access for Non-Agricultural Products—Negotiating Proposal on Export Taxes: Communication from the European Communities, TN/MA/W/11/Add.6, para 1.

3
Services Coverage in TPP, TiSA and GATS

A Comparative Analysis and Implications for India

Pralok Gupta

3.1 Introduction

Services negotiations are happening more intensively outside the World Trade Organization (WTO) multilateral trading architecture than within it. Two important trade agreements seeking ambitious services liberalization are the Trans-Pacific Partnership (TPP) Agreement and the Trade in Services Agreement (TiSA). The TPP had been signed by its members in February 2016, but the United States of America (USA) withdrew from it after Donald Trump assumed Presidency of the USA in January 2017. Recently, Japan has indicated that it is ready to go ahead with the TPP without the USA ('Japan wants...' n.d.). TiSA negotiations are happening secretly and not much information is available on it except some leaked documents and news releases by a few members of the TiSA. Whereas the TiSA is a stand-alone agreement pertaining to services, the TPP is a comprehensive agreement covering all areas of trade including goods, investment, intellectual property rights (IPRs) and others. In addition to an overarching chapter (Chapter 10) dealing with liberalization of services markets among member countries, the TPP also contains specific chapters devoted to financial services (Chapter 11), temporary entry of business persons (Chapter 12), telecommunication services (Chapter 13) and electronic commerce (Chapter 14).

Though the TPP has been abandoned by the USA and its future is uncertain given the recent indications by Japan, it is important to understand and analyse its services-related provisions as these provisions are most likely to slip into other trade agreements and probably even into the WTO in future. Moreover, many of these provisions are also there in the TiSA. Against this backdrop, this chapter seeks to analyse the TPP and TiSA provisions and compare these with the General Agreement on Trade in Services (GATS) provisions. It also brings out the implications of these provisions for India if India wishes to meet these provisions.

3.2 Services Provisions in the TPP

Comparison with the GATS

The framework of services liberalization envisaged in Chapter 10 of the TPP Agreement (henceforth referred to as 'the Agreement') is significantly different from that under the GATS at the WTO. There are at least 12 specific ways in which the TPP provisions are different from those under the GATS. First, while the GATS prescribes a positive list approach for scheduling commitments, the Agreement has adopted a negative list approach. This has turned the GATS architecture on its head. Second, unlike the GATS, the provisions under the Agreement seek to commit countries to significant liberalization in the future through 'ratchet' by curtailing their flexibility to go back to the earlier restrictive regulations and similar other measures. Third, in comparison to the GATS, under the Agreement the member countries are required to adhere to more stringent obligations in respect of the so-called 'most favoured nation' (MFN) treatment. Fourth, unlike the GATS, under the Agreement, rules and disciplines of the investment chapter will also apply to the supply of services through commercial presence under mode 3. Thus, disputes arising from investments related to services would be subject to the 'investor–state dispute settlement' (ISDS) mechanism. Fifth, as compared to the GATS, the coverage of air services has been expanded under the Agreement. Sixth, the measures to which cross-border trade in the services chapter applies differ from the GATS. Seventh, unlike the GATS, which does not contain detailed rules on either government procurement (GP) of services or subsidies to services, the Agreement contains rules in these two areas. Eighth, unlike the GATS, measures taken at the regional level of government have been brought specifically within the ambit of rules under the Agreement. Ninth, unlike the GATS, the Agreement has a specific provision delinking supply of service through mode 1 from local commercial presence. Tenth, the Agreement has a specific provision recognizing the right of the government to regulate in order to meet policy objectives. Eleventh, the provisions on transfers and payments in the Agreement are different from those under the GATS. Twelfth, the Agreement contains certain sector-specific annexes that are not included in the GATS. These departure points of the TPP as compared to the GATS are discussed in the subsequent subsections.

TPP Turns the GATS Architecture on Its Head: Shifting from the Positive List Approach to Negative List Approach

The GATS follows a positive list approach, whereby commitments of each of the WTO members are inscribed in their individual schedule of commitments. These commitments are in respect of market access (MA), national treatment and additional commitments. If a sector has been excluded in a member's schedule, it implies that the particular WTO member has not made any commitment in that sector. Thus, under the positive list approach, sectors and sub-sectors that are not included in a member's schedule are exempt from commitments related to MA and national treatment. In respect of sectors included in its schedule of commitments, the WTO member is required to provide MA and national treatment subject to the terms, limitations and conditions contained in the schedule. In contrast, the TPP follows a negative list approach for national treatment (Article 10.3), most-favoured-nation treatment (Article 10.4), MA (Article 10.5) and local presence (Article 10.6).

Under the negative list approach, member countries' markets are fully open to services suppliers from other member countries, unless they have taken exceptions for non-conforming measures (NCMs) in one of two country-specific annexes attached to the Agreement. Thus, a member country would be required to allow unconditional access to services suppliers from other member countries, except in respect of NCMs which have been inscribed as exceptions in the schedule. Therefore, under the negative list approach, there is an underlying presumption that country has fully liberalized all services, unless otherwise explicitly stated in the country's schedule of NCMs.

The NCMs provide two types of flexibilities: first, Annex-I NCMs, wherein member countries can continue to maintain some existing measures that do not conform to the rules of the Agreement, provided they are not made more restrictive in the future (referred to as standstill); and second, Annex-II NCMs in respect of certain sectors/sub-sectors for which members have retained full regulatory flexibility for introducing new measures in the future by permanently excluding them from the Agreement. It should be noted that while a country may resort to NCMs for various obligations, such NCMs are subject to negotiations and are not a choice to be exercised unilaterally by the concerned country.

While the implications of the negative list approach are manifold, two important aspects need to be highlighted. First, negotiations based on a negative list approach are more challenging than those based on a positive list approach. The former approach requires a country to prepare a comprehensive and exhaustive inventory of all services-related measures, examine whether each of the measures allows unconditional access to service suppliers from the partner countries and seek exceptions under the NCM for those measures that may not provide for such access. It is quite possible that a country may have inadvertently overlooked an existing measure that results in a restriction or discrimination not permitted under the agreement and not negotiated for its inclusion in the list of NCMs. In case the country fails to secure an exception in the form of an NCM for an existing measure that does not provide for unconditional access, that measure cannot be continued to be maintained after implementation of the trade agreement. Thus, the negative list approach can be extremely onerous for developing countries that are constrained by inadequate technical capacity and are generally deficient in human resources. In contrast, under the positive list approach of the GATS, commitments do not apply if a sector/sub-sector is not inscribed in the member's schedule of commitments.

Second, the negative list approach can significantly curtail the policy flexibility available to countries to liberalize services trade and regulate it in the future. Under the negative list approach, a country cannot make an existing measure more restrictive, even if the market realities so demand. Further, a country may not be able to regulate a new service that is just emerging, or might develop in future, if it has not included it in the list of NCMs. As most of the new services are likely to originate in the developed countries, this would prevent developing countries from building the capacities of their nascent and emerging domestic service suppliers by protecting them from import competition from service suppliers of the developed countries. This is particularly relevant for services in dynamic industries, such as information technology, financial services and telecommunication services. Thus, developing countries that may want to develop new services in these sectors may be considerably disadvantaged by the negative list approach.

TPP Commits Countries to Future Liberalization and Erodes Policy Space

In respect of NCMs contained in Annex-I, the TPP template requires that any amendment to these measures shall not decrease the conformity, as existed immediately before the amendment, in respect of provisions related to national treatment, MFN treatment, MA and local presence (Article 10.7.1(c)). This affects future liberalization of NCMs in two specific ways. One, the amendment to an NCM cannot make it more restrictive than what existed on the date of implementation of the Agreement. Thus, the NCMs are locked in, based on their current domestic regime (known as the 'standstill' mechanism). The standstill mechanism ensures that NCMs cannot become more restrictive in future, compared to what existed on the date of implementation of the Agreement. Two, any amendment to an NCM can proceed in only one direction—making the NCM progressively less restrictive. In other words, if an amendment to an NCM makes it less restrictive, this autonomous liberalization gets locked in (known as the 'ratchet' mechanism). Any subsequent amendment cannot make the NCM more restrictive than what existed prior to the amendment. Standstill and binding of autonomous liberalization through the ratchet mechanism will significantly reduce the policy space for member countries to experiment with liberalization of NCMs, as the liberalization cannot be rolled back even if it causes a severe adverse impact on the economy of the concerned member. It may be noted that NCMs listed in Annex-II are not subject to standstill and ratchet obligations and hence a member may maintain the existing measures or adopt new or more restrictive ones, in respect of the Annex-II NCMs.

More Onerous MFN Provision in the TPP Would Constrain Progressive Liberalization Through FTAs with Non-TPP Countries

The GATS provisions permit a WTO member to deviate from MFN obligations and grant preferential treatment to other members through MFN exemptions or on the basis of provisions related to economic integration. However, the TPP does not permit deviations from MFN obligations. The MFN provision of the TPP (Article 10.4) requires each member to accord to services and service suppliers of another member treatment no less favourable than that it accords, in like circumstances, to services and service suppliers of any other member or a non-member. Thus, a TPP member is obliged to give to other members the treatment that it gives to its existing FTA partners (commonly referred to as backward MFN) as well as to its future FTA partners (forward MFN). However, a TPP member can negotiate NCMs for such MFN treatment. The onerous MFN obligation, as envisaged in the TPP, is likely to constrain a country from entering into an economic integration agreement on services in future with non-member countries, wherein it provides more favourable treatment to non-members as compared to the treatment provided to the existing members.

Foreign Service Investor Can Sue the Host Country Under Investor–State Dispute Settlement

The GATS covers all four modes of services trade but TPP services chapter covers only mode 1, mode 2 and mode 4 of services trade. Mode 3 of services trade—through commercial presence—is covered under the investment chapter in the TPP.[1] However, some articles of the services chapter, namely, Article 10.5 (Market Access), Article 10.8 (Domestic Regulation) and Article 10.11 (Transparency), apply to measures adopted or maintained by a member affecting the supply of a service in its territory by a covered investment. The inclusion of mode 3 within the investment chapter implies that any investment in the services sector made by foreign service providers can be subject to the provisions

---

[1] TPP services chapter defines cross-border trade in services or cross-border supply of services as the supply of a service (a) from the territory of a party into the territory of another party; (b) in the territory of a party to a person of another party; or (c) by a national of a party in the territory of another party, but does not include the supply of a service in the territory of a party by a covered investment. On the other hand, the GATS defines trade in services as the supply of a service (a) from the territory of one member into the territory of any other member; (b) in the territory of one member to the service consumer of any other member: (c) by a service supplier of one member, through commercial presence in the territory of any other member; (d) by a service supplier of one member, through presence of natural persons of a member in the territory of any other member.

of the investment chapter including ISDS provisions. Any future regulation that adversely affects foreign investment in services, including having an adverse impact on future profits, may be challenged under the investor–state dispute mechanism as envisaged in the investment chapter of the TPP. Further details regarding the implications of ISDS are provided in Chapter 6 of this book.

TPP Expands the Coverage of Air Services

As in the case of the GATS, the services covered under the TPP services chapter exclude air services from its ambit. However, certain categories of services related to air services are excluded from the ambit of air services and thereby are covered under the GATS and the TPP. Under the GATS three services—aircraft repair and maintenance services; selling and marketing of air transport services; and computer reservation system services—are subject to the rules of the agreement. However, in the TPP, in addition to the three services covered by the GATS, three other services—specialty air services; airport operation services; and ground handling services—are included. Thus, the TPP expands the category of services that are included within its ambit. Broadening the exclusions from the ambit of air services increases services coverage under the TPP, thereby implying the liberalization mandate for more services sectors under the TPP as compared to the GATS.

Measures to Which Cross-border Trade in Services Chapter Apply Differ from the GATS

The scope of the cross-border trade in services chapter defines the measures to which this chapter shall apply, adopted or maintained by a member affecting cross-border trade in services by service suppliers of another member. These measures differ from the GATS in two ways.[2]

---

[2] As per GATS, 'measures by Members affecting trade in services' include measures in respect of (a) the purchase, payment or use of a service, (b) the access to and use of, in connection with the supply of a service, services which are required by those members to be offered to the public generally, (c) the presence, including commercial presence, of persons of a member for the supply of a service in the territory of another member. TPP measures

First, the TPP exclusively defines the services, in connection with the supply of a service, to which these measures will be applicable. These are distribution, transport or telecommunications networks and services. On the other hand, the GATS does not define these services exclusively, rather includes services required by members to be offered to the public generally. Thus, whereas the TPP exclusively defines the input services to be considered for the said purpose, the GATS does not do so. Though telecommunication services are covered under a separate chapter in the TPP, this may imply that these services acting as inputs to other services also come within the purview of this chapter. Second, the TPP adds a new type of measure within its scope that was not included in the GATS. These include measures affecting the provision of a bond or other form of financial security as a condition for the supply of a service. It implies that minimum capital requirements for cross-border trade in services will also be subject to TPP provisions.

Unlike the GATS, the TPP Includes Rules on Government Procurement of Services and Subsidies to Services

The GATS has articles on GP and subsidies though relevant disciplines in these two areas are yet to be developed. GP and subsidies are out of the scope of the services chapter in the TPP, however, GP of services is covered in a separate chapter on GP. Under the GP chapter of the TPP, member countries of the TPP cannot discriminate in favour of their domestic service suppliers. However, the TPP member countries have negotiated the services that will be subject to GP disciplines. Rules on subsidies to services are covered in the Agreement's chapter on state-owned enterprises. These rules curtail the flexibility of TPP members to provide government support to services, if the support results in adverse effects.

---

include measures affecting: (a) the production, distribution, marketing, sale or delivery of a service; (b) the purchase or use of, or payment for, a service; (c) the access to and use of distribution, transport or telecommunications networks and services in connection with the supply of a service; (d) the presence in the member's territory of a service supplier of another member; and (e) the provision of a bond or other form of financial security as a condition for the supply of a service.

TPP Brings Measures at the Regional Level of Government to the Forefront

The GATS has an overarching condition of its applicability to central, regional and local governments. TPP NCMs can also be maintained at central, regional and local levels. However, the TPP specifically mentions measures affecting trade in services adopted at the regional level of government in the article on national treatment (Article 10.3(2)) and article on non-conformity measures (Article 10.7(3)). Thus, the TPP brings the regulations applied at the regional level of government to the forefront of the agreement. Though it may not have any significant implications in practice as the GATS also covers measures at the regional level of government, TPP members may require to be more cautious about regional level regulations and take exceptions (non-conformity measures) for such regulations while signing the agreement if they wish to apply these regulations in practice.

TPP Delinks Cross-border Supply of Services from Local Presence

The TPP has an article on local presence (Article 10.6) that does not find place in the GATS. This article specifies that no member shall require a service supplier of another member to establish or maintain a representative office or any form of enterprise, or to be resident, in its territory as a condition for the cross-border supply of a service. This provision is likely to facilitate mode 1 trade as it delinks mode 1 from commercial presence requirements. However, local presence may be required for mode 1 delivery of certain services, such as, accredited professional services and telecom services to ensure regulatory comfort, accountability and consumer protection and in financial services for prudential reasons. The countries either need to take non-conformity measures or do away with the requirement of local presence for such services.

Right to Regulate

The article on domestic regulation (Article 10.8) of the TPP services chapter requires that all measures of general application affecting trade in services are administered in a reasonable, objective and impartial manner, whereas under the GATS, these requirements are applicable only for the measures pertaining to the sectors where specific commitments are undertaken. Thus, whereas domestic regulation (DR) disciplines are applicable to all sectors under the TPP, these are applicable under the GATS only to the sectors committed by a member.

Article 10.8 of the TPP recognizes the right to regulate and to introduce new regulations on the supply of services in order to meet a member's policy objectives. However, it does not define the kinds of policy objectives to be served in order to introduce new regulations. This may enable member countries to apply new restrictions in the form of domestic regulations in order to protect their services markets.

Article 10.8 also requires each member to ensure that any authorization fee charged by any of its competent authorities is reasonable, transparent and does not, in itself, restrict the supply of the relevant service. These requirements on the authorization fee charged are not included in the GATS.

The GATS requires that each member shall maintain or institute, as soon as practicable, judicial, arbitral or administrative tribunals or procedures which provide, at the request of an affected service supplier, for the prompt review of, and where justified, appropriate remedies for, administrative decisions affecting trade in services. This provision is not available in the TPP.

TPP Erodes the Flexibility to Apply Restrictions on Payments and Transfers Related to Supply of Services

TPP provisions on 'Payments and Transfers' (Article 10.12) are different from that of the GATS from two perspectives.[3] Whereas the GATS

---

[3] TPP provisions on payments and transfers: (1) Each party shall permit all transfers and payments that relate to the cross-border supply of services to be made freely and without delay into and out of its territory. (2) Each Party shall permit transfers and payments that relate to the cross-border supply of services to be made in a freely usable currency at the market rate of exchange that prevails at the time of transfer. (3) Notwithstanding paragraphs 1 and 2, a party may prevent or delay a transfer or payment through the equitable, non-discriminatory and good faith application of its laws that relate to: (a) bankruptcy, insolvency or the protection of the rights of creditors; (b) issuing, trading or dealing in securities, futures, options or derivatives; (c) financial reporting or record keeping of

requires that a member shall not apply restrictions on international transfers and payments for 'current transactions' relating to specific commitments, the TPP requires permitting 'all transfers and payments' relating to cross-border supply of services. Thus, the TPP expands the payment and transfer obligations of not applying restrictions on international payments and transfers to capital transactions as well. This article of the TPP also does not have reference to the rights and obligations of the members of the International Monetary Fund (IMF). It implies that a country may not impose restrictions on payments and transfers based on balance of payments (BoP) grounds—a right that is contained in the GATS.

TPP Contains Sectoral Annexes for Liberalization of Specific Services

The TPP services chapter has an annex on professional services and express delivery services, which is not in the GATS. Whereas Annex 10-A of the TPP specifically deals with engineering and architectural services; temporary licensing or registration of engineers; and legal services, Annex 10-B deals with express delivery services. These annexes chart out specific liberalization approaches for selected professional services and express delivery services considering their peculiar characteristics.

3.3 TPP Chapters on Specific Issues Pertaining to Services

Financial Services

As mentioned earlier, apart from the overarching chapter dealing with services trade, the TPP also has specific chapters on financial services, telecommunication services, e-commerce and temporary entry of business persons. Financial services are dealt in a significantly greater detail under the TPP as the chapter on financial services is the lengthiest

---

transfers when necessary to assist law enforcement or financial regulatory authorities; (d) criminal or penal offences; or (e) ensuring compliance with orders or judgements in judicial or administrative proceedings.

Services Coverage in TPP, TiSA and GATS **87**

chapter out of all the services chapters. As in the case of the overarching services chapter discussed earlier, the chapter on financial services also has provisions that depart significantly from GATS obligations. Salient features of the chapter on financial services and deviations from the GATS are discussed in this section. In addition, the final subsection discusses the implications for India if it would like to adhere to the disciplines contained in the TPP template.

TPP Expands the Scope of Financial Service Supplier

In the GATS Annex, a financial service supplier means any natural or juridical person of a member wishing to supply or supplying financial services but the term 'financial service supplier' does not include a public entity. On the other hand, the TPP chapter defines financial service supplier of a member as a person of a member that is engaged in the business of supplying a financial service within the territory of that member. Therefore, the TPP does not exclude 'public entities' from the definition of a financial service supplier. It is to be noted that the term 'public entities' under the GATS means (a) a government, a central bank or a monetary authority, of a member, or an entity owned or controlled by a member, that is principally engaged in carrying out governmental functions or activities for governmental purposes, not including an entity principally engaged in supplying financial services on commercial terms; or (b) a private entity, performing functions normally performed by a central bank or monetary authority, when exercising those functions. Thus, the scope (Article 11.2) of this chapter is widened as compared to the GATS Annex on financial services by not excluding 'public entities' from the ambit of financial service supplier.

TPP Includes Activities Conducted by a Central Bank or Monetary Authority

Activities conducted by a central bank or monetary authority or by any other public entity in pursuit of monetary or exchange rate policies are considered as 'services supplied in the exercise of governmental authority' under the GATS and hence these are excluded from the scope of the GATS Annex on financial services. However, the exclusions mentioned in the TPP financial services chapter does not exclude activities performed by a central bank or monetary authority from the scope of this chapter.

TPP Brings New Financial Services within the Ambit of Its Rules

The TPP also includes 'new financial services' within its ambit. A new financial service means a financial service not supplied in the member's territory that is supplied within the territory of another member, and includes any new form of delivery of a financial service or the sale of a financial product that is not sold in the member's territory. The TPP requires each member to permit a financial institution of another member to supply a new financial service that the member would permit its own financial institutions, in like circumstances, to supply without adopting a law or modifying an existing law. It is to be noted that as per this definition, a new financial service is not an innovative financial service, rather it is a financial service not supplied in a member's territory but supplied in another member's territory. Thus, the newness of a financial service depends on the availability or non-availability of such service in a particular territory. In contrast 'new financial services' are not a part of the GATS Annex on financial services.

TPP Permits Countries to Subsidize Financial Sector

The TPP chapter on financial services excludes subsidies or grants with respect to the cross-border supply of financial services, including government-supported loans, guarantees and insurance from its scope. The GATS Annex on financial services does not have any mention of subsidies. However, as mentioned earlier, the GATS has an article on subsidies which stipulates that members shall enter into negotiations with a view to developing the necessary multilateral disciplines on subsidies to avoid trade-distortive effects of subsidies. Keeping subsidies completely out of the scope of the TPP overarching services chapter and financial services chapter will allow members to continue with large amount of subsidies given in various forms to their financial sector which may eventually result into creation of big banks that fall into 'too big to fail' category.[4]

TPP Prohibits Countries from Imposing Market Access Restrictions

MA commitments in the TPP chapter on financial services specifies that no member shall adopt or maintain, with respect to financial institutions of another member or investors of another member seeking to establish those institutions, either on the basis of a regional subdivision or on the basis of its entire territory, measures that (a) impose limitations on: (i) the number of financial institutions whether in the form of numerical quotas, monopolies, exclusive service suppliers or the requirement of an economic needs test (ENT); (ii) the total value of financial service transactions or assets in the form of numerical quotas or the requirement of an ENT; (iii) the total number of financial service operations or the total quantity of financial services output expressed in terms of designated numerical units in the form of quotas or the requirement of an ENT; or (iv) the total number of natural persons that may be employed in a particular financial service sector or that a financial institution may employ and who are necessary for, and directly related to, the supply of a specific financial service in the form of numerical quotas or the requirement of an ENT; or (b) restrict or require specific types of legal entity or joint venture through which a financial institution may supply a service. Thus, unless any NCM is claimed by a member, financial services are fully open for foreign service providers (negative list approach). This is in contrast to the GATS positive list approach wherein a country specifies the sub-sectors and the extent to which it wants to open its services. The other deviation from the GATS is that the TPP chapter does not include foreign equity limits within the scope of the above-mentioned measures while the GATS has foreign equity limits as one of the six MA limitations.

---

[4] 'Too big to fail' theory stipulates that certain corporations, particularly financial institutions, are so large and interconnected that their failure would be disastrous to the greater economic system, and therefore, they must be supported by the government when they face potential failure.

Implications for India If It Adheres to the TPP Template on Financial Services

The TPP chapter on financial services intends to set rules which would assist the expansion of financial multinationals of developed countries into other nations by preventing regulatory barriers. Instead of advocating sound prudential norms for financial services, the TPP would expose many financial stability measures to investors' challenges. The scope of financial services chapter is enlarged by having provisions for new financial services. India may find it difficult to meet the ambitious obligations that are associated with opening up financial services, as envisaged in the TPP template. This subsection examines the implications for India if it were to adhere to the TPP template of rules and obligations pertaining to financial services.

Existing Policy of RBI Pertaining to Foreign Banks Not in Accordance with TPP Obligations

On two grounds the existing policy of Reserve Bank of India (RBI) pertaining to foreign banks diverges from the MA rules of the TPP. First, at present, eligible foreign banks are allowed by the RBI to set up business in India through a single mode of presence—either branch mode or a wholly owned subsidiary (WOS) mode. The foreign banks have to choose one of the above two modes of presence and are governed by the principle of single mode of presence. Second, the RBI also considers that providing the extent of national treatment to a WOS of foreign banks needs to be considered from the financial stability perspective. From the perspective of financial stability and concentration of market power, downside risk may arise if the foreign banks, that is, WOSs of the foreign banks and foreign bank branches together come to dominate the domestic financial system. To address this risk, restrictions can be placed on further entry of new WOSs of foreign banks, when the capital and reserves of the foreign banks (that is, WOSs and foreign bank branches) in India exceed 20 per cent of the capital and reserves of the banking system. In such eventuality, prior approval of the RBI will be required for capital infusion into the existing WOSs of foreign banks (Reserve Bank of India 2013). If the TPP provisions enter into future agreements to which India wishes to be a party, it would need to negotiate both these requirements as non-conformity measures.

Adhering to the TPP Provisions on Senior Management can Compromise Financial Stability

The financial stability may further be compromised if the TPP article on senior management and boards of directors (Article 11.9) is to be followed. According to this article, no member shall require financial institutions of another member to engage natural persons of any particular nationality as senior managerial or other essential personnel. Also, no member shall require that more than a minority of the board of directors of a financial institution of another member be composed of nationals of the member, persons residing in the territory of the member, or a combination thereof. These requirements go beyond the GATS obligations.

At present in India, apart from other requirements, the composition of the board of directors of a WOS should meet two requirements based on nationality. First, not less than 50 per cent directors should be Indian nationals/non-resident Indians (NRIs)/persons of Indian origin (PIOs) subject to the condition that one-third of the directors are Indian nationals resident in India; and second, the chief executive officer (CEO) would be appointed on full-time basis and should be resident in India. Again, if India has to adhere to the TPP template in any future agreement, it would need to negotiate both these requirements as non-conformity measures.

Adhering to the Negative List Approach Would Severely Restrict India's Ability to Regulate Services, Particularly in the Future

The 'negative list' approach for MFN, MA and national treatment limitations would require India to anticipate all possible financial regulations, including future regulations applicable for financial services not yet invented, at the time of signing the concerned trade agreement. If India fails to anticipate these future regulations and does not get such regulations exempted through NCMs, its ability to regulate its financial services sector in future would be severely curtailed.

Adhering to Notification Obligations of the TPP Would Make it More Onerous to Implement New Measures

Prior notification of proposed new measures (Article 11.13 on transparency and administration of certain measures) is likely to add opportunities to influence governments and launch lobbying and public campaigns against or in support. As it applies to the whole range of 'measures', it will impose compliance obligations, especially at lower levels of government, which are onerous and expensive to satisfy. Providing an opportunity to comment assumes a process and criteria for decision-making, which means it is easier to subject those decisions to review and challenge. It is also feared that the response mechanism for inquiries raised by 'interested persons' could open the door for a constant stream of enquiries from services firms that may paralyse a ministry or agency. It would also allow them to collect information to form the basis of a review or dispute.

Adhering to the TPP Template Will Make Measures Taken for Financial Stability Susceptible to Challenge Under ISDS

The TPP allows foreign firms to use extra-juridical tribunals to challenge financial stability measures that do not conform to their expectations as the financial services chapter together with the investment chapter would grant foreign banks and other foreign financial firms new substantive rights and privileges to challenge financial stability measures. Moreover, foreign firms can challenge such policies even if they apply to domestic and foreign firms alike and have been reviewed and affirmed by domestic courts. Similarly, 'restrictions to safeguard the BoP' are constrained by two limitations. First, capital controls are subject to ISDS challenges as indirect appropriations. It implies that a country imposing capital controls may be required to compensate a foreign investor if the controls result in a significant reduction in the value of an investment. The GATS does not have a comparable obligation to compensate private investors. Second, the TPP does not allow capital controls to be applied to payments or transfers relating to foreign direct investment (FDI). It is due to this provision that in the TPP Chile had to negotiate for a separate carve-out of its policies that allow long term limits on capital flows ('TPP—a threat to financial' n.d.).

3.4 TPP Chapter on Temporary Entry for Business Persons

Chapter 12 of the TPP pertains to cross-border movement of business persons. Business persons in the TPP chapter are meant to include not only persons who are engaged in the supply of service but also in trade in goods and the conduct of investment activities. Thus, the scope of business persons is widened in the TPP as compared to the GATS by including persons engaged in trade in goods and investment activities.

Article 12.3 (Application Procedures) of this chapter requires that each member shall make a decision on the application and inform the applicant of the decision including, if approved, the period of stay and other conditions as expeditiously as possible after the receipt of a completed application for an immigration formality. It also requires that each member shall ensure that fees charged by its competent authorities for the processing of an application for an immigration formality are reasonable in that they do not unduly impair or delay trade in goods or services or conduct of investment activities. Members are also required to promptly publish online if possible or, otherwise, make publicly available information on (a) current requirements for temporary entry, including explanatory material and relevant forms and documents that will enable interested persons of the other members to become acquainted with those requirements, and (b) the typical time frame within which an application for an immigration formality is processed. They shall establish or maintain appropriate mechanisms to respond to enquiries from interested persons regarding measures relating to temporary entry (Article 12.6: Provision of Information).

The chapter also envisages easing business travel by incorporating that the members affirm their commitments to each other in the context of Asia-Pacific Economic Cooperation (APEC) to enhance the mobility of business persons, including through exploration and voluntary development of trusted traveller programmes, and their support for efforts to enhance the APEC Business Travel Card programme (Article 12.5: Business Travel).

Annex 12-A of this chapter contains the commitments made by TPP members with regard to temporary entry of business persons, and outlines the conditions and limitations for entry and temporary stay, including length of stay, for each category of business persons specified by the concerned member. It is to be noted that the USA has not submitted any commitment in this annex, thereby implying that the USA has not committed anything with regard to temporary entry of business persons except the obligations envisaged in the main text of this chapter.

It is also to be noted that dispute settlement may not be available for cases involving temporary entry of business persons (Article 12.10) as the chapter specifically mentions that no member shall have recourse to dispute settlement under the chapter on dispute settlement regarding a refusal to grant temporary entry unless (a) the matter involves a pattern of practice, and (b) the business persons affected have exhausted all available administrative remedies regarding the particular matter.

It seems from the text of this chapter that there is not much in this chapter to facilitate mode 4 movement as the obligations of this chapter are not far reaching and rather superficial. However, some provisions of this chapter seem to be positive for India. For instance, the article on application procedures (Article 12.3) and the one on provision of information (Article 12.6) contain obligations that may facilitate temporary movement of business persons.

3.5 TPP Chapter on Telecommunications Services

This chapter applies to (a) any measure relating to access to and use of public telecommunications services, (b) any measure relating to obligations regarding suppliers of public telecommunications services, and (c) any other measure relating to telecommunications services. This chapter does not apply to any measure relating to broadcast or cable distribution of radio or television programming, except that (a) article on access to and use of public telecommunications services applies with respect to a cable or broadcast service supplier's access to and use of public telecommunications services, and (b) article on transparency applies to any technical measure to the extent that the measure also affects public telecommunications services. The GATS Annex on telecommunications also excludes the measure affecting broadcast or cable distribution of radio or television programming from its scope but this annex does not mention the two exceptions to it as included in the TPP and outlined above.

It contains detailed obligations related to telecommunication services and has provisions that are not included in the GATS Annex on telecommunications. The provisions not included in the GATS Annex are—approaches to regulation (Article 13.3), obligations relating to suppliers of public telecommunications services (interconnection, number portability and access to numbers [Article 13.5]), international mobile roaming (Article 13.6), treatment by major suppliers of public telecommunications services (Article 13.7), competitive safeguards (Article 13.8), unbundling of network elements by major suppliers (Article 13.10), interconnection with major suppliers (Article 13.11), provisioning and pricing of leased circuits services by major suppliers (Article 13.12), co-location by major suppliers (Article 13.13), access to poles, ducts, conduits and rights-of-way owned or controlled by major suppliers (Article 13.14), international submarine cable systems (Article 13.15), independent regulatory bodies and government ownership (Article 13.16), universal service (Article 13.17), allocation and use of scarce resources (Article 13.19), enforcement (Article 13.20), resolution of telecommunications disputes (Article 13.21) and flexibility in the choice of technology (Article 13.23).

Even for the provisions finding a place both in the TPP and the GATS Annex, there are differences in the obligations covered under the TPP and the Annex. For instance, the TPP provisions pertaining to access to and use of public telecommunications services (Article 13.4) are a bit different from the GATS Annex on telecommunications. Whereas the GATS Annex specifically mentions its applicability to only committed sectors, the TPP does not use words 'committed sectors'. Therefore, the TPP provisions will be applicable to all telecommunication services even if some of these are not committed. Apart from this, as compared to the GATS Annex, the TPP requires each member to ensure that any service supplier of another member is permitted to (a) provide services to individual or multiple end-users over leased or owned circuits and (b) perform switching, signalling, processing and conversion functions. The TPP provisions also do not include two of the six conditions for access to and use of public telecommunications transport networks and services, mentioned in the GATS Annex. These two conditions are: (a) restrictions on resale or shared use of such services, and (b) restrictions on interconnection of private leased or owned circuits with such networks or services or with circuits leased or owned by another service supplier.

This chapter has an article (Article 13.6) on international mobile roaming, which till date remained a relatively less discussed area within the domain of telecommunication services trade and not even mentioned in the GATS Annex. This article requires that members shall endeavour to cooperate on promoting transparent and reasonable rates for international mobile roaming services that can help promote the growth of trade among the members and enhance consumer welfare. A member may choose to take steps to enhance transparency and competition with respect to international mobile roaming rates and technological alternatives to roaming services, such as (a) ensuring that information regarding retail rates is easily accessible to consumers, and (b) minimizing impediments to the use of technological alternatives to roaming whereby consumers, when visiting the territory of a member from the territory of another member, can access telecommunications services using the device of their choice. It also requires that each member shall provide to the other members information on rates for retail international mobile roaming services for voice, data and text messages offered to consumers of the member when visiting the territories of the other members.

The telecommunication services chapter requires that no member shall prohibit the resale of any public telecommunications service (Article 13.9). The GATS Annex on telecommunications does not have this onerous requirement. This article provides the flexibilities that each member may determine, in accordance with their laws and regulations, which public telecommunications services must be offered for resale by major suppliers based on the need to promote competition or to benefit the long-term interests of end users. Though this article provides the flexibilities to choose the services to be offered for resale, the intent is to open all, or most, of the services for resale.

The provisions on licensing (Article 13.18) and transparency (Article 13.22) are likely to increase administrative burden on the government as licensing provisions require that reasons for denial of licence, imposition of supplier-specific conditions on a licence, revocation of a licence, or refusal to renew a licence be provided to an applicant on request. These requirements do not exist in the GATS Annex. Similarly, transparency provisions also have provisions going beyond the GATS. In addition to the transparency provisions as included in the GATS Annex,[5] this chapter has other transparency provisions that requires each member to ensure that when its telecommunications regulator body seeks input for a proposal for a regulation, that body shall (a) make the proposal public or otherwise available to any interested persons, (b) include an explanation of the purpose of and reasons for the proposal, (c) provide interested persons with adequate public notice of the ability to comment and reasonable opportunity for such comment, (d) to the extent practicable, make

---

[5] Transparency provisions in the GATS Annex requires that each member shall ensure that relevant information on conditions affecting access to and use of public telecommunications transport networks and services is publicly available, including: tariffs and other terms and conditions of service; specifications of technical interfaces with such networks and services; information on bodies responsible for the preparation and adoption of standards affecting such access and use; conditions applying to attachment of terminal or other equipment; and notifications, registration or licensing requirements, if any.

publicly available all relevant comments filed with it and (e) respond to all significant and relevant issues raised in comments filed, in the course of issuance of the final regulation.

3.6 TPP Chapter on E-commerce

The chapter on electronic commerce is applicable to measures adopted or maintained by a member affecting trade by electronic means. However, it does not define categorically what is 'e-commerce' or 'trade by electronic means'. It only defines 'digital product' as a computer programme, text, video, image, sound recording or other product that is digitally encoded, produced for commercial sale or distribution, and that can be transmitted electronically. However, a digital product does not include a digitized representation of a financial instrument, including money.

The provisions of this chapter do not apply to (a) GP, or (b) information held or processed by or on behalf of a member, or measures related to such information, including measures related to its collection. Use of electronic means for GP is covered in a separate chapter on GP.

This chapter contains articles on custom duties, non-discriminatory treatment of digital products, domestic electronic transactions framework, electronic authentication and electronic signatures, online consumer protection, personal information protection, paperless trading, principles on access to and use of the internet for e-commerce, cross-border transfer of information by electronic means, Internet interconnection charge sharing, location of computing facilities, unsolicited commercial electronic messages, source code, and international cooperation.

The TPP advocates permanent moratorium on custom duty on digital products as the article on custom duties (Article 14.3) requires that no member shall impose customs duties on electronic transmissions, including content transmitted electronically, between a person of one member and a person of another member. Though India is a party to the existing temporary moratorium under the WTO, which prohibits countries from imposing custom duty on electronic transmissions, agreeing to a permanent moratorium, as envisaged in the TPP template, may not be good for India. India could use this moratorium flexibility as a bargaining tool for negotiating some other provisions either within e-commerce or outside it.

Non-discriminatory treatment of digital products (Article 14.4) requires that no member shall accord less favourable treatment to digital products created, produced, published, contracted for, commissioned or first made available on commercial terms in the territory of another member, or to digital products which have a person of another member as their author, performer, producer, developer or owner, than it accords to other like digital products. However, it does not apply to broadcasting and subsidies or grants provided by a member, including government-supported loans, guarantees and insurance. In order to support innovation and developments of digital products, India may require giving preferential treatment to its domestic digital products or producers of digital products.

This chapter also requires that each member shall allow the cross-border transfer of information by electronic means, including personal information, when this activity is for the conduct of the business of a covered person (Article 14.11). These provisions grant businesses the freedom to outsource data storage and processing to any other TPP jurisdiction without any limitation. As the chapter does not require members to adopt privacy laws, this could create meaningful barriers for the protection of privacy. These provisions significantly undermine the ability of governments to secure their citizens' data against unauthorized or unlawful processing or accidental loss or destruction of, or damage to, personal data in these contexts. Though there is a provision to maintain measures inconsistent with the cross-border transfer of information, the exception seems to be difficult to use and insufficient to safeguard privacy as the language of such exceptions has many layers of qualifications. Moreover, the exception is negatively worded. It is drafted in such a way that the data localization restrictions apply unless it can be demonstrated that a government's legitimate public policy objective can justify a departure from the general restriction. Therefore, not only does the government bear the burden of demonstrating that the restriction does not restrict trade or discriminate, but it must also prove that its chosen public policy objectives are legitimate (Kilic and Israel 2015).

In this context, it must be noted that the Supreme Court of India had set up a five-judge bench in April 2017 to decide on the petition challenging the privacy policy of WhatsApp on sharing data with its parent company Facebook. Under WhatsApp's new privacy policy, the company will share some user data, including phone number of the user, with its parent company Facebook ('Based on "WhatsApp…"' n.d.).

In the present age, almost each action of individuals and businesses, whether a simple online search, a social media activity or an online transaction, generates data. This data contains important information about human behaviour and customer tastes and preferences. For instance, if one searches flight options for a particular destination in Google, he gets promotional messages in his Facebook account. Hence, the data generated by individuals' actions is of high commercial value. The pertinent questions in this regard are: Should data having such high commercial value be transferable freely across borders? Will this benefit only multinational companies operating across borders or are there any gains to countries that allow such free cross-border transfer of data?

This chapter prohibits governments to require a covered person to use or locate computing facilities in that member's territory as a condition for conducting business in that territory (Article 14.13). Having a provision that prohibits imposing localization requirements may not be a good idea as localization may be required in future for national security or consumer protection purposes. Localization of servers may also be required from a dispute resolution perspective. Cloud computing is rapidly gaining popularity among service providers, which raises important questions regarding accountability of service providers. Any dispute pertaining to data/server will be subject to the rules of the territory where the server is located. It implies that if a member's data is stored in servers located outside its territory, it is subject to the jurisprudence of that country where the server is located.

E-commerce chapter also requires that no member shall require the transfer of, or access to, the source code of software owned by a person of another member, as a condition for the import, distribution, sale or use of such software, or of products containing such software, in its territory (Article 14.17). Software subject to this provision is limited to mass-market software or products containing such software and does not include software used for critical infrastructure. There are many situations other than in the critical infrastructure context in which it might be desirable from a public policy or national security perspective to require access to software. For instance, a few years ago, the Indian Government's internal security and intelligence services were not able to break the encryption of the BlackBerry device, which made countering terror threats and national security matters difficult. While the Indian Government wanted BlackBerry to allow monitoring of e-mails and short message service (SMS), Research In Motion (RIM) has said that the security architecture for its enterprise customers is based on a symmetric key system whereby the customers create their own key and only they possess the copy of the encryption. RIM said the security architecture for customers was designed to exclude RIM or any third party from reading encrypted information under any circumstances ('RIM refuses to…' n.d.). The recent episode of Apple taking 'unlocking phone' battle to US Congress is another glaring example of how denying access to source code may jeopardize national security. Responding to an order which compelled Apple to help weaken the security on a phone used by a terrorist and give access to its contents, Apple has said that the US government is seeking 'dangerous power' by forcing the company to unlock a terrorist's phone, in landmark legal filings that challenged the Obama administration and the Federal Bureau of Investigation (FBI; Griffin 2016).

3.7 Implications of the TPP Type Provisions for India

The provisions of the services chapter as well as the four specific chapters may have wide-scale implications for the services sector in India if these provisions are adopted in other trade agreements. Some of these implications are highlighted in the preceding discussion. The following paragraphs discuss other important implications of these provisions for India.

Some of the services-related provisions of the TPP may be beneficial to India. For instance, the TPP talks about taking steps to implement a temporary or project-specific licensing or registration regime based on a foreign supplier's home licence or recognized professional body membership, without the need for further written examination. This may be advantageous for professionals in India who intend to provide their services in overseas markets. Similarly, the provisions related to authorization and licensing may prove beneficial to India.[6] The TPP also

---

[6] These provisions require a member to ensure that its competent authorities: (a) within a reasonable period of time after the submission of an application is considered complete under its laws and regulations, inform the applicant of the decision concerning the application; (b) to the extent practicable, establish an indicative time frame for the processing of an application; (c) if an application is rejected, to the extent practicable, inform the applicant of the reasons for the rejection, either directly or on request, as appropriate; (d) on request of the applicant, provide, without undue delay, information concerning the status of the application; (e) to the extent practicable, provide the applicant with the opportunity to correct minor errors and omissions in the application and endeavour to provide guidance on the additional information required; and (f) if they deem appropriate, accept copies of documents that are authenticated in accordance with the member's laws in place of original documents.

requires members to ensure that any authorization fee charged by any of its competent authorities is reasonable, transparent and does not, in itself, restrict the supply of the relevant service. This is also one of the demands of India in international trade agreements and has also been included in India's proposal on trade facilitation in services.

However, there are a number of provisions that may adversely affect India's services sector or that may require significant changes in India's services regulations. For instance, binding of autonomous liberalization and ratchet mechanism will significantly reduce the policy space for India and, hence, India's ability to experiment with liberalizing regulatory measures for various services will be adversely affected. Past experiences suggest this may not be warranted given the regulatory structure and politico-economic realities of India. For instance, FDI in banking services in India was allowed up to 74 per cent through automatic route in 2005 (Government of India 2005) but after the global financial crisis, the government has stipulated in 2010 that FDI in banking services is allowed through automatic route only up to 49 per cent, and beyond 49 per cent and up to 74 per cent, it is allowed through Government route (Government of India 2010). Similarly, government allowed 51 per cent FDI in multi-brand retail (MBR) in November 2011 but withdrew it after strong opposition. It again allowed 51 per cent FDI in MBR in 2012. Such back and forth on regulatory measures will not be possible in the presence of the ratchet mechanism.

As mentioned earlier, mode 3 of services trade is covered under the investment chapter in the TPP rather than in the services chapter. The USA follows this model in its free trade agreements (FTAs), whereas India does not follow this model as its FTAs cover mode 3 within the services chapter and not under the investment chapter. As mentioned earlier, any future regulation that adversely affects foreign investment in services may be challenged under the investor–state dispute mechanism as envisaged in the investment chapter of the TPP. This may again not be desirable given the evolving nature of regulations in various services in India.

Domestic rule-making would also be heavily pressurized by transparency provisions as it will be subject to not only advance publications but also review by foreign service providers. Therefore, autonomy with respect to rule-making is likely to be affected by such reviewing. Moreover, it will increase administrative burden on the government as foreign service providers may hire a battery of lawyers and other professionals to raise questions on the proposed regulations of the government. The government may not have enough resources to respond to all these queries.

The chapter on temporary entry of business persons does not have provisions on issues that are important for India with regard to mode 4. For instance, working of dependent members is not incorporated. It must, however, be noted that provision to apply reasonable fees for processing applications for temporary entry and stay of the service providers is positive for India, though the interpretation of the word 'reasonable' is subjective.

It seems that many of the provisions of the telecommunication chapter have already been implemented in India. However, detailed investigation of implications of the TPP-like obligations is required to assess the possible impact of such obligations on India. The main sticking point in this chapter could be about defining 'major suppliers' (Articles 13.7, 13.10, 13.11, 13.12, 13.13 and 13.14). As India does not have any definition of 'major suppliers', these obligations need to be assessed to understand whom they should apply on. The article on unbundling (Article 13.10) may also be very contentious.

For the chapter on e-commerce, consumer protection to foreign consumers is already available in India as the Consumer Protection Act, 1986, does not differentiate between an Indian or a foreign national. Provisions related to cross-border movement of information, transfer or access to source code, location of computing facilities, etc., require detailed discussion with appropriate bodies. It seems that diverse positions are taken by various stakeholders on many of these issues. For instance, some segments of the Indian industry do not favour localization of computing facilities restriction. Considering the interests of the Indian industry, India may not support imposing localization requirements but at the same time it should also not support prohibition on imposing such requirements so as to keep the flexibility to impose these requirements in future if required.

The annex on professional services has a provision related to temporary licensing or registration of engineers. It also specifically discusses opening up legal services and allowing transnational legal services (a) on a temporary fly-in, fly-out basis, (b) through the use of web-based or telecommunications technology, (c) by establishing a commercial presence and (d) through a combination of fly-in, fly-out and one or both of the other modes listed in (b) and (c). As the Advocates Act, 1961, does not allow foreign law firms to practice law in India, suitable regulatory changes may need to be brought in order to comply with such requirements.

3.8 Trade in Services Agreement (TiSA)[7]

The stalling of the Doha Development Round (DDR) led some of the members of the WTO to think of an alternative approach to open up services markets across countries, in the early 2012. The TiSA is an attempt, led by developed countries, in this direction. The USA, the European Union (EU) and Australia, along with some other like-minded members, called the Really Good Friends of Services, have proposed this new approach to services trade. The TiSA is currently being negotiated by 23 members of the WTO, including the EU. Together, the participating countries account for 70 per cent of world trade in services.[8]

TiSA negotiations are being undertaken in considerable secrecy and the official text of the agreement is not yet in the public domain. However, some leaked documents pertaining to the core text as well as its annexes are available in the public domain. The core text contains the most general provisional language agreed by the existing negotiating members, establishing the overall legal architecture of the TiSA. Specialized areas, such as maritime transport services, or electronic commerce, are dealt within 'annexes', which are being negotiated alongside the core text. A review of these leaked documents reveals that many of the provisions are similar to the TPP. Though many provisions are borrowed from the GATS, the TiSA also has a GATS-plus architecture, as in the case of the TPP, because a number of provisions are either very different from GATS provisions or are newly introduced in the TiSA. For instance, the TiSA has four parts of the agreement, namely, general provisions, scheduling commitments, new and enhanced disciplines and institutional provisions. On the other hand the GATS includes six parts, namely, scope and definition, general obligations and disciplines, specific commitments, progressive liberalization, institutional provisions and final provisions. The deletion of progressive liberalization provisions in the TiSA may not be in the interest of developing countries including India. Provisions of 'new and enhanced disciplines' may require regulatory changes in many of the services in India.

Similarly, 'MA', national treatment and 'additional commitments' are part of specific commitments in the GATS but of general provisions in the TiSA. As part of specific commitments, MA, national treatment and additional commitments are applicable only for the sectors committed in

---

[7] Analysis in this section is primarily based on the leaked documents available at WikiLeaks.
[8] Source: http://ec.europa.eu/trade/policy/in-focus/tisa/ (last visited 7 December 2016).

the schedule of commitments. However, these may become obligatory irrespective of sectors committed if general provisions in the TiSA are interpreted as general obligations of the GATS.

Unlike the TPP, which follows a negative list approach, the TiSA follows a hybrid approach for scheduling of commitments. The format for listing individual commitments in the TiSA builds on the format for scheduling commitments under the GATS. With respect to MA, the individual commitments of the TiSA participants are to be scheduled as under the GATS. However, the novelty compared to the GATS is that the TiSA incorporates a horizontal national treatment. This is the reason why the TiSA scheduling is called the 'hybrid' approach ('How to read the TiSA…' n.d.).

As in the case of the GATS, the TiSA also has annexes on various important issues pertaining to services trade. Some of these annexes are taken from the GATS and have been modified, whereas some are newly introduced.

TiSA and GATS Annexes

The following subsections analyse various annexes of the TiSA that are taken from the GATS.

Annex on Movement of Natural Persons Supplying Services under the Agreement

The first four paragraphs of the annex on movement of natural persons supplying services are the same as in the GATS Annex. However, the TiSA Annex also has another article on 'general obligations', though the provisions of this article are not yet finalized. This article prescribes that all measures related to or concerning the entry and temporary stay of service providers are administered in a reasonable, objective and impartial manner and are not applied in a manner which would constitute a means of arbitrary or unjustifiable discrimination or a disguised restriction on trade in services to nullify or impair the benefits accruing to any member under the terms of a specific commitment. The USA is opposing this paragraph.

The period of temporary stay envisaged in this annex is minimum one year for intra corporate transferee (ICT), contract service suppliers (CSS) and independent professionals (IP). Extension of temporary stay as well as working of dependent members is not considered under this annex. The provision regarding not to apply the ENT is under negotiation.

Therefore, it seems from the available text of the annex on movement of natural persons that there is not much in this annex to facilitate mode 4 movement. However, it must also be noted that much of this annex is still under negotiations.

Annex on Air Transport Services

The annex on air transport services included three new types of services that are covered by this agreement under air transport services. These are: ground handling services, airport operation services and specialty air services. The scope of these three services is under negotiation.

Thus, the annex on air transport services intends to significantly enlarge the scope of air transport services to which the agreement will apply. Most of these services are those in which developed countries' service suppliers, particularly the USA and the EU ones, have an edge over the developing countries' service suppliers. Therefore, the provisions of this annex are likely to benefit developed countries more.

Annex on Financial Services

An important departure from the GATS Annex on financial services is that it has provisions related to temporary entry of personnel including specialists from other professions such as computer services, telecommunication and accounts of the financial service supplier and actuarial and legal specialists. Thus, the provisions of this annex will also be applicable to other service suppliers who are engaged in providing back office support to the financial service supplier.

MA and national treatment commitments for financial services are also discussed in this annex. More importantly, MFN and national treatment provisions for financial services purchased by public entities are also introduced. This annex also negotiates transfer of information in electronic form, into and out of the territory of a country for data processing where such processing is required in the financial service supplier's ordinary course of business.

Annex on Maritime Transport Services

The annex on maritime transport services negotiates inclusion of multimodal transport within the scope of the annex. It also negotiates commitments without limitations to permit cross-border supply (mode 1) and commercial presence (mode 3) for international maritime transport services as well maritime auxiliary services.

There is also a provision under negotiation that requires members not to adopt or maintain cargo-sharing arrangements in any agreement concerning international maritime transport services. Any such arrangements in any agreement in force or signed prior to the date of entry into force of this agreement are required to be terminated upon the entry into force of this agreement.

This annex also introduces national treatment and MFN obligations with regard to the access to ports, use of infrastructure and port services, and the access to and use of maritime auxiliary services and related services.

Annex on Telecommunications Services

This annex proposes an article on openness of telecommunication services markets and negotiates full foreign participation without limitations of foreign capital not only in telecommunication services but also in electronic services. It also proposes not to impose any MA or national treatment limitations on supply of telecommunications services on a cross-border basis.

There also exist articles on telecommunication regulatory body, technological neutrality, interoperability, regulatory flexibility, licensing and other authorizations, transparency, resolution of domestic telecommunication disputes, access to and use of public telecommunications networks and services, obligations relating to suppliers of public telecommunications services, obligations relating to major suppliers, undersea cables and landing facilities and services, universal service, allocation and use of scarce resources, international mobile roaming, international standards and organizations, international cooperation, and review of these provisions. The GATS has an annex on negotiations on basic telecommunications, which is not included in the TiSA.

New Annexes in the TiSA

Apart from the annexes that are taken from the GATS and discussed earlier, the TiSA also has a number of new annexes. As the negotiations progress, some of these annexes may become a part of the core text of the TiSA. These new annexes are discussed as follows.

Annex on Competitive Delivery Services

The annex on competitive delivery services requires each member that maintains a postal monopoly to define the scope of the monopoly on the basis of objective criteria, including quantitative criteria such as price and/or weight thresholds. It also requires that each member should ensure that any supplier of services covered under a postal monopoly does not use its monopoly position to engage, either directly or indirectly, in anticompetitive practices in a non-monopolized market in its territory that adversely affect the supply of competitive delivery services by as service supplier of another member.

This annex prohibits cross-subsidization as it mentions that no member may allow a supplier of services covered by a postal monopoly to cross-subsidize its own, or any other supplier's, competitive delivery services with revenues derived from monopoly postal services.

It also requires that members should ensure that the regulatory authority responsible for regulating competitive delivery services should be separate from and not accountable to any supplier of competitive delivery services.

Thus, the annex on competitive delivery services intends to limit the scope of the postal monopoly, to prevent misuse of monopoly power and to curb cross-subsidization.

Annex on Transparency

The annex on transparency is one of the most important annexes of the TiSA. As per this annex, each member is required to ensure that its laws, regulations, procedures and administrative rulings of general application respecting any matter covered by the TiSA are promptly published, or otherwise made available, in such a manner as to enable interested persons and members to become acquainted with them. A member is also required to publish in advance any measure referred to as earlier that it proposes to adopt. Some members also proposed that interested persons and other members should also be given a reasonable opportunity to comment on such proposed measure. It is also proposed that to the extent possible, a member should include in the publication an explanation of the purpose of and rationale for the proposed regulation. If a member does not provide advance notice and opportunity for comment, it shall, to the extent possible, address in writing the reasons for the same.

It is to be noted that some paragraphs of the article on transparency under the GATS are not included in the TiSA. These paragraphs have provisions pertaining to informing the Council for Trade in Services of the WTO about any new regulations or changes in the existing regulations affecting trade in services covered by specific commitments and some flexibility for developing countries with regard to responding promptly to any request of other members. The absence of these paragraphs clearly indicates a lack of concern for the interests of developing countries.

Annex on Professional Services

This annex enlarges the scope of services to be considered as professional services. For instance, domestic law (host country) is proposed to be included within legal services. Similarly, private education services are also proposed to be included within the category of professional services.

In order to secure the existing MA, it proposes that in sectors where commitments are undertaken in accordance with the article on MA, any terms, limitations and conditions on MA affecting trade in professional services shall be limited to measures that a member maintains on the date the TiSA will take effect, or the continuation or prompt renewal of any such measures. Thus, it prescribes binding the existing level of autonomous liberalization in professional services.

For cross-border supply (mode 1) of professional services, it proposes to undertake commitments without limitations. Similarly, it proposes no limitations on foreign equity. Thus, this annex prescribes that both mode 1 and mode 3, the most important modes for developed countries' professional services suppliers, should be completely liberalized and there should not be any limitations on these two modes. It must, however, be noted that this annex does not talk about mode 4 (cross-border movement of professionals). This is one of the most important modes for developing countries for professional services given their labour abundance and human resources.

Annex on Government Procurement

The annex on GP mandates that foreign service suppliers that have established a commercial presence in the host country should be accorded national treatment as regards GP of services in the host country. It also requires that each member should ensure that the GP of services is conducted in a transparent and impartial manner that (a) ensures that the service market is opened up to competition, (b) avoids conflicts of interest and (c) prevents corruptive practices.

It also requires that a procuring entity shall promptly inform participating suppliers of the entity's contract award decision. Where national legislation provides for a review procedure, a procuring entity shall, on request, provide an unsuccessful supplier with an explanation of the reasons why the entity did not select its tender and the relative advantages of the successful suppliers tender in sufficient detail to allow for the review of the decision on the request of an unsuccessful supplier. This requirement is likely to increase administrative burden on the government.

Annex on E-commerce

This annex contains articles on cross-border information flow, online consumer protection, personal information protection, unsolicited commercial electronic messages, transfer or access to source code, open networks, network access and use, local infrastructure, electronic authentication and electronic signatures, custom duties on electronic deliveries and international cooperation.

It also has new provisions applicable to all services. The articles included in this section are on local presence, local management and board of directors, local content, local technology, and scheduling of localization commitments, among others. It suggests prohibition on using local infrastructure conditions and also prohibition on using transfer of technology or local technology conditions. It is proposed that the terms, conditions, limitations and qualifications referred to in articles on local presence, local management and boards of directors, local content and local technology shall be set out in each member's schedule and shall be limited to measures that a member maintains on the date the TiSA will take effect, or the continuation or prompt renewal of any such measures.

Annex on Domestic Regulations

Most of the text of the annex on domestic regulations is under negotiation. An important point of this annex is that it proposes a definition of 'technical standards'. As per this proposal, 'technical standards' are measures that lay down the characteristics of a service or the manner in which the service is supplied. Technical standards also include the procedures relating to the compliance with and enforcement of such standards. Thus, it seems that 'technical standards' are defined in a way that not only regulation of services but also of goods used in supplying a service is included within the scope of technical standards. It must be noted that though the GATS makes use of 'technical standards' at a number of places in the provisions related to domestic regulations, it does not define 'technical standards'.

Another important observation about the annex on domestic regulations is that most of the provisions contains 'to the extent possible' or 'to the extent practicable' words. Similarly, 'reasonable' word is also used frequently. As the interpretation of these words is very subjective, the frequent use of such words dilutes the provisions of DRs and makes them amenable to get misused by various countries to protect their services markets in a disguised manner.

3.9 Conclusion

Both the TPP and TiSA restrict public policies and reduce policy space and the ability of the governments to experiment with liberalization. Both agreements include similar language, mechanisms or provisions, be it 'DR' (TiSA) or regulatory coherence (TPP) and transparency, which may result in corporations challenging and hampering almost any state policy to protect the public good. The TiSA and TPP also intend to have extensive liberalization of public procurement in member countries, restricting governments' ability to support sustainable local food systems, jobs or local production of clean energy ('Secret TISA...' n.d.).

The TPP and TiSA are envisaged as the gold standard trade architecture and intend to significantly open services markets among the member countries. Some of the provisions of the TPP or TiSA may be beneficial for India but other provisions may affect its ability to reform and liberalize various services. India will be required to make significant changes in its domestic regulatory framework affecting various services to align them with higher standards as envisaged in these agreements.

Notwithstanding the compulsions of any trade agreement, India needs to prepare itself for higher level of regulatory coherence and could consider liberalizing some services not yet opened for foreign service providers on its own. Such liberalization is likely to improve efficiency in these services by bringing in competition without compromising autonomy or policy space available to the government.

References

'How to Read the TiSA Initial Offer of the European Union?' Retrieved 18 July 2017, from http://trade.ec.europa.eu/doclib/docs/2014/july/tradoc_152691.pdf

Friends of the Earth. 2016. 'Secret TiSA Trade Deal: Equally as Dangerous as TPP and TTIP'. Global Research, Centre for Research on Globalization. Retrieved 4 December 2016, from http://www.globalresearch.ca/secret-tisa-trade-deal-equally-as-dangerous-as-tpp-and-ttip/5559797

Government of India. 2005. *FDI Policy 2005*. New Delhi: Department of Industrial Policy and Promotion, Ministry of Commerce.

———. 2010. *FDI Policy 2010*. New Delhi: Department of Industrial Policy and Promotion, Ministry of Commerce.

Gramer, Robbie. 2017. 'Japan Wants to Revive the TPP Sans US'. *The Dawn*, April 30. Retrieved 18 July 2017, from https://www.dawn.com/news/1330197/japan-wants-to-revive-the-tpp-sans-us

Griffin, Andrew. 2016. 'Apple Being Forced to Unlock a Terrorist's iPhone is an Unprecedented Grab for Power by the Government, Company Says in Court'. *The Independent*, February 26. Retrieved 18 July 2017, from http://www.independent.co.uk/life-style/gadgets-and-tech/news/apple-being-forced-to-unlock-a-terrorists-iphone-is-an-unprecedented-grab-for-power-by-the-a6897266.html

Kilic, B., and T. Israel. 2015, November 5. *The Highlights of the Trans-Pacific Partnership E-commerce Chapter*. Washington, DC: Public Citizen.

Reserve Bank of India. 2013. 'Scheme for Setting Up of Wholly Owned Subsidiaries (WOS) by Foreign Banks in India'. Retrieved 18 July 2017, from https://www.rbi.org.in/Scripts/bs_viewcontent.aspx?Id=2758

Singh, Shalini. 2010. 'RIM Refuses to Help India on Security'. *The Economic Times*, August 4. Retrieved 18 July 2017, http://articles.economictimes.indiatimes.com/2010-08-04/news/27597255_1_security-architecture-customers-encryption-rim

Soni, Anusha. 2017. 'WhatsApp Privacy: Supreme Court Sets Up 5-judge Bench to Hear Plea Challenging the Policy'. *India Today*, April 5. Retrieved 3 May 2017, from http://indiatoday.intoday.in/story/supreme-court-whatsapp-facebook-privacy-policy-challenged/1/920824.html

Third World Resurgence. 2015. 'TPP A Threat to Financial and Economic Stability'. *Third World Resurgence* (303/304): 29–30.

4
IPR and New Rule-making
Chandni Raina

4.1 Introduction

The scope and extent of intellectual property rights (IPRs) protection in countries are entirely defined by the underlying domestic legal regime and its complementing administrative machinery. Countries can frame a legal regime that best serves their purpose while also ensuring compliance with any multilateral or international regime the concerned country may be party to. Prior to the Agreement on Trade-Related Intellectual Property Rights (TRIPS or TRIPS Agreement), the available policy space enabled countries to have vastly differing levels of protection modulated in accordance with their level of development, stakeholder requirements and sector-specific demands. The conclusion of the TRIPS Agreement in 1995 brought in its wake a complete overhaul in the level of protection required to be provided by the members of the World Trade Organization (WTO). But like it is in any multilateral treaty, it also provided countries the policy space to adapt to the minimum norms set while crafting a legal framework that reflected their level of development and addressed public policy concerns on technology transfer, protection of public health and other sectors of vital importance. The policy space enshrined in TRIPS has promoted a healthy diversity in legal regimes. The divergence in the compliance to the TRIPS Agreement is visible, for instance, in the higher threshold of the inventive step adopted by India to address public health concerns related to evergreening of patents; it is also reflected in the fairly low threshold of inventive step in most IPR-creating countries—a response perhaps to the large constituency of inventors and the pharmaceutical multinational corporation (MNCs) that have thrived on patenting small improvements. Variety is also visible in the compliance to norms set for protection of geographical indications (GIs)—with the European Union (EU) at one end of the spectrum, providing three types of protection, for wines and spirit, agricultural goods and food products, and the United States of America (USA) at the other end, seeking to protect GIs through their trademark system.

The TRIPS Agreement can be considered a game changer in many respects. While it sets down the minimum threshold level of protection only, allowing countries to go beyond these, the most critical contribution has been to the architecture of free trade agreement (FTA) negotiations. It has brought IPR norm setting firmly into the fold of FTA negotiations allowing countries to be pushed and pressurized into accepting commitments much beyond the extant regulations in their countries for perceived benefits in trade. With the General Agreement on Tariffs and Trade (GATT) exception for FTAs not applicable to the IPR chapter, it has meant that any ratcheting of norms through later bilateral or regional trade agreements have to be unilaterally made available to the entire membership of the WTO with no quid pro quo or examination of the long-term impact on priority/vital sectors of the economy such as, inter alia, health, education and food security. In a sense, the TRIPS Agreement has become a basis for the continuous narrowing down of the policy space. New norms setting in the creation, protection and enforcement of IPR through trade agreements is now a standard expectation rather than an exception to the rule.

The Trans-Pacific Partnership Agreement (TPP or the Agreement), which is perhaps the most significant plurilateral agreement both in terms of the number of countries that are a part of it and the quantum of world trade that is likely to get impacted, seeks to reduce the policy space provided by TRIPS. The objective of the IPR chapter is to seek higher levels of minimum commitments than specified under TRIPS and to reduce or remove safeguards while also substantially enhancing the enforcement provisions. The process, thus, aims to reduce the flexibilities of TRIPS. Although the chapter impacts all IPRs, yet the most critical among these are patents—more specifically pharmaceutical patents, and protection of information submitted to the market regulator. One of the main objectives of the provisions on patents appears to be to reduce competition from generic medicines.

The raison d'être of the TRIPS Agreement was to promote technological innovation and enable the transfer and dissemination of technology. The understanding behind the IPR chapter in the TPP is also similar with Article 18.4 delineating the public policy objectives to be: to promote innovation and creativity, facilitate the diffusion of information, knowledge, technology, culture and the arts, and foster competition and open efficient markets. The rationale for the rights-based system is derived from the utilitarian theory that protection is good for innovation because in its absence the competitor would 'drive the inventor out of the market' (Bentham 1839). Pigou went on to explain that government-created monopoly rights bring marginal private benefit and marginal social benefit closer and by so doing enable optimization of inventive activity (Pigou 1924). However, the discussion about the impact of IPR on innovation is not without opposing views. The renowned mathematician and physicist Penrose (1951) made a telling statement when he noted that 'if national patent laws did not exist, it would be difficult to make a conclusive case for introducing them; but the fact that they do exist shifts the burden of proof and it is equally difficult to make a really conclusive case for abolishing them.' Bessen and Maskin (2000) found that strong patent protection may make subsequent innovations more difficult. They concluded that strong patent protection may hinder innovation vis-à-vis a situation of no patent protection. Boldrin and Levine (2008) in their book *Against Intellectual Monopoly* discuss how extensive patent protection leads to enhancement in costs which could be a drag to further innovation. Williams (1994) tried to estimate the impact of patent protection on innovation and found that this effect is very modest. The study found that a 10 per cent increase in patent life would boost productivity by less than one-tenth of 1 per cent (Lerner 2002).

While whether or not the TPP will ever come into force is a question that plagues many in these times, it can be said with some conviction that the text will form the basis of future engagement for the USA—be it the multilateral forum such as the WTO or in bilateral treaty discussions. This is so because the content of the IPR chapter in the TPP is completely consistent with the US positions as reflected in the Special 301, its earlier engagements through bilateral and plurilateral treatises (such as the Anti-Counterfeiting Trade Agreement), the positions it has adopted in the World Intellectual Property Organization (WIPO) and the disputes raised by it in the WTO Dispute Settlement Body. Therefore, it is important to assess what the IPR chapter in the TPP plans to do even if the future of the Agreement is uncertain. The objective of this chapter is to assess the impact of the TPP template on IPRs—on the real economy and the social costs it will impose even if India is never a part of this.

4.2 General Provisions: A General Enhancement in Norms (Articles 18.1–18.11)

The section on general provisions broadly covers definitions (Article 18.1), objectives (Article 18.2), principles (Article 18.3), national treatment clause (Article 18.8) and establishes the overall understandings regarding certain public health measures (Article 18.4). In addition, it covers commitments in respect of specific international agreements that have been taken on by the members of the Agreement (Article 18.7). Issues concerning transparency (Article 18.9) and exhaustion of IP rights (Article 18.11) are also covered.

The basic rationale behind the general provisions is to leverage the existing international agreements on IPRs, many of which were finalized after TRIPS, to build a TRIPS-plus regime. The treaties to which mandatory commitments through accessions are being sought include Protocol Relating to the Madrid Agreement Concerning the International Registration of Marks (Madrid Protocol), Singapore Treaty on the Law of Trademarks (Singapore Treaty), Union for the Protection of New Plant Varieties 1991 (UPOV 1991), WIPO Copyright Treaty (WCT) and the WIPO Performances and Phonogram Treaty (WPPT). These treaties, with the exception of the Madrid Protocol (which is a filing treaty), have substantive implications. The Singapore Treaty seeks to cover non-traditional marks covering sound, smell and feel as subject matter of a trademark. It also seeks harmonization in administrative procedures and specifies maximum requirements for several actions of the Trade Marks Registry. Of the 12 TPP countries, only 4 (that is, USA, Singapore, Australia and New Zealand) have acceded to this treaty. The UPOV 1991, on the other hand, establishes the rights of the plant breeders in a manner that reduces the freedom of the farmers to exchange and sell seeds among each other or to reproduce seeds (for multiplication) or to propagate or stock seeds. Malaysia and Brunei, among the 12 TPP countries, are the only two countries that have yet to accede to the treaty. The WCT and WPPT are internet treatises addressing copyright protection in the digital environment. They seek institutions of strong technology protection measures (TPMs) and rights management information (RMI) for protection of copyrighted work. Vietnam, Brunei and New Zealand are the only outliers that have yet to accede to the treaty. Table 4.1 brings out the transition periods given to some member countries of the TPP for complying with commitments under the IPR chapter.

Table 4.1

Transition periods for the IPR chapter in the TPP

Countries	International Agreements	Non-traditional TM	Data Exclusivity Agro-chem	Pharma	Biologics	Patent Linkage	Internet Service Providers	Patent Term Extension	Copyright Term
Brunei	UPOV—3 yrs	3 yrs	18 months	4 yrs	4 yrs	2 yrs	3 yrs		2
Malaysia	Madrid Protocol—4 yrs Budapest Treaty—4 yrs Singapore Treaty—4 yrs UPOV-4 yrs	3 yrs			5 yrs	4.5 yrs		4.5 yrs	
Mexico	UPOV—4yrs			5 yrs	5 yrs		3 yrs		
New Zealand	UPOV—3 yrs*								8 yrs
Peru				5 yrs	10 yrs				
Vietnam	Budapest—2 yrs WCT—3 yrs WPPT—3 yrs	3 yrs	5 yrs	10 yrs**	10 yrs**	3 yrs	3 yrs	5yrs for patent office delays for patents claiming pharmaceutical and agro chemical product*** 3yrs for patent office delays in other technologies 5 yrs for market regulator delay	5 yrs

Countries	Enforcement					
	Confusingly similar TM	Ex-officio export and in-transit	Encrypprog	Criminal	Anti-camcording/ TPM/RMI	Trade secret
Brunei						
Malaysia	4 yrs	4 yrs	4 yrs			
Mexico						
New Zealand						
Peru						
Vietnam		Exports—3 yrs	Criminal remedies—3 yrs	Ex-officio action—3 yrs	Anti-camcording—3 yrs	3 yrs
		In-transit—2 yrs	Cable signals—3 yrs	Importation of pirated copyright goods—3 yrs	TPM—3 yrs	
				With respect to exportation—3 yrs	RMI—3 yrs	

Notes: For the other countries not listed here the obligations are from the date of entry into force of the agreement. For obligations other than for which transition periods have been mentioned, implementation is from the date of entry into force of the Agreement.

*Can adopt a sui generis system that gives effect to UPOV 1991. Nothing shall preclude New Zealand from adopting measures deemed necessary to protect indigenous plant species in fulfilment of its obligations under the Treaty of Waitangi, provided these are not arbitrary or unjustified discrimination against a person of another party. Consistency of this with UPOV 1991 will not be subject to dispute settlement provisions of this agreement. Interpretation of the Treaty of Waitangi including the nature of the rights and obligations arising under it shall not be subject to the dispute settlement provisions of the Agreement.

**Can be extended by two additional years on justified request and an additional one year thereafter. Vietnam not to be subject to dispute settlement for three years after conclusion of the first extension period of two years.

***Request for extension by one additional year would be considered on written request with justification.

India has not acceded to the WCT, WPPT, Singapore Treaty and UPOV 1991. It is, however, interesting to note that bringing the copyright law in conformity with the WCT and WPPT was one of the stated objectives and reasons of the Copyright (Amendment) Bill, 2010. This is clearly brought out in the record of discussion/debate in the Rajya Sabha on the occasion of the passing of the 2012 amendments[1] to the Copyright Act. Despite this, the accession did not happen. As for the Singapore Treaty, there is no official document in public domain that examines the compatibility of the Indian trademark law with it or whether the accession would benefit the country. But the fact that the treaty requires member countries to grant smell and feel trademarks and also restricts the maximum information that can be sought by the Trade Marks Registry probably makes it difficult for India to accept the commitment at this stage when the Indian Registry has yet to take that technology leap. Perhaps the most significant treaty that India will find impossible to accede to is UPOV 1991. With estimates indicating that Indian farmers provide 87 per cent of the total requirement of seeds (Sahai 2003), the said instrument which seeks to make this illegal is not only in complete contradiction to the Indian law on Protection of Plant Varieties and Farmers Rights Act but is also divorced from the realities of subsistence agriculture. The Indian law on plant variety protection on the other hand has tried to safeguard farmers' interest treating them as breeders in their own rights.

The second and perhaps a more critical implication of extensive listing in the TPP text of independent international agreements to which mandatory accession is being sought, even where member countries of the Agreement may have already acceded to it, is that enforcement of these agreements would now be open to application of the dispute settlement chapter under the TPP. Considering that most of these international treatises lack effective enforcement mechanisms, inclusion of these as mandatory commitments under the TPP seeks to address that gap.

---

[1] Debate on the passing of the Copyright (Amendment) Bill, 2010. Available at rsdebate.nic.in/bitstream/12345678/603476/1/ID_225_17052012_p443_p496_25.pdf#search=copyright amendment bill 2012 (last visited 7 August 2017).

4.3 Cooperation: Harmonization of Procedures and Processes of the Patent Offices (Articles 18.12–18.17)

In a separate section on cooperation (Section B), there is a listing of activities that could be carried out between intellectual property offices (Article 18.13) upon request. Besides this, there is also a mandate that parties harmonize procedures for grant of patents (Article 18.14) and consider acceding to the Patent Law Treaty (PLT) or maintain standards consistent with it to bring uniformity of procedures (Article 18.14).

Cooperation

Preventing Countries from Seeking Information from Patent Applicants

The Agreement aims at reducing the complexity and cost of obtaining a patent across all the members of the TPP by harmonizing procedures and processes. In this direction, an endeavour would be made to comply with the PLT or maintain procedural standards consistent with the PLT. While this is a best endeavour clause probably because at present, of the 12 countries only the USA and Australia have acceded to it, the inherent implication of such an understanding however needs to be looked at more carefully. The PLT sets down the maximum information that can be sought by a patent office from an applicant, thus not allowing countries to address any unique concern they may have.

For India this has special significance as the Indian patent law requires that the applicants mandatorily disclose whether the claims sought to be protected are derived from a genetic resource and associated traditional knowledge and also indicate the source or origin of the resource. If a genetic resource is disclosed to be the basis for the invention, a no objection certificate (NOC) from the National Biodiversity Authority is required to be furnished by the applicant before the patent is granted. The authority gives the NOC only after seeking prior informed consent from the concerned community(s) and subsequent to establishing the terms of access and corresponding benefit sharing. If PLT is acceded to, then these unique features aimed at addressing the specific concerns of countries would be difficult to be incorporated. It is also important to point out that complying with this obligation will prevent further negotiation on the TRIPS Convention on Biological Diversity (CBD) linkage issue at the WTO by undermining or prohibiting mandatory disclosure requirements in patent applications.

Cooperation: A Weak Attempt to Address Biopiracy

The cooperation section encourages patent offices to enhance understanding of issues connected with traditional knowledge associated with genetic resources and genetic resources (Article 18.16). In this direction, there is a general endorsement of using publicly available documented information related to traditional knowledge associated with genetic resources and the possibility of a third-party observation in writing while evaluating the patentability of invention. The use of digital libraries or databases on traditional knowledge and cooperation in the training of patent examiners has also been advocated.

While this is a positive development to the limited extent of recognizing that patents may get granted wrongly on existing traditional knowledge and that this needs to be corrected through an examination system that utilizes publicly available traditional knowledge information, it does not cover traditional knowledge that may not be publicly available or codified such as oral knowledge. Besides, the clauses are not mandatory, thus carry no force.

Again, it is perhaps relevant to state that the provision does not foresee addressing mandatory disclosure of origin or source of genetic resource, evidence for prior informed consent and access and benefit sharing in patent applications. The TPP merely recognizes the fact that patents may be wrongly granted due to asymmetry of information between the patent examiner and applicant. It aims to correct this by making available databases on this information to the patent office.

4.4 Trademarks: Focus on Non-traditional Trademarks and Strengthening Protection of Well-known Trademarks (Section C: Articles 18.18–18.28)

At the normative level, the focus of the trademark section in the TPP is on broadening the coverage of what can be protected as trademarks and to augment the protection to trademarks in general and well-known trademarks in particular. The term of protection is kept at 10 years to be renewed indefinitely (Article 18.26).

At the procedural level (Articles 18.23 and 18.24), it seeks uniformity in actions to be taken by the trademark offices in communication with the applicants, contestation of an initial opinion of the office, opportunity for opposition and cancellation and that administrative decisions are reasoned and conveyed in writing. It also requires that the members provide for a system of electronic filing and maintenance besides maintaining a publicly available online database of trademark applications and registered trademarks. The basic emphasis is, therefore, on improving efficiency and transparency in the functioning of the trademark offices.

TRIPS allows member States the flexibility to restrict registration of trademarks to those that are visually perceptible. The coverage of protection for trademarks under the TPP is sought to be expanded in three different ways. First, the TPP makes protection of non-traditional trademarks—such as feel, sound and smell marks that are not visually perceptible—mandatory (Article 18.18). Second, strengthening of protection is being achieved by allowing the owners the right to protect not only against use of a similar sign or word (Article 18.20) to market identical or similar goods but also when it is applied to related goods. It may be noted that TRIPS allows protection of trademarks for identical or similar goods, but not for related goods. This is supported by the interpretation adopted on classification of goods and services (Article 18.25). The countries are required to follow the Nice Agreement on International Classification of Goods and Services for the Registration of Marks (Nice Classification) which is a classification of goods and services established by the Nice Classification and applied for registration of trademarks. It is interesting to note that the text discusses at great length the extent of impact this classification should have in determining similarity among goods and services. It clarifies that classification would not have legal sanctity in determining whether the products are similar or not. That is, even when products belong to different classes they may be considered to be similar. Conversely, those belonging to the same class may not be considered as similar. This interpretation ensures that the class to which the product belongs would have no role as an argument in infringement cases and that it would be left to the right-holder to establish the similarity and relatedness of a product where none may seem to exist. While the Nice Agreement is broadly accepted to be a tool for the trademark offices to enable registration of goods and services with no specific legal implications, the text aims at correcting the myriad ways in which classification is used in disputes to establish similarity or otherwise. The discussion on its application draws in the clarity provided by the Trademark Law Treaty and the Singapore Treaty but goes beyond that to establish guidelines on how classification should be looked at in case of disputes. Third, the TPP seeks to strengthen the right of a trademark owner over a GI by allowing him the right to prevent a subsequent GI from being marketed on the grounds that it is likely to cause confusion (Article 18.20).

At another level, the text expands on the provision of the TRIPS Agreement to cover issues such as what could be classified as well-known trademarks (Article 18.22) and the type of protection that should be provided. Towards this end, the Agreement leverages on the Joint Recommendations of the WIPO on Well-known Trademarks (1999) to harmonize the manner in which the concept of well-known trademarks would be administered in the 12 countries. The agreement requires that well-known trademark be protected even without registration and that the protection be available against use in dissimilar goods and services provided there is a connection with the goods and services of the trademark owner and the harm that is likely to happen. On well-known trademarks, the Indian system follows the Joint Recommendations of the WIPO; therefore, compliance may not be a problem. However, the TPP does have a notable difference in respect of the treatment given to GIs which is contrary to the legal position in India (discussed in greater detail in the section on GIs).

On domain names (Article 18.28), the agreement seeks to establish a procedure for settlement of disputes on the lines established in the Uniform Domain-Name Dispute-Resolution Policy as adopted by the Internet Corporation for Assigned Names and Numbers (ICANN) which is a US-based private organization. It also requires domain name registrants to disclose contact information and make this publicly accessible. While this appears to be innocuous, it is clear that members of the Agreement would not only be encouraged to accept practices developed by a US organization and thereby to accept the extra-judicial process which may unduly benefit trademark owners over the users but also to disclose contact information of domain name registrants, exposing them to the risk of being misused.

4.5 GIs—Arresting the EU Onslaught (Articles 18.30–18.36)

The section on GIs tries to address the discomfort of the USA with the concept of sui generis protection for GIs promoted by the EU in its various FTAs. One very significant demand from the EU in its FTAs with other countries has been mutual recognition of GIs. Mutual recognition essentially means that countries exchange a list of GIs that they wish to get protected in the trading partner country. The GIs so indicated in the list get protection in the partner country without these having to go through a full examination and registration process as long as they are registered as GIs in the country of origin. The protection is therefore accorded on the basis of the home country registration allowing only for an opposition process in the case of existing trademarks. The second significant ask from the EU from their trading partners is commitment to provide higher level of protection to other agricultural GIs such as cheese. In this way, the EU seeks to promote the concept of a multilateral register and GI extension—which are both issues that are still under discussion in the WTO (Drexl et al.). On the relationship between GIs and trademarks, EU free trade agreements (EUFTAs) have established the supremacy of a GI over a trademark by explicitly providing that parties should refuse to register a trademark or have procedures to invalidate a trademark if it causes confusion in respect of a protected GI. Only in the case of reputed or well-known trademarks can a party have no obligation to protect a GI if the protection is liable to mislead consumers about the true identity of the product.[2]

The TPP text addresses each one of these concerns albeit from a different perspective. It begins by recognizing that GIs could be protected through a trademark or sui generis system or through other legal means (Article 18.30). It clearly establishes that the GI registration should be sought by the concerned applicants and that no involvement of the State would be encouraged in the matter (Article 18.31). While requiring that the processes adopted to examine GI applications are not overly burdensome, it sets down procedures and mechanisms for enabling publication, opposition and cancellation. The text lays down the minimum grounds for opposition and cancellation of a GI; however, these would not apply to wines and spirits (Article 18.32). The

---

[2] Article 211 EU–Peru Columbia FTA.

text mandates following minimum grounds for opposition and cancellation of a GI: (a) a likelihood of confusion on grounds of a trademark that is the subject of a pre-existing good faith pending application or registration, (b) pre-existing trademark right acquired in accordance to the party's law or (c) when the GI is a customary term in the common language and denotes a common name in that territory. Where protection is provided to the translation or transliteration of that GI, grounds for cancellation and opposition as specified earlier would apply. Thus at one end of the spectrum, the EU is trying to restrict oppositions to GI applications only from well-known trademarks, while at the other end, the USA has stipulated through the TPP that existing trademarks or even pre-existing good faith trademark applications would be grounds for opposition. It is important to note that these are just the minimum grounds in the TPP; countries could have other specific grounds for opposition and cancellation.

In the context of eligibility for or the validity of registration of a trademark, it is relevant to compare the grounds for opposition and cancellation of GIs as contained in the TPP with the corresponding provision of TRIPS. Article 24.5 of TRIPS addresses exceptions for prior trademark rights or where the trademark has been applied for, or the rights have been acquired through, use in goods. However, these exceptions are narrow and apply only in two situations. First, the exception is applicable in respect of the rights that were obtained or applied for before the date of application of TRIPS in that country; and second, if the trademark protection is obtained before the GI is protected in its country of origin (Taubman et al. 2012). As discussed in detail in the preceding paragraph, the extensive carve-outs provided to trademarks in the TPP seem to be non-compliant with the TRIPS Agreement.

Interestingly, the TPP text also specifies that a GI could be cancelled or could cease to exist if the recognized term ceases to meet the conditions upon which it was originally granted in that country (Article 18.32 (3)). This is unlike the formulation under TRIPS where the obligation to protect a GI ends only when it ceases to be protected in the country of origin or has fallen into disuse in that country. The provision in the TPP effectively implies that a GI can become generic in the country where it is registered even when it continues to be protected as a GI in the country of origin.

The TRIPS Agreement allows members the flexibility to exclude customary terms with respect to goods and services from being protected as GIs. With a view to bring uniformity in the definition, the TPP sets down detailed guidelines (Article 18.33) for determining whether or not a term is customary in the common language. The parties would have to take into account how consumers understand the term in that country and whether it refers to a type of a good/product and the manner in which it is marketed to determine whether the term is customary in the common language. Besides this, the text tries to address situations arising out of GIs that involve multi-component terms (Article 18.34). In such cases, the agreement specifies that if one component of the multi-component term is customary or common in a party, then that component would not be protected as a GI in that party. On the whole, the emphasis under the TPP is to reduce the flexibilities countries may have had under TRIPS and in that sense to harmonize the rules across the member countries of the TPP.

The TPP tries to address the EU system of seeking mutual recognition through a list approach by requiring (Article 18.36) that when protection is given to a GI pursuant to an international agreement and administrative procedures similar to those as set out in Article 18.31 are not followed or GIs are protected through a sui generis system by means of judicial procedures, parties would still need to provide for opposition procedures and specify grounds for opposition that at least cover the minimum grounds as specified in Article 18.32.1 of the text. In such cases, the judicial authority will have the authority to deny protection if any of the circumstances as specified under the minimum grounds are established. GIs for wines and spirits and international agreements between a party and a non-party that predate the TPP are exempted from the commitment.

Under the Indian GI system, registration of a GI is dependent on the evaluation of the Committee of Experts and after opposition, if any, is disposed of. To that extent the TPP provision may seem similar; however, the similarities end there. Important divergence from the TPP provisions relate to the precedence given to trademarks in the TPP text vis-à-vis GIs when it is quite the opposite under the Indian GI Law, which prohibits registration of GIs as trademarks and allows institution of invalidation proceedings against a trademark for causing confusion or for misleading the consumer. There are, however, some concessions that have been given to trademarks that were registered prior to the GI legislation coming into existence or those that were registered prior to the filing of the GI application or acquiring of rights through use in good faith. This implies that there could be a possibility in India that trademark and GI may coexist—which is not foreseen in the TPP.

4.6 Patents and Undisclosed Test or Other Data: Substantive Rule-making for Curtailing TRIPS Flexibilities and Restricting Competition from Generics (Section F: Articles 18.37–18.56)

Patent protection has arguably been the most contentious issue among countries. While TRIPS tried to set down some minimum norms, it left countries with space to enable adoption of the requirements in a manner that was in harmony with the level of development of the country or the public interest issues it was faced with. The most potent flexibility, perhaps, has been in the terms 'novelty', 'inventive step' and 'industrial application'. Since none of these terms have been defined in TRIPS, it provides the countries the flexibility to determine the criteria for the application of the norms in order to address their concerns. India clearly made a carve-out under 'novelty' for traditional knowledge (section 3(p) of the Patents Act, 1970). It has also specified a criterion for inventive step under Section 3(d), which mandates that any new form of a known substance could be patented only if it showed enhanced efficacy. As an explanation to the provision, further clarification was also provided in the case of chemical entities on what could be considered forms equal to the known substance. This has been a strong provision which has helped the country address problems of evergreening of patents—a malaise that besets the world today. The example of Gleevec is excellent to prove the stellar contribution this provision has had on the prices in India vis-à-vis the rest of the world (for details, see Section 5.2.1).

If predictability, policy space to address public interest concerns in sectors of vital importance and promotion of technological innovation were perhaps the raison d'être for the TRIPS Agreement, the contrary is true in the case of the TPP. The objective of the TPP text is to reduce or remove the existing flexibilities with a clear intent to tilt the balance in favour of the IPR holders. It does so in myriad ways–by bringing in greater uncertainty about the term of patent protection, mandating lower thresholds for patentability and allowing evergreening of patents and of data exclusivity. While doing so, the text in parts not only goes beyond TRIPS but also violates the very spirit on which the TRIPS Agreement is based.

As far as exceptions and possibility of issue of compulsory licence are concerned, the IPR chapter (Article 18.40 and Article 18.41) echoes the provisions of Article 30 and Article 31 of TRIPS (including with amendments).

Keeping a Low Threshold for Patent Grant (Subsection A: Article 18.37)

As the TRIPS does not define 'inventive step', countries have the flexibility to set the bar low and treat minor or incremental developments as being patentable. This approach has been adopted by the developed countries and some developing countries. From the public health perspective, an important consequence of this approach is that large pharmaceutical companies become eligible for patenting derivatives or variants of existing products or their method of use—such as formulations, dosages, salts esters, ethers, polymorphs, metabolites, isomers and combinations (Correa 2010, 47). Consequently, through this process of evergreening of patents, competition from generic pharmaceutical products is either delayed or even blocked. On the other hand, some developing countries consider only substantial departures from prior art to be eligible for patentability (ibid.). Section 3(d) of the Indian Patents Act is a good illustration of the latter approach towards patentability. This has sought to contain evergreening of patents, thereby facilitating introduction of generics in the market. Over time, Philippines, Argentina and Indonesia have amended their patent law to incorporate strong provisions aimed at discouraging evergreening of patents. Brazil and South Africa are in the process of reforming their patent law for adopting India's approach against evergreening. As these developments have been a source of considerable concern to its pharmaceutical industry, the USA is seeking to ensure that countries do not raise the bar on patentability for preventing evergreening of patents. Some of the provisions on patents in the TPP should be viewed as a concerted attempt at facilitating evergreening of patents.

The manner in which the text on patentable subject matter is worded (Article 18.37), it is clearly an attempt by the USA to prevent any misadventure among the 12 members to amend their patents act to further raise the standards of patentability. It is also an endeavour of the USA to export the provisions it already has to the other 11 trading partners.

The fact that the formulation is the exact antithesis of Section 3 (d) of the Indian Patents Act also indicates that the impact of this provision on disallowing patents for insignificant improvements is something that the TPP countries would not like to import into their region. The concern that the USA has may also stem from the fact that both Australia and New Zealand have recently amended their patent law to bring in substantive improvements to raise the quality of patents granted. The amendments[3] which aim at raising standards for an inventive step, enhance disclosure requirements and strengthen the usefulness requirements have been brought about in response to strong criticism about the threshold of an inventive step being too low resulting in patents being granted for insignificant improvements also.

The fact that Canada faces an Investor State Dispute Settlement (ISDS) proceeding under NAFTA for the invalidation of the patents for pharmaceutical products—Strattera and Zyprexa—held by M/s Eli Lily, a US based Pharma Company, on account of violation of NAFTA Articles relating to expropriation and minimum standards of treatment adds to the mystery. The measure can also be seen to reassure the Big Pharma about the certainty of the regime that will be followed in the TPP countries especially after the Indian Supreme Court Judgement in the *Novartis vs. Union of India* and the Eli Lily case in Canada.

According to paragraph 2 of Article 18.37 of the TPP, any new use of a known substance or a new process or method of using a known substance would be a subject matter of a patent—effectively implying that new forms of a known substance would be patentable without any qualifications related to efficacy. This could well mean that an off-patent molecule could get patented again if a new use is found of the same substance, thus enabling evergreening of an old molecule and thereby extension of patent monopolies. The rationale for this would be derived from the fact that the new use would add to the novelty aspect of the invention for which clear literature was not available earlier. Sustained release forms of existing molecules and new dosage forms as also new methods such as the injectible form or fixed dose combinations of drugs are the possible examples of new process or method of using a known substance. This provision of the TPP would facilitate filing of secondary patents based on minor or merely incremental developments on the main patent.

---

[3] https://www.legislation.gov.au/Details/C2011B00114/Explanatory%20Memorandum/Text#_Toc295897373 (last visited 18 July 2017).

Kapczynski, Park and Sampat (2012) examined the effects of secondary patents on the US pharmaceutical industry and concluded that 'secondary claims are common in the industry'. The study goes on to mention that independent secondary patents (these are the ones really responsible for evergreening) tend to be filed after the main patent, are 'more likely to be filed after the drug approval' and 'are more common for best-selling drugs'. According to the study, formulation patents add on an average 6.5 years to the patent life, independent method of use patents add 7.3 years to the patent life and patents on polymorphs, isomers, prodrug, ester and/or salt claim add 6.3 years to the patent life. The final report on the pharmaceutical sector inquiry launched by the European Commission on 15 January 2008 (2009) also reveals that the whole strategy to seek secondary patents is to create uncertainty for the generic industry. The study quotes an originator company as saying,

> The entire point of the patenting strategy adopted by many originators is to remove legal certainty. The strategy is to file as many patents as possible on all areas of the drug and create a 'minefield' for the generic to navigate. All generics know that very few patents in that larger group will be valid and infringed by the product they propose to make, but it is impossible to be certain prior to launch that your product will not infringe and you will not be the subject of an interim injunction.

The study goes on to show that

> [the purpose behind secondary patents is to] establish an effective barrier to generic competition by extending the term of the existing compound patent and by filing patents on further inventions that last beyond the expiry of the compound patent.... The objective [of scope of patent claims] is to secure an optimal competitive position for [our company's] products in the market by blocking competitors.

Another originator company is quoted as saying that '[s]econdary patents will not stop generic competition indefinitely but may delay generics for a number of years, at best protecting the originator's revenue for a period of time.'

The TPP by seeking lax patentability criteria is in fact trying to facilitate weak patents which in turn can create substantial social costs and affect access to medicines by restricting or even disallowing generic competition.

Box 4.1

Evergreening: Some examples and impact

> Evergreening of patents has been a concern because this allows innovators to get extensions on their monopoly right or may even result in a monopoly being given to an already existing molecule in the public domain. The concern is largely two-folds—the first arises from the fact that this would restrict generic competition, affect prices of medicines and thereby impact access to medicines. The second is a larger policy implication of promoting research and development around an existing molecule because of the low risk and high returns involved as against promoting research in new chemical/molecular entities.
>
> Moir and Gleeson (2014) illustrate this point well in the context of Australia and the medicine 'Venlafaxine' (Efexor). This drug which is used for treating depression was 'granted patent in 1983'. Towards the end of the patent period, an extended release version of the same drug (Efexor XR), was patented with validity till 2023. The obviousness of the invention led to post grant challenge and the patents on Efexor XR were invalidated in 2011. However, even during the short period of protection, the cost of the extension of protection to the public was reported to be AUS$ 209 million. Still further, the patent owner went on to seek a patent on Desvenlafaxine, which is naturally formed in the human body when Venlafaxine (Efexor) is absorbed. This 'patent lasts till 2023'. Even though there are no additional benefits over Efexor-XR, in 2013–14 itself, the cost to the taxpayer of doctors prescribing this metabolite called Pristiq rather than Efexor-XR exceeded Aus$ 21 million.
>
> Another distinctive example is that of 'Insulin' (Gordon 2015). Insulin was 'first discovered in 1921' by Dr Frederick Banting and Charles Best. The patent was sold to the University of Toronto for US$1. In 1970, first human insulin was invented. In 1990, first synthetic insulin was invented. In 2000, first long acting insulin was invented. First 'patent on long acting insulin expired in 2014'. Incremental improvements in insulin were granted patents in the USA and this has continued to date, making it impossible for generic competition to enter. Cost of insulin for those not covered by insurance in the USA is US$120–400 per month.

Patent Term Extension for Patent Office Delays: Uncertain Term of Protection (Article 18.46)

Patent office delays are to be accounted for through an enhanced term of protection. Article 18.46 of the Agreement quantifies unreasonable delay to be more than five years from the date of filing of the application in the territory of the party or three years after a request for examination has been received, whichever is later. In determining the additional period of protection, a party is allowed to exclude the delays that are not directly attributable to the granting authority.

This is an interesting provision because most patent offices require a request, along with a specified fee, to be filed before the application joins a queue for examination. In reality, request for examination is not received for all applications and for these, the applications keep languishing. This could be because the applicant realizes that the invention is not patentable, therefore does not pursue the matter further. However, the Agreement now makes it mandatory to process such applications even when a request is not received, thereby adding to the burden of the office.

The compensation for the delays in the patent office was an important argument given by the developed countries during the TRIPS negotiations for seeking a 20-year period of patent protection. The same argument is now being extended by them to seek a protection beyond 20 years. However, in the bargain, the attempt creates uncertainty because unlike under TRIPS, where a patent had 20 years protection from the date when it was first filed irrespective of the country in which it was filed, the term of protection in TPP countries will vary depending on the delays in different country jurisdictions. So it would not be uncommon to see that terms of protection vary across TPP countries. Again, if evergreening of patents is to be allowed, then even these molecules could be eligible for patent term extension for any delays in processing of their applications. Of course the question about whether there was any delay would itself be a subject matter of dispute under the ISDS mechanism as would be the substantive issue of creation or revocation of a right.

In essence, the patent provisions hit at the bedrock on which TRIPS was said to be based. Uncertain term of protection and lax patentability standards will adversely impact the robustness of the public domain which has been so sacrosanct in any patent-related debates, affecting thereby the future development of technologies. It will unfavourably affect technology adoption by enterprises for there would be no surety of the patent status given the possibility to evergreen patents.

Besides this, it will negatively impinge on the investment decisions of enterprises and affect competition and public interest adversely. But perhaps the most significant impact would be on creativity and innovation itself. The text clearly places inventions at the margin or weak improvements on the same plane as inventions that bring about a significant improvement or are path breaking. Given that companies work to minimize risks and maximize returns, it would be reasonable to expect that they would have greater incentive to work at the margins of existing patents so that the risks and expenditure incurred are lower. On the whole, the provisions work towards creating an unpredictable, non-transparent environment that works against creativity and innovation.

Regulatory Data Protection

Fixed Term Protection, Evergreening and Extension of Protection (Articles 18.47–50, 18.52)

Regulatory data protection or data exclusivity is discussed in the IPR chapter in respect of data submitted for agrochemicals, pharmaceuticals and biologics. Article 39.3 of TRIPS deals with the undisclosed test or other data submitted for seeking marketing approvals for pharmaceutical/agrochemical products that utilize new chemical entities. It says that data submitted on new chemical entities, the origination of which had involved considerable effort, should be protected from unfair commercial use. TRIPS provision allows countries to determine the mechanism for protection of this undisclosed information. Countries such as India ensure that the data is never disclosed either to the public or to an individual company so that there is no unfair commercial use. However, in India, the marketing regulator is allowed to rely on the information he already has from the data submitted by the originator to grant a regulatory approval to a second applicant of the same product. In situations where there is no data exclusivity, a second applicant can seek regulatory approval by showing bioequivalence on the basis of a small size data for an existing molecule already approved by the marketing regulator. This provision benefits society at large because such an interpretation promotes competition by allowing generics to enter the market faster while ensuring the confidentiality of the data.

In the developed countries such as the USA and EU, Article 39.3 has been translated to imply that data submitted to the regulator would not be relied upon by the regulator to provide approval to the second applicant for a certain period of time. This is also called data exclusivity or fixed-term data protection. This protection is provided irrespective of the patent status of the drug or agrochemical product, that is, it may exist independent of a patent. The implication of the provision is that if a second applicant wants to bring the drug already approved and for which data exclusivity protection has been given to the market, it would have to conduct all phases of the clinical trial. The obvious effect is that the approval by a marketing regulator to the first applicant becomes the grounds to create monopoly for a certain period of time, denying the public access to lower priced generic versions of the drug.

Article 39.3 of TRIPS provides extensive flexibilities. The first of those is in determining what would be included in 'New Chemical Entity'. The second flexibility lies in the fact that member countries of the WTO can assess whether or not the origination of the data required considerable effort. The third lies in determining what type of protection the data would be provided to be considered as being protected from unfair commercial use. Most FTAs and Comprehensive Economic Partnership Agreements (CEPA) have tried to reduce the flexibilities available under TRIPS by removing the three flexibilities ensconced in Article 39.3 of TRIPS. The TPP is no different in this regard. The definition adopted for agrochemical product, pharmaceutical product and biologic (Articles 18.47.3 and 18.53) and the fact that expenditure incurred in the origination of the data is not to be a consideration ensure that any addition of a chemical entity that has not been approved earlier would qualify to be protected. Even improvements such as single dosage combinations of existing drugs, which may otherwise not be patentable, will get protected because of the fixed-term protection being provided for clinical trial data submitted to establish that the medicine is safe and efficacious. Further, since such innovation and improvements are a continuous process, it may actually lead to evergreening of protection and hence a continuous extension of the protection period. This would in its turn either delay investment decisions of generic manufacturers or they may have to bear the cost of this uncertainty in case they do go ahead to manufacture the product.

The TPP lays down the period of protection that would need to be provided to the undisclosed data that is submitted. The term of protection varies from 10 years for agrochemicals to 5 years of initial period of protection for pharmaceuticals which can be extended by 3 years if new clinical information is submitted covering new indication, new formulation or new method of administration of an existing medicine. Protection for sustained release or fixed dose combinations of molecules and for paediatric dose of an existing molecule or developments that improve the administration of the same medicine could get extended data exclusivity protection of 3 years which could get extended further if there is innovation on the margin satisfying the conditions for application of data exclusivity. Biologics get protection of 8 years (countries also have the flexibility to provide 5 years of data exclusivity and 3 years of marketing exclusivity so that the total outcome remains unchanged at 8 years of protection) from the time of registration in the concerned country (Article 18.52).

The desire to export provisions on data exclusivity to other countries has a strong foundation in the commercial interest of large producers of pharmaceuticals, biologics and agricultural chemicals in the developed countries. In pharmaceuticals, data exclusivity provision with the possibility to evergreen this protection allows companies to circumvent the uncertainty of patent protection. A white paper on the US invalidity cases for the period 2007–11 brings out the precarious nature of patent grant (Smyth 2012) even in the so-called Mecca of innovation. According to this paper, 'out of the 283 cases pertaining to patent validity challenges brought before the US Federal District Courts in 2007–2011, only in 39 cases was the patent held valid.' With data exclusivity provisions having limited or no possibility of being challenged, this protection will guarantee certainty of monopoly right. With certainty comes the possibility to seek rent. Many researchers have widely documented this tendency in the context of other FTAs that were signed by the USA. An Oxfam briefing paper (Malpani 2007) documents how medicine prices rose by 20 per cent in Jordan since 2001 threatening the public health system in the country. The paper cites the example of Plavix (an anti-thrombotic agent), which saw an increase in price from 12 Jordanian dinars (JD) per unit to JD 50 per unit by 2006, an increase of approximately 400 per cent. This was when the drug did not have a patent in Jordan. The increase was primarily due to data exclusivity protection brought in 2001 as an outcome of the FTA with the USA. In comparison, the paper brings out the fact that the drug was available in India for JD 0.12 per unit, where there is no patent protection or data exclusivity protection for the medicine. Expanding on this further, the paper has identified 81 medicines out of 108, sales of which are reported in the paper to be US$31.49 million from 2002 to mid-2006, where generic versions do not exist because of data exclusivity. It is also pertinent to mention that the higher prices did not lead to increased registration of new medicines in Jordan nor did it lead to increased FDI flows. The paper brings out that only 33 of the 82 products of the Big Pharma[4] were registered in Jordan. Another study brought out in Health Affairs (Shaffer and Brenner 2009) studied

---

[4] Pfizer, Bristol-Myers Squibb, Merck, Genzyme, Roche and Genetech.

the impact of Central American Free Trade Agreement (CAFTA) on the drug prices in Guatemala. The paper, inter alia, compared the prices of drugs that were protected by data exclusivity vis-à-vis those drugs that were for treatment of the same disease but did not get data exclusivity. The study states that in each case those drugs that were protected by data exclusivity were more expensive. Citing examples of this difference, the study states,

> For example, the insulin Lantus costs 846% more that isophane insulin; the antifungal Vfend costs 810 per cent more than the non data protected amphotericin B; and the intravenous antibiotic Invanz costs 342 percent more than the non data protected meropenem (Meronem).

In the agrochemical sphere, it is instructive to note that nearly 200 major active agrochemical ingredients have gone off patent between 2000 and 2015 with another 28 molecules to go off patent by 2019.[5] Data exclusivity protection of 10 years (Article 18.47) for agrochemicals from the date of market approval in that country will provide a fresh lease of life to old molecules that may not even be patented. While as an outcome, this should see registration of many old molecules in new markets, it will come at a huge social cost in terms of high prices.

While data exclusivity will delay entry of the generic version and affect access to medicines and pesticides, there are other implications of this system. The commencement of the data exclusivity period and the compensation for regulatory delays are two other areas of concern. As the protection will be from the time of marketing approval in a country, one can expect that the year when such protections would come to an end may vary from country to country depending upon when the medicine or pesticide was approved. Since most companies seek regulatory approvals first in the developed country markets and then in the developing countries, we may have situations when data exclusivity protection may extend beyond the patent protection. If more countries become party to the TPP, the magnitude of the uncertainty created due to these provisions may affect decisions from generic manufacturers, thereby impacting the competition adversely, and affect access.

Article 18.48 of the TPP aims at compensating the applicant for any delays in receiving a marketing approval. Unlike the patent term

---

[5] Enigma Marketing Research on agrochemical patents approaching expiry; http://enigma-marketingresearch.com/collections/reports (last visited 18 July 2017).

extension provision, there is no average period specified beyond which delays would need to be suitably taken into account. Although it may not be unrealistic to assume that the delays may be counted from the time the application is filed, one could at the least expect some variety in how the mandate is complied with. Since the registration date would vary across countries and different jurisdictions may have diversity in the extent of delays, one can expect variations in the date of expiry. Variations such as this will lead to indecision on part of the generic industry and could be an effective barrier to development.

An exception has been provided under Articles 18.50 and 18.52 to enable implementation of measures to protect public health in accordance with the Declaration on TRIPS and Public Health or any amendment of the TRIPS Agreement to implement the declaration or any waiver of any provision of the TRIPS Agreement granted by the WTO members to implement the declaration. This carve-out applies only to issue of compulsory license, whereas the Doha Declaration on TRIPS and Public Health is much more extensive and substantive as it reassures members about their ability to use all flexibilities under the TRIPS Agreement. The TPP takes this flexibility away from the member countries of the Agreement. To be explicit, if countries interpret Article 39.3 in a manner as to provide data exclusivity and allow lowering of patentability, they have effectively given up the flexibility that the Doha Declaration so clearly articulated. Since compulsory license may not issue very often and, whenever such an occasion arises, will be constantly mired in litigation, the carve-out has limited applicability and utility, if any.

It is also important to point out that the date exclusivity protection will run independent of the term of patent protection (Article 18.54). This implies that even when a patent is revoked, protection for the data submitted to the regulators would continue, thus perpetuating a monopoly even when it is recognized that there is no real innovation. In fact, data exclusivity protection may be allowed for a molecule that may never have had a patent protection. We have earlier discussed the situation of the agrochemical industry, but this is equally true for the pharmaceutical sector. An example (Pugatch 2004) is the anti-cancer drug Taxol (Paclitaxel). This is a 1962 molecule derived from the Pacific Yew bark by the National Cancer Institute and licensed exclusively to Bristol-Myres Squibb in 1991 for commercial development. While the molecule did not have a patent protection, the data exclusivity protection in the USA expired only in 2004. Other examples (Ibid.) include Eprex (epeotinalpah) and Arava (leflunomide) for treatment of severe anaemia and rheumatoid arthritis, respectively. The patents on these expired in the USA in 2004 and 2001, respectively, but data exclusivity protection continued till 2005 and 2003 in that order.

Since data exclusivity protection cannot be challenged in any court of law, it makes it a stronger right than the patent right. More significantly, in India where Section 3(d) sets higher standards for patentability, data exclusivity if adopted will provide protection to pharmaceutical medicines which may not qualify the patentability criteria set by Section 3(d) and in fact are frivolous inventions. Besides the egregiousness of the impact it has on the industry and accessibility, data exclusivity also hits at the very principles on which the IPR chapter in the TPP is to be established—that is, to promote innovation and creativity because data exclusivity has nothing to do with creativity.

Patent Linkage: Delay in the Entry of Generics (Article 18.51)

When a country allows marketing approval to a second applicant of a pharmaceutical product on the basis of the information on safety and efficacy submitted by the first applicant, the TPP requires that the concerned authority inform the patent holder before granting the approval to the second applicant. The authority would then need to give adequate opportunity to the patent holder. The process would be subject to judicial procedures of provisional measures, preliminary injunctions and resolution of disputes concerning validity or infringement of the patent.

Market approval and patent grant are two separate processes which require different skill sets. Patent rights are to be enforced by the right-holders through the legal channels provided in the laws of the land. Whether or not a patent infringement has occurred can be decided through a quasi-judicial or judicial process. On the other hand, marketing approval is given by a public authority which certifies that the product is safe and effective in the treatment of the disease. Linking marketing approvals to existing patents will place the onus on an authority ill-equipped to assess a patent to do this comparison and enforce the patent right, thereby changing the nature of TRIPS obligation.

4.7 Copyright and Related Rights: Extending Term of Protection, Technology Protection Measures, Rights Management Information and Absence of Fair Use Clauses (Section H: Articles 18.57–18.70)

Term of Protection: Enhanced (Article 18.63)

Copyright protection has been witness to continuous strengthening of norms through the adoption of a number of copyright treatises such as the WCT and the WPPT in 1996 which was then followed by the Beijing Treaty on Audiovisual performances in 2012. The enhancement in norms has also been witnessed in most countries as part of commitments under an FTA or CEPAs.

Under the TPP Agreement, the USA has tried to transmit its provisions to other members of the group. One of the most significant measures relates to increase in the term of copyright protection on the basis of the life of a natural person by 20 years to life plus 70 vis-à-vis life plus 50 years as specified in TRIPS. In the case of other than the life of a natural person, the term shall be not less than 70 years from the end of the calendar year of the first authorized publication of work, performance or phonogram. Also if there is no authorized publication within 25 years from the creation of the work, performance or phonogram, the period of protection will be 70 years from the end of the calendar year of the creation of the work, performance or phonogram.

The enhancement in copyright term works against accessibility of literary works and affects the robustness of the public domain which is the main source of learning for people. Increase in copyright protection much beyond the life of the person creates situations where it would be difficult to address problems related to out of print books[6] where the authorized publisher is either not interested in bringing out reprints or has ceased to exist. No other publisher may be willing to go ahead because of the possibility of a dispute. Similarly, long copyright terms make it more difficult to address orphan works where the copyright owner is not known affecting, thereby, the accessibility to this resource.

---

[6] Electronic Frontier Foundation: Copyright Term Extensions and the Public Domain.

The literature on copyright protection indicates that an ideal period of protection for copyright is about 14 years (Pollock 2009). Another study by Levine put the ideal period of copyright protection as 2 years (Kinsella 2011). The trend, on the contrary, to continuously extend protection has tilted the balance considerably in favour of the copyright owners and works against the growth and development of the society which undoubtedly depends on the availability of literary and artistic works in public domain.

Digital Rights Management: Wide Powers Under Technology Protection Measures (TPM) (Article 18.68)

Article 18.68 of the TPP requires that the member States implement a regime that would protect against copyright infringement in the internet environment. This is sought to be carried out by not only making the act of accessing copyrighted material without authorization an offense but also making development of such technologies, their manufacture and sale illegal. In the absence of fair use exceptions, the provision can have a significant impact on research in the area, affect consumer's access and may even jeopardize security.

The text in the TPP is an adaptation of the US law on digital rights measures, and analysts[7] believe that the exception clause in Article 18.68 is too weak and will not cover manufacture, distribution and sale of technologies that could also be used for accessing copyrighted material. Their belief is based on the implementation of the US law which has itself been a testimony to the weak application of the exception and limitation clauses. In any case, the provision is in direct conflict with the recently amended Indian law on copyright which, while providing for TPM, has tried to utilize the flexibility under the WCT to restrict the offense of circumvention to the final act. It clearly makes an exception for manufacture, distribution and sale of technologies that could be used for circumventing copyrighted material. The only requirement being that the person who assists in the circumvention must maintain a list of person who were helped and the purpose. Other areas of exception

---

[7] Electronic Frontier Foundation: Digital Content Locks.

to the protection of technology measures delineated in the Indian law include conduct of encryption research or lawful investigations or anything required for testing the security of the computer system or network with the authorization of the owner or for surveillance or if measures are required to be taken in national interest.

Rights Management Information

Protection also Provided Against Removal Which Is Unknowingly Done (Article 18.69)

According to Article 18.69 of the TPP, RMI is that information that identifies a work or performance to the author or the performer and includes the terms and conditions of the use of the work. Any removal of this information carried out knowingly will be protected against through both criminal and civil procedures. While this is a TRIPS-plus provision in itself, the fact that countries have been given the flexibility to extend the protection even against persons who may have been importing or distributing works without the knowledge that the RMI has indeed been altered is likely to have a chilling impact in the concerned country. In the Indian case, strict criminal and civil enforcement is available but only to the extent that the activity has been carried out with full knowledge that RMI has been removed by either a third party or by the individual himself. Effectively under the TPP, member countries have been encouraged to give up fair use exceptions wherever possible.

4.8 Internet Service Providers (Section J: Articles 18.81–18.82): Strong Liability for Internet Service Providers

Internet service providers (ISPs) host information of all kind—news, opinion or images—in the internet environment. In doing so, they provide a very critical service and have direct bearing on the freedom of speech and expression in society. It is, therefore, important to ensure that they are protected so that there is no disincentive to curb the flow of information. Much of what the ISPs host may also contain copyright content.

With enhancement of copyright protection being the byword these days, there is pressure on setting down the liabilities of the intermediate service providers. This has been the trend in most FTAs and it is also true for the TPP. It requires signatory countries to provide legal remedies in their domestic law for right-holders against copyright infringement in the online environment, and to create safe harbours for ISPs.

Article 18.82 of the TPP provides the framework for legal remedies and safe harbours that the signatory countries are mandated to adhere to. The framework has three essential elements—first, legal incentives for ISPs to cooperate with copyright owners in order to deter unauthorized storage and transmission of copyrighted materials; second, limitations in law that preclude monetary relief against ISPs for copyright infringement that they do not control, initiate or direct; and third, conditions for ISPs to qualify for the limitations against monetary relief or conversely the circumstances when the limitation will not hold. One of the conditions that the ISP would necessarily have to follow when storing information, or directing users to a particular site including through hyperlinks and directories, is to expeditiously remove or disable access to material residing in their systems on receipt of notice or if they make their own determination of a likely infringement. Under this notice and take-down procedure the ISPs would also be required to promptly inform the concerned/alleged infringer about the action. In countries which provide for counter notices, the material would be restored on receiving such a notice from the user unless the person giving the original notice gets judicial relief within a reasonable time.

India does have the notice and take-down procedures and in some ways more onerous than in the TPP, especially in the light of the *Star India Pvt. Ltd v. Haneeth Ujwal*, Delhi High Court, CS (OS) 2243/2014 where the court has held that the ISP is liable for hosting material that infringes the IPR of the third party.

4.9 Enforcement: Strengthening the Strong (Section I: Articles 18.71–18.80)

The TRIPS Agreement has perhaps the most comprehensive, largest number of articles and the most onerous provisions on enforcement covering all conceivable situations and remedies. The enforcement sections have been systematically worked upon in most FTAs/CEPAs with the single purpose of reducing the flexibilities and limitations that may have been specified in the TRIPS with the view to strengthen the hands of the right-holders vis-à-vis the users.

The sections on enforcement in the TPP selectively quote the provisions of TRIPS while removing, or diluting, the safeguards in the multilateral agreement. Important provisions that dilute the safeguards and are also not compliant with the Indian law are as follows.

Enforcement Practices (Article 18.73)

While specifying that final judicial decisions and administrative decisions be made available in writing and published, Article 18.73 of the TPP mandates that parties make available to the public efforts made by them to enforce IPRs effectively in the civil, administrative and criminal systems. The content required to be provided is quite extensive and could be a difficult proposition to comply with for most developing countries. India, at present, only documents criminal enforcement measures in respect of copyright infringement. Considering that the country has a federal set up, documentation at one place of all the civil, administrative and criminal actions in respect of patents, trademarks, copyrights, designs and GIs is indeed a tall task.

Civil and Administrative Procedures and Remedies (Article 18.74)

Article 18.74 of the TPP covers issues concerning damages, other remedies, right of information and injunctive relief. The concerns on these issues are discussed further.

Damages: The TPP has a concept of pre-established damages which are similar to statutory damages for violations relating to copyright and related rights and trademarks. It requires that parties should provide for pre-established damages that are sufficiently high to be a deterrent and also compensate the right-holder for the harm caused and/or provide for additional damages that include exemplary damages. It states that at least in case of counterfeit trademark or pirated copyright goods, judicial authorities should have the authority to pay the right-holder the infringer's profits that are attributable to the infringement. The Indian law gives the judicial authorities the right to determine the quantum of damages that can be imposed and whether or not account of profits can be sought. There is, therefore, no concept of pre-established damages in India. Besides this, there are safeguards under the Indian law when infringement happens unknowingly or when the infringer desists from further use of the trademark after becoming aware of the existence and nature of the rights of the plaintiff. These safeguards do not exist in the TPP. TRIPS itself does not mandate pre-established damages. It allows parties the flexibility to decide for themselves whether it could be considered and seeks to restrict this to only appropriate cases.

Other remedies: TRIPS Article 46, while addressing effective deterrence to infringement, provides that the judicial authorities should have the right to order disposal of the goods outside the channels of commerce so as to avoid any harm to the right-holder or unless this is, would be contrary to constitutional requirements, the good be destroyed. The flexibility is sought to be removed under the TPP by requiring parties to destroy the infringing material.

Right of information: Under the TPP, the signatory countries have an obligation to give the judicial authorities the right to seek information regarding persons involved and the means of production or the channel of distribution without consideration of the extent of infringement or whether there really was an infringement. Under TRIPS (Article 47) the commitment to provide authority to the judiciary to seek information is not only non-mandatory but also has to be utilized using the lens of 'proportionality of the seriousness of the infringement' and also only when the infringement has been clearly established. In the TPP, on the other hand, the commitment is mandatory and will apply to the alleged infringer without taking into consideration the seriousness of the infringement.

Enforcement against circumvention of TPM and RMI: The text provides that judicial authorities should be allowed to impose provisional measures including custody of the devices and products suspected to be involved in the prohibited activity. The provision is in direct conflict with the recently amended Indian law on copyright which while providing for TPM has tried to utilize the flexibility under the WCT to restrict the offense of circumvention to the final act. It clearly makes an exception for manufacture, distribution and sale of technologies that could be used for circumventing copyrighted material. The only requirement is that the person who assists in the circumvention must maintain a list of person who were helped and the purpose. In respect of RMI also, the Indian law has no provision for seizure or custody of the devices used for the infringement but only seeks to take action against the person involved in altering the RMI.

Provisional Measures (Article 18.75)

Article 18.75 of the TPP allows a right-holder to prevent the infringing product from entering the channels of commerce, and this measure can be awarded *inaudita altera parte*, that is, ex parte. When judicial authorities are given the powers to take action without hearing the defending side, there needs to be in place sufficient safeguards to ensure that justice is not denied. In TRIPS (Article 50), these have been duly accounted for. Under it the defending party has to be given notice without delay after the execution of the measure and a right for review within a reasonable period of time. Besides this, the right-holder could be asked to provide more information to establish its case, and the measures can be revoked if proceedings are not initiated by the right-holder within a reasonable period of time specified as 20 working days or 31 calendar days. In case the measures are revoked if there was no case of infringement, the judicial authorities have the authority to order the applicant upon request of the defendant to compensate him for the injury. Unfortunately, the TPP has none of these safeguards. It only requires that the security or the equivalent assurance that would need to be given by the applicant be reasonable enough not to deter the use of the measure. Clearly, the balance is tipped in favour of the right-holder.

Special Requirements Related to Border Measures (Article 18.76)

Article 18.76 of the TPP requires that signatories to the Agreement allow right-holders to seek, through an application, the suspension of the release of any 'suspected' counterfeit or 'confusingly similar' trademarks or pirated copyright goods that are imported into their country. The right-holder initiating this procedure must furnish adequate evidence to satisfy the authorities that there is a prima facie case and provide sufficient information to make the suspected goods 'reasonably recognizable' by the authorities. The article also mandates that confidential information relating to the defendant, such as name and address of the consignor, exporter, consignee or importer and the quantity of the goods, could be provided to the right-holder without undue delay and without waiting for determination of infringement. Where this is not provided in the laws, the parties would need to allow this information to be divulged in the case of imports within 30 days of the seizure or determination that the goods are counterfeit trademark goods.

Under the TRIPS, member countries have to adopt procedures to enable suspension of imported counterfeit trademarks and pirated copyright goods. The scope of this measure has been expanded in the TPP to cover suspected counterfeit and even confusingly similar trademarks. Not only does the Agreement extend the scope but it also places a much lower level of obligation on the right-holder by requiring that he give sufficient information to 'reasonably establish' that the product is a counterfeit as against a much more rigorous requirement in TRIPS of the information being sufficiently detailed to make it 'readily recognizable' as counterfeit by custom authorities. Further, a mandatory requirement—that the authorities divulge confidential information about the defendant to the right-holder even before the determination is made as to it being a counterfeit or within 30 days of the seizure or determination—severely skews the balance in enforcement in favour of the right-holder. The expansion in the scope, the relatively lower information requirement and the possibility that confidential information may be compromised makes the provision far reaching in its implications.

Absence of any articulation on safeguards has been a casualty in the TPP. There is no discussion of the rights of other stakeholders in the enforcement procedures. The need to promptly inform the importer along with the applicant seeking imposition of measures is conspicuous by its absence. TRIPS mandates that within a period not exceeding 10 working days after the applicant has been served notice of suspension, the authorities have to be informed of initiation of proceedings by the right-holder. In case this does not happen, the goods are liable to be released. While this period can be extended to another 10 working days, it is an important measure to ensure that detentions do not happen at the free will of the right-holder and despite inaction on his part. Sadly, this aspect is completely ignored in the TPP. Considering the fact that TPP mandates that secret commercial information be divulged to the right-holder without delay and without waiting for a determination on whether there is indeed an infringement or not, the fact that the absence of safeguards in the form of compensation to the importer in case of wrongful detention has not been addressed in the text is a cause of concern. Other precautions such as review of decision are also not specifically mentioned.

The TPP seeks to enable ex-officio action on part of the competent authorities for goods imported, destined for exports or 'in transit'. The requirements specified are beyond TRIPS as TRIPS covers not only border measures for 'in transit' goods and those meant for exports, but also ex-officio action in this regard. Besides, Article 58 of TRIPS indicates that these actions can only be taken if the border authorities have acquired prima facie evidence of such an infringement. In the TPP, there is no such clarity being provided with the measures required to be used where authorities suspect infringement.

Criminal Procedures and Penalties (Articles 18.77 and 18.78)

Articles 18.77 and 18.78 of the TPP provides for criminal enforcement for wilful trademark counterfeiting and copyright and related rights piracy on a commercial scale. While the provision appears similar to the TRIPS provision (Article 61), the major deviation is the attempt to define 'on a commercial scale' to mean acts carried out for commercial advantage or financial gains and acts that may not be for commercial advantage but are likely to impact the interest of copyright and related right-holder in relation to the market place. This would include non-authorized uses of protected works, performances and phonograms, irrespective of whether they are for commercial advantage or not. Criminal enforcement would also be due on wilful importation of labelling and packaging to which a trademark has been applied without authorization, that is, either identical to or cannot be distinguished from a registered trademark and is intended for use on identical goods and services.

Criminal enforcement is also sought for copying of cinematographic works in movie theatres (anti-camcording) and unauthorized and wilful misappropriation of a trade secret (Article 18.78). These are all TRIPS-plus provisions and also not compatible with the Indian law.

It is important to note that the definition of 'on a commercial scale' adopted in the TPP is based on the interpretation that the USA sought to give to the terms 'commercial scale' in the WTO dispute 'China-Intellectual Property Rights' (DS 362). In this dispute before the panel, the USA submitted that the word 'commercial' in the context of Article 61 refers to engaged in commerce; pertaining to, or bearing on commerce, interested in financial return rather than artistry; regarded as a mere matter of business; and likely to make a profit. The panel asserted that the enforcement mechanism envisaged in 'Article 61' does not cover all commercial acts. The panel rejected the US interpretation of these terms, which would have included 'all activity for financial gain or profit' (para 7.541 and para 7.542 WT/DS362/R). Instead, the panel found that the word 'commercial' has been used in the context of 'Article 61' as a qualifier for the scale of activity and not to refer to commercial purpose of the activity. Thus, the definition of 'on a commercial scale' adopted in the TPP is based on an interpretation advanced by the USA, but rejected by the panel.

Government Use of Software (Article 18.80)

The provision requires that every party adopt appropriate laws, regulations, policies, orders, guidelines of executive decree mandating that the central government only use non-infringing computer software and in a manner authorized by the relevant licence. Considering that the entire chapter would also be applicable to how the governments conduct their work, the provision is puzzling.

4.10 Indonesia and Philippines: Impact of Acceding to the TPP

There have been newspaper reports about the possible accessions by Indonesia and Philippines to the TPP. These appear to be interesting developments considering the position taken by the concerned countries on patents so far and in the light of certain recent developments. On inventive step, Philippines and now Indonesia have features broadly identical to the Section 3(d) of the Indian Patents Act. While Philippines enacted a law in 2008 called the Universally Accessible Cheaper and

Quality Medicines Act,[8] which incorporates safeguards against evergreening (Section 22.1) identical to Section 3(d) of the Indian Patents Act, 1970, Indonesia took this plunge as recently as 28 July 2016 when it excluded new use of a known product and new form of a pre-existing compound which does not offer significant increase in efficacy from being patented.[9] Data exclusivity protection would be another area that would require legislative changes in both Indonesia and Philippines, as they do not have a provision on fixed term regulatory data protection.

Accession to the TPP will effectively imply complete overhaul of the patent and regulatory system in Indonesia and Philippines with extensive impact on the cost of medicines and access to health.

4.11 Conclusions: Implications for India

The IPR chapter in the TPP seeks to harmonize the laws and regulations on the subject with those that exist in the USA and in other developed countries of the region. The objective of the exercise is to allow firms and the corporate of the developed world a regime that protects and enforces their IPR in a similar manner across the TPP region, thereby bringing in greater certainty for these companies and enhancing the prospects of profits generated through monopoly market conditions. Further, the IPR provisions entail a concomitant reduction in policy space available under TRIPS to the signatory countries of the TPP, particularly the developing countries. On a more specific note, the TPP provisions curb the freedom of signatory countries to adopt regimes that promote their specific sectors of vital importance or support domestic corporate interests or/and deal with issues of larger policy significance such as health and access to medicines.

Although the rationale of the chapter (Article 18.4) is to promote creativity and innovation, advance technology transfer and diffusion, increase competition and improve transparency, yet as discussed in the previous sections many of the provisions impact the stated principles negatively. Whether it is setting low boundaries on 'inventive step' to allow evergreening of the patents or it is to allow data exclusivity and

---

[8] http://www.lawphil.net/statutes/repacts/ra2008/ra_9502_2008.html (last visited 18 July 2017).

[9] www.hhp.co.id/files/uploads/documents/type%202/hhp%al-jakarta-enactmentnewpatentlaw-Aug16.pdf (last visited 18 July 2017).

evergreening of data exclusivity, the thrust is on benefitting certain stakeholders at the cost of others including the society at large. The chapter is about commercial benefits for a set of stakeholders that predominantly reside in the developed countries. For the developing countries, such provisions are likely to increase the cost of medicines, limit policy space to address sector-specific concerns and lead to higher levels of enforcement with little or no safeguards.

It is important to understand the implications for India if it were to adhere to the obligations contained in the IPR chapter of the TPP. When India amended its patent regime through the Patents Act of 1970 (which came into force in 1972) to disallow product patents in food, medicines or drugs or substances produced by chemical process, it was a decision taken to address high prices of medicines and improve access. The outcome was a spurt in generic competition, enhanced availability of medicines at lower prices and a concomitant expansion of the Indian generic pharmaceutical industry which is now regarded as the 'pharmacy of the world'. Consequent to the TRIPS Agreement, the country was faced with a situation where it had to bring back product patents for pharmaceuticals/chemical-based substances or drugs. While this was fait accompli, the amendments to the Patents Act, 1970, were crafted so as to comply with the TRIPS requirements while ensuring against evergreening (amendments to Section 3(d) of the Act is a case in point), thus safeguarding access to medicines. This became possible because of significant flexibilities and policy space available under TRIPS. The flexibilities and policy space has allowed countries to come up with patent regimes that address their unique situation. This diversity in compliance with the TRIPS requirements has been a cause of concern for the Big Pharma since its very inception in 1995. The IPR text in the TPP speaks to these concerns directly. The text as discussed earlier removes the flexibility and policy space by seeking to adopt a 'one size fits all' model. Most significantly, the Agreement aims at lowering the criteria for grant of pharmaceutical patents to enable patents to be allowed for new use of a known substance or a new process or method of using a known substance. This is the exact antithesis of Section 3(d) of the Patents Act, 1970, which if the country agrees to comply with at some point in time will render a body blow to India's pharmaceutical industry which has been nurtured over a number of decades to reach a point where it is considered among the best manufacturers of generic medicines. This in turn will adversely affect access to medicines for our teeming millions.

Disciplines on data exclusivity, patent term extension and patent linkage have been the other significant contributions of the TPP specifically impacting the pharmaceutical and agrochemical sector. These are clearly TRIPS-plus measures whose objective is to perpetuate the monopoly of innovator pharmaceutical and agrochemical companies. Since the data exclusivity protection exists irrespective of a patent, it is an award for no real innovation. Ironically, it is a much stronger right than patent, as the former can never be revoked, while the latter can be. The Indian law does not address issues such as data exclusivity, patent term extensions and linkage. On the question whether the country should move on a path based on the IPR provisions of the TPP, it would perhaps not be amiss to state that continuation of a legal monopoly through provisions on criteria for patentability, data exclusivity, patent term extensions and patent linkage will result in all the infirmities of monopoly behaviour. This is something the country can ill-afford at this juncture, given the human angle and the industry structure that exists. It is important to note that the TPP position on this has been guided by the interests of US pharmaceutical companies. The Agreement is not about innovation but about promoting business interests. The question that India must answer is whether such a push also comes from its domestic generic industry and whether it has the capacity to bear the costs that such measures will naturally entail. The fact that the Indian Government does not in any way subsidize or pay for the expenses entailed in medical treatment should also be kept in mind before giving up one's position in favour of commercial interest of stakeholders of another country. Taking that argument further, even full subsidization of medical costs by the government, would not be reason enough to go down that route for the simple reason that the high costs of medicines, in the absence of generic competition, would then have to be borne by the government.

Other areas of concern are the extensive enforcement provisions that almost mirror the provisions of the highly controversial Anti-Counterfeiting Trading Agreement which did not come into force because of the opposition from the EU. The remedies provided in the TPP aim at strengthening the TRIPS provisions in various ways such as by the removal of safeguards, by mandating judicial authorities to behave in a certain manner, by extension of border measures including allowing ex-officio action on exports and goods in transit as also extending this measure to confusingly similar trademarks. The objective of the exercise is to reduce transaction costs for the right-holders by removing, as far as possible, the subjectivity that normally comes into and should come into implementing enforcement actions. The other problem is that the TPP provisions by and large are confined to the protection of the right-holder interests without due regard to the need for balance in the enforcement

IPR and New Rule-making   151

proceedings. Considering that implementation of enforcement procedures in India has an inherent balance and the fact that the judicial authorities in India cannot be directed to act in a certain manner, it would be difficult for India to agree to these very prescriptive provisions.

Coming to the extension of border measures to exports and goods in transit, one can say that this is really about creating effective barriers to trade, particularly of generic pharmaceutical products. Enforcing border measures on goods to be exported implies application of enforcement measures twice. This is so because by its very nature, products due for exports are produced in the territory of the exporting country in compliance with the existing laws of the country. If these products are to be checked again at the ports for violation of IPRs as per the laws of the exporting country, it is an unnecessary additional procedure leading to higher transaction costs for the exporter. But more significantly, if IPR violations have to be assessed by the exporting country as per the laws of the importing country, then it is an extra-territorial application of the measure and is completely undesirable and inconsistent with TRIPS which recognizes IPRs as territorial rights. In both cases it is a clear barrier to trade. In the case of goods in transit, the product is not meant for the market of the country through which it is transiting. In such cases, it is unacceptable that this country through which the product is transiting should take measures against IPR violations, if any, in the product that is meant for a third market. If we go along with the argument, the question that needs to be answered is whether the country through which the product is transiting has the jurisdiction to take action and, if it has, which law would need to be applied—whether it would be the importing or exporting countries or its own laws. In all cases, it would be an unwarranted action leading to delay, uncertainty and enhanced transaction costs for the exporting country besides it being an extra-territorial application of laws. Should India ever consider such a commitment is a question that needs to be answered by the policymakers, but the implications of such actions are fairly apparent and, to say the least, the measures are undeniably effective barriers to trade.

The TPP Agreement aims at changing the rules of the game drastically. While the text lays down the understanding that member countries have behind including such a chapter, it is not clear from the details how this understanding will be achieved. While the chapter deals with most of the existing IPRs, the emphasis really is on giving a better deal to the innovator pharmaceutical industry, addressing the technological developments in the copyright regime, enhancing substantially the enforcement provision even at the cost of creating effective barriers to trade and addressing misappropriation of trade secrets in a manner not done before. Norm setting in most of these areas is influenced largely by the position the USA has taken—which is also articulated well in their Special 301 Reports—on these issues. The question we must answer is whether the discourse articulated by US interests is to be accepted as being appropriate for countries that are at a completely different development stage. The IPRs regime is an institutional framework that has deep linkages with the real sector. To understand the likely impact of India adhering to a template for IPR protection based on the TPP provisions, two crucial developments need to be borne in mind. First, the amendments to bring the Patents Act of 1970 in line with the recommendations of Justice Ayyangar Committee energized a complete industry and has made India the global pharmacy. Second, the Australia–US FTA, which brought in TRIPS-plus standards such as patent term extensions, completely changed the pharmaceutical industry structure (Centre for WTO Studies 2015) in Australia and impacted the generic competition adversely. It would, thus, be appropriate to say that as far as the IPR is concerned, the TPP provisions are less about promoting innovation and competition, and instead are aimed at restricting competition and facilitating windfall profits through perpetuating monopoly market conditions. It is important for India to weigh domestic concerns, particularly the impact on access to affordable medicine, and assess commercial interest of its domestic stakeholders before any decision is taken, to align its IPR regime with the IPR template contained in the TPP.

Notes on Exceptions and Concessions Given to Certain Countries in the IPR chapter of the TPP

> *Chile:* For protection of undisclosed information, Chile has negotiated a safeguard that allows them not to provide this protection (in accordance with Article 91 of the Law no. 19.039) if there is corrupt practice or when compulsory license is issued or on justified grounds of public health, national security, non-commercial public use, national emergency or other extremely urgent circumstances or if registration has been obtained in another country more than 12 months before the application is filed in Chile or if the product has not been marketed within 12 months from the date of registration in Chile.

Malaysia: In case of Malaysia, for protection of undisclosed information (Articles 18.50.1, 18.50.2 and 18.52.1), the applicant must initiate the process for obtaining approval for pharmaceutical products within 18 months from the date when the product is first granted marketing approval in any country. Protection will begin from the date of registration in Malaysia.

Peru: It has been given the flexibility to seek waiver from the Andean Community for providing patent term extensions for delays by the patent office and the market regulator. In case this waiver is not received, Peru will need to ensure that there is no discrimination with respect to availability or enjoyment of patent rights based on the field of technology, the place of invention and whether products are imported or locally produced. In addition, Peru will apply the provisions of the US–Peru Trade Promotion Agreement in respect of data exclusivity protection which will be counted from the time of first approval anywhere in the world (provided Peru can grant regulatory approval within six months' of the date of filing of a complete application in the country).

References

Bentham, Jeremy. 1839. *A Manual of Political Economy*. New York: G.P. Putnam.

Bessen, James, and Erik Maskin. 2000. 'Sequential Innovation, Patents and Imitation'. Working Paper No. 00–01, Department of Economics, Massachusetts Institute of Technology, Cambridge, MA.

Boldrin, M. and David L. Levine. 2008. Against Intellectual Monopoly, Cambridge University Press, The Edinburgh Building, Cambridge CB28RU, UK. Published in USA by the Cambridge University Press New York www.cambridge.org/9780521879286

Centre for WTO Studies. 2015. Report of the International Workshop on the Impact of the TRIPS Agreement on Key Sectors and its Relevance in the Context of Bilateral and Regional Trading Agreements, 26–27 October. Retrieved 18 July 2017, from wtocentre.iift.ac.in/books_reports.asp

Correa, Carlos M. 2010. 'Patentability Standards: When Is an Invention Patentable?' In *Intellectual Property and Access to Medicines*. Geneva: World Health Organization and South Centre.

Josef, Drexel, Grosse Ruse Khan, Henning, Nadde-Phlix, Souheir, eds. 2014. *EU Bilateral Trade Agreements and Intellectual Property: For Better or Worse?* MPI Studies on Intellectual Property and Competition Law. Berlin, Heidelberg: Springer-Verlag.

European Commission. 2009, 8 July. *Pharmaceutical Sector Inquiry: Final Report*. European Commission. Retrieved 17 August 2017, from ec.europa.eu/competition/sectors/pharmaceuticals/inquiry/staff_working_paper_part 1.pdf

Gordon, Serena. 2015. 'How Drug Companies Keep Insulin Prices High'. *CBS News*, March 19. Retrieved 18 July 2017, from http://www.cbsnews.com/news/how-drug-companies-keep-insulin-prices-high/

Kapczynski, A., C. Park, and B. Sampat. 2012. 'Polymorphs and Prodrugs and Salts (Oh My!): An Empirical Analysis of "Secondary" Pharmaceutical Patents'. *PLoS ONE* 7(12): e49470. doi:10.1371/journal.pone.0049470

Kinsella, Stephen. 2011. 'Optimal Patent and Copyright Term Length'. Mises Wire. Retrieved 18 July 2017, from https://mises.org/blog/optimal-patent-and-copyright-term-length

Lerner, Josh. 2002. 'Patent Protection and Innovation Over 150 Years'. Working Paper No. 8977, National Bureau of Economic Research, Massachusetts Ave, Cambridge.

Malpani, R. 2007. 'All Costs, No Benefits: How TRIPS-plus Intellectual Property Rules in the US–Jordan FTA Affect Access to Medicines'. *Oxfam Briefing Paper*. Oxford: Oxfam.

Moir, Hazel, and Deborah Gleeson. 2014. 'Explainer: Evergreening and How Big Pharma Keeps Drug Prices High'. *The Conversation*, November 6. Retrieved 18 July 2017, from http://theconversation.com/explainer-evergreening-and-how-big-pharma-eeps-drug-prices-high-33623

Penrose, Edith Tilton. 1951. *The Economics of the International Patent System*. Baltimore, MD: John Hopkins University Press.

Pigou, A.C. 1924. *The Economics of Welfare*. New York: Macmillan. Retrieved 17 August 2017, from www.morganlewis.com/-/media/files/publication/presentation/speech/smyth_uspatentinvalidity_sept12.ashx.

Pollock, Rufus. 2009. 'Forever Minus a Day? Calculations on Optimal Copyright Term Lengths'. Retrieved 18 July 2017, from https://rufuspollock.org/papers/optimal_copyright_term.pdf

Pugatch, Meir Perez. 2004. 'Intellectual Property and Pharmaceutical Data Exclusivity in the Context of Innovation and Market Access'. Retrieved 17 August 2017, from www.iprsonline.org/unctadictsd/bellagio/docs/pugatch_bellagio3.pdf

Sahai, Suman. 2003. 'India's Plant Variety Protection and Farmers Rights Act, 2001'. *Current Science* 84 (3), 407–12.

Shaffer, Ellen R., and Joseph E. Brenner. 2009. 'A Trade Agreement's Impact on Access to Generic Drugs'. *Health Affairs* 28 (5): w957–68.

Smyth, R. 2012. US Patent Invalidity Study presented at the IPO Annual Meeting, September.

Taubman, A., H. Wager, and J. Watal, eds. 2012. *A Handbook on the WTO TRIPS Agreement*. Cambridge: Cambridge University Press.

Williams, John D. 1994. 'Patent Protection, Taxation, and the Supply and Demand for R&D'. Unpublished working paper, Federal Reserve Board. Reference cited in Lerner, Josh (2002) Patent Protection and Innovation over 150 years, Working Paper 8977, National Bureau of Economic Research, Massachusetts Ave, Cambridge.

5
Conforming India's IPR Laws to the TPP's IPR Standards

Issues and Concerns for India

Jayant Raghu Ram*

5.1 Introduction

The Trans-Pacific Partnership Agreement (TPP) created ripples in the world trading system when it was concluded on 4 October 2015. Negotiated by over 12 countries across the Pacific Ocean including the United States of America (USA; which was the driving force behind the negotiations), and covering nearly 40 per cent of the world's gross domestic product (GDP), the TPP was touted to be the world's largest trade agreement concluded outside the World Trade Organization (WTO). However, the inauguration of a new president in the USA in January 2017 sounded a death knell for the TPP, when the administration announced its withdrawal from the TPP. As a result, the TPP, in its current structure, is unlikely to come into force.

Even though the possibility of the TPP translating into an enforceable agreement among the twelve signatory countries seems unlikely, its normative contents remain highly relevant in understanding what could be the contents of prospective free trade agreements (FTAs) and also of future negotiations at the WTO. It has been widely speculated

---

* I am grateful to Professor Abhijit Das, Amb. V.S. Seshadri, Ms Kajal Bharadwal and Mr Pei-Kan Yang for helpful comments on previous drafts of this chapter. I would also like to thank Akhil Raina for research and editorial assistance.

that the TPP's normative contents would definitely serve as a template for future negotiations in the world trading system on WTO-plus norms such as competition, environment, labour, and e-commerce (Fergusson et al. 2015). However, before discussions on such issues become underway at the respective forums, it becomes important to understand the nature of these norms, and the implications for countries that align their domestic laws to such norms.

This chapter is an attempt to understand one of the most contentious chapters of the TPP—its intellectual property right (IPR) chapter. The TPP's IPR chapter covers six categories of intellectual property—geographical indications, patents, undisclosed commercial information, copyrights, trademarks and industrial designs. The IPR chapter also mandatorily requires TPP Members to join the Union for the Protection of New Plant Varieties (UPOV) Convention.

Existing literature on the subject points out that the TRIPS-plus FTAs signed with the USA mandating higher standards of independent professionals (IP) protection impede access to medicines in countries. A study by Shaffer and Brenner (2009) on the impact of Central American Free Trade Agreement (CAFTA)-mandated norms on data exclusivity and patents found that these norms led to denial of access of several cheaper generic drugs to the Guatemalan market in the place of costlier brand-name drugs. A number of studies have been conducted on the impact of the Jordan–US FTA signed in 2001 on medicine prices in Jordan. A study by Abbot et al. (2012) found an increase of 17 per cent in total price of medicines from 1999 to 2004. Their study also estimated that delayed market entry of generics due to enhanced IP protections cost Jordan's retail market approximately US$18 million in 2004, representing 14 per cent of the total annual pharmaceutical spending in Jordan's private sector. A working paper by the Abrol et al. (2016) points out that delayed implementation of product patents in India as required by TRIPS positively impacted the ability of the domestic generic industry to compete with foreign originator firms in the Indian pharmaceuticals market.

The impact of TRIPS-plus provisions in FTAs has also been felt in developed countries. According to a study by Faunce et al. (2010), changes brought about by the AUSFTA not only dented the profitability of the generic sector, but also appeared to have contributed to an unwillingness of generic manufacturers to establish or invest substantially in research facilities in Australia. Their study also concludes that these provisions would result in higher prices for patented drugs than would have been in the absence of the AUSFTA.

This chapter analyzes the issues and concerns that would arise if India conformed its laws on patents, clinical trial data and trademarks to the TPP's IPR chapter. This chapter also discusses the issues and concerns that would arise if India conformed its plant variety protection laws to the 1991 Act of the UPOV Convention. In the course of this chapter's analysis, TRIPS has been taken as the benchmark for a comparative understanding of India's IP protection obligations under the WTO and the available flexibilities.

5.2 India's Patent Laws vis-à-vis the TPP's IPR Chapter

This section reviews the provisions in the TPP's IPR chapter pertaining to patents and assesses the changes that would be required in the Indian Patents Acts. This chapter also discusses the implications arising from conformity in the Indian context.

Expanding the Scope of Patentability of an Invention

As per Article 27.1 of the TRIPS, the criteria for patenting an invention—whether a product or a process—is novelty, industrial applicability and the presence of an inventive step. TRIPS does not define or stipulate the standard for any of these three criteria. Each WTO Member has been given the flexibility to determine its own standards in its applicable domestic IPR laws. As a result, each Member has been able to establish its own standards of patentability for an invention.

From the Indian perspective, this flexibility has been crucial in allowing patentability only for those inventions that are truly innovative and involve real effort, and disallowing patents for insignificant inventions. Section 3 of the Patents Act, 1970, establishes criteria as to what does not constitute a patentable invention of a given product. Section 3(d) is by far one of the most important provisions in the Indian patent law as it aims to prevent evergreening of pharmaceutical products, such that it would extend the monopoly of a patent holder beyond the term of the patent, namely, 20 years. Section 3(d) fundamentally disqualifies from patentability the mere discovery of the following:

1. A new form of a known substance which does not result in the enhancement of the known efficacy of that substance.
2. Any new property or new use for a known substance.
3. Mere use of a known process, machine or apparatus, unless such known process results in a new product or employs at least one new reactant.

Furthermore, the explanation to section 3(d) clarifies that chemical derivatives of a known substance shall be considered to be the same substance unless there is a significant difference in the efficacy of the derivative and the original substance. According to Gopalakrishnan (2010), these standards of patentability in India's Patents Act show that the legislative intent has been to exclude inventions that are not based on value addition from the scope of patentability. It would seem that legislators intended to ensure a high threshold for an invention to receive patent protection.

It would be important to note that section 3(d) was not immune from judicial challenge. In *Novartis v. Union of India* ((2013) 6 SCC 1), pharmaceutical major Novartis challenged the provisions of section 3(d) while assailing the rejection of its patent application for the beta crystalline form of imatinib mesylate (for treating leukaemia and tumours) by the patent authority. However, both the Madras High Court and the Supreme Court of India (later in appeal) rejected Novartis' claims. Holding that there was no enhanced efficacy of the drug, the Supreme Court traced the history of patent law in India, discussed the TRIPS Agreement and India's obligations under it, and referred to the concerns raised in parliament over access to medicines. Commenting on section 3(d), the Supreme Court stated:

> ... The amended portion of section 3(d) clearly sets up a second tier of qualifying standards for chemical substances/pharmaceutical products in order to leave the door open for true and genuine inventions but, at the same time, to check any attempt at repetitive patenting or extension of the patent term on spurious grounds.

The Supreme Court's jurisprudence reiterates that the scope of patentability under the Patents Act does not extend to an invention which is akin to old wine in a new bottle, unless there is an enhancement of efficacy.

While the patentability standards laid down in the Patents Act are reasonably strong, a review of some of the provisions in the TPP's IPR chapter shows that these countries are attempting to erode the TRIPS flexibility by expanding the scope of patentability under the domestic IPR regime and concomitantly diluting high standards of patentability.

Article 18.37 of the IPR chapter requires parties to allow patentability for inventions claimed as at least one of the following: (a) new uses of a known product, (b) new methods of using a known product or (c) new processes of using a known product. This provision is clearly in opposition to the sum and substance of section 3(d) of the Patents Act; conformity would mean deleting section 3(d). Flynn et al. (2011), are of the opinion that these provisions are probably targeted against India, and drafted with a purpose to counter the policy embedded in section 3(d) even though India was not a TPP party.

Conformity of section 3 to the above standard would dilute the fundamental standard of patentability which Indian legislators have sought to preserve. The TPP standard aims at granting patents for inventions which are merely variations and not just entirely new. However, as per generally accepted patent jurisprudence, patents are to be granted only for inventions that meet the 'novelty' criterion. According to Correa (2010a), the expansion of the patentability scope by means such as admitting broad claims and diluting patentability requirements would profoundly distort the patents system. Correa (ibid.) also is of the opinion that 'as incremental inventions prevail in most sectors, the patent system has increasingly moved away from its objective of stimulating genuine "invention" towards a system for the protection of investment in incremental invention, whether truly incentive or not.'

The second concern pertains to the implications for access to medicines in India. The above conformity steps would open the floodgates for evergreening of pharmaceutical patents in India through new forms/ new uses of a pharmaceutical drug even if there is no enhanced efficacy of the drug. According to Gopalakrishnan (2010), a country's patentability standards should be commensurate with its development interests which include the physical health and well-being of its people. A standard which puts generic pharmaceutical products out of reach for a significant proportion of its population on account of monopoly vested with the originator would be inimical to the health interests of its people.

Extending Patent Terms

The minimum term of a patent under TRIPS Article 33 is 20 years from the date of filing. The TPP's IPR chapter does not specify the term of a patent. However, unlike TRIPS, there are provisions in the TPP's IPR chapter which provide for extension of the patent term in certain circumstances. While TPP Article 18.46 requires parties to provide for patent term extension to compensate for delays in issuing patents, a party is permitted to exclude delays that occur during the processing or examination by the patent authority, those that are not directly attributable to the granting authority and those that are attributable to the patent applicant.

However, the real pinch concerning patent term extension arises not on account of delay in granting patents, but on account of delays in granting marketing approval by the regulator. TPP Article 18.48 requires each party to extend the term of a pharmaceutical patent to compensate for delays arising as a result of the marketing approval process. A conspicuous difference is that unlike adjustment of patent terms where delays not attributable to the patent office and delays attributable to the patent applicant can be factored, Article 18.48 provides no flexibility in adjusting patent terms extension on account of such delays.

Section 53 of India's Patents Act provides that the term of a patent shall be 20 years from the date of filing the application for grant of patent. There are no provisions in either the Patents Act or the Drugs and Cosmetics Act to grant patent term extension due to unreasonable delay in grant of patent or marketing approval. Conformity of these statutes to the TPP will mean that they will have to be amended to allow for patent term extension in the case of delays on account of grant of marketing approval.

The argument propounded by demandeurs of patent terms is that due to delays in granting regulatory approval, the effective period of a patent's exploitation is curtailed. However, the demandeurs for such provisions may be rushing to place the onus on drug regulators for delaying the approvals of pharmaceutical drugs without understanding the reason for delays in granting regulatory approvals. In the USA, the Food and Drug Authority (FDA) has faced heavy criticism for the delays in granting regulatory approvals for pharmaceutical drugs. However, a study (Sacks et al. 2014) conducted by researchers associated with the FDA on regulatory and scientific reasons for delay in the FDA granting regulatory approvals for new molecular entities (NMEs) for the period 2000–12 concludes,

Several potentially preventable deficiencies, including failure to select optimal drug doses and suitable study end points, accounted for significant delays in the approval of new drugs. Understanding the reasons for previous failures is helpful to improve the efficiency of clinical development for new drugs.

The study states that that many drugs are not approved by the drug regulator because the information supplied by the applicant is unsatisfactory to determine safety or efficacy, as a result of which, the applicant has to resubmit the information, thereby delaying the process. Such factors do not justify patent term extension.

On the flip side, extension of patent terms on account of administrative or regulatory delays is a serious issue not just in the context of development of generic medicines but for the development of originator drugs. Patent term extension may pressurize drug regulators to expedite the approval of drugs; this may compromise the regulator's responsible assessment of the drug's safety, quality and efficacy. Drug approval is a major legal and moral responsibility; drug regulators need to exercise extreme caution in an objective manner without being pressurized by commercial concerns. As the infamous thalidomide case reminds us, it is better to be safe than sorry.

Besides the above factors, it is important to note that the current term of 20 years for patents itself came to be established on account of administrative and regulatory delays. If one compares the history of patent laws of developed countries such as the USA, patents were for a terms of much less than 20 years (United States Patent and Trademark Office n.d.). Under the US Patents Act, 1790, patents were granted for a term of 14 years (ibid.). It was then increased in 1836 to 21 years taking into account a 7-year term extension (ibid.). However, again in 1861, the USA brought it down to 17 years without the possibility of extension (ibid.). The very purpose of rationalizing patent terms to 20 years under the TRIPS Agreement was to factor administrative and regulatory delays.

Drug regulators in both developed and developing countries are burdened due to the increasing number of applications for regulatory approval while being faced with a shortage of resources such as manpower. In the USA for instance, the process of approving generic drugs has slowed down to hit a 6-year low (ET Bureau 2014). However, efforts are being made in the wrong direction by way of patent term extension to address the issue of regulatory delays. Augmenting the resources of a constrained regulator, and improving the quality of clinical trial data provided by pharmaceutical companies, would go a long way in reducing the time required for processing regulatory approvals.

5.3 India's Drug Regulatory Laws vis-à-vis the TPP's IPR Chapter

5.3.1 Data Exclusivity Norms

The concept of data exclusivity is not explained here since the author of the previous chapter has done a fine job with that. It would suffice to say that the option of not allowing for data exclusivity is a flexibility which developing countries are entitled to under TRIPS.

Article 39 of TRIPS obliges Members to take steps for the protection of 'undisclosed commercial information'. Demandeurs argue that this provision mandates data exclusivity for clinical trial data. However, there are two qualifications inherent in Article 39.3. First, Article 39.3 requires data protection only against 'unfair commercial use'. It is difficult to construe the reliance on previously submitted clinical trial data as an 'unfair commercial use'. Furthermore, it is important to note that the drug regulators are only making a 'reference' to the clinical trial data; there is no use as such by the drug regulator or any other entity which is proscribed by Article 39.3.

Second, Article 39.3 allows Members the flexibility to refuse data protection for purposes of 'protection of the public', yet another term which is undefined under TRIPS. This is a broad phrase which by all means could be interpreted to refuse data exclusivity for public health purposes. Indeed, such an interpretation is possible in the light of the provisions of Articles 7 and 8 of the TRIPS Agreement, which envisage the protection of public interests, and also the Doha Declaration on TRIPS and Public Health. It would appear that developing countries such as India have refused data exclusivity based on these flexibilities.

In the TPP, however, it would appear that there in an attempt to entirely circumvent such flexibilities and ensure data exclusivity. Article 18.50 requires parties to provide data exclusivity for five years from the date of marketing approval of the pharmaceutical product in the territory of a TPP party. The above-discussed provisions prima facie appear to restrict the objectives of access to medicine and public health since they limit the ability of generic drug manufacturers from using clinical trial data previously submitted to the drug regulator.

The legal framework for regulatory approval of pharmaceuticals is contained in the Drugs and Cosmetics Act, 1940, and the Drugs and Cosmetics Rules, 1945 (Drug Rules), framed thereunder. Under the Drug Rules, the regulator is permitted to rely upon or refer to previously submitted clinical trial data or evidence of prior marketing approval in other countries demonstrating quality, safety and efficacy of the generic drug.

What the Indian legal framework conveys is that the originator consent is not a prerequisite for the use of third-party clinical trial data. Data exclusivity provisions are in effect absent from Indian law as far as pharmaceuticals are concerned.[1] On the other hand, originator consent is at the heart of the data exclusivity provisions in the TPP's IPR chapter. If India intends to conform to the TPP's standards, it may require amending the Drugs and Cosmetics Rules. This would definitely curtail India's policy space with regard to access to medicines.

It is possible to understand the rationale underlying data exclusivity from the text of TRIPS Article 39.3, which requires the protection of data from 'unfair commercial use'. Owing to the pressure from the originator pharmaceutical manufacturers, demandeurs might cite the proprietary nature of data and the huge investments made into the research and development that goes into developing new drugs. However, as Reichman (2009) points out, 'given that originator pharmaceutical companies would have recouped their investments and made their profits by charging high prices in developed countries, it is hard to justify any further protection of investments in R&D beyond territorial patents in the developing countries.'

Correa too addresses this issue from the perspective of legal injury. According to Correa (2010b):

> The law condemns taking advantage of another's efforts when it is the result of an illegal act, or of an act, which although legal, is dishonest or unfair. In other words, what the law condemns is not the effect of a commercial behaviour (reducing a competitor's market share), but the manner in which such effect is obtained.

---

[1] In comparison, there is a legislative proposal pending for data exclusivity in agrochemicals. Sub-clause (6), clause 12 of the Pesticides Management Bill, 2008, pending in the Indian Parliament provides for data exclusivity for a period of three years in respect of pesticides.

Correa (2010b) also gives an insightful economic perspective against data exclusivity rules:

> Companies follow attentively what their competitors do and, within the framework of commercial and industrial freedom, attempt to use all the means they can to increase the number of their own customers. If all use of another's efforts were to be considered as legally prohibited, the market economy, as we know it today, would cease to function. In fact, the dynamics of competition suppose that all economic agents will attempt to take advantage of their competitor's efforts, which would certainly not be illegitimate, unless they were to engage in illegal or morally reprehensible behaviour which could be considered as 'unfair'.

Patent Linkage Norms

The mandate of the drug regulatory authority is to act as a checkpoint for the safety, quality and the efficacy of a pharmaceutical product. However, the TPP's IPR chapter contains provisions which impose patent-related enforcement obligations on drug regulators. Article 18.51 imposes certain obligations on a TPP party if it permits third parties to rely on evidence or information concerning safety or efficacy (such as evidence of prior marketing approval) of a pharmaceutical product that has been previously approved by a party or in another territory (which need not be a TPP party). If a party permits such reliance, then clause (a) requires a party to provide a system to give notice to a patent holder or allow for a patent holder to be notified of the marketing of the pharmaceutical product informing about the third party seeking to market the product during the term of the patent. Clause (b) read with clause (c) of Article 18.51 in addition requires the party to give the patent holder adequate time and opportunity to seek administrative and judicial remedies such as injunction prior to the marketing of an allegedly patent infringing pharmaceutical.

From the above-discussed provisions, it is very clear that the drug regulatory authority is being vested with additional obligations which pertain to patent enforcement. There are several problems with this proposition. First, this burdens an already burdened regulator that has been constituted primarily for the purpose of reviewing pharmaceutical products for quality, safety and efficacy. Patent linkage goes against the nature of duties and the purpose for which the drug regulator has been constituted. A related issue is that the patent-linkage mechanism can further delay a system that is already faced with delays.

Second, an important point to be made is that the onus of surveillance, which is essentially the duty of the right-holder, is being shifted from a private person to a public authority. This is an unnecessary diversion of public resources, which can instead be used to strengthen the drug regulatory authority. Third, not only is the drug regulator required to inform the patent-holder of possible infringement, but he/she is also required to not grant marketing approval till issues of patent infringement are adjudicated. There is, thus, no reason to associate grant of marketing approval with the existence of a patent. The appropriate remedy would be for the right-holder to seek an injunction when the third party has initiated steps to launch the generic pharmaceutical after receipt of marketing approval, which is already available under Indian law. Further, adjudication of patent infringement may take inordinate period of time for settlement. This is bound to further delay the entry of generic pharmaceuticals.

India's Drugs and Cosmetics Act does not take cognizance of the status of a patent for the purposes of granting regulatory approval. Conformity to the TPP provisions would mean introducing, by way of amendment to the Drugs and Cosmetics Act, provisions for patent linkage. However, Indian jurisprudence on the subject of patent linkage gives valid reasons against patent linkage. In *Bayer Corporation v. Cipla*,[2] the Delhi High Court held that no such system could be read into Indian law. The court expressly recognized the difference in objectives of the patent law and the drug regulation law in the country. According to the Delhi High Court, the Drug Controller General of India (DCGI), which was established for the purpose of checking drugs for their safety, efficacy and quality, could not be expected to discharge obligations under the Patents Act.

The TPP's provisions on patent linkage, which are clearly TRIPS-plus, are intended to block the entry of generic pharmaceuticals into the market. While it may seem legitimate for a patent holder to expect that his patent not be exploited by another person except with his consent, or in accordance with the patent laws if without his consent, it may be excessive to expect the drug regulator to take on obligations akin to enforcement.

---

[2] 2009 (41) PTC 634 (Del.).

5.4 India's Trademark Laws vis-à-vis the TPP's IPR Chapter

Besides implications for the patents regime and the drug regulatory regime, conformity in the context of the Indian trademark regime as contained in the Trade Marks Act, 1999, could also pose serious implications. These are discussed below.

Border Measures Against 'Confusingly Similar' Goods

Counterfeiting and trade in counterfeited trademark goods, and piracy and trade in pirated copyright goods are perhaps one of the biggest challenges faced by IP enforcement and customs officials the world over. IP-related border measures exercised by customs officials are important in eliminating trade in counterfeited trademark goods and pirated copyrighted goods. TRIPS allows Members considerable flexibility in designing the mechanisms for enforcement of IP rights at the borders. However, provisions have been included in the TPP's IPR chapter which distort what is intended under the TRIPS Agreement.

Article 18.76 of the TPP's IPR chapter requires parties to provide for applications to suspend the release of, or to detain, any suspected counterfeit or 'confusingly similar trademark' or pirated copyright good that is imported into the territory of a party.

The provisions on border measures in the TPP prima facie seem benign and legitimate for the protection of the right-holders. It also seems consistent with the TRIPS norms. However, what needs to be understood is the extension of the scope of these measures to 'confusingly similar' trademarked goods. Article 51 of the TRIPS Agreement requires, as part of border measures concerning IPR protection, the suspension of release of goods which are 'counterfeited trademark goods'. On the other hand, the TPP's IPR chapter goes a step ahead in extending the scope of the measures to 'confusingly similar' trademarked goods. The effect of Article 18.76 is that it would result in including goods (generics) similar to trademarked goods within the definition of counterfeit goods, even if they are not counterfeit. This is clearly a TRIPS-inconsistent measure.

The above-discussed provision would have the effect of throwing a huge net around generic medicines as customs officials even from countries with such a legal regime would be compelled to seize imported generic drugs for the reason that they are 'confusingly similar' to the parent drug. The effect of such provisions is that it would be a deterrent to legitimate trade in generic drugs between countries. The provision also reminds countries of the troubling incidents that took place in May 2009 when European customs authorities seized generic drug consignments manufactured by Indian companies and destined to Vanuatu on the grounds of alleged trademark infringement. In this instance, the customs authorities seemed ignorant of the fact that the goods in question were not 'counterfeited trademark goods' and instead conflated the phrase with 'confusingly similar' goods. Though the consignments were ultimately released, it highlights the problems that could arise if 'confusingly similar' was the global norm as against the extant TRIPS norm.

Another problem pertains to the destination of the goods in question. Article 18.76 requires that the border enforcement authorities of TPP countries should have the power to initiate border measures ex officio for goods that are not only imported or destined for export but also in transit. This norm is TRIPS plus in nature as it requires TPP Members to mandatorily extend border measures to in-transit goods. whereas in the case of the WTO, TRIPS Article 51 read with footnote 13 makes the application of border measures to in-transit goods optional for WTO Members.

The threats to legitimate trade in generic drugs as a result of the aforesaid TPP's provisions pertaining to border measures in respect of in-transit goods can be understood by the same example of the 2009 seizure by the European Union (EU) customs authorities of Indian-manufactured generic drugs destined to South American countries transiting through Europe. If the scope of destination with respect to 'confusingly similar' goods were to extend to in-transit goods, this would entail TPP countries across both sides of the Pacific Ocean to seize such drugs, further hindering legitimate trade in generic drugs. Generic drug exporters from countries such as India would have to be wary of transiting through countries with such border measures.

Border measures pertaining to the protection of IPRs in India are contained in the Customs Act, 1962, the IPR (Imported Goods) Enforcement Rules, 2007, among other instruments. The border measures in the Indian legal framework do not recognize the category of 'confusingly similar goods'. The legal framework in respect of border measures described above is consistent with the TRIPS norms and will not affect legitimate trade. However, the provisions in Article 18.76 pertaining to 'confusingly similar' goods raise serious questions.

Furthermore, conformity by India to the TPP standards discussed above will sound the death knell for legitimate trade in generic drugs. Hailed as the pharmacy to the developing world, India's exports of generic drugs are crucial to several developing countries which do not have a mature manufacturing base for generic drugs in their countries. Provisions of such a nature also militate against the spirit and text of the Doha Declaration on Public Health.

Expanded Scope of Trademark Registrability

The very notion of trademark has been understood to be a sign that is visually perceptible. However, the TPP's IPR chapter seeks to enlarge the scope of trademark by requiring parties to allow for marks other than those of visual perception such as sound marks and smell marks. According to Article 18.18 of the IPR chapter, no party may deny registration of a trademark for the reason that the sign of which it is composed of is a sound. Additionally, parties are required to make best efforts to register scent marks.

The implication of acceding to the above-discussed provisions for India's trademark regime is that definitional changes will be required to the Trade Marks Act, 1999, which currently limits the essence of the definition of trademark to visual representation. If India decides to conform to the TPP's IPR chapter, India may be required to amend its Trade Marks Act to allow for non-traditional trademarks. A serious implication of including scents within the ambit of trademarks is that a generic drug having a scent similar to a parent drug could be susceptible to IPR enforcement on grounds of trade mark infringement. Such implications for access to medicines are better described by Gopakumar and Smith (2010):

> Non-traditional trademarks have direct implications for access to medicines, because the medicine market is highly brand driven. Physicians often prescribe by brand name, leaving consumers little choice. Moreover, consumers may be reluctant to switch to a product with a different taste or smell. Meanwhile, due to the monopoly that results from patent protection, the originator company has ample time to build brand awareness. The pharmaceutical industry may try to use a taste mark or smell mark

to block generic competition. This could delay generic competition, and result in prices of medicines remaining high even in the absence of patent monopoly.

Gopakumar and Smith's concerns are not unfounded. Given how attempts are being made by certain countries to expand the scope of trademark infringement and also the scope of enforcement action in respect of trademark infringement, extending non-traditional trademarks for scents could pose a problem for access to medicines. Though there has been no case yet involving enforcement action in respect of generic medicines for violation of a non-traditional trademark, the same should not be taken lightly; there is a need to examine carefully the implications for access to medicines that would follow if registrability of trademarks for scents are allowed. In this context, India should tread cautiously in allowing for the registrability of non-traditional trademarks such as scents.

5.5 India's Plant Varieties Protection Law vis-à-vis UPOV Convention

The TRIPS Agreement does not contain any specific provisions in terms of detailed rights and obligations concerning the protection of plant varieties. In fact, Members are not obliged to grant patentability of plants and animals (other than microorganisms) in their national legislations. However, TRIPS requires WTO Members to provide for the protection of plant varieties either by patents or by an effective sui generis system or by any combination thereof. On the basis of this provision, many WTO Members provide for the protection of the plant varieties by way of their respective national legislations. In India, legal provisions concerning plant varieties protection are contained in the Protection of Plant Varieties and Farmers' Rights Act, 2001 (PPVFR Act).

Even though TRIPS does not contain specific provisions concerning the protection of plant varieties other than in Article 27.3(b), efforts have been made at other venues for developing multilateral legal instruments concerning the protection of plant varieties. In 1961, the International Convention for the Protection of New Varieties of Plants (UPOV Convention) was signed. While the UPOV Convention has been in existence since 1961, its membership as of October 2015 does not exceed 74.[3] Out of these 74 Members, not all are party to the 1991 Act, which is the last revised version of the UPOV Convention.[4]

Conspicuously, India is not a party to any versions of the UPOV Convention. India's PPVFR Act has been framed keeping in mind the need to balance the interests of farmers with that of plant variety breeders. However, under an international regime (such as the TPP) where India would have to conform to the UPOV Convention, India would have to revise its PPVFR Act to conform its provisions to the UPOV Convention. This section reviews the legal issues and concerns that would arise if India took steps towards conforming its PPVFR Act to the UPOV Convention of 1991.

Scope of Varieties that Can Be Registered

Section 14 of the PPVFR Act defines the scope of the 'variety' that can be registered under the PPVFR Act. Under section 14, clauses (b) and (c) recognize the registrability of an extant variety and a farmers' variety, respectively. In respect of a new variety, however, clause (a) of section 14 read with subsection (2) of section 29 recognizes the registrability of only such genera and species that the Central government has notified. This policy space under the PPVFR Act is at odds with the provisions of the UPOV Convention as discussed below.

Under paragraph (2)(ii), Article 3 of the UPOV Convention, Members of the UPOV are required to allow the applicability of the UPOV Convention to all plant genera and species. The implication of this provision is that the PPVFR Act may have to be amended to provide protection even for living modified organisms (LMO) plant varieties. However, it is to be noted that Article 18 of the UPOV Convention recognizes that a grant of protection does not entail the right of the breeder to production, market or import/export of an LMO plant variety.

---

[3] Members of the International Union for the Protection of New Varieties of Plants, International Union for the Protection of New Varieties of Plants (UPOV), Status on 22 October 2015, http://www.upov.int/export/sites/upov/members/en/pdf/pub423.pdf

[4] The other versions are that of the 1961 text revised in 1972 and 1978.

Conditions of Protection

Criteria for Registration

The criteria for registration of a new plant variety under the PPVFR Act are broader under the UPOV Convention as compared to the PPVFR Act from at least two perspectives.

Under the PPVFR Act, section 15 establishes the criteria for registrability of a new plant variety. Under subsection (1), these are novelty, distinctiveness, uniformity and stability. These criteria and the definitions of each of these criteria are substantially similar to the criteria and their respective definitions laid down in the UPOV Convention. There are, however, certain differences. First, with regard to the definition of 'distinctness', clause (b) of subsection (3) deems a variety to be distinct if it is clearly distinguishable 'by at least one essential characteristic' from any other variety whose existence is a matter of common knowledge in any country at the time of filing of the application. This is slightly different from the language of Article 7 of the UPOV Convention, which deems a variety to be distinct if it is clearly distinguishable from any other variety whose existence is a matter of common knowledge in any country at the time of filing of the application.

The PPVFR Act uses a clear, qualitative criterion (of at least one essential characteristic) for establishing distinctness. This basis is narrower than the criterion stipulated in Article 7 of the UPOV Convention. The use of only a clear, qualitative criterion under the PPVFR Act establishes a narrower threshold for a variety to be eligible for protection.

In the case of the definitions of uniformity and stability, clauses (c) and (d) of the PPVFR Act define 'uniformity' and 'stability' in terms of essential characteristics, whereas the UPOV Convention defines these two criteria in terms of relevant characteristics. This is a broader threshold for being eligible for protection than that in the PPVFR Act.

Under clause (h) of section 1 of the PPVFR Act, 'essential characteristics' has been defined to mean 'such heritable traits of a plant variety which are determined by the expression of one or more genes of other heritable determinants that contribute to the principal features, performance or value of the plant variety'. The UPOV Convention itself does not define 'relevant characteristic'; its meaning has been clarified in the General Introduction to the Examination of Distinctness, Uniformity and Stability (DUS) and the Development of Harmonized Descriptions of

New Varieties of Plants (General Introduction) developed by the UPOV Council. According to the General Introduction,

> [R]elevant characteristics of a variety include at least all characteristics used for the examination of DUS or included in the variety description established at the date of grant of protection of that variety. Any obvious characteristic may be considered relevant, irrespective of whether it appears in the Test Guidelines or not.

Prohibition of 'Further or Different Conditions'

An important legal aspect of the UPOV Convention is clause (2) of Article 5, which restricts the imposition of 'further or different conditions' for the grant of the breeders' right apart from the criteria of novelty, distinctness, uniformity, and stability stipulated in clause (1) of Article 5. The implication of clause (2) is that it restricts the regulatory space for a national government to define any conditions other than novelty, distinctness, uniformity, and stability for registration of a plant variety, such as disclosures pertaining to genetic material used in the development of the plant variety. In fact, that a prohibition on registration on failing to meet this particular disclosure obligation is inconsistent with the UPOV Convention has been unequivocally clarified by the UPOV in its reply to the Notification of 26 June 2003 issued by the Executive Secretary to Convention on Biological Diversity.[5] According to the UPOV,

> [I]f a country decides, in the frame of its overall policy, to introduce a mechanism for the disclosure of countries of origin or geographical origin of genetic resources, such a mechanism should not be introduced in a narrow sense, as a condition for plant variety protection. A separate mechanism from the plant variety protection legislation, such as that used for phytosanitary requirements, could be applied uniformly to all activities concerning the commercialization of varieties, including, for example, seed quality or other marketing related regulations.

The nature of the aforesaid provisions inherently conflicts with some of the aspects of the PPVFR Act. Under section 14 of the PPVFR Act, a

---

[5] *Reply of UPOV to the Notification of 26 June 2003, from the Executive Secretary of the Convention on Biological Diversity (CBD)*, adopted by the Council of UPOV at its 37th ordinary session on 23 October 2003, International Union for the Protection of New Varieties of Plants. Available at http://www.upov.int/news/en/2003/pdf/cbd_response_oct232003.pdf (last visited 18 July 2017).

breeder seeking registration of a variety under the PPVFR Act is required to make an application to the Plant Varieties Registry (Registry). As per subsection (1) of section 20 of the PPVFR Act, the Registrar, on receipt of the application, after making the necessary inquiry, may accept the application either absolutely, or subject to such conditions or limitations he deems fit. Subsection (2) of section 20 further states that the Registrar may either require the applicant to amend the application for registration, or he/she may reject the application if he/she is satisfied that the application does not comply with the requirements of the PPVFR Act or the rule and regulations made thereunder.

An instance of a statutory requirement that will have to be fulfilled by an applicant-breeder is stipulated in subsection (1) of section 40 of the PPVFR Act, which requires disclosure of information regarding the use of genetic material conserved by any tribal or rural families in the breeding or development of such variety. Failure on part of the applicant-breeder entitles the Registrar to reject the application for registration. The purpose of the subsection is ostensibly to ensure transparency in the sharing of any potential benefits that may accrue to the breeder from commercial exploitation of the variety, with the tribal or rural community concerned with the particular genetic material.

The other important provisions relevant for the purposes of registration/protection under the PPVFR Act pertain to pre-grant and post-grant opposition. Under clause (1) of section 21 of the PPVFR Act, the Registrar may, after accepting an application for registration, invite post-grant opposition. Clause (3) of section 21 allows such interested persons to oppose registration on grounds including[6] that the grant of registration may not be in public interest or that the variety in concern may have adverse effect on the environment. After taking into account all aspects of the due process stipulated in section 21, the Registrar may either uphold or reject the opposition.

Another important restriction in applying for registration under the PPVFR Act is that clause (c) of subsection (1) of section 18 prohibits registration of a plant variety containing any gene or gene sequence involving terminator technology. This technology, better known as 'genetic use restriction technology (GURT)', has been subject to a lot of criticism. According to a study by the Food and Agricultural Organization (2002), 'GURTs could have considerable impacts, both positive and negative,

---

[6] The other two grounds are opposition to entitlement of the application to the breeder's right as against the applicant, and that the variety is not registrable under the PPVFR Act.

on agricultural biodiversity and agricultural farming systems: these impacts, together with possible policy considerations.'

It may be argued that the provisions discussed above are in the nature of 'further or different' conditions in the context of paragraph 2 of Article 5 of the UPOV Convention. If India revised the PPVFR Act to conform to the UPOV Convention, it will have to delete or amend many of these important provisions.

Prohibition Against Seed Saving

The UPOV Convention substantially deals with the rights of only one stakeholder—the breeder. There is hardly any substantial provision in the UPOV Convention that deals with the rights of the farmer or of any other stakeholder. This is not the case with the PPVFR Act which explicitly recognizes the rights of farmers with regard to plant varieties. An important farmer right which has been recognized under the PPVFR Act is the right to save seeds. Under clause (iv), subsection (1) of section 39, farmers have been given the express right to save, use, resow, exchange, share or sell their farm produce including seed of a protected variety. They are only prohibited from selling branded seed[7] of any protected variety.

The PPFVR Act also expressly lays down the rights of a breeder on registration of a plant variety. Under subsection (1) of section 28, a breeder has the exclusive right to produce, sell, market, distribute, import or export the variety.[8] The PPFVR Act simply does not recognize the right of a breeder to prohibit stocking of seeds, that is, seed-saving without the breeder's authorization.

The UPOV Convention on the other hand does not permit farmers to exercise their right to stock seeds without authorization of the breeder. Article 14(1)(a) expressly lists those acts in respect of the propagating material of the protected variety which requires authorization of the breeder, one of which—sub-clause (vii) deals with the stocking of the propagating material, that is, seeds. Without being able to save and exchange seeds, costs will go up for the farmers as they would have to keep buying seeds from the breeder.

---

[7] According to the 'explanation' to clause (iv), 'branded seed' means any seed put in a package or any other container and labelled in a manner indicating that such seed is of a variety protected under the PPVFR Act.

[8] The definition of 'variety' under clause (za) of section 2 includes propagating material of the variety.

'Limitations and Conditions' of Authorization by the Breeder

When authorizing the exploitation of a variety, a breeder may wish to impose certain limitations and conditions such as remuneration, period of authorization, method of authorization, and quality and quantity of the production. The difference between the UPOV Convention and the PPFVR Act in respect of authorization by the breeder to exploit the plant variety pertains to the limitations and conditions that may be imposed by the breeder. Under Article 14(1)(b) of the UPOV Convention, these limitations and conditions are the decision of the breeder with no proscription by the local legislation on plant variety protection.[9] Under the PPVFR, however, subsection (2) of section 28, which grants the breeder the right to authorize any person to produce, sell, market or deal with the registered variety, permits the breeder to impose limitations and conditions only to the extent specified in the PPFVR Regulations.

Under Regulation 13(1) of the PPFVR Regulations, an authorization by a registered breeder to exploit a variety has to be made in Form 1A annexed to the PPFVR Regulations. The terms and conditions contained in Form 1A pertain to term, territory, revision, termination and single instrument. Indian law also consists of provisions governing the price/royalty/license fee that can be demanded by the breeder. The relevant legislation in this regard is the Essential Commodities Act of 1955. Under this statute, the Central government has the power to control the price of a product notified as an essential commodity.

From the above discussion, it is clear that the limitations and conditions, which a breeder can make his authorization for exploitation of the variety subject to, are controlled by the applicable laws. However, Article 14(1)(b) of the UPOV Convention may have seemingly large implications for these legal provisions if India joined the UPOV Convention, since neither the law nor the government would be able to impose any conditions or limitations in respect of authorization of exploitation by the breeder.

---

[9] *Guidance for the Preparation of Laws Based on the 1991 Act of the UPOV Convention*, UPOV/INF/6/4, International Union for the Protection of New Varieties of Plants (UPOV), adopted by the Council at its 49th ordinary session on 29 October 2015. Available at http://www.upov.int/edocs/mdocs/upov/en/c/43/upov_inf_6_1_draft_3.pdf (last visited 18 July 2017).

Compulsory Licensing: Scope of Compensation

Section 47 of the PPVFR Act recognizes the space for compulsory licensing of breeders rights in public interest. Subsection (1) allows any interested person to make an application for compulsory licensing on the grounds that the reasonable requirement of the public for seed or other propagating material of the variety has not been satisfied, or that the seed or other propagating material of the variety is not available to the public at a reasonable price.

Section 51(1) of the PPVFR Act requires that reasonable compensation should be given to a breeder whose variety has been subject to compulsory license. Clause (i) stipulates that the reasonable compensation should be secured having regard to the nature of the variety, the expenditure incurred by the breeder and other relevant factors.

The UPOV Convention also recognizes space for compulsory licensing of plant varieties. Article 17(1) recognizes the right of a UPOV Member to issue compulsory licenses on grounds of public interest. However, in terms of compensation to the licensor, there is an important difference between the UPOV Convention and the PPVFR Act. Under Article 17(2), UPOV Members are required to ensure that the concerned breeder receives 'equitable remuneration'.

If India were to revise the PPVFR Act to conform to the compulsory license provisions of the UPOV, the standard of compensation that it may have to provide to the breeder will have to be one of 'equitable remuneration'. However, it may be possible to argue that the term 'equitable remuneration' is equivalent to the term 'reasonable remuneration', and hence no revision may be required. This ambiguity is because neither of these terms have actually been defined in any of the texts nor in international legal jurisprudence.

Term of Protection

Under the PPVFR Act, the term of protection for registered plant varieties is two-tiered. Under section 24, there is first an initial period of validity accruing under the certificate of registration granted under the Act for a new variety. After the expiry of this initial period, the registration of the plant variety may be reviewed and renewed for a further period. Under subsection (6) of section 24, the initial period of validity of registration for a variety in the case of trees and vines is 9 years, while in the case of others it is for a period of 6 years. Clauses (i), (ii) and (iii) of subsection (6) lay down the total period of validity (the sum of the initial period of validity and extended validity) to be not more than 18 years in the case of trees and vines, 15 years in case of an extant variety, and 15 years in other cases.

Under the UPOV Convention, however, there is no two-tier period of validity like in the PPVFR Act. Paragraphs (1) and (2) of Article 19 requires right to be granted to the breeders for a fixed period of not less than 25 years from the date of grant of the breeders' right, and 20 years in other cases.

The ostensible reason for a review-based extension of the validity of protection for a plant variety under the PPVFR Act is ostensibly to review whether granting a longer term of protection for the registered plant variety would be in public interest, though the PPVFR Act does not stipulate such criteria. This policy discretion has been retained keeping in mind the vitality of the agriculture sector for a developing country such as India. The UPOV Convention, however, erodes this policy and goes a step further in requiring a term of protection longer than in the PPVFR Act. While it is understandable that a long-enough duration of protection is required to enable breeders to recover their investments in developing the plant variety, the longer monopolistic protection under the UPOV Convention may not be justified and is at odds with India's policy space in this regard.

5.6 Conclusion

The TPP's IPR chapter is undoubtedly a part of the series in the history of efforts to introduce TRIPS-plus norms through non-WTO agreements with most of the standards of IP protection in the TPP being more favourable to IPR holders in comparison to the norms contained in the TRIPS Agreement. Given the opposition to a maximalist negotiating agenda for TRIPS at multilateral forums such as the WTO, demandeurs who had responded by pursuing such an agenda earlier through bilateral trade agreements are now doing so by way of mega-FTAs such as the TPP (Flynn et al. 2011).

Given the TPP's probable use as a template for future negotiations at the WTO, this chapter has analyzed and discussed the implications that would arise if India revises its IPR laws to conform to the TPP's protectionist IPR standards. This chapter finds that the changes that would have to be brought about in India's patents laws, plant protection laws, trademark laws and drug regulatory laws are of such fundamental nature that they would compromise India's public policy interests.

Some of the major changes that would have to be carried out include deleting or amending section 3(d) of the Patents Act and thereby allowing for evergreening of pharmaceutical patents. It is important at this juncture to highlight that such a norm is actually TRIPS-minus as it lowers the threshold for patentability rather than maintaining a strong standard which is what IP jurisprudence advocates. Coupled with obligations on patent linkages and extending patent terms on account of delays in grant of patents, these measures would extend the monopoly over vital pharmaceuticals.

Given the strong opposition to more protectionist standards of patents for pharmaceutical products, it would now seem that different channels for maintaining protectionist grip on pharmaceuticals are being made. Some of these are attempt to extend such protection through the regulatory front. In the TPP context, this would include data exclusivity, which is especially becoming an increasingly acceptable alternative to patent protection for pharmaceutical products (Reichman 2009).

The TPP also has major implications for legitimate international trade in generic medicines given that the TPP's IPR chapter intends to expand the scope of trademark protection-related border measures to 'confusingly similar' trademarked goods. Like how blocking rivers could dry up the oceans, similarly, blocking export, import and even transit of generic drugs on the grounds of being 'confusingly similar' goods could halt legitimate international trade and thereby access to generic pharmaceuticals.

An important aspect of the provisions concerning border measures is that India will face problems not only on account of conforming to these provisions, but also if other countries conformed their border measures to the TPP's protectionist standards. This will certainly have an adverse impact on Indian exports which in turn will have an adverse impact on other developing countries critically dependent on the supply of generic medicines from India. Also, as explained earlier, this is clearly TRIPS-inconsistent and falls afoul of WTO Members' commitments.

The presence of public health safeguards—the references to interpret and implement the provisions of the TPP's IPR chapter in a manner consistent with the objectives to protect public health and promote access to medicines—has been inserted ostensibly to assuage any concerns. However, the absence of the requisite flexibilities in the TPP's IPR chapter as compared to the TRIPS Agreement makes these safeguards moot; the space for interpreting and implementing these provisions simply do not exist. The protectionist IP standards could spell negative effects for India's generic drugs industry by slowing and halting the production of generic medicines.

Besides the discussion on IPR provisions pertaining to pharmaceuticals, this chapter has also discussed the IPR provisions pertaining to plant variety protection. For the right reasons, India has avoided joining the UPOV Convention which is strongly geared towards protecting breeders' rights at the cost of other stakeholders including farmers and the local communities. However, conforming its plant variety protection laws to the UPOV Convention, which is required by the TPP's IPR chapter, will seriously prejudice India's food sovereignty.

Given the initiatives by certain countries at various forums, there would be pressure on all countries to reshape their IPR laws to conform to the standards espoused in the TPP's IPR chapter. However, based on the analysis and the reasons discussed in this chapter, India should exercise great caution in acceding to these norms. It would be in India's best interests to resist any pressure towards conforming to the IPR provisions of the TPP in its current form. It is unlikely that any benefits are to be derived from conforming to such protectionist standards. Furthermore, like how Ha Joon Chang described the First World's attempts in 'kicking away the ladder' for the developing world, conforming to the TPP's protectionist standards would mean that India itself would be 'kicking away the ladder' without even having reached the top.

Appendix: Comparative Table

S. no.	Issue	TPP Article	Relevant Indian Law	Comments
1.	Scope of patentability	Paragraph 2 of Article 18.37	Section 3(d) of Indian Patents Act, 1972	Indian law provisions prohibiting evergreening will have to be deleted to allow for a broader scope of patentability of pharmaceutical products.
2.	Extension of patent term	paragraph 3 of Article 18.46	Indian Patents Act, 1972	Indian law does not provide for extension of patent terms on any ground whatsoever.
3.	Clinical trial data exclusivity	Article 18.50	Drugs and Cosmetics Rules, 1945, under Drugs and Cosmetics Act, 1940	Indian law does not provide for data exclusivity in the context of pharmaceuticals.
4.	Patent linkage	Article 18.51	Indian Patents Act, 1972; Drugs and Cosmetics Act, 1940	Neither the patents law nor the drug regulatory laws provide for patent linkage.
5.	Border measures pertaining to trademarks	Article 18.76	Notification No. 51/2010—Customs (N.T.) dated 30th June 2010 r/w IPR (Imported Goods) Enforcement Rules, 2007 AND Circular No. 41/2007—Customs dated 29th October 2007 AND Trade Marks Act, 1999	Indian laws only recognize border measures in respect of 'false trademark' as defined in the Trade Marks Act, 1999.
6.	Scope of trademark registrability	Article 18.18	Clause (zb) r/w clause (m) of Subsection (1) of section Trade Marks Act, 1999	The definition of trademark in Indian law will have to be amended to include non-visual trademarks.

7.	Plant varieties protection—scope of registrability of varieties	paragraph (2)(ii), Article 3 of the UPOV Convention	clause (a) of section 14 read with subsection (2) of section 29 of the Protection of Plant Varieties and Farmers' Rights Act, 2001	Indian law will have to be amended to allow for registrability of all plant varieties.
8.	Criteria for registration of a plant variety	Article 7 of the UPOV Convention	clause (b) of subsection (3) of section 15 of the PPVFR Act	Indian law requirement that a new plant variety have at least one essential characteristic for registrability will have to be amended.
9.	Seed saving	sub-clause (vii) of clause (a) under paragraph (1) of Article 14 of the UPOV Convention	Clause (iv), subsection (1) of section 39 of the PPVFR Act Subsection (1) of section 28 of the PPVFR Act	Indian law will have to be amended to prohibit seed saving.
10.	Prohibition of 'further or different conditions' for registrability	clause (2) of Article 5 of the UPOV Convention	Subsection (1) of section 20 of the PPVFR Act Subsection (1) of section 40 of the PPVFR Act clause (1) r/w clause (3) of section 21 of the PPVFR Act clause (c) of subsection (1) of section 18 of the PPVFR Act	
11.	Term of protection	Paragraphs (1) and (2) of Article 19	Subsection (6) of the section 24 of the PPVFR Act	Indian law will have to be amended to allow for longer periods of protection to a breeder.

References

Abbott, Ryan B., Rania Bader, Lina Bajjali, Taher Abu El Samen, Thamer Obeidat, Hanan Sboul, Mustafa Shwayat, and Ibrahim Alabbadi. 2012. 'The Price of Medicines in Jordan: The Cost of Trade-Based Intellectual Property'. *Journal of Generic Medicines* 9(2): 75–85. doi:10.1177/1741134312447499.

Abrol, Dinesh, Sivakami Dhulap, Malini Aisola, and Nidhi Singh. 2016, March. 'Pharmaceuticals, Product Patent and TRIPS Implementation'. Working Paper No. 191, Institute for Studies in Industrial Development, New Delhi.

Correa, Carlos M. 2010a. 'Patentability Standards: When is an Invention Patentable'. In *Intellectual Property Rights and Access to Medicines*, 39–50. New Delhi: World Health Organization, Regional Office for South-East Asia. Retrieved 7 July 2014, from http://apps.who.int/medicinedocs/documents/s19580en/s19580en.pdf

———. 2010b. 'Protection of Data Submitted for the Registration of Pharmaceutical Products: TRIPS Requirements and "TRIPS-Plus" Provisions'. In *Intellectual Property and Access to Medicines*, 131–40. New Delhi: World Health Organization, Regional Office for South-East Asia.

Economic Times Bureau. 2014. 'US Generic Drug Approval Delays Hit Growth Plans of Indian Firms'. *The Economic Times*, December 2. Retrieved 2 February 2015, from http://articles.economictimes.indiatimes.com/2014-12-02/news/56649153_1_drug-approval-usfda-drug-applications

Faunce, Thomas, Jimmy Bai, and Duy Nguyen. 2010. 'Impact of the Australia-US Free Trade Agreement on the Australian Medicines Regulation and Prices'. *Journal of Generic Medicines* 7 (1): 1–12. Retrieved 2 April 2017, from http://ssrn.com/abstract=1547563

Fergusson, Ian F., Mark A. McMinimy, and Brock R. Williams. 2015, 20 March. 'The Trans-Pacific Partnership (TPP) Negotiations and Issues for Congress'. Congressional Research Service Report, prepared for members and committee of Congress. Retrieved 2 April 2017, from https://fas.org/sgp/crs/row/R42694.pdf

Flynn, Sean, Margot Kaminski, Brook Baker, and Jimmy Koo. 2011. 'Public Interest Analysis of the US Trans Pacific Partnership Proposal for an IP Chapter'. *PIJIP Research Paper Series* 21: 1–56. Retrieved 20 June 2015, from http://digitalcommons.wcl.american.edu/research/21

Gopakumar, K.M., and Sanya R. Smith. 2010. 'IPR Provisions in FTAs: Implications for Access to Medicines'. In *Intellectual Property and Access to Medicines*. New Delhi: World Health Organization, Regional Office for South-East Asia.

Gopalakrishnan, N.S. 2010. 'TRIPS Flexibilities: The Case of India'. In *Intellectual Property and Access to Medicines*, 63–74. New Delhi: World Health Organization: Regional Office for South-East Asia. Retrieved 8 June 2014, from http://apps.who.int/medicinedocs/documents/s19580en/s19580en.pdf

Reichman, Jerome H. 2009. 'Rethinking the Role of Clinical Trial Data in International Intellectual Property Law: The Case for a Public Goods Approach'. *Marquette Intellectual Property Law Review* 13 (1): 1–68.

Sacks, Leonard V., Hala H. Shamsuddin, Yuliya I. Yasinskaya, Khaled Bouri, Michael L. Lanthier, and Rachel E. Sherman. 2014. 'Scientific and Regulatory Reasons for Delay and Denial of FDA Approval of Initial Applications for New Drugs,

2000–2012'. *Journal of American Medical Association* 311 (4): 378–84. doi:10.1001/jama.2013.282542.

Shaffer, Ellen R., and Joseph E. Brenner. 2009. 'A Trade Agreement's Impact on Access to Generic Drugs'. *Health Affairs* 28 (5): w957–w968. doi:10.1377/hlthaff.28.5.w957.

United Nations. 2002, October. 'Potential Impacts of Genetic Use Restriction Technologies (GURTs) on Agricultural Biodiversity and Agricultural Production Systems'. Technical Study, Food and Agriculture Organization of the United Nations, Commission on Genetic Resources for Food and Agriculture. Retrieved 20 May 2016, from https://www.cbd.int/doc/meetings/cop/cop-07/information/cop-07-inf-31-en.pdf

United States Patent and Trademark Office. n.d. 'Patent Term Calculator: History of Changes to Patent Terms'. Retrieved 10 September 2014, from http://www.uspto.gov/patent/laws-and-regulations/patent-term-calculator

6

Investment Protection in TPP

Analysis from an Indian Perspective

Shailja Singh

6.1 Background and Introduction

The Trans-Pacific Partnership Agreement (TPP) contains a detailed chapter enshrining the rules governing investment in the TPP signatory countries. The stated objective of the TPP's investment chapter is to set out 'rules requiring non-discriminatory investment policies and protections that assure basic rule of law protections, while protecting the ability of signatory countries' governments to achieve legitimate public policy objectives'.[1] At its core, this chapter is not much different from other existing international investment agreements (IIAs).[2] In fact, a plain reading of the chapter brings out several similarities between the TPP and other IIAs, especially those signed by the United States of America (USA) in recent years. Hence, any evaluation of the TPP's investment chapter cannot be done in isolation. It has to be carried out in the larger context of the current international investment law regime, and the various well-documented ills that plague it.

The international investment law regime has been facing criticism on several counts. The broad and often vague substantive obligations, limited regulatory flexibility for pursuing public policy objectives, coupled with an

---

[1] See Summary of the TPP, available at https://ustr.gov/about-us/policy-offices/press-office/press-releases/2015/october/summary-trans-pacific-partnership (last visited 16 May 2017).

[2] The term IIA includes investment chapters in comprehensive economic partnership agreements, as well as stand-alone bilateral investment treaties (BITs).

investor–state dispute settlement (ISDS) mechanism that has a propensity to come out with inconsistent rulings—without an appellate mechanism—are just some of its problems. The TPP does not seek to dramatically reform this system. Hence, to a large degree, these problems extend to the TPP framework as well. While the TPP's future might be uncertain—with Japan pushing for a TPP-11 Agreement sans the USA—its investment chapter template will continue to be relevant for future agreements, and therefore requires a closer analysis, especially from an Indian perspective.

India is no stranger to IIAs—having signed 83 bilateral investment treaties (BITs; 72 in force) and 4 comprehensive economic partnership agreements (CEPAs) having an investment chapter. Of the TPP signatory countries, India has an existing BIT with Vietnam, Australia, Brunei and Malaysia. India also has a CEPA with Malaysia, Singapore and Japan.

This chapter aims to analyse some of the key provisions of Chapter 9 of the TPP that deals with investment. It is divided into four parts, the first being background and introduction. The second part provides a brief overview of the relationship between IIAs and foreign investment. The third part discusses select provisions of the TPP's investment chapter—their scope, coverage and implications on the regulatory space of the TPP signatory countries. It also analyses how the TPP compares with India's own model BIT[3] and the India–Japan CEPA (India–Japan CEPA).[4] The last part provides some concluding thoughts on the subject.

6.2 IIAs and Foreign Investment Flows: Myths and Realities

The international investment regime has seen a proliferation of IIAs in recent years. There are currently 2,563 BITs and other IIAs in force.[5] This network of IIAs provides foreign investors and their investments in

---

[3] The Indian Model BIT is available at http://finmin.nic.in/sites/default/files/ModelText-India_BIT%20%281 %29.pdf?download=1(last visited 16 May 2017).

[4] The India–Japan CEPA was signed on 15 February 2011 and came into force on 1 August 2011.

[5] See http://investmentpolicyhub.unctad.org/IIA (last visited 16 May 2017).

the host countries a range of protection, including international remedies in the form of ISDS. Countries sign IIAs and thereby cede national sovereignty on certain economic policies with an aim to promote foreign investment. It is, however, far from evident that these IIAs have resulted in the promised increase in foreign direct investment (FDI; Bernasconi-Osterwalder et al. 2012, 8), leading to the threshold issue of whether an IIA is required at all to attract FDI. The existing literature on this is divided. Neumayer and Spess (2005, 28) conclude from their quantitative analysis that developing countries signing a higher number of BITs with major capital exporting developed countries are likely to have received more FDI in return. They, however, caution that whether the demonstrated benefits from signing a BIT are higher than the substantial costs developing countries incur in negotiating, signing, concluding and complying with obligations typically contained in such treaties is impossible to tell (ibid.). Some scholars argue that it is not the signing of a BIT per se, rather the inclusion and strength of key investment provisions that determine FDI flow in a State. Berger et al. (2010, 19) found strong evidence that liberal admission rules promote bilateral FDI, and the existence and coverage of national treatment provisions in the pre-establishment phase had a highly significant and positive impact on FDI flows, independent of the method employed for the evaluation. On the contrary, studies have also shown that there is no significant correlation between IIAs and foreign investment (Padmanabhan 2012, 65), and the IIAs alone are neither necessary nor sufficient for attracting foreign investment (Bernasconi-Osterwalder et al. 2012, 9; Sachs and Sauvant 2009).

The United Nations Conference on Trade and Development (UNCTAD), too, has undertaken a number of studies on the issue. According to one such study, the decision to make foreign investment in a country is guided by a host of factors, such as the favourable economic conditions, financial incentives, political stability, and sound domestic judicial system (UNCTAD 2009, 109).[6] Moreover, one of the most recent studies on the subject, the UNCTAD's *Trade and Development Report* (2014a, 159), based on a rigorous empirical exercise concludes

---

[6] The UNCTAD has identified three broad types of host country determinants, namely: (a) the general policy framework for foreign investment, including economic, political and social stability, the legislation affecting foreign investment and any other policies affecting FDI locational decisions; (b) economic determinants, such as the market size, cost of resources and other inputs or the availability of natural resources; and (c) business facilitation, including investment promotion.

that international investment treaties 'appear to have no effect on bilateral North–South FDI flows'.

This can be seen from the example of Brazil, which is one of the highest recipients of FDI globally. Brazil had not ratified a single BIT till 2015. In 2014, Brazil was ranked 6th in the list of top host economies in the world for FDI (ibid. 2015, 5). Brazil's example illustrates that there are other factors at play that make a country a favoured destination for foreign investors. The IIA is not the panacea for all problems that a country faces in attracting foreign investment. Similarly, South Africa, Ecuador and India are some of the countries that have either suspended their IIAs or are undertaking a comprehensive review.

6.3 Analysis of Key TPP Provisions and Their Implications

Definition of Investment

Analysis of the TPP Provision

The TPP contains a broad asset-based definition of 'investment' under Article 9.1, with a non-exhaustive list of examples contained in the definition. Investment means every asset owned or controlled by an investor, either directly or indirectly. Importantly, such an asset should have the characteristics of an investment such as commitment of capital or other resources, the expectation of gain or profit or the assumption of risk. The TPP excludes an order or judgement entered in a judicial or administrative action from the scope of investment. The arbitral tribunals have given a very broad interpretation to such asset-based definitions. Certain types of assets that may make little or no contribution to the host State's economy or sustainable development can, in fact, benefit from the 'heightened rights and protections offered by the investment agreement' (Bernasconi-Osterwalder et al. 2012, 10). Notably, these protections are not available to domestic investments.

There are two specific points of concern in the TPP definition. First, the TPP text includes intellectual property rights (IPRs) as part of investment. Though fairly common now, such an inclusion continues to pose challenges for host countries, especially developing ones. While protection of IPRs is part of a separate chapter in the TPP, its inclusion in the form of investment means that an investor holding an IPR can benefit from the substantive protections in the investment chapter and gain access to the ISDS mechanism laid there. Compulsory licenses, however, have been excluded from the scope of expropriation.[7] Other measures affecting IPR can be subject to an ISDS dispute. Recently, in *Eli Lilly v. Canada*,[8] pharmaceutical company Eli Lilly took Canada to an ISDS dispute under North American Free Trade Agreement (NAFTA),[9] challenging the Canadian court's interpretation of the utility doctrine in grant of a patent which it claimed amounted to a 'radical change' in the Canadian patent law, thus warranting an ISDS claim. Eli Lilly's ISDS challenge followed two rulings against it by the Canada's Federal Court of Appeal on the same issue. Eli Lilly claimed US$500 million CAD by claiming a violation of minimum standard of treatment, indirect expropriation and national treatment. Though the award in this dispute went in Canada's favour, it shows how investors are using the inclusion of IPR in the investment decision to challenge the domestic patent regime of a country.

The second point of concern is the non-exclusion of portfolio investment from the definition. Portfolio investment is a type of foreign investment that is of a purely financial character, where the investor remains passive and does not control the management of the investment (UNCTAD 2011, 29). Portfolio investment is considered to be less desirable than FDI because it generally does not bring with itself technology transfer, training or other benefits (ibid. 2004, 77). Moreover, a portfolio investment can be easily withdrawn during adverse economic situation, leading to capital volatility. Extending IIA protection to such an investor negates the very reason for entering an IIA from a host country perspective.

TPP Provision vis-à-vis Indian IIAs

The India–Japan CEPA incorporates a broad asset-based definition of investment, quite similar to that in the TPP. The Indian Model BIT, however, has incorporated an enterprise-based definition of a hybrid nature,

---

[7] See Article 9.8.5 of the TPP.
[8] *Eli Lilly and Company v. The Government of Canada*, 2017. UNCITRAL, ICSID Case No. UNCT/14/2; http://www.italaw.com/cases/1625#sthash.gj1ATjdo.dpuf (last visited 18 July 2017).
[9] The NAFTA between Canada, USA and Mexico.

with the list of assets such an enterprise can possess listed there. This definition is narrower than the asset-based definition found in the TPP and India–Japan CEPA. It defines investment as an enterprise constituted, organized and operated in good faith by an investor in accordance with law of the host country. IPR is included as a type of investment the enterprise can possess. A copyright, know-how and IPRs, such as patents and trademarks, are included only to the extent they are 'recognized under the law of a Party'. With this qualification, it may be difficult to pursue an *Eli Lilly v. Canada* like dispute under the Indian Model BIT. The model BIT also excludes portfolio investments from the definition. Taxation measures are also outside the scope of the Indian Model BIT.

National Treatment

Analysis of the TPP Provision

National treatment obligation has been described as the 'single most important standard of treatment' enshrined in an IIA (ibid. 1999, 1). Essentially a principle of non-discrimination, national treatment principle is fairly common in IIAs. It imposes an obligation on the State to treat foreign investors/investment 'no less favourable' than how it treats their domestic counterparts in 'like circumstances'.[10] In essence, the national treatment principle is geared towards providing a level playing field for foreign investors when compared to domestic investors.

The stage of investment where the national treatment obligation applies has been intensely debated in recent years. Traditionally, IIAs have applied the national treatment obligation to investors that are already operating in the host country (post-establishment national treatment), thus retaining the right to regulate the entry of investors (pre-establishment). Limiting the obligation to only the post-establishment stage allows host States, especially the economically vulnerable ones, to 'dictate which forms of foreign economic activity [they are] willing to permit within [their] borders, according to [their] own economic and social requirements;

---

[10] The Drafters' Note on Interpretation of 'In Like Circumstances' Under Article 9.4 (national treatment) and Article 9.5 (most-favoured-nation treatment) is available at https://www.tpp.mfat.govt.nz/assets/docs/Interpretation%20of%20In%20Like%20 Circumstances.pdf (last visited 16 May 2017).

a crucial manifestation of national sovereignty' (Collins 2013, 11). Pre-establishment national treatment is present in relatively fewer IIAs, with the USA and Canada investment agreements forming a large bulk of the same (Bernasconi-Osterwalder et al. 2012, 21).[11] The TPP predictably goes for an expansive national treatment in Article 9.4, with both pre- and post-establishment stages included. Thus, the obligation extends to 'establishment', 'acquisition' and 'expansion' of investment in addition to the usual post-establishment stages of management, conduct, operation, etc., of investment. This will ensure market access for foreign investors on terms equal to those enjoyed by national investors (UNCTAD 1999, 4). The pre-establishment national treatment curtails the very right of a sovereign nation to decide what investments can enter its market, and if such entry is permitted, what conditions are to be imposed in respect of it. Not surprisingly, the extension of national treatment to the pre-establishment stage has been called a 'revolution' for many countries (ibid., 4).

The consequence of having an expansive national treatment provision such as in the TPP is significant as it hits at the very core of the regulatory powers of the TPP signatory countries, especially the capital importing ones. This curtailment on the regulatory space is assuaged to a certain extent by Article 9.12 of the TPP that provides the signatory countries an opportunity to record their existing non-conforming measures and measures with respect to sectors, sub-sectors or activities that they wish to be treated as an exception to the national treatment obligation in the form of a negative list. However, this is only a limited exception. The TPP signatory countries cannot add sectors, sub-sectors or activities at a later stage without following the procedure laid down in the TPP. Any future amendment to the already listed non-conforming measures can also not decrease the conformity of the measure with the national treatment obligation, prior to such an amendment. Thus, the hands of the TPP signatory countries are tied if due to changed circumstances, they desire at a later stage to exclude a new sector or sub-sector from the scope of the national treatment obligation.

TPP Provision vis-à-vis Indian IIAs

Most BITs signed by India provide the post-establishment national treatment only. However, the investment chapter in India's CEPAs reflect a model similar to the TPP. For instance, in the India–Japan CEPA, the

---
[11] For reference, see Article 11.3, KORUS FTA.

national treatment obligation extends to all 'investment activities'.[12] 'Investment activities' has been defined to include establishment, acquisition and expansion of investment.[13] The new Indian Model BIT, however, proposes the post-establishment national treatment model.[14]

At present, the entry of FDI into India can either take place through the automatic route or through the government approval route (Consolidated FDI Policy 2016, Chapter 3.4). While under the former, no prior approval of the government is required, under the government approval route, proposals for foreign investment need to be made before the Foreign Investment Promotion Board (FIPB) of India.[15] However, in the Union Budget for 2017–18, an overhaul of this system has been planned with the government proposing the abolition of the FIPB, which will be accompanied by a number of related policy reforms.[16] The Consolidated FDI Policy of India prescribes the entry conditions in various sectors/activities (ibid., Chapter 3.4). For India to agree to a pre-establishment national treatment, these entry conditions will have to be reflected as part of non-conforming measures of an IIA. Once particular entry conditions are enshrined as part of an IIA exception, any change or addition in these conditions can lead to a potential violation of IIA obligations, including the national treatment.

Most-favoured Nation

Analysis of the TPP Provision

The most-favoured nation (MFN) principle in Article 9.5 aims to provide the TPP signatory countries a no less favourable treatment than that accorded to any other TPP signatory country or any non-signatory country to the TPP in like circumstances. This is meant to ensure an equality of competitive conditions between foreign investors of different nationalities. Like the provision on national treatment, the TPP's provision on MFN applies to both investors and investment. Furthermore, coverage

---

[12] See Article 85, India–Japan CEPA.
[13] Article 3(j), India–Japan CEPA.
[14] See Article 4, Indian Model BIT.
[15] See http://fipb.gov.in/ (last visited 15 May 2017).
[16] Key Features of Budget, 2017–18, available at http://indiabudget.nic.in/ub2017-18/bh/bh1.pdf (last visited 15 May 2017).

of the MFN obligation under the TPP extends to both pre- and post-establishment phases of investment.

There have been several instances where the investors have imported substantive and procedural commitments from other IIAs signed by the host country (Bernasconi-Osterwalder et al. 2012, 24). Thus, even if the IIA of the investor's home country and the host country does not contain a particular commitment, some arbitral tribunals have permitted investors to bring successful claims on the basis of commitments made by the host country in its other IIAs, relying on the MFN principle. This is of significance because a host country may have several IIAs signed at different points in time. The obligations under a particular IIA is moulded by the timing of the IIA, relative economic and political strength of the other party (for instance some countries like the USA always insist their model be used for negotiations) and host of other reasons that are at play then. There are currently 2563 BITs and other IIAs in force.[17] Thus, analysts fear that cherry-picking obligations from other IIAs of the host country will create a kind 'super treaty' with strong protection for the investors, unhinged from their associated limitations and exceptions (ibid., 26).

The TPP has excluded import of procedural provisions from other IIAs. However, investors from a TPP signatory country will be free to import more favourable substantive obligations from IIAs signed by the other TPP signatory countries. For instance, in *MTD v. Chile*,[18] the investor brought a dispute under the Chile–Malaysia BIT, and invoked the MFN principle therein to import the fair and equitable treatment (FET) obligation in Chile's BITs with Denmark and Croatia which was more expansive (*MTD v. Chile* 2004). Thus, the current trend of importing more favourable substantive provisions from other IIAs akin to 'treaty shopping', on the basis of the MFN provision, is a matter of concern.

TPP Provision vis-à-vis Indian IIAs

Most Indian IIAs contain an MFN provision. The India–Korea CEPA and the India–Singapore Economic Partnership Agreement have omitted the MFN provision. On the other hand, the India–Japan CEPA, while including the MFN obligation, restricts it to only the post-establishment stage of management, conduct and operation of the investment.[19]

---

[17] See http://investmentpolicyhub.unctad.org/IIA (last visited 16 May 2017).
[18] *MTD Equity Sdn. Bhd. & MTD Chile S.A. v. Chile*, 2004. ICSID Case no. ARB/01/7.
[19] See Article 86, India–Japan CEPA.

India has already faced adverse consequences of having an expansive MFN clause in its IIAs. In *White Industries v. India*,[20] the Australian claimant took India to arbitration on the grounds that the inordinate delay in Indian courts to enforce an earlier arbitration award was in violation of the Australia–India BIT, by invocation of the MFN principle. White Industries successfully used the MFN cause in the Australia–India BIT to import substantive protections from the India–Kuwait BIT that guaranteed 'effective means of asserting claims and enforcing rights'. In the first known investment treaty ruling against India, the tribunal ruled that India had violated the MFN obligation and awarded White Industries 4 million Australian dollars.

Not surprisingly, the recent Indian Model BIT altogether omits the MFN provision from the model text. Hence, if India were to join an IIA with the TPP template, it will not only go against the current Indian position on the presence of MFN obligation but also make India susceptible to treaty shopping by potential claimants.

Minimum Standard of Treatment

Analysis of the TPP Provision

The minimum standard of treatment to which the investors are entitled under the TPP is provided in Article 9.6. The provision states that the investors will be treated in accordance with the applicable customary international law principles. Annex 9A states that the signatory countries confirm their shared understanding that 'customary international law' results from general and consistent practise of Sates that they follow from a sense of legal obligation. In particular, the TPP mentions two kinds of treatment that investors are entitled to, namely, FET and full protection and security. The first is discussed in detail in this chapter.

The FET principle has attracted much discussion in the context of IIAs. This is primarily because the principle is invoked regularly in the investment disputes by claimants, with a 'considerable rate of success' (UNCTAD 2012b, xiv). In fact, the FET obligation has emerged as a 'catch-all' clause, coming to the rescue of the investors when their claim

---

[20] *White Industries Australia Ltd. v. The Republic of India*, 2011; available at http://www.italaw.com/sites/default/files/case-documents/ita0906.pdf (last visited 16 May 2017).

under other provisions has failed (Bernasconi-Osterwalder et al. 2012, 12). One of the prime reasons for this is the fairly vague understanding of the principle without any clear set of legal prescriptions as to what constitutes an FET. Over time, this has led to various inconsistent rulings by the arbitral tribunals and this has, in turn, made the inclusion of the FET obligation a fairly risky prospect for the States. Past arbitral tribunals have even found a violation of FET in cases where the investor has suffered loss due to a new measure introduced by the host State on environmental grounds- indicating the vast reach of FET.

The UNCTAD has, from its study of various arbitral panel awards, broadly identified the following as forming a part of the FET obligation (UNCTAD 2012b, xvi):

1. Prohibition of manifest arbitrariness in decision-making, that is, measures taken purely on the basis of prejudice or bias without a legitimate purpose or rational explanation;
2. Prohibition of the denial of justice and disregard of the fundamental principles of due process;
3. Prohibition of targeted discrimination on manifestly wrongful grounds, such as gender, race or religious belief;
4. Prohibition of abusive treatment of investors, including coercion, duress and harassment;
5. Protection of the legitimate expectations of investors arising from a government's specific representations or investment inducing measures, although balanced with the host State's right to regulate in the public interest.

There is a long-standing debate whether the FET principle is an autonomous obligation, or if it is interchangeable or part of the customary international law (Schreuer 2005, 357). To put rest to this debate and to discipline the wide scope of this obligation, many IIAs, starting with the NAFTA, have linked the FET principle to the customary international law minimum standard of treatment of aliens as the standard of treatment to be afforded to investments. The TPP follows the same path. However, it is noteworthy that this linking of FET with a minimum standard of treatment is also not free from drawbacks. For one, there is no consensus on what precisely constitutes a minimum standard of treatment of aliens in the customary international law (UNCTAD 2012b, 28). The differing approaches adopted by arbitral tribunals in dealing with the subject have led to much confusion and inconsistency in the interpretation of the concept. Despite limiting the FET concept by linking it to the customary international law principle, there appears to be a tendency on part of the arbitral tribunals to interpret the principle by ignoring the actual State practice, giving precedence to previous arbitral rulings, thus negating the effect of such a linkage (Porterfirled 2013).[21]

The TPP specifically mentions that FET includes the obligation to not deny justice in criminal, civil or administrative adjudicatory proceedings in accordance with the principle of due process embodied in the principal legal systems of the world. While fairly straightforward, the TPP does not identify which legal systems it is referring to.

Additionally, there is a new exclusion to the principle of FET. The TPP states that the 'mere fact' that a party takes or fails to take an action that may be inconsistent with an investor's expectations does not constitute a breach of the provision, even if there is loss or damage to the covered investment as a result. Such a provision is absent in the KORUS FTA[22] as well as the US Model BIT of 2012.[23] As stated above, protection of legitimate expectation of the investors has been interpreted to be a key aspect of the FET doctrine. In fact, a study of arbitral practice indicates that there is an over-reliance on the doctrine of legitimate expectations in cases dealing with an FET claim, with the arbitral tribunals going for very wide sweeping interpretations, where any change in the government policy leading to an adverse economic effect on the investments is treated as a violation of FET. Hence, the said exclusion appears to be an attempt by the TPP signatory countries to further rein in the tendency of arbitral tribunals to go for broad interpretation of the doctrine of legitimate expectations under the FET principle. However, the success of this language will only be tested in future disputes. By mentioning, 'investor's expectations' and not the 'legitimate expectations', it can be argued that the new explanation in the TPP is unnecessary, adding nothing new to the legal discourse on the subject. 'Investor's expectations' being wider in scope than the much controversial 'legitimate expectations' does not clarify the latter term.

There have been numerous disputes invoking the FET clause till date involving huge payouts by the host States. For instance, in *TecMed*

---

[21] See also *RDC v. Guatemala* (ICSID CASE NO. ARB/07/23, Award [29 June 2012]), where the arbitral tribunal rejected the arguments of Guatemala and others that the interpretation of customary international law linked to FET standard should be undertaken by consideration of state practice and opinio juris.

[22] The KORUS FTA was signed on 30 June 2007 and came into force on 15 March 2012.

[23] Available at http://www.state.gov/documents/organization/188371.pdf (last visited 16 March 2016).

v. Mexico,[24] the arbitral tribunal found that the decision of Mexico to not re-license an operating waste treatment plant was in violation of Mexico's FET obligation under its BIT with Spain, even though no assurance was provided by Mexico regarding the continuation of the existing legal and regulatory regime. Similarly, in a series of cases against Argentina in the aftermath of its peso crisis of 2000–2002, the arbitral tribunals found that the emergency measures undertaken by Argentina in the form of dismantling of its tariff guarantees regime was a breach of its FET obligation. This was primarily because Argentina had failed to provide a stable investment regime, going against the legitimate expectation of the investors.[25] In *Occidental Petroleum v. Ecuador*,[26] Ecuador was found to violate the FET and was asked to pay a penalty of US$2.4 billion. The government had annulled a contract with the company because the latter had violated a clause that it would not sell its rights to another firm without permission. The tribunal agreed that the violation took place but ruled that the annulment did not constitute FET to the company.

These disputes show that any measure of the host country that changes the economic and regulatory framework in which the investor's investments operate, putting it into an economic disadvantageous situation can lead to a violation of the FET obligation of the State.

TPP Provision vis-à-vis Indian IIAs

The India–Japan CEPA contains a minimum standard of treatment linked to the customary international law, not much different in essence to the TPP text. The India–Singapore Comprehensive Economic Cooperation Agreement (CECA), on the other hand, omits the FET provision. The Indian Model BIT does not mention 'minimum standard of treatment' but contains a 'treatment of investment' clause under Article 3. It states that no party shall subject investments made by investors of the other party to measures which constitute a violation of the customary international law through:

---

[24] ICSID Case No ARB (AF)/00/2, Award, 29 May 2003.
[25] See *CMS Gas Transmission Company v. The Republic of Argentina* (ICSID Case No. ARB/01/8); *Enron v. The Republic of Argentina* (ICSID Case No. ARB/01/3).
[26] ICSID Case No. ARB/06/11, available at http://www.italaw.com/cases/767 (last visited 16 May 2017).

1. denial of justice in any judicial or administrative proceedings, or
2. fundamental breach of due process, or
3. targeted discrimination on manifestly unjustified grounds, such as gender, race or religious belief, or
4. manifestly abusive treatment, such as coercion, duress and harassment.

The Indian Model BIT has stayed clear of mentioning the FET principle as part of treatment to be meted out to the investments, thus limiting the discretion of the arbitral tribunals to interpret it. Instead, the Indian Model BIT lists down four precise scenarios that will lead to a violation of a party's obligations relating to treatment of investment. The Indian Model BIT also states that investments will be provided full protection and security, where the term 'full protection and security' only refers to the physical security of investors and to investments made by the investors. The TPP does not limit the full protection and security to physical security only. The Indian Model BIT appears to have addressed some of the concerns relating to the FET provisions in the form they appear in the TPP. Joining an IIA with a TPP-like text on FET will be a step-back from India's current position.

Expropriation and Compensation

Analysis of the TPP Provision

The TPP contains a standard clause on expropriation in Article 9.8, with four grounds of expropriation listed there, namely, public purpose; non-discrimination; payment of prompt, adequate and effective compensation; and in accordance with the due process of law. Expropriation under TPP includes both direct and indirect expropriation.[27] Direct expropriation involves a formal transfer of title or outright seizure, as in the case of nationalization. Indirect expropriation refers to a 'total or near-total deprivation of an investment but without a formal transfer of title or outright seizure' (UNCTAD 2012a, 7). Indirect expropriation has garnered severe criticism and controversy, primarily because of the vague scope of the term and overreaching interpretation given by arbitral tribunals.

---

[27] Annex 9-B, Expropriation, TPP.

The TPP lists down indicative factors that can guide in determining whether there is indirect expropriation, namely, the economic impact of the government action, the extent to which the government action interferes with distinct, reasonable investment-backed expectations, and the character of the government action.[28] These factors are cumulative in nature and can guide the arbitral tribunals in their interpretation. However, the inclusion of 'reasonable investment-backed expectations', similar to 'legitimate expectations', can be used to widen the concept of indirect expropriation if the same erodes the economic value of the investment (Suzy 2012, 12). Under the expansive approach taken to interpret indirect expropriation, any regulatory measure, such as ones dealing with the production process, or technological addition or ban on harmful material, could be determined to be indirect expropriation (Kinda 2015).

For instance, in *Metalclad v. Mexico*,[29] a case under NAFTA, Metalclad was authorized by the federal government to operate a waste disposal project. However, the construction permit was denied by the provincial government on environmental grounds after a geological audit showed that the facility would contaminate the local water supply. The site was then declared to be part of a 600,000-acre ecological zone. An International Centre for Settlement of Investment Disputes (ICSID) arbitral tribunal found this to be expropriation and Mexico was ordered to pay US$16.7 million as compensation.

The TPP excludes compulsory licensing and non-issuance, non-renewal, etc., of a government's subsidy scheme from the scope of expropriation. The TPP also provides a public policy exception to indirect expropriation. It states that 'Non-discriminatory regulatory actions by a Party that are designed and applied to protect legitimate public welfare objectives, such as public health, safety and the environment, do not constitute indirect expropriations, *except in rare circumstances.*'[30] The exception is a much desired one and a step in the right direction. However, inclusion of 'except in rare circumstances' adds a degree of impreciseness to the provision, leaving it to the mercy of arbitral tribunals and their interpretations. As stated earlier, issuance of compulsory licenses is another exception to expropriation.

---

[28] Article 3(a), Annex 9-B, Expropriation, TPP.
[29] *Metalclad Corporation v. The United Mexican States*, ICSID Case No. ARB(AF)/97/1, available at http://www.italaw.com/cases/671#sthash.jlc5j124.dpuf (last visited 29 March 2016).
[30] Article 3(b), Annex 9-B, Expropriation, TPP.

With regard to compensation, the TPP, *inter alia,* provides that the same shall be paid without delay, equivalent to the fair market value and be fully realisable and freely transferable. This is quite similar to the language found in the KORUS FTA.[31]

TPP Provision vis-à-vis Indian IIAs

The India–Japan CEPA includes a language quite similar to the TPP on expropriation. The Indian Model BIT also lays down a set of factors that are to be considered in determining whether there is indirect expropriation. It states that for indirect expropriation to exist, there has to be a substantial or permanent deprivation of the fundamental attributes of property in the investment. This is a stricter requirement for indirect expropriation when compared to the TPP, which only mentions that the economic impact of government action is one of the factors to be considered for indirect expropriation. Furthermore, the Indian Model BIT provides that non-discriminatory regulatory measures by a party or measures or awards by judicial bodies of a party that are designed and applied to protect legitimate public interest or public purpose objectives such as public health, safety and the environment shall not constitute expropriation.[32] This is an unqualified exception, not limited by the phrase 'except in rare circumstances', as seen in the case of the TPP.

Thus, on the whole, the Indian Model BIT seems better placed to restrict the expansive interpretation of indirect expropriation by the arbitral tribunals, and provides much more policy space to States to introduce non-discriminatory public welfare measures.

Performance Requirements

Analysis of the TPP Provision

Performance requirements are 'governmentally imposed stipulations that firms meet certain specified goals with respect to their operations within the Government's jurisdiction' (UNCTAD 2001, 11). They are

---

[31] See 11.6 of the KORUS FTA.
[32] Article 5.5 of the Indian Model BIT.

important tools in the hand of countries, especially developing countries, to align the FDI made in their countries with their own economic, social and developmental goals. The aim of an investor is to maximize profits from its investment. It is up to the State to influence the FDI entering its market in such a manner so as to promote the general welfare of its population. Though performance requirements have been criticized as having a distorting effect on international trade and investment, empirical study has shown that many countries, including Japan, Singapore, Taiwan and Korea, have used them extensively at certain times in their history while continuing to attract high FDI (Suzy 2014, 3).

Imposition of certain performance requirements is already prohibited at the multilateral level. The Agreement on Trade-Related Investment Measures (TRIMs Agreement) of the WTO lists certain prohibitions on trade-related investment measures. These relate to local content, trade balancing, foreign-exchange balancing and export restrictions. The TRIMs Agreement covers measures related to trade in goods only. Thus, performance requirements imposed on trade in services are not prohibited by the TRIMs Agreement.

At the bilateral level, traditionally, most IIAs did not include any additional prohibition or restriction on imposition of a performance requirement by the host State. In recent times, IIAs entered into by the USA and Canada have come to include these restrictions. The NAFTA has a detailed list of prohibited performance requirements. The TPP under Article 9.10 follows a similar model. The performance requirements prohibited by the TPP extend to both pre-establishment and post-establishment stages, with an elaborate list of exceptions.

A tabular representation of the performance requirements covered under the TPP, compared to the India–Japan CEPA, is provided in Table 6.1. The Indian Model BIT contains none of the below-listed prohibitions.

As can be seen in Table 6.1, the TPP contains an extensive list of performance requirements, the imposition of which by the host State is prohibited. However, these prohibitions should be read with their corresponding exceptions. The list of exceptions to these prohibitions is provided in Table 6.2.

The TPP has a number of exceptions to the list of prohibited performance requirements. Additionally, the TPP text specifically permits certain performance requirements. These relate to performance requirements imposed as a condition of receipt or continued receipt of an

Table 6.1

List of prohibited performance requirements

List of Prohibitions	TPP	India–Japan CEPA
A. In connection with establishment, acquisition, expansion, management, conduct, operation or sale of an investment if an investor:		
Export requirement (export a certain percentage of goods and services)	▪	▪
Export restrictions		▪
Domestic content	▪	▪
Purchase, use or accord preference to domestic goods/purchase goods from persons in its territory	▪	▪ (includes services too)
Export–import balance/foreign exchange balance	▪	▪
Restriction on sales of goods or services linked to exports/foreign exchange earnings	▪	▪
Transfer of technology	▪	▪
Exclusive supply from the territory of party	▪	▪
Requirement relating to purchase, use or accordance of preference	▪	
Amount of royalty under a license contract	▪	
Duration of the term of a license contract	▪	
Management from a particular nationality	▪ (Article 9.11)	▪
B. In relation to receipt or continued receipt of an advantage, in connection with establishment, acquisition, expansion, management, conduct, operation or sale of an investment if an investor:		
Domestic content	▪	
Purchase, use or accord preference to domestic goods/purchase goods from persons in its territory	▪	
Export–import balance/foreign exchange balance	▪	
Restriction on sales of goods or services linked to exports/foreign exchange earnings	▪	

Source: Author.

Table 6.2

List of performance requirements under TPP with the exceptions.
Please see Notes below the table for the significance of numbers '1, 2, 3, 4, 5, 6, 7, 8, 9, 10'.

TPP Prohibitions	Exceptions									
Article 9.10.1: In connection with establishment, acquisition, expansion, management, conduct, operation or sale of an investment if an investor:										
	1	2	3	4	5	6	7	8	9	10
Export requirement (1(a))							▪			
Domestic content (1(b))				▪	▪	▪	▪	▪		
Purchase, use or accord preference to domestic goods/purchase goods from persons in its territory (1(c))				▪	▪	▪	▪	▪		
Export–import balance/foreign exchange balance (1(d))										
Restriction on sales of goods or services linked to exports/foreign exchange earnings (1(e))										
Transfer of technology (1(f))	▪	▪		▪	▪	▪		▪		
Exclusive supply from the territory of party (1(g))							▪			
Requirement relating to purchase, use or accordance of preference (1(h))	▪	▪						▪	▪	
Amount of royalty under a license contract (1(i)(i))	▪	▪	▪					▪	▪	
Duration of the term of a license contract (1(i)(ii))	▪	▪	▪					▪	▪	
Article 9.10.2: In relation to receipt or continued receipt of an advantage, in connection with establishment, acquisition, expansion, management, conduct, operation or sale of an investment if an investor:										
Domestic content (2(a))			▪	▪	▪	▪	▪	▪		
Purchase, use or accord preference to domestic goods/purchase goods from persons in its territory (2(b))			▪	▪	▪	▪	▪	▪		
Export–import balance/foreign exchange balance (2(c))										
Restriction on sales of goods/services linked to exports/foreign exchange earnings (2(d))										

Source: Author.

Notes:
1. Covered under Articles 31 and 39 of the TRIPS Agreement.
2. If found anti-competitive by domestic courts.
3. If equitable remuneration under copyright laws.
4. Necessary to secure compliance with laws.
5. Necessary to protect human, animal or plant life/health.
6. Conservation of exhaustible natural resources.
7. With respect to export promotion and foreign aid programmes.
8. Government procurement.
9. To qualify for preferential tariffs/quotas.
10. To protect legitimate public welfare objectives.

advantage on compliance with a requirement to locate production, supply a service, train or employ workers, construct or expand particular facilities, or carry out research and development, in its territory.[33]

The prohibition of these performance requirements will considerably curtail the regulatory flexibility of the TPP signatory countries to use FDI as a tool to attain their developmental objectives. Though the TPP provides a limited list of permitted performance requirements, a country taking refuge under such provisions should be wary due to inconsistent rulings by arbitral tribunals in the past on the issue of which of the two should be given preference—the objective of the measure (which could be a permitted ground for performance requirement under the treaty text) or the effect of the said measure in question.[34]

TPP Provision vis-à-vis Indian IIAs

Quite like the TPP, the India–Japan CEPA contains a fairly elaborate list of performance requirements that are prohibited. However, one aspect where both these agreements differ is on the imposition of performance requirement for receipt or continued receipt of an advantage. While the TPP provides a number of requirements that cannot be imposed in this regard, the India–Japan CEPA clarifies that nothing in the text prevents a party from imposing a performance requirement for the receipt of continued receipt of an advantage.

The Indian Model BIT, in contrast, proposes full regulatory powers with the State on imposition of performance requirements by omitting

---
[33] Article 9.10.3(a) of the TPP.
[34] See *Lemire v. Ukraine* and *Mobil Oil v. Canada*. For a detailed discussion, see Suzy (2014).

any provision relating to its prohibition. Such an approach allows the State to retain flexibility with respect to its economic policy. Furthermore, this approach also enables States 'to avoid complex, uncertain formulations and to guard themselves against the unpredictability of tribunal interpretations, while avoiding having to take a cut-and-dried position on the effectiveness of performance requirements.'[35] It should also be noted that the most economically distortive performance requirements are already prohibited under the TRIMs Agreement, which equally applies to all WTO members, irrespective of whether such stipulation is made in the IIA of such a member.

Thus, while India has in the past undertaken prohibition of performance requirements as part of its obligations under IIAs, the current Indian position on the subject, as reflected in the Indian Model BIT, is just the opposite.

Transfers

Analysis of the TPP Provision

Article 9.9 of the TPP contains a list of transfers related to the covered investments that are to be necessarily permitted out of the territory of the TPP signatory country freely and without delay. The TPP also contains a list of transfers that may be prevented or delayed by a TPP signatory country through the equitable, non-discriminatory and good faith applications of the law. Both these kinds of transfers are listed and compared with the corresponding provisions in the India–Japan CEPA and the Indian Model BIT.

The TPP like other IIAs permits a number of transfers to be made out of the host country freely and without delay. This allows foreign investors to freely move their investment-related capital out of the host country. The kinds of free transfers under the TPP, the Indian–Japan CEPA and the Indian Model BIT are largely overlapping. The TPP also lists a number of transfers that may be declined by the host country if certain conditions arise. Governments may have a number of legitimate reasons for regulating transfer of capital in and out of the country,

---

[35] Ibid.

namely, 'to protect the stability of their currency and markets, to minimize effects of global economic crises, to restrict funding of terrorism or regressive regimes and to ensure the collection of taxes, fines of judgments' (Bernasconi-Osterwalder et al. 2012, 30). Under the TPP, these grounds mainly relate to bankruptcy, domestic-law-mandated scenarios and transfers in the time of balance-of-payment difficulties or the threat of the same being faced by the host country.

TPP Provision vis-à-vis Indian IIAs

The list of mandatorily permitted transfers in the India–Japan CEPA, the Indian Model and the TPP is not much different, with similar type of transfers present in these three agreements (Table 6.3). However, there are noticeable differences in the kinds of transfers that may be denied by the host country (Table 6.4). The Indian Model BIT provides several additional grounds for restricting transfers, thus providing more flexibility to host States than the TPP.

Table 6.3

List of transfers that cannot be prohibited/restricted or delayed by the host country

Type of Transfers	TPP	India–Japan CEPA	Indian Model BIT
Contributions to capital	▪	▪	▪
Profits, dividends, interest, capital gains, royalty payments, management fees, technical assistance fees and other fees	▪	▪	▪
Proceeds from the sale of covered investment or from the partial or complete liquidation of the covered investment	▪	▪	▪
Payments made under a contract, including a loan agreement	▪	▪	▪
Payments made pursuant to treatment in case of armed conflict or civil strife and expropriation and compensation	▪	▪	
Payments arising out of a dispute	▪	▪	
Earnings and remuneration of personnel from the other party who work in connection with investments	▪	▪	▪

Source: Author.

Table 6.4

List of transfers that may be prevented or delayed by the host country

Transfers Relating to	TPP	India–Japan CEPA	Indian Model BIT
Bankruptcy, insolvency or the protection of the rights of creditors	▪	▪	▪
Issuing, trading or dealing in securities, futures, options or derivatives	▪	▪	▪
Criminal or penal offences	▪	▪	▪
Financial reporting or record keeping of transfers when necessary to assist law enforcement or financial regulatory authorities	▪		▪
Ensuring compliance with orders or judgements in judicial or administrative proceedings	▪	▪	▪
Obligations of investors on account of social security, pubic retirement and compulsory savings scheme		▪	▪
Compliance with labour obligations			▪
Severance entitlements of employees		▪	▪
Requirement to register and satisfy other formalities imposed by the Central Bank and other relevant authorities of a party; and			▪
Requirements to lock-in initial capital investments, as provided in FDI policy, where applicable, provided that, any new measure which would require a lock-in period for investments will not apply to existing investments			▪
Temporary safeguard measures on account of balance of payment problem, payments or transfers relating to capital movements cause or threaten to cause serious difficulties for macroeconomic management.	▪ (Article 29.3 of the TPP)		▪

Source: Author.

Public Policy Exceptions

Analysis of the TPP Provisions

The TPP contains exceptions that relate to different aspects of public policy, including public welfare. Such provisions are necessary to remove regulatory constraints that prevent a country from attaining its public welfare objectives. This section will look into the merits and demerits of the provisions present in the TPP relating to this. Provided below is a compilation of the major public policy/welfare exceptions present in the TPP on investment.

The TPP contains two general carve-outs relating to public welfare measures. The first is a carve-out for tobacco control measures. The second is a mere reiteration that nothing in Chapter 9 of the TPP prevents a signatory country from imposing a measure that ensures that investment activity in its territory is undertaken in a manner sensitive to environmental, health or other regulatory objectives, provided such measures are consistent with the TPP. This is a curious provision to be included in the text. While on the one hand it begins with the declaration that 'nothing in this Chapter shall be construed to prevent a Party [...]' from maintaining a measure for environment, health or other regulatory objectives, on the other hand it states that such a measure should be 'otherwise consistent' with the investment chapter. This second qualification makes the inclusion of this provision meaningless.

As seen in Box 6.1, apart from these two general provisions, the TPP includes certain specific exceptions. For instance, exceptions to specific prohibitions on imposition of performance requirement are fashioned along the lines of General Agreement on Tariffs and Trade, 1994 (GATT) Article XX of the WTO, with a chapeau and list of exceptions. Similarly, a non-discriminatory action taken by a State to protect legitimate public welfare objectives is construed to be an exception to indirect expropriation, 'except in rare circumstances'. Though a major improvement on existing IIAs, the TPP does not clarify what these rare circumstances are; thus, leaving it to the arbitral tribunal to decide on the same in a future dispute.

An overall assessment of these exceptions shows that the TPP's carve-outs for public welfare objectives are not very strong in nature. These do not equip the TPP signatory countries sufficiently to introduce public welfare regulations without the fear of being dragged to an investor–State dispute. An overarching exception to the chapter, along the lines of GATT Article XX, would have better preserved the regulatory space of a party and helped it to use its policy to attain the sustainable development goals. Such an exception is available for Chapter 2 (National Treatment and Market Access for Goods), Chapter 3 (Rules of Origin and Origin Procedures), Chapter 4 (Textile and Apparel), Chapter 5 (Customs Administration and Trade Facilitation), Chapter 7 (Sanitary and Phytosanitary Measures), Chapter 8 (Technical Barriers to Trade) and Chapter 17 (State-Owned Enterprises and Designated Monopolies) of the TPP.[36]

---

[36] Article 29.1 of the TPP.

Box 6.1
Public policy exceptions in the TPP

I. General Exceptions

a. *Article 9.16: Investment and Environmental, Health and other Regulatory Objectives*

Nothing in this Chapter shall be construed to prevent a Party from adopting, maintaining or enforcing any measure **otherwise consistent** with this Chapter that it considers appropriate to ensure that investment activity in its territory is undertaken in a manner sensitive to environmental, health or other regulatory objectives.

b. *Article 29.5: Tobacco Control Measures*

A Party may elect to deny the benefits of Section B of Chapter 9 (Investment) with respect to claims challenging a tobacco control measure [12] of the Party. Such a claim shall not be submitted to arbitration under Section B of Chapter 9 (Investment) if a Party has made such an election. If a Party has not elected to deny benefits with respect to such claims by the time of the submission of such a claim to arbitration under Section B of Chapter 9 (Investment), a Party may elect to deny benefits during the proceedings. For greater certainty, if a Party elects to deny benefits with respect to such claims, any such claim shall be dismissed.

Footnote 12 A tobacco control measure means a measure of a Party related to the production or consumption of manufactured tobacco products (including products made or derived from tobacco), their distribution, labelling, packaging, advertising, marketing, promotion, sale, purchase, or use, as well as enforcement measures, such as inspection, recordkeeping, and reporting requirements. For greater certainty, a measure with respect to tobacco leaf that is not in the possession of a manufacturer of tobacco products or that is not part of a manufactured tobacco product is not a tobacco control measure

II. Specific Exceptions

a. *Expropriation*
   (i) **Compulsory License** (Article 9.8.5)
   (ii) Non-issuance, renewal, continuation, maintenance, modification or reduction of a **subsidy** (Article 9.8.6)

b. *Minimum Standard of Treatment*
   (i) Non-issuance, renewal, continuation, maintenance, modification or reduction of a **subsidy** (Article 9.6.5)

c. *Performance Requirements*
   (i) Provided that such measures are not applied in an arbitrary or unjustifiable manner, or do not constitute a disguised restriction on international trade or investment, paragraphs 1(b), 1(c), 1(f), 2(a) and 2(b) shall not be construed

> to prevent a Party from adopting or maintaining measures, including **environmental measures:**
>
> (a) necessary to secure compliance with laws and regulations that are not inconsistent with this Agreement;
> (b) necessary to protect human, animal or plant life or health; or
> (c) related to the conservation of living or non-living exhaustible natural resources. (Article 9.10.3(d))
>
> (ii) **Government procurement** (Article 9.10.3(f))
> (iii) Paragraphs (1)(h) and (1)(i) shall not be construed to prevent a Party from adopting or maintaining measures to protect legitimate **public welfare objectives**, provided that such measures are not applied in an **arbitrary or unjustifiable manner**, or in a manner that constitutes a disguised restriction on international trade or investment. (Article 9.10.3(h))
>
> d. *National Treatment and MFN*
> **Government procurement** and subsidies or grants provided by a Party, including government supported loans, guarantees and insurance. (Article 9.12.6)
>
> e. *Indirect Expropriation*
> Non-discriminatory regulatory actions by a Party that are designed and applied to protect **legitimate public welfare objectives**, such as public health,[37] safety and the environment, do not constitute indirect expropriations, **except in rare circumstances.**
>
> *Footnote 37* For greater certainty and without limiting the scope of this subparagraph, regulatory actions to protect public health include, among others, such measures with respect to the regulation, pricing and supply of, and reimbursement for, pharmaceuticals (including biological products), diagnostics, vaccines, medical devices, gene therapies and technologies, health-related aids and appliances and blood and blood-related products.
>
> *Note:* Emphasis added.

TPP Provision vis-à-vis Indian IIAs

The Indian Model BIT incorporates exceptions clauses modelled on GATT 1994's Article XX (General Exceptions) in Article 31, and Article XXI (Security Exceptions) in Article 33. As discussed above, these umbrella exceptions provide better regulatory space to governments in attaining their public welfare goals.

6.4 Relation of the Investment Chapter with Other TPP Chapters

Article 9.3 of the TPP states that in the event of inconsistency between the TPP's investment chapter and any other chapter, the other chapter shall prevail, to the extent of such inconsistency. The investment chapter shall also not apply to measures adopted or maintained by a party, to the extent they are covered by the TPP's chapter on financial services. This is different than the approach in the India–Japan CEPA, which provides that the chapter on services prevails over the chapter on investment, if inconsistency relates to national treatment, MFN and general treatment provisions under the investment chapter. For all other inconsistencies the investment chapter will prevail. In the TPP, mode 3 of services is part of the investment chapter and not the chapters dealing with services. This is a major shift from the Indian approach of including mode 3 in the services chapter of CEPAs. For a more detailed discussion, please refer to Chapter 3 on services.

6.5 Investor–State Dispute Settlement

Section B of the TPP's investment chapter deals with ISDS. It lays down the procedure for consultation and negotiations, submission of a claim to the arbitration, selection of arbitrators, conduct of arbitration, governing law, awards, etc. The ISDS is a unique recourse because it provides a private party, that is, the investor, an access to the international arbitration against the host country, without first approaching the home country. The functioning of ISDS has been severely criticized on several counts and the same has been well-documented. The UNCTAD identifies four main problems with ISDS (UNCTAD 2014b, 22). These are briefly summarized further. Each problem is followed by the TPP's response to the same.

- *Legitimacy and transparency:* There have been several instances of investors challenging public welfare regulations of the State dealing with environmental and health grounds. This raises the question 'whether three individuals, appointed on an ad hoc basis, have sufficient legitimacy to assess the validity of States' acts, particularly if the dispute involves sensitive public policy issues' (ibid.).

UNCTAD estimates that till 2014, host countries have faced ISDS claims of up to US$114 billion and awards of up to US$1.77 billion (ibid.). Furthermore, the ISDS system lacks on ground of transparency since procedures can continue to be fully confidential. Boxes 6.2 and 6.3 provide a glimpse of the kind of measures challenged at ISDS, along with the quantum of arbitral awards.

The TPP does not attempt to revamp the ISDS mechanism on ground of legitimacy. It provides for the international investment arbitration in the case of an investor–State dispute. Article 9.23 of the TPP, however, provides for strong transparency measures, by making ISDS-related documents public and providing for an open hearing of disputes.

- *Inconsistent and erroneous arbitral decisions:* The ISDS arbitral panels have often given inconsistent rulings on similar or same provisions. These inconsistent rulings have added uncertainty and unpredictability on interpretation of core IIA obligations. Also, the ISDS does not provide an effective review or the appellate mechanism in the case of an erroneous arbitral decision. The TPP's ISDS provisions do not rule out inconsistent ruling by arbitral tribunals in the future. Furthermore, at present no appellate mechanism is available under the TPP, though in the event such a

Box 6.2

Illustrative measures that have been challenged at the ISDS

- **Bank regulators' response to the global financial crisis** (*Ping An v. Belgium*)
- **Debt restructuring** (*Cyprus Popular Bank v. Greece*)
- **Ban on nuclear power** after the Fukushima meltdown (*Vattenfall v. Germany*)
- **Land reforms** (*Border Timbers v. Zimbabwe*)
- **Health and medicines and tobacco regulations:** *Eli Lilly v. Canada* (patents); *Philip Morris v. Australia* (tobacco) and *Philip Morris v. Uruguay* (tobacco); *Ethyl v. Canada* (toxic gas additive), settled (resulted in payment to investor and toxics ban reversed).
- **Environmental regulations:** *Vattenfall v. Germany I* (coal); *Lone Pine v. Canada* (on fracking); *Chevron v. Ecuador*; *Renco v. Peru* (metal smelter pollution); *Metalclad v. Mexico* (toxic waste); *S.D. Myers v. Canada* (toxic waste).

Source: Kinda (2015).

Box 6.3
Arbitral awards in ISDS

- *Yukos v. Russia*: US$ 50 billion (three awards for three former Yukos majority shareholders, 2014)
- *Occidental v. Ecuador:* US$ 1,769,625,000 (ICSID, 2012)
- *Al Kharafi and Sons v. Libya:* US$ 935 million (ad hoc, 2013, with interest, fixed at 4 per cent per annum, the sums owing under the 22 March 2013 award are increasing, topping US$ 1 billion at the end of 2014)
- *Gold Reserve v. Venezuela:* US$ 713 million plus costs (ICSID, 2014)
- *Wagih Siag v. Egypt*: 74,550,795 US$ (ICSID, 2009)
- *Duetsche Bank v. Sri Lanka:* US$ 60,368,993 (ICSID, 2012)
- *Bernandus Henricus v. Zimbabwe:* US$ 10,637,000 (ICSID, 2009)
- *France Telecom v. Lebanon:* US$ 266,349,600 (UNCITRAL, 2005)
- *Argentina:* US$ 1,140,819,547 in 15 cases

Source: Kinda (2015).

mechanism develops, the TPP signatory countries shall consider the applicability of the same to awards under the TPP.[37]

- *Concerns relating to arbitrators:* There's a growing concern regarding the impartiality of arbitrators constituting the tribunals in the ISDS. A specific concern rises from the fact that an arbitrator sitting on an ISDS panel can simultaneously act as a counsel or expert in another ISDS dispute donning 'multiple hats' (Bernasconi-Osterwalder et al. 2014, 13). The TPP in Article 9.22.6 provides that TPP signatory countries shall, prior to the entry into force of this Agreement, provide guidance on the application of the Code of Conduct for Dispute Settlement Proceedings under Chapter 28 (Dispute Settlement) to arbitrators selected to serve on ISDS tribunals pursuant to this article, including any necessary modifications to the code of conduct to conform to the context of ISDS. How such a code will operate in the context of the TPP's investment chapter remains to be seen.
- *Cost and time related to arbitration:* UNCTAD provide that the average, costs, including legal fees (which on an average amount to approximately 82 per cent of the total costs), and tribunal expenses in an ISDS dispute, have exceeded $8 million per party per case (UNCTAD 2014, 28). With the field being dominated by

---

[37] See Article 9.23.11 of the TPP.

large law firms charging extraordinarily high fees, and disputes proceedings spanning several years, the system is tilted against developing countries. This being more an issue of systemic concern on the practical side of matters is not addressed by the TPP.

Lastly, Annex 9J of the TPP provides a 'fork in the road' clause relating to submission of an arbitration claim against Chile, Peru, Mexico or Vietnam. If an investor elects to submit a claim before the domestic court or administrative tribunal of these countries, that election is definitive and exclusive and the investor may not thereafter submit the claim to arbitration.

All Indian IIAs have an ISDS mechanism similar to the TPP. The Indian Model BIT proposes recourse to ISDS only on exhaustion of local remedies. It is noteworthy that the various problems faced by ISDS have led to the European Union (EU) proposing an alternate investment tribunal system in its Comprehensive Economic Trade Agreement (CETA) with Canada.[38]

6.6 Conclusion

The TPP's investment chapter does not bring any substantial new element to the existing IIA table. It replicates, to a large extent, the faults in the current international investment law regime, along with the ISDS arbitration mechanism—with only a feeble attempt to address the various concerns and criticisms. The substantive obligations of the TPP, especially relating to national treatment, FET and indirect expropriation, greatly curtail the regulatory space of its signatory countries to pursue public welfare objectives. Past arbitral rulings in favour of the investors through expansive and sometimes inconsistent interpretations discourages States from introducing new measures, even if they address legitimate concerns of the governments. The public welfare exceptions in the TPP, though a slight improvement on the existing regime, appear to be weak and qualified. IIAs like the TPP can thus trigger a regulatory chill on policy making of a State. Furthermore, expansive coverage of the investment chapter means that measures relating to IPR and services are

---

[38] See Chapter 8 of the EU–Canada CETA; available at http://ec.europa.eu/trade/policy/in-focus/ceta/ceta-chapter-by-chapter/ (last visited 16 May 2017).

covered under it and measures relating to these can be subjected to an ISDS challenge.

India has signed several IIAs, some not quite different to the TPP. Therefore, from the Indian policy perspective, it can be argued that the TPP provisions are in no way more onerous than what India has already committed to in its previous IIAs. Hence, the TPP's investment provisions will not pose a major hurdle, should India decide to join a TPP-style Agreement in future. Notwithstanding the fact that there is no conclusive evidence of IIAs by themselves leading to more foreign investment, such an argument ignores two points. First, though India has undertaken equally demanding and self-defeating obligations in the past, the problems with the international investment regime has become more evident and understood only in the last few years. This has prompted India to review its IIAs and come out with the Indian Model BIT, which has incorporated improvements in the treaty text. The Indian Model BIT differs starkly to the TPP text in several areas. Thus, accepting the investment chapter of the TPP at the current stage will take India several steps back in its IIA reform process. Second, the State with which such a TPP-style agreement may be signed also becomes relevant. For instance, investors from some countries, such as the United States of America (USA) and Canada are the most active users of the ISDS. The USA is also a big investor in India. Hence, if and when such an agreement is signed with these countries, India will become susceptible to a flurry of potential ISDS disputes.

Last but not the least, though the TPP's fate remains undecided on account of USA's withdrawal, which was its key driver at one point, the investment chapter template will continue to shape and guide future investment agreements. With India in the midst of negotiating a 16-countries Regional CEPA and contemplating a BIT with the USA, lessons from the TPP's investment template are more relevant than ever.

References

Berger, Axel, Matthias Busse, Peter Nunnenkamp, and Martin Roy. 2010. 'Do Trade and Investment Agreements Lead to More FDI? Accounting for Key Provisions inside the Black Box'. Kiel: Kiel Institute of World Economy. Retrieved 18 July 2017, from https://www.ifw-members.ifw-kiel.de/publications/do-trade-and-investment-agreements-lead-to-more-fdi-accounting-for-key-provisions-inside-the-black-box/kwp_1647.pdf

Bernasconi-Osterwalder, Nathalie, Aaron Cosbey, Lise Johnson, and Damon Vis-Dunbar. 2012. 'Investment Treaties & Why they matter to Sustainable Development: Questions and Answers'. International Institute for Sustainable Development. Retrieved 18 July from http://www.iisd.org/library/investment-treaties-and-why-they-matter-sustainable-development-questions-and-answers

Bernasconi-Osterwalder, Nathalie, and Diana Rosert. 2014. 'Investment Treaty Arbitration: Opportunities to Reform Arbitral Rules and Processes'. IISD. Retrieved 18 July 2017, from http://www.iisd.org/pdf/2014/investment_treaty_arbitration.pdf

Collins, D.A. 2013. *National Treatment in Emerging Market Investment Treaties*. London: The City Law School of City University London. Retrieved 18 July 2017, from http://openaccess.city.ac.uk/2395/

Government of India. 2016. *Consolidated FDI Policy of India* (effective from 7 June 2016). New Delhi: Department of Industrial Policy and Promotion, Ministry of Commerce and Industry. Retrieved 5 April 2017, from http://dipp.nic.in/English/Policies/FDI_Circular_2016.pdf

Mohamadieh, Kinda. 2015. *The Rapidly Changing Situation in Investment Agreements—Presentation*. South Centre. Retrieved 18 July 2017, from http://www.southcentre.int/wp-content/uploads/2015/03/Ev_150312_KMohamadieh.pdf

Neumayer, Eric, and Laura Spess. 2005. *Do Bilateral Investment Treaties Increase Foreign Direct Investment to Developing Countries?* LSE Research Online. Retrieved 18 July 2017, from http://eprints.lse.ac.uk/archive/00000627

Nikiema, Suzy. 2012. *Indirect Expropriation: Best Practices Series*. International Institute of Sustainable Development. Retrieved 18 July 2017, from http://www.iisd.org/pdf/2012/best_practice_indirect_expropriation.pdf

———. 2014. *Performance Requirements in Investment Treaties: Best Practices Series*. International Institute for Sustainable Development. Retrieved 18 July 2017, from http://www.iisd.org/sites/default/files/publications/best-practices-performance-requirements-investment-treaties-en.pdf

Padmanabhan, Aishwarya. 2012. 'Relationship Between FDI inflows and Bilateral Investment Treaties/International Investment Treaties in Developing Economies: An Empirical Analysis'. *International Journal of Economic Sciences* 1 (1), 65–84.

Porterfirled, Mathew. 2013. *A Distinction Without a Difference? The Interpretation of Fair and Equitable Treatment Under Customary International Law by Investment Tribunals*. Retrieved 18 July 2017, from https://www.iisd.org/itn/2013/03/22/a-distinction-without-a-difference-the-interpretation-of-fair-and-equitable-treatment-under-customary-international-law-by-investment-tribunals/

Sachs, Lisa E., and Karl P. Sauvant. 2009. 'BITs, DTTs, and FDI Flows: An Overview'. In *The Effect of Treaties on Foreign Direct Investment: Bilateral Investment Treaties, Double Taxation Treaties and Investment Flows*. Oxford: Oxford University Press. Retrieved 18 July 2017, from http://ccsi.columbia.edu/files/2014/01/Overview-SachsSauvant-Final.pdf

Schreuer, Christoph. 2005. 'Fair and Equitable Treatment in Arbitral Practice'. *Journal of World, Investment and Trade* 6 (3), 357–86.

UNCTAD. 1999. 'National Treatment'. In *UNCTAD Series on Issues in International Investment Agreement*. New York and Geneva: United Nations. Retrieved 18 July 2017, from http://unctad.org/en/Docs/psiteiitd11v4.en.pdf

UNCTAD. 2009. 'The Role of International Investment Agreements in Attracting Foreign Direct Investment to Developing Countries'. In *UNCTAD Series on International*

Investment Policies for Development. New York and Geneva: United Nations. Retrieved 18 July 2017, from http://unctad.org/en/Docs/diaeia20095_en.pdf

———. 2011. 'Scope and Definition'. In *UNCTAD Series on Issues in International Investment Agreement II*. New York and Geneva: United Nations. Retrieved 18 July 2017, from http://unctad.org/en/Docs/diaeia20102_en.pdf

———. 2015. 'Global Investment Trends'. In *World Investment Report*. Retrieved 18 July 2017, from http://unctad.org/en/PublicationChapters/wir2015ch1_en.pdf

———. 2001. 'Host Country Operational Measures'. In *UNCTAD Series on Issues in International Investment Agreements*. New York and Geneva: United Nations. Retrieved 18 July 2017, from http://unctad.org/en/Docs/psiteiitd26.en.pdf

UNCTAD. 2004. *International Investment Agreements: Key Issues*. New York and Geneva: United Nations. Retrieved 18 July 2017, from http://unctad.org/en/Docs/iteiit200410_en.pdf

———. 2012a. 'Expropriation: A Sequel'. In *UNCTAD Series on International Investment Agreements II*. New York and Geneva: United Nations. Retrieved 18 July 2017, from http://unctad.org/en/Docs/unctaddiaeia2011d7_en.pdf

———. 2012b. 'Fair and Equitable Treatment: A Sequel'. In *UNCTAD Series on International Investment Agreements II*. New York and Geneva: United Nations. Retrieved 18 July 2017, from http://unctad.org/en/Docs/unctaddiaeia2011d5_en.pdf

———. 2014a. 'Do Bilateral Investment Treaties Attract FDI Flows to Developing Economies?' In *Trade and Development Report*. New York and Geneva: United Nations. Retrieved 18 July 2017, from http://unctad.org/en/PublicationsLibrary/tdr2014_en.pdf

———. 2014b. 'Investor State Dispute Settlement: A Sequel'. In *UNCTAD Series on Issues in International Investment Agreements II*. New York and Geneva: United Nations. Retrieved 18 July 2017, from http://unctad.org/en/PublicationsLibrary/diaeia2013d2_en.pdf

7
Standards under the TPP
Much Ado about Nothing?
R.V. Anuradha*

7.1 Introduction

The Trans-Pacific Partnership (TPP) Agreement, concluded between the United States of America (USA) and 11 other countries in the Asia-Pacific region—Australia, Brunei Darussalam, Canada, Chile, Japan, Malaysia, Mexico, New Zealand, Peru, Singapore, and Vietnam, has been hailed as a 'high-standards' agreement that sets 'a new standard for global trade while taking up next-generation issues'.[1] This broadly refers to the elaboration and consolidation of provisions of the World Trade Organization (WTO) relating to technical regulations and standards and sanitary and phytosanitary measures. In addition to this, the TPP Agreement deals in substantial detail with standards on WTO-plus areas, namely labour and the environment.

Notwithstanding the USA's withdrawal from the TPP, the approach and the provisions of the TPP continue to hold relevance for the types of provisions on standards that are likely to find reflection in free trade agreements (FTAs) negotiated by the other TPP countries.

A study for the World Bank has documented that measures related to technical barriers to trade (TBTs) and to sanitary and phytosanitary

---

* The author gratefully acknowledges the valuable research assistance provided by Ronjini Ray, Associate at Clarus Law Associates, New Delhi.

[1] See, for example, the Press Releases on Summary of the TPP Agreement announced by Australia, and the USA: http://dfat.gov.au/trade/agreements/tpp/outcomes-documents/Pages/summary-of-the-tpp-agreement.aspx; https://ustr.gov/about-us/policy-offices/press-office/press-releases/2015/october/summary-trans-pacific-partnership (last visited 18 July 2017).

(SPS) standards and regulations have become important dimensions of FTAs (Maur and Shephard 2011). These are driven by a variety of policy objectives ranging from consumer safety, to environmental protection, to food quality, or consumer information through labelling, etc. The approach that the TPP has adopted is specification of benchmark international standards in a few sectors, which has been the US approach to FTAs. This is in contrast to the European Union's (EU) approach to FTAs which emphasizes more on harmonization with its own standards. Overall, the impact on developing country exporters is the need to ramp up and adhere to any higher level of standards, in the interest of continued market access. This aspect, as will be explained in further detail in this chapter, is something which was true before the TPP and continues to prevail after the TPP as well.

This chapter will present an analysis of these aspects under Chapters 7 ('Sanitary and Phytosanitary Measures') and 8 ('Technical Barriers to Trade) of the TPP Agreement.

7.2 Technical Barriers to Trade

Overview of the TBT Chapter

Chapter 8 on TBT emphasizes the implementation of the WTO TBT Agreement (hereinafter the 'TBT Agreement'). Additionally, it specifically incorporates certain paragraphs of Article 2 (Technical Regulations) and Article 5 (Conformity Assessment Procedures) of the TBT Agreement. It emphasizes on the important role that international standards can play in supporting greater regulatory alignment and in this regard refers to the 'TBT Committee Decision on Principles for the Development of International Standards, Guides and Recommendations'. The main WTO-plus elements of the TPP Agreement can be said to fall under three broad categories: conformity assessment, transparency and sector-specific annexes. Each of these aspects is discussed below.

Conformity Assessment

The TBT chapter elaborates several elements of the WTO's TBT Agreement on conformity assessment. It then lays out principles for recognition of conformity assessment by conformity assessment bodies

(CABs) from other TPP parties. The overall impact of these provisions is the narrowing down of the level of discretion that an authority in a country would have in rejecting the assessments done by CABs from other TPP parties, and thereby reducing the necessity of duplicating tests for conformity assessment. This essentially would translate to ease of acceptance of products in a TPP party, which have been certified by CABs from another TPP party. Such possibility exists even under the WTO's TBT Agreement, in the form of mutual recognition agreements on conformity assessment.

Under Article 6.4 of the WTO's TBT Agreement, WTO members are obligated to allow participation of CABs from other members under principles of national treatment and most favoured nation (MFN) treatment. The TPP TBT chapter takes this one step further and specifies that such an obligation would entail that each party applies the same or equivalent procedures, criteria and conditions while considering accreditation, approval, licensing or any other form of recognition of the relevant CAB.[2] It further mandates that there shall be no requirement for local presence of such body within the territory of the approving party.[3]

Transparency

The transparency provisions of the chapter (Article 8.7) are far more elaborate than in the WTO TBT Agreement. For example, each party is required to allow persons of any other party to participate in the development of technical regulations, standards and conformity assessment procedures by central government bodies, on a national treatment basis.[4] Parties are also required to publish in a single website all new regulations, conformity assessment procedures and proposals for amendments.[5] Publication on the WTO's official website has been specified as constituting sufficient compliance with this obligation.

Sector-specific Annexes

The other significant TBT-plus elements are primarily those relating to provisions on cooperation and trade facilitation (Article 8.9), and the

---

[2] Article 8.6.1, Chapter 8 on technical barriers to trade, TPP.
[3] Article 8.6.4, Chapter 8 on technical barriers to trade, TPP.
[4] Article 8.7.1, Chapter 8 on technical barriers to trade, TPP.
[5] Article 8.7.4, Chapter 8 on technical barriers to trade, TPP.

seven product-specific annexes which outline the basic principles for standards and regulations for the concerned sectors.

Each annex emphasizes on consideration of scientific or technical guidance documents in the development of standards and regulations. Under the WTO's TBT Agreement, 'scientific and technical information' is listed as one of the elements that WTO members 'may' consider for risk assessment.[6] In contrast, the TPP TBT Annexes specify mandatory legal obligations on parties to consider scientific information in the following provisions:

1. Each party shall consider relevant scientific or technical guidance documents developed through international collaborative efforts with respect to the annexes on pharmaceutical products, cosmetics, and medical devices; and[7]
2. The parties shall seek to apply relevant scientific guidance documents developed through international collaborative efforts with respect to inspection of pharmaceuticals.[8]

Product-specific Annexes

The product-specific annexes under the TBT chapter are as follows:

- Annex 8-A: Wine and Distilled Spirits
- Annex 8-B: Information and Communications Technology Products
- Annex 8-C: Pharmaceuticals
- Annex 8-D: Cosmetics
- Annex 8-E: Medical Devices
- Annex 8-F: Proprietary Formulas for Prepackaged Foods and Food Additives
- Annex 8 G: Organics

Under these annexes, there is no obligation to harmonize or mandate for mutual recognition of each other's standards or regulations. Instead the annexes encourage the TPP parties to consider certain principles while developing standards/regulations. Each annex emphasizes that parties

---

[6] Article 2.2, TBT Agreement.
[7] Annex 8C—Pharmaceuticals, para 8; Annex 8D—Cosmetics, para 8; Annex 8E—Medical Devices, para 8.
[8] Annex 8C—Pharmaceuticals, para 18.

should collaborate in international initiatives regarding the specific product, including on international standards. As discussed above, the annexes on pharmaceutical products, cosmetics and medical devices mandate the TPP parties to consider relevant scientific or technical guidance documents developed through international collaborative efforts. Specific international standards are referenced in some of the annexes, not all of which are mandatory requirements, and the relevant TPP parties have the ability to consider the relevant standards based on the specific terms of the annex. Brief summaries of each of the annexes are provided below:

1. The wine and distilled spirits annex provides guidance on labelling including specific minimum requirements for labels for wine and spirits products. Consumer information such as product name, country of origin, net contents and alcohol content need to be clearly displayed within a 'single field of vision' on the bottle. The annex does not limit a TPP party's ability to impose other labelling requirements. A party has the discretion to determine whether certification is necessary to protect human health and safety or to achieve other legitimate objectives, and in that regard, shall consider the *Codex Alimentarius* 'Guidelines for Design, Production, Issuance and Use of Generic Official Certificates' (CAC/GL 38-2001).
2. The annex on proprietary formulas for prepackaged foods and food additives provides TPP parties with guidance to ensure the confidentiality of commercially sensitive information for proprietary formulas and in implementing technical requirements such as labelling. The annex stipulates that nothing shall prevent a TPP party from applying labelling standards in accordance with international standards, such as those set by codex.
3. The annex on pharmaceutical products mandates each party to review safety, efficacy and manufacturing quality information submitted by a person seeking marketing authorization in a format that is consistent with the principles found in the International Conference on Harmonization (ICH) of Technical Requirements for Registration of Pharmaceuticals for Human Use Common Technical Document (CTD), including any amendments thereto. At the same time, the annex recognizes that the CTD does not necessarily address all aspects relevant to a party's determination to approve marketing authorization for a particular product, and allows flexibility for inclusion of such other elements in any consideration

for marketing authorizations. In this regard it is interesting to note that India participates at ICH meetings as an observer.[9]

4. Under the annex on medical devices, while each party to the TPP is free to define the scope of the 'medical devices' subject to its statutes and regulations in its territory, the annex specifies that the scope of medical devices should be consistent with the meaning of 'medical device' as per the Global Harmonization Task Force (GHTF) Final Document (GHTF 2012). The GHTF, which is now referred to as the International Medical Device Regulators Forum (IMDRF), is a voluntary group of medical device regulators from around the world who have come together to accelerate international medical device regulatory harmonization and convergence. The World Health Organization (WHO) is an affiliate organization of IMDRF. India is not a member. Its current members are (a) Australia, (b) Brazil, (c) Canada, (d) China, (e) Europe, (f) Japan, (g) Russia and (h) USA.[10] The GHTF definition of 'medical device' is a broad 'purpose-based' definition that includes any instrument, apparatus, machine, etc., intended by the manufacturer to be used for one or more of the specific medical purposes such as diagnosis, prevention, monitoring, treatment or alleviation of diseases.

5. The annex on cosmetics requires the TPP parties to adopt a risk-based approach to testing unnecessary duplication in approvals processes, testing and marketing authorization for such products.

6. The annex on information and communications technology (ICT) products provides guidance on the application of technical requirements and conformity assessment obligations to ICT products that use cryptography or that have an electromagnetic capability. Parties are encouraged to implement the Asia-Pacific Economic Cooperation (APEC) Mutual Recognition Arrangement for Conformity Assessment of Telecommunications Equipment (MRA-TEL) and the APEC Mutual Recognition Arrangement for Equivalence of Technical Requirements (MRA-ETR) with respect to each other or other arrangements to facilitate trade in telecommunications equipment.

7. The organic products annex encourages parties to exchange information on matters relating to organic production and certification and to work towards improved international guidelines and

---

[9] http://www.ich.org/about/organisation-of-ich/coopgroup.html (last visited 18 July 2017).
[10] 'About IMDRF', available at: http://www.imdrf.org/about/about.asp (last visited 24 August 2016).

standards. It further encourages parties to consider expeditiously a request for equivalence of standards and technical regulations or conformity of procedures.

As noted above, some of the annexes reference specific international standards that need to be conformed with. A tabular assessment on this aspect is provided in Table 7.1, which discusses implications for non-TPP countries such as India. There are no mandatory standards that are imposed as a result of the TBT annexes under the TPP agreement. The reference to international standards is generally worded as a best endeavour requirement.

The possible alignment of regulatory practices in TPP parties along these standards cannot be confined to TPP parties alone. Exporters from non-TPP parties will, therefore, have to adhere to any such evolution of technical regulations. But this is true in the non-TPP world also, where every country is free to implement technical regulations that are consistent with the elements of the WTO's TBT Agreement. There is nothing in the TPP's TBT chapter that deviates from this. In this regard, the possible harmonization of any regulatory standard across TPP parties could possibly have spillover benefits for exporters from non-TPP parties who can access multiple TPP markets by adhering to a single standard.

7.3 Sanitary and Phytosanitary Measures

Overview of the SPS Chapter

TPP's Chapter 7 on SPS measures builds on the WTO SPS Agreement. It places emphasis on the use of 'scientific principles' in arriving at SPS measures.[11] It, however, strengthens the obligation in this regard to some extent beyond the WTO's SPS Agreement. For example, like Article 5.7 of the WTO's SPS Agreement, a party can adopt certain emergency measures.[12] The difference, however, is that while the WTO SPS Agreement refers to a need for review of such measure within a 'reasonable period of time', the TPP SPS chapter mandates parties to review the scientific basis of the measure within 6 months. Furthermore, the party adopting the emergency measure is obliged to take into consideration information provided by other parties.

---

[11] Article 7.9, Chapter 7 on SPS measures, TPP.
[12] Article 7.14, Chapter 7 on SPS measures, TPP.

Table 7.1

Impact of specific international standards

Reference of Specific Standard in TPP Annex	Impact on Exports from a Non-party such as India	Impact on Parties to the TPP
Annex 8-B, Information and Communications Technology Products: APEC Mutual Recognition Arrangement for Conformity Assessment of Telecommunications Equipment (MRA-TEL) and the APEC Mutual Recognition Arrangement for Equivalence of Technical Requirements (MRA-ETR)	India is not a member of these APEC MRAs. Mutual recognition will facilitate easier market access for APEC members and TPP members who adhere to the APEC MRAs.	The obligation on TPP parties is an encouragement to implement the APEC MRAs. This is expected to be a voluntary exercise which can be considered when required.
Annex 8-C, Pharmaceuticals: Person seeking marketing authorization is required to submit information in a format that is consistent with the principles found in the International Conference on Harmonization of Technical Requirements for Registration of Pharmaceuticals for Human Use CTD, including any amendments thereto.	India's drug regulatory authority participates at ICH meetings as an observer.[a] In this regard, it is interesting to note that in 2002, the WHO had commented on the then prevailing version of the ICH guidelines and noted that technical complexity of these guidelines could be cumbersome for industry in developing countries to comply with.[b] Since then, however, it appears that ICH requirements have gradually been implemented, and ICH requirements for good clinical practice form the basis of India's GCP guidelines.[c] India's requirements for documentation of market authorization do not appear to be based on the CTD.	Compliance with the CTD requirements are mandatory for TPP parties.

Reference of Specific Standard in TPP Annex	Impact on Exports from a Non-party such as India	Impact on Parties to the TPP
	As of now, Indian exporters seeking market access in any country would in any event be required to adhere to the regulatory requirements for market authorization in that country. Any harmonization of such requirements across TPP members could work to India's advantage.	
Annex 8-E, Medical Devices: While each Party to the TPP is free to define the scope of the 'medical devices' subject to its statutes and regulations in its territory, the annex specifies that the scope of medical devices should be consistent with the meaning of 'medical device' as per the GHTF Final Document (GHTF 2012).	The GHTF definition of 'medical device' is a broad 'purpose based' definition that includes any instrument, apparatus, machine, etc., intended by the manufacturer to be used for one or more of the specific medical purposes such as diagnosis, prevention, monitoring, treatment or alleviation of diseases, etc.	A key regulatory mandate under the annex is that each TPP party has to define 'medical devices' based on the definition proposed by the GHTF. The GHTF, which is now referred to as the IMDRF, is a voluntary group of medical device regulators from around the world who have come together to accelerate international medical device regulatory harmonization and convergence.

(Continued)

Table 7.1

(Continued)

Reference of Specific Standard in TPP Annex	Impact on Exports from a Non-party such as India	Impact on Parties to the TPP
	India is not a member of the GHTF. Indian exporters seeking market access in any TPP country would in any event be required to adhere to the regulatory requirements for market authorization in that country. Any harmonization of such requirements across TPP parties could work to India's advantage.	The WHO is an affiliate organization of IMDRF. The GHTF definition of 'medical device' is a broad 'purpose based' definition that includes any instrument, apparatus, machine, etc., intended by the manufacturer to be used for one or more of the specific medical purposes such as diagnosis, prevention, monitoring, treatment or alleviation of diseases, etc. (GHTF 2012, para 5.1). TPP parties would need to adhere to the broad contours of the GHTF definition.

Source: Author.

[a] 'Membership: Current Members and Observers'; available at http://www.ich.org/about/membership.html (last visited 24 August 2016).
[b] 'Implementation of ICH Guidelines in Non-ICH Countries'; available at http://apps.who.int/medicinedocs/en/d/Jh2993e/6.2.html (last visited 24 August 2016).
[c] Regulations and Guidelines, Indian Pharmaceuticals Association; available at http://www.ipapharma.org/regulations.aspx (last visited 24 August 2016).

The TPP chapter is the WTO's SPS-plus in several respects; it has more elaborate provisions than the WTO SPS Agreement on adaptation to regional conditions, including pest- or disease-free areas,[13] as well as on audits[14] and import checks.[15] For instance, the provisions on import checks mandate that these are required to be carried out on the basis of risk assessments, and without any undue delay, in order to ensure that exporters are not disadvantaged.[16] Any finding of non-conformity is required to be limited to what is reasonable and necessary and rationally related to available science. There is also a need for ensuring prompt and clear communication, including providing the exporter with necessary information on testing procedures to allow for resolution of any issues of detention at the border.

On the issue of certification, the provisions mandate that these requirements are limited to information essential for the protection of human/animal/plant life or health and, further, TPP parties are encouraged to work together to develop model certificates to accompany specific commodities and to promote electronic certification.

Unlike the TPP's TBT chapter, however, there are no product-specific annexes to the SPS chapter.

The chapter provides for the concept of recognition of equivalence, based on the provisions of the WTO's SPS Agreement. The WTO principles are further elaborated with specific obligations on procedures for equivalence, timelines and communication to be provided to parties regarding the same. No definitive outcomes for equivalence are envisaged, and this has been left to discussions between the parties.

Institutional Provisions, Transparency, etc.

The TPP parties are committed to improve information exchange related to equivalency or regionalization requests and to promote systems-based audits to assess the effectiveness of regulatory controls of the exporting party. The chapter also puts in place a mechanism for consultation between governments to resolve SPS matters.[17]

---

[13] Article 7.7, Chapter 7 on SPS Measures, TPP.
[14] Article 7.10, Chapter 7 on SPS Measures, TPP.
[15] Article 7.11, Chapter 7 on SPS Measures, TPP.
[16] Ibid.
[17] Article 7.17, Chapter 7 on SPS Measures, TPP.

Conformity with International Standards: Science and Risk Analysis

The TPP SPS provisions on science and risk analysis mandate that parties will conform to international standards.[18] Under the transparency provision of the TPP chapter, there is a requirement of providing rationally related objective scientific evidence to another party when a measure does not conform to international standards.[19] This requirement under the TPP SPS chapter places a higher standard than that provided under Article 5.8 of the WTO SPS Agreement which only requires for an explanation in case the measure is not based on an international standard.

Dispute Settlement

The dispute settlement chapter of the TPP has been made applicable in a phased manner to some of the SPS provisions. With regard to provisions on equivalence,[20] audits[21] and import checks,[22] dispute resolution can be invoked only one year after the date of entry into force of the TPP; and with regard to science and risk analysis,[23] the disputes chapter would apply two years from the date of entry into force.

7.4 Implications of the TPP's TBT and SPS Chapters

The TPP's TBT and SPS chapters are based on the WTO agreements on TBT and SPS, and are largely facilitative in that they provide the framework for moving towards specified international standards, especially those specified in their product-specific annexes. The TBT chapter's product-specific annexes (ranging from pharmaceuticals to cosmetics to IT products) provide an outline for elements of mutual recognition and standardization.

---

[18] Article 7.9, Chapter 7 on SPS Measures, TPP.
[19] Article 7.13.6, Chapter 7 on SPS Measures, TPP.
[20] Article 7.8, Chapter 7 on SPS Measures, TPP.
[21] Article 7.10, Chapter 7 on SPS Measures, TPP.
[22] Article 7.11, Chapter 7 on SPS Measures, TPP.
[23] Article 7.9, Chapter 7 on SPS Measures, TPP.

The WTO-plus commitments of the TBT chapter pertain to aspects such as higher emphasis on consideration of science for the purpose of enacting technical regulations. With regard to SPS measures, the liberty to these on grounds of precaution (when there is scientific uncertainty) is possible as is the case under the WTO's SPS Agreement. The difference however is the willingness that such member needs to show to listen and consult with another TPP member when science-based assessments are provided. The other WTO-plus provisions of these chapters are a higher degree of transparency obligations, and timelines for response systems that countries must have for conclusion of equivalence assessment and mutual recognition of each other's regulatory systems relating to technical regulations and SPS measures. A broad assessment of TBT and SPS obligations for TPP members is that these contain incrementally more specific obligations than the WTO's SPS and TBT Agreements; but in substance and essence, they follow the WTO principle that each country has the right to enact its TBT and SPS measures pursuant to legitimate policy objectives, provided that the overall framework of disciplines (such as reliance on international standards, where available, and use of science-based factors for enacting such measures, etc.) is adhered to.

Impact on Non-TPP Countries

With regard to non-TPP parties, it is important to note, in relation to standards, that a generalization that is sometimes made is that the TPP would lead to alignment of standards among TPP parties, which will reduce the costs for businesses in TPP countries and increase the costs for non-TPP parties such as India (Meltzer 2016). However, it should be emphasized that standards, unlike tariffs, are not multilateralized within the TPP (or for that matter even within the WTO Agreements). The TPP, like the WTO, simply creates the platform for countries to enter into agreements of mutual recognition and/or equivalence, based on certain international standards. The WTO's TBT and SPS Agreements provide for this liberty for countries. In this context, the provisions of the TPP Agreement can be seen as a simple reiteration of pre-existing WTO principles.

Complex regulations are an existing feature of most developed economies. Other than regulatory frameworks, businesses also impose their own requirements in order to ensure the quality of inputs, sourcing requirements, health and labour certifications, etc.

Developing countries like India are also known to be 'standard takers' rather than 'standard makers'. The success of exporters from countries like India depends on their ability to match up to the standards. Trade-related product standards typically apply only to products destined for specific destinations, and a firm can choose whether to meet them (World Bank 2016). As noted in a recent analysis of this aspect, in general, exporters are known to have conformed their goods or services to the most stringent rules of the largest, most affluent consumer markets, that is, the USA or the EU, rather than incur the expense of differentiating their production for each market (Bollyky and Bradford 2013).

Matching up products to the higher standards of the US market, therefore, may not be a significant problem for exporters from non-members like India. As discussed earlier, technical regulations and standards is not an aspect on the basis of which TPP members can differentiate between imports from members and non-members of the TPP. In such a scenario, if the TPP actually results in harmonization of regulations and standards in TPP members' markets, it could possibly have spillover benefits for exporters from non-members like India, since gearing up products for the US market access would mean that their products are suitable for sale in other TPP member countries as well.

An exporter in any country seeking to export to a TPP member would necessarily need to match up to standards required under the TPP. Building of technical capacities to achieve better manufacturing processes, and effectively meet standards, is but a given to ensure greater market access.

The underlying point is that unlike the issue of tariffs, where being a TPP party entitles another TPP party to market access at a lower tariff rate, and non-TPP parties are excluded from such access, the issue of standards will operate differently, since TPP parties cannot exclude products from market access on account of differential regulations or standards in their home countries. The recognition of conformity assessment, equivalence and minimization of multiple testing requirements could certainly mean lowering of costs for exporters from TPP parties. Any move towards mutual recognition or harmonization of standards would have the obvious and logical consequence of exporters from such countries not having their products tested multiple times in the country of origin and the county of import. Reduction of costs is, therefore, a likely consequence of such a development; but this cannot be characterized as a consequence of the TPP, since this practice exists currently, and the TPP does not create any exclusionary 'TPP members only club' on TBT and SPS measures. In fact, such a move would arguably not sustain scrutiny under WTO obligations under the SPS and TBT

Agreements, since neither of these agreements allow deviation from the national treatment principle in respect of FTAs that are entered into.

Another aspect to be taken into consideration is that any mutual recognition or other agreement for recognition of equivalence is something that cannot be confined under the WTO Agreement to members of a regional agreement. For example, under Article 4 of the WTO SPS Agreement, members have an 'obligation' to accept equivalent SPS measures that are objectively demonstrated by the exporting member as achieving the importing member's appropriate level of SPS protection. A similar obligation exists under Articles 2.7, 6.1 and 6.3 of the WTO TBT Agreement.

7.5 Conclusion

In conclusion, standards for TBT and SPS under the TPP Agreement are likely to lead to greater harmonization among TPP members, but they cannot exclude market access for exporters from non-TPP members if such exporter meets the standard of the concerned TPP member. This is the situation in the current world, whether with or without the TPP. The possible harmonization of standards between TPP members may actually work to the benefit for exporters from non-TPP members, who may be able to access multiple markets by conforming their product standards to that of one of the TPP members.

References

Bollyky, Thomas J., and Anu Bradford. 2017. 'Getting to Yes on Transatlantic Trade'. *Foreign Affairs*.

Global Harmonization Task Force. 2012. *Final Document: Definition of the Terms 'Medical Device' and 'In Vitro Diagnostic (IVD) Medical Device*. GHTF/SG1/N071:2012. Global Harmonization Task Force. Retrieved 10 August 2017, from http://www.imdrf.org/docs/ghtf/final/sg1/technical-docs/ghtf-sg1-n071-2012-definition-of-terms-120516.pdf

Maur, Jean-Christophe, and Ben Shephard. 2011. 'Product Standards'. In *Preferential Trade Agreement Policies for Development: A Handbook*, edited by Jean-Pierre Chauffour and Jean-Christophe Maur. Washington, DC: World Bank.

Meltzer, Joshua. 2016. 'Standards and Regulations in the TPP Negotiations: Implications for India'. In *TPP and India* (pp. 225–79), edited by Harshvardhan Singh. New Delhi: Wisdom Tree.

World Bank. 2016. 'Potential Macro-economic Implications of the Trans-Pacific Partnership'. In *Global Economic Prospects January 2016*. Washington, DC: World Bank.

8
Addressing 'Labour' in Trade Agreements
The TPP Approach
R.V. Anuradha

8.1 Trade and Labour: A Conceptual Journey

Chapter 19 of the Trans-Pacific Partnership (TPP) Agreement on 'labour' is essentially a crystallization of labour provisions across various US free trade agreements (FTAs). Before delving into the contents and assessing the implications of this chapter, it would be useful to first set out the perspectives underpinning the trade and labour linkage, which is a sensitive and controversial issue for many countries and one that India has been a strong opponent of.

The trade and labour debate is characterized by two conflicting strands of thought: one favouring the inclusion of labour standards in trade negotiations and the other discrediting and denouncing any kind of trade–labour linkage. The intellectual foundation of these divergent sets of viewpoints is in alignment with the contradictory stands of the developed and industrialized nations on the one hand, and the developing nations on the other. The divergence of views was most visible during the World Trade Organization (WTO) Ministerial Conference at Singapore in 1996, and at Seattle in 1999, when the developing nations Brazil, Egypt, India and Malaysia vehemently opposed the pressure from the developed nations to include labour standards within the ambit of the WTO (Panagariya 2003). While this resistance has been responsible for

Addressing 'Labour' in Trade Agreements **233**

lack of any labour standards being incorporated under the WTO, labour provisions have increasingly found reflection in bilateral and regional FTAs, especially those entered into by the United States of America (USA) and the European Union (EU).

The literature discussing the presence of any linkage between trade and labour issues can be grouped on the basis of the following two considerations: (a) the nature of economic relationship between trade and labour standards (the economic dimension), and (b) the need and rationale, if any, for incorporation of legal principles addressing labour standards in trade negotiations the legal and institutional dimension (Block, Roberts and Clarke 2003).

The Economic Dimension

The discussion on the economic relationship between trade and labour standards is grounded on basically two issues. Firstly, whether lower labour standards result in an unfair competitive edge and secondly, whether due to this 'unfair advantage', a 'race to the bottom' regarding labour standards would occur. Proponents of the trade and labour standards linkage argue that countries with relatively low labour standards would have lower costs of production which would give them an unfair advantage over countries which provide for higher labour standards. While this competitive advantage may be rewarding in the short run, it is argued that the overall and long-term effect of low labour standards would be workplace violations (Hiatt and Greenfield 2004). It has been observed that lower labour standards are associated with higher trade (Granger and Siroen 2006). It has also been argued that since labour is a factor of production of goods that are traded internationally, violations of international labour standards should be enforced through trade sanctions (Ehrenberg 1995).

However, there is a significant body of literature that debunks this argument (Block, Roberts and Clarke 2003). An Organisation for Economic Co-operation and Development (OECD 2003) study on the trade and labour linkage has observed that while countries which strengthen their core labour standards can increase economic growth and efficiency by raising skill levels in the workforce and by creating an environment which encourages innovation and higher productivity, there is no evidence to suggest that countries with low core labour standards enjoy a better export performance. A prominent voice in this regard is Paul Krugman (1994), a strong proponent of trade liberalization, who regards the demands for labour standards in trade agreements as a protectionist measure in the guise of humanitarian concerns. This view is linked with the concept of consumer welfare maximization which encourages a particular economy to be at its efficient best by producing at minimum possible cost (Block, Roberts and Ormiston 2002). Some scholars argue that the immediate imposition of international labour standards would lead to a reduction in the total economic welfare worldwide in developing nations, as well as developed and industrialized nations (see, for example, Trebilcock and Howse 2005). It has been noted that attaching labour standards to the WTO and other trade agreements will not achieve the goal of better wages or labour standards, nor will it have the desired effect of keeping more jobs in the industrialized countries (Stern and Turrell 2003). On the contrary, it has also been argued that such a policy could make things worse for many workers in developing countries (ibid.).

Another argument, often related with the unfair competition, by proponents of the trade and labour linkage, is that in the absence of coercive international labour standards, all the nations of the world would deliberately start to continuously lower their labour standards so as to benefit from the comparative advantage. Supporters of trade–labour linkage fear that competition from imports made in low-wage developing countries will lead to loss of jobs for workers in developed countries, and would drive the developed countries to lower their labour standards (see discussions in Bhala 1998).

The opponents of such a linkage, however, argue that there is no clear basis for this argument and there is little empirical support for a link between increased world trade and a decline in labour conditions (Gould 2001). It has also been noted that if mandatory standards raise the cost of labour above its level of productivity, this will not improve wages and working conditions of workers in poor countries; on the contrary, workers may actually suffer negative consequences when their wages are raised above the market value of their productivity (Stern and Turrell 2003).[1]

Hence, according to scholars like Jagdish Bhagwati (2001), the demand for linkage that reflects these unsupported concerns can then

---

[1] Stern and Turrell refer to numerous empirical studies which have measured the degree to which workers were displaced when mandated minimum wages were raised by different amounts.

be interpreted legitimately as protectionist. Further, it is also argued that improvements in actual labour conditions may raise productivity and hence compensation, but the analysis finds no evidence that adoption of international labour standards has produced such improvements (Flanagan 2002).

The Legal and Institutional Dimension

One of the major points of contention in the trade–labour linkage debate is that providing for appropriate labour standards is essentially a function of the state, and imposition of international labour standards is against the concept of state sovereignty. In this sense, trade–labour linkage has also been referred to as a form of political imperialism (see, for example, discussions in Barry and Reddy 2006). It has been argued that there is no need for linkage since developing countries may improve their labour standards without endangering their comparative advantage (Elliott and Freeman 2003).

The advocates of trade–labour linkage, however, argue that an absolutist concept of national sovereignty is unsustainable in the modern context of integrated world economy (Erickson and Mitchell 1999). It has also been argued that international labour standards and international trade law could contribute to a modification or a shift in the concept of state sovereignty and that this would enable better labour protection (Macklem 2002).

At the WTO, there has been strong opposition to the linkage of labour standards to trade. The Singapore Ministerial Declaration in 1996, as discussed earlier, unequivocally rejected the use of labour standards for protectionist purposes. Specifically, the Singapore Ministerial Declaration stated,

> [E]conomic growth and development fostered by increased trade and further trade liberalization contribute to the promotion of these standards. We reject the use of labour standards for protectionist purposes, and agree that the comparative advantage of countries, particularly low-wage developing countries, must in no way be put into question.

It is with this in view that the WTO and International Labour Organization (ILO) secretariats were asked to continue their existing collaboration.

Those in favour of such inclusion are of the view that the trade agreements should incorporate labour standards because labour is a factor of production, and failure by a government to regulate the means by which labour is utilized constitutes a trade distortion (Zaheer 2004). A slightly different view, though favouring inclusion, is that though trade sanctions should be viewed as a last resort, labour issues should be considered by in-trade agreements with focus on incentives and preferences to developing nations to promote higher labour standards (Howse and Mutua 2000).

On the other hand, several scholars have written about the dangers of incorporation of labour standards in trade agreements (Bhagwati 1995; also see Srinivasan 1996). This is largely premised on the fear of the coercive nature of the dealings in trade agreements such as the WTO and also the relative inability of the developing nations, on account of limited resources, to adequately defend their position (Basu 2001). The use of trade sanctions for imposition of labour standards is not regarded as the best approach to ensure better domestic labour standards (Maskus 1997).

Opponents of a trade and labour linkage at the WTO also emphasize that the empirical literature suggests that mandating unsustainably high labour standards will not improve average wages and working conditions in poor countries or even improve trade of developing countries (Stern and Turrell 2003). Such mandates can create further inequality, by reducing the number of workers with better pay and working conditions and increasing the number in poorer conditions (ibid.).

8.2 Labour Under the TPP Agreement

The debates on trade and labour notwithstanding, labour chapters are increasingly finding reflection in trade agreements. A study done for the ILO notes an increasing trend in use of labour provisions in FTAs since the global financial crisis of 2008 (Ebert and Posthuma 2011).

The ILO study notes that the use of labour provisions is no longer confined to FTAs entered into by the USA and the EU, and that agreements entered into by countries such as Chile, New Zealand and various regional integration organizations have also used such provisions. The scope and approach adopted by FTAs vary widely, ranging from referencing specific ILO Conventions to the general ILO Declaration on Fundamental Principles and Rights at Work and its follow-up (ILO

1998 Declaration), to a general commitment by parties to enforce labour standards under their own national labour law.

As noted in the beginning of this chapter, the TPP chapter on labour reflects the US approach across its FTAs. The interesting aspect to note is that the USA itself does not have a commendable record in terms of ratification of the international labour conventions of the ILO. The ILO's Governing Body has identified eight conventions as 'fundamental' covering subjects that are considered as fundamental principles and rights at work: freedom of association and the effective recognition of the right to collective bargaining, the elimination of all forms of forced or compulsory labour, the effective abolition of child labour and the elimination of discrimination in respect of employment and occupation. The ILO fundamental conventions are legally binding international treaties applicable for countries that have ratified the same.

The USA has ratified only two out of the eight fundamental ILO conventions, those pertaining to forced labour and child labour. But there are six fundamental ILO conventions that the USA has not ratified and these are the conventions on forced labour,[2] freedom of association,[3] collective bargaining,[4] equal remuneration,[5] employment discrimination[6] and minimum age.[7]

Ratifications of the fundamental ILO conventions by the developed countries which were engaged in the TPP (including the USA) are highlighted in Table 8.1.

It is interesting to note that India has four ratifications, that is, two more than the USA. As a consequence, the reference under the TPP's Chapter 19 on labour is not to specific ILO conventions, but to the ILO Declaration on Fundamental Principles and Rights at Work of 1998 (ILO 1998 Declaration). A 'declaration', by its very nature, is not a binding legal instrument but represents soft law obligations. The text of the declaration recognizes that even when ILO members have not ratified the fundamental ILO conventions, they would need to adhere to the principles of these conventions.

---

[2] C029—Forced Labour Convention, 1930 (No. 29).
[3] C087—Freedom of Association and Protection of the Right to Organise Convention, 1948 (No. 87).
[4] C098—Right to Organise and Collective Bargaining Convention, 1949 (No. 98).
[5] C100 Equal Remuneration Convention, 1951 (No. 100).
[6] C111—Discrimination (Employment and Occupation) Convention, 1958 (No. 111).
[7] C138—Minimum Age Convention, 1973 (No. 138).

Table 8.1 Status of ratifications of fundamental ILO conventions by developed countries under the TPP (including the USA)

Country	Freedom of Association		Forced Labour		Discrimination		Child Labour	
	Freedom of Association and Protection of the Right to Organize Convention, 1948	Right to Organize and Collective Bargaining Convention, 1949	Forced Labour Convention, 1930	Abolition of Forced Labour Convention, 1957	Equal Remuneration Convention, 1951	Discrimination (Employment and Occupation) Convention, 1958	Minimum Age Convention, 1973	Worst Forms of Child Labour Convention, 1999
USA	X	X	X	1991	X	X	X	1999
Canada	1972	X	2011	1959	1972	1964	2016	2000
Australia	1973	1973	1932	1960	1974	1973	X	2006
New Zealand	X	2003	1938	1968	1983	1983	X	2001
Japan	1965	1953	1932	X	1967	X	2000	2001
Singapore	X	1965	1965	Denounced: 1979	2002	X	2005	2001

Source: Author.

Nature of Labour-related Obligations

The labour-related obligations that are required under Chapter 19 of the TPP are threefold:

1. A general obligation to maintain rights under ILO Declaration on Fundamental Principles and Rights at Work. As noted above, this declaration essentially reiterates the principles of ILO's fundamental conventions pertaining to freedom of association and collective bargaining; elimination of all forms of compulsory labour; effective abolition of child labour, and elimination of employment-related discrimination. The labour chapter does not make direct reference to any of these conventions; instead, the focus is on the declaration whose legally binding status falls in the realm of soft law, as opposed to the more legally binding provisions of the conventions.
2. The TPP chapter refers to an additional obligation to adopt and maintain laws and practices governing 'acceptable conditions of work'. This relates to minimum wages, hours of work, and occupational safety and health as determined by each party.
3. Each party is required to guarantee enforcement of labour laws within its territory, including by maintaining impartial and independent judicial and quasi-judicial tribunals.

In relation to the above obligations, the labour chapter provides that to establish the violation of an obligation, the complaining party needs to demonstrate that the other party has 'failed to adopt or maintain a statute, regulation or practice in a manner affecting trade or investment between the parties'. The term 'affecting trade or investment' is broad and would be open to interpretation. Given that labour is an integral factor of any manufacturing or services-related activity, labour in itself would 'affect' trade and investment. How this is linked to 'failure to adopt or maintain' specific labour-related obligations would need to be examined in a given set of circumstances. Whether competitiveness of labour can be questioned through such an open-ended provision is yet to be seen. As explained above, the fundamental aspects that have been highlighted in the trade and labour discussion at the WTO have been that: (a) labour standards cannot be used for protectionist purposes, and (b) the comparative advantage of countries, particularly low-wage developing countries, must in no way be put into question. In the absence of these safeguards under the TPP Chapter 19, the overall focus and implementation of this chapter will need to be seen in practice.

More specifically, with regard to the obligation on 'acceptable conditions of work', Note 5 in the labour chapter clarifies that what constitutes 'acceptable conditions of work' will be determined by each party. This appears to imply that aspects such as minimum wages, hours of work, etc., are to be determined by each party, and appears to suggest a certain degree of sovereign policy space in the determination of what would constitute 'acceptable conditions'. However, the definition of 'labour laws' under Article 19.1 brings in the concept of 'internationally recognized labour rights' as part of the overarching framework for 'acceptable conditions of work'. This leaves room open for further scrutiny as regards whether a country's determination of wages or hours of work is 'internationally recognized'.

Labour Consistency Plans for Three TPP Members

A unique feature of the labour chapter of the TPP Agreement is the bilateral 'consistency plans' that have been entered into between the USA and Brunei Darusalam, Malaysia and Vietnam. Each plan is worded as a letter between the representatives of the USA, on the one hand, and the TPP member, on the other, and states that it 'create rights and obligations' only between the two signatories to the letter. The letters state that they are being entered into pursuant to Chapter 19 on labour of the TPP Agreement; but not all TPP members are parties to these letters. It is only commitments that each of the three countries have taken vis-à-vis the USA. The USTR has noted in its summary on Labour provisions under the TPP that[8]:

> ... the United States has concluded bilateral implementation plans with several individual TPP countries to ensure that their laws and practices are consistent with international standards, including through reforms of laws, regulations, institutions, and practice. The commitments in the implementation plans are subject to TPP dispute settlement procedures, meaning they are fully enforceable and backed up by trade sanctions.

---

[8] USTR Summary of Chapter 19, Labour: https://ustr.gov/sites/default/files/TPP-Chapter-Summary-Labour-1.pdf (last visited 7 August 2017).

Each plan of action specifies commitments towards legal reform, undertakes relevant institutional reform and capacity building, and ensures full transparency in implementation of each step of the action plan. The legislative amendments are to be put into place before the coming into effect of the TPP Agreement. Each plan envisages an expert panel comprising of members from the governments of the USA and the country undertaking the consistency obligations, as well as the ILO.

Institutional Mechanisms

Public Submissions

Dispute settlement relating to labour provisions under Chapter 19 are confined to State-to-State mechanisms. However, the institutional mechanisms established under the TPP allow for interventions by non-governmental organizations and any other person from any of the parties which have been given rights to make 'public submissions'. Each party is required to put in place the mechanism for such submissions and communicate these to the other parties. Each of such submissions needs to be considered and responded to 'in a timely manner', in writing.[9] Each submission, as well as the results of the party's consideration of such submission, also needs to be made publicly available.[10]

Cooperative Labour Dialogue

A party may request a labour dialogue with another party on any matter arising under the chapter. Outcomes may include the development and implementation of action plans or cooperative programmes. They may also include capacity building to encourage or assist parties to identify and address labour matters.

Each party is mandated to establish or maintain, and consult, a national labour consultative or advisory body or similar mechanism, for members of its public, including representatives of its labour and business organizations, to provide views on matters regarding the chapter.

---

[9] Article 19.9, Chapter 19.
[10] Ibid.

Labour Council

A labour council, composed of senior governmental representatives as designated by each party, provides the forum to discuss matters of common interest and consider activities under the chapter, including being able to receive public submissions on issues covered by the chapter.

Consultation and Dispute Settlement

All obligations in the chapter are subject to the same dispute settlement chapter that applies to the broader TPP Agreement. However, the labour chapter has specific procedures for labour consultation that must be used before the dispute settlement provisions of TPP are employed. The procedures provide the timelines within which parties are required to endeavour to arrive at mutual resolution to the matter.

Corporate Social Responsibility

The chapter provides that each party shall endeavour to encourage enterprises to voluntarily adopt corporate social responsibility (CSR) initiatives on labour issues that have been endorsed or are supported by that party. In essence, this requirement appears to promote private labour standards based on labour standards that are supported by the government.

8.3 Impact of the TPP's Labour Chapter

As discussed in the introductory part of this chapter, there are significant differences of views on the economic and legal underpinnings of the trade–labour linkage. Labour provisions are, however, an integral part of several trade agreements, and with them, there is the prospect of trade sanctions being imposed on countries on account of non-compliance with labour-related provisions. The approach of the TPP chapter in this regard is similar to the approach in US FTAs so far. A unique aspect of the TPP's labour chapter is the side agreements for labour consistency plans that are applicable on Vietnam, Malaysia and Brunei Darussalam, under which each country has committed to specific labour law reform prior to the coming into force of the TPP Agreement.

For non-parties to the TPP Agreement, it has been estimated that the higher labour standards across TPP parties would result in rise in wages for unskilled labour even in non-TPP parties (Narayanan and Ciuriak 2016, Table 1.2). The manner in which this could possibly occur is if labour standards actually mandate any specific wage-related standards that need to be implemented. However, given that the TPP's labour chapter itself does not mandate any specific wage-related standard that needs to be adhered to, it is difficult to envisage a situation wherein this can be predicted to be a consequence of the TPP's labour chapter. Rising wages has been a natural consequence of economic growth, as well as a result of government intervention in countries like India.

The TPP Agreement would likely result in greater scrutiny of labour laws and their enforcement in TPP member countries; but there is no product- or production-related labour standard that is mandated in respect of all imports into TPP countries. In a hypothetical instance that TPP parties arrive at an industry-wide standard that mandates that all products imported into TPP countries will need to carry labour certification of certain uniformity of specific labour standards, such requirements could possibly be challenged as violating such TPP parties' WTO obligations (under General Agreement on Tariffs and Trade [GATT] and the technical barriers to trade [TBT] Agreement). As of now, it must be underscored that all this is mere conjecture and speculation. Nothing in the TPP's labour chapter suggests that such a consequence is indeed possible. It is, however, possible that private standards incorporating labour-related requirements, certification and labelling could gradually increase across TPP parties.

As noted above, the provision on CSR under the labour chapter requires parties to encourage private enterprises to 'voluntarily adopt CSR initiatives on labour issues' that have been endorsed or are supported by that party. This could provide the basis for private standards relating to labour-related requirements. To the extent that such requirements, under the TPP provision on CSR, have the blessing of the government, given the wording of the TPP's provision in this regard, the evolution of such provisions should be closely tracked in order to consider an appropriate challenge under the WTO's TBT Agreement.

What Would Be the Implications of Adhering to an FTA with TPP-type Provisions on Labour?

A key aspect of the TPP-type labour provisions in an FTA is the systemic and institutional implications. The issue is not that labour is an unimportant issue. The key issue is—what is the institution that is best positioned to set labour standards and monitor compliance? As members of the ILO, most countries today have a close institutional relationship between their labour ministries and the ILO. The ILO plays an active role in monitoring and providing advice to its members on compliance with labour laws. The approach is consultative and cooperative, rather than adversarial.

By making labour provisions as part of an FTA, however, the biggest impact would mean that, other than the ILO keeping track of and monitoring and reviewing a country's obligations, any accession to a TPP-type FTA would lead to another layer of scrutiny through 'consultations' and 'cooperation' by the FTA members. Obligations such as 'implementation of action plans' or cooperative programmes could become pressure points on labour-related issues.

More fundamentally, any perceived non-compliance with requirements under the chapter, for example, 'acceptable conditions of work', within a country could also become the subject matter of dispute resolution which can be remedied through trade sanctions. Taken to its logical conclusion, the very principle that the WTO's Singapore Ministerial Declaration sought to address, that is, not using labour conditionalities to question the comparative advantage of low-wage nations, could itself be put into question under such dispute settlement under a trade agreement.

References

Barry, Christian, and Sanjay G. Reddy. 2006. 'International Trade and Labour Standards: A Proposal for Linkage'. *Cornell International Law Journal* 39: 545–64.
Basu, Kaushik. 2001. 'Compacts, Conventions, and Codes: Initiatives for Higher International Labour Standards'. *Cornell International Law Journal* 34: 487–92.
Bhagwati, Jagdish. 1995. 'Trade Liberalisation and "Fair Trade" Demands: Addressing the Environmental and Labour Standards Issues'. *The World Economy* 18: 745.
———. 2001. Free Trade and Labour. Retrieved 18 July 2017, from http://www.uoit.ca/sas/Globalization%20and%20WTO/Free%20Trade%20and%20Labour.pdf
Bhala, Raj. 1998. 'Clarifying the Trade-Labour Link'. *Columbia Journal of Transnational Law* 11 (17).

Block, Richard N., Karen Roberts, and Ronald Oliver Clarke. 2003. *Labor Standards in the United States and Canada*. Kalamazoo, MI: W.E. Upjohn Institute.

Block, Richard N., Karen Roberts, and Russell Ormiston. 2002. 'Economic Perspectives on International Labour Standards'. *Journal of International Law* 11 (3): 417, 420.

Ebert, Franz Christian, and Anne Posthuma. 2011. *Labour Provisions in Trade Arrangements: Current Trends and Perspectives*. Geneva: International Labour Organization.

Ehrenberg, Daniel S. 1995. 'The Labour Link: Applying the International Trading System to Enforce Violations of Forced and Child Labour'. *Yale Journal of International Law* 20: 361–64.

Elliott, Kimberly A., and Richard B. Freeman. 2003. *Can Labour Standards Improve Under Globalization?* Washington, DC: Institute for International Economics.

Erickson, Christopher L., and Daniel J.B. Mitchell. 1999. 'The American Experience with Labour Standards and Trade Agreements'. *Journal of Small and Emerging Business Law* 3: 41–43.

Robert J. Flanagan, Labour Standards and International Competitive Advantage (International Labour Standards Conference, Stanford Law School, May 20, 2002). Retrieved 10 August 2017, from https://www.researchgate.net/publication/237309583_Labor_standards_and_international_competitive_advantage

Gould, William B., IV. 2001. 'Labour Law for a Global Economy: The Uneasy Case for International Labour Standards'. *Nebraska Law Review* 80: 715, 725–26.

Granger, Clotilde, and Jean-Marc Siroen. 2006, October. 'Core Labour Standards in Trade Agreements from Multilateralism to Bilateralism'. Retrieved from http://econpapers.repec.org/paper/nerdauphi/urn_3ahdl_3a123456789_2f255.htm

Hiatt, Jonathan P., and Deborah Greenfield. 2004. 'The Importance of Core Labour Rights in World Development'. *The Michigan Journal of International Law* 26 (1): 39–62. Retrieved 10 August 2017, from http://repository.law.umich.edu/mjil/vol26/iss1/3

Howse, Robert, and Makua Mutua. 2000. 'Protecting Human Rights in a Global Economy: Challenges for the World Trade Organization'. International Centre for Human Rights and Democratic Development, Canada. Retrieved 10 August 2017 from http://www.ichrdd.ca/english/commdoc/publications/globalization/wtoRightsGlob.html#r59

Krugman, Paul. 1994. 'Does Third World Growth Hurt First World Prosperity?' *Harvard Business Review*, 72 (4 [July–August]): 113–21.

Macklem, Patrick. 2002. 'Labour Law Beyond Borders'. *Journal of International Economic Law* 5 (August): 605–45.

Maskus, Keith E. 1997. 'Should Core Labour Standards Be Imposed Through International Trade Policy?' Policy Research Working Paper No. 1817, World Bank, Geneva. http://www.worldbank.org/html/dec/Publications/Workpapers/WPS1800series/wps1817/wps1817.pdf

Narayanan, G. Badri, Harsha Vardhana Singh and Dan Ciuriak. 2016. *Chapter 4 in 'TPP and India: Implications of Mega-regionals for Developing Economies'*, (pp. 133–197) edited by Harsha V. Singh. New Delhi: Wisdom Tree.

OECD. 2000. *International Trade and Core Labour Standards*. Paris: OECD.

Panagariya, Arvind. 2003. *Trade-Labour Link: A Post-Seattle Analysis*. Retrieved 10 August 2017, from http://www.columbia.edu/~ap2231/Policy%20Papers/zdenek PANAGARYAYA%20(Chapter%203.doc).pdf

Srinivasan, T.N. 1996. 'International Trade and Labour Standards from an Economic Perspective'. In *Challenges to the New World Trade Organization*, edited by Pitou van Dijck and Gerrit Faber. The Netherlands: Brill Academic Publications.

Stern, Robert and Katherine Turrell, 2003. 'Labour Standards and the World Trade Organization'. Retrieved 10 August 2017, from available https://www.wto.org/english/forums_e/ngo_e/labor_standards_e.doc

———. 2003. 'Labour Standards and the World Trade Organization'. Retrieved 18 July 2017, from https://www.wto.org/english/forums_e/ngo_e/labor_standards_e.doc

Trebilcock, Michael J., and Robert Howse. 2005. 'Trade Policy and Labour Standards'. *Minnesota Journal of Global Trade* 14: 261, 268.

Zaheer, Daniel A. 2004. 'Breaking the Deadlock: Why and How Developing Countries Should Accept Labour Standards in the WTO'. *Stanford Journal of Law, Business and Finance* 9: 69–73.

9
Trade and Environment under the TPP

R.V. Anuradha

9.1 Trade and Environment

Environment is a critical issue for an international agreement. A fundamental question, however, is whether this issue is better addressed in standalone environmental agreements, with its separate institutional framework, or whether trade agreements are suitable for addressing environmental concerns. A background paper prepared by the World Trade Organization (WTO) Secretariat in 1997 observed that trade instruments are 'not' the first-best policy for addressing environmental problems (WTO Secretariat 1997; also see WTO 2004).

Environmental problems have, till recently, been addressed in standalone multilateral environmental agreements (MEAs), under the aegis of the United Nations. Notable MEAs include the United Nations Framework Convention on Climate Change (UNFCCC), the Convention on Biological Diversity, the Vienna Convention on protection of the Ozone Layer, the Convention on International Trade in Endangered Species of Wild Fauna and Flora (CITES), etc. Such a specialized approach to 'environment' encompasses the elaboration of obligations for countries with respect to the environment and the means to achieve it through concrete steps. Agreements such as the UNFCCC's Kyoto Protocol and the Vienna Convention's Montreal Protocol also embody differential approaches to the obligations for developed and developing countries, taking into account their respective roles in contributing to the environmental problem in the first place, as well as the need for different transitional periods, capacity building, and technical and financial assistance for developing countries.

The first trade agreement to integrate a 'side agreement' on the environment was the North American Free Trade Agreement (NAFTA), entered into by the United States of America (USA), Canada and Mexico. The apparent motivation for this approach was to assuage concerns that the entry into the trade agreement would not lead to the relocation of polluting industries from the USA to Mexico, where the costs of compliance with environmental norms would be cheaper.

Proponents of the trade and environment linkage primarily use this 'pollution haven' hypothesis, as the reason why environment should be addressed within trade agreements. This hypothesis is essentially that firms whose main concern is to maximize profits may be inclined to move their operations to developing countries, where pollution control is inexpensive and lax (see, for example, Daly 1993). The validity of this assumption, however, has been questioned in several studies which have demonstrated that lower environmental regulations do not necessarily lead to a race to the bottom and that environmental regulations are not the only factors that guide investment decisions (see, for example, Friedman, Gerlowski and Silberman 1992).

The trade and environment linkage is questioned by economists such as Professor Jagdish Bhagwati who argue that free trade would eventually lead to economic growth and better income levels, which would translate into investment in higher environmental standards (Bhagwati 1993). He also points out that trade should not be used as a tool to impose environmental standards, as the welfare implications of free trade are independent of environmental standards (Bhagwati and Srinivasan 1996).

Environment Under the WTO

The WTO recognizes the importance of addressing environmental issues, but it does not seek to enforce any specific environmental standards or regulations through trade sanctions.

The Marrakesh Agreement Establishing the World Trade Organization (WTO Agreement) in its preamble states that members recognize that

> their relations in the field of trade and economic endeavour should be conducted with a view to raising standards of living, ensuring full employment and a large and steadily growing volume of real income and effective

demand, and expanding the production of and trade in goods and services, while allowing for the optimal use of the world's resources in accordance with the objective of sustainable development, seeking both to protect and preserve the environment and to enhance the means for doing so in a manner consistent with their respective needs and concerns at different levels of economic development.

This broad and generic reference to environment, in the context of sustainable development, also recognizes that while the preservation and protection of the environment is an important objective, it will be done 'in a manner consistent with their respective needs and concerns at different levels of economic development'. There is a clear recognition, therefore, that protection of the environment as an ideal in itself is not the WTO's objective, rather its focus is on the overall principle of sustainable development.

Other than the preamble to the WTO Agreement, environmental provisions find a place under the general exceptions to trade obligations,[1] and the WTO Agreements relating to technical barriers to trade (TBT) and sanitary and phytosanitary (SPS) measures. GATT Article XX on general exceptions lays out a number of specific instances in which WTO members may be exempted from GATT rules. Two exceptions are of particular relevance to the protection of the environment: paragraphs (b) and (g) of Article XX. Pursuant to these two paragraphs, WTO members may adopt policy measures that are inconsistent with GATT disciplines, but necessary to protect human, animal or plant life or health (paragraph (b)), or relating to the conservation of exhaustible natural resources (paragraph (g)). The GATS under Article XIV provides for an exception related to environment that is worded similar to Article XX(b).

The WTO Agreement on TBT seeks to ensure that product specifications, whether mandatory or voluntary (known as technical regulations and standards), as well as procedures to assess compliance with those specifications (known as conformity assessment procedures), do not create unnecessary obstacles to trade. In its preamble, the Agreement recognizes countries' rights to adopt such measures to the extent they consider appropriate—for example, to protect human, animal or plant life or health, or the environment.

The WTO Agreement on SPS measures deals with food safety, and human, animal and plant health and safety regulations. It recognizes

---

[1] Article XX of the General Agreement on Tariffs and Trade and Article XIV of the General Agreement on Trade in Services.

members' rights to adopt SPS measures but stipulates that they must be based on a risk assessment, should not create unnecessary obstacles to trade (should be applied only to the extent necessary to protect human, animal or plant life or health) and should not arbitrarily or unjustifiably discriminate between members where similar conditions prevail.

There have been several prominent disputes at the WTO dealing with the trade and environment interface, which have confirmed that measures relating to environment, which are inconsistent with trade obligations, can be adopted and maintained only when these are subject to the specified conditions under the WTO Agreements. These conditions seek to ensure that the environmental measures imposed do not constitute arbitrary or unjustifiable discrimination, or a form of disguised restriction on trade. There is also an emphasis on countries to demonstrate that they could not have relied on a less trade-restrictive alternative measure.

The questions on the trade–environment linkage notwithstanding, 'environment' has been making a rapid transition from an 'exception' to a trade agreement, to a core obligation of a trade agreement. Since the NAFTA, not only free trade agreement (FTAs) entered into by the USA but those entered into by Canada and New Zealand also incorporate environmental obligations. The European Union's (EU) approach in FTAs in the early 21st century was to include provisions on 'sustainable development', as a recognition of the interplay of economic, environmental and social concerns. The EU's more recent approaches reflect a move towards the US approach.

This stands in stark contrast to the approach of developing countries. Regional economic groups of several developing economies, such as the Mercado Común del Sur (MERCOSUR; Southern Common Market), Andean Community, Association of Southeast Asian Nations (ASEAN), South Asian Association for Regional Cooperation (SAARC), Caribbean Community (CARICOM) and the South African Development Community (SADC), recognize 'environmental issues' as an important aspect which countries need to collectively address. However, environmental issues are dealt by these groups in separate agreements or understandings, and not as part of an FTA.

9.2 TPP's Environment Chapter

The recently concluded, but yet to be enforced, mega-FTA—the Trans-Pacific Partnership (TPP) Agreement—mirrors the US approach to environmental provisions. With the TPP Agreement, the positions of the USA, Canada, Australia, Japan, and New Zealand, as well as the developing country members such as Vietnam, Malaysia and Brunei Darussalam, have now all been aligned with the US approach.

The objective of the TPP's Chapter 20 on environment is to promote 'high levels of environmental protection and effective enforcement of environmental laws, and enhance the capacities of the parties to address trade-related environmental issues'.[2] The term 'environmental laws' is defined to include both domestic laws, as well as a party's obligations under MEAs.[3] Each party's sovereign right to establish its own level of domestic environmental protection and environmental priorities is recognized[4]; but this is subject to the obligation of parties not to weaken or reduce protection under their environmental laws, or derogate from it, or weaken environmental protection to encourage trade and investment.[5]

With regard to MEAs, there is a general provision whereby parties reaffirm their commitment to implement the MEAs they have joined.[6] Specific obligations with regard to MEAs are specified with regard to commitments to undertake the following: measures to control production or trade in substances that can deplete or modify the ozone layer in accordance with the Montreal Protocol[7]; measures to prevent pollution of the marine environment from ships[8]; adopt, maintain and implement laws, regulations and other measures to fulfil obligations under the CITES, and take measures to combat and cooperate to prevent trade in wild fauna and flora that has been done illegally.[9]

TPP parties have further agreed to promote sustainable forest management, and to protect and conserve wild fauna and flora that they have identified as being at risk in their territories, including through measures to conserve the ecological integrity of specially protected natural areas, such as wetlands.

---

[2] Article 20.2 'Objectives'.
[3] Article 20.1 'Definitions'.
[4] Article 20.3(2).
[5] Article 20.3(46).
[6] Article 20.4.
[7] Article 20.5.
[8] Article 20.6.
[9] Article 20.17.

Fisheries Management and Elimination of Fisheries Subsidies

A key area where the TPP goes beyond other US FTA provisions is in its obligations on fisheries management and regulation of fisheries subsidies.[10] The TPP parties have committed to undertaking implementation of a fisheries management system that is designed to prevent overfishing and overcapacity. Parties have further committed to promote the recovery of overfished stocks through control, reduction and eventual elimination of all subsidies that contribute to overfishing and overcapacity. They have further agreed to sustainable fisheries management and promote conservation of important marine species. They are also obligated to prohibit fisheries subsidies that negatively affect fish stocks and that support illegal, unreported or unregulated fishing. To achieve the above, there are detailed provisions on transparency related to such subsidy programs and commitment on parties to make best efforts to refrain from introducing new subsidies that contribute to overfishing or overcapacity.[11]

Environmental Goods

The TPP Agreement commits parties to address and remove non-tariff barriers in respect of environmental goods, and also commits them to address these issues on a bilateral and plurilateral basis. Several of the TPP members are also participants in the negotiations for an environmental goods agreement in the sidelines of the WTO.

The parties may develop bilateral and plurilateral cooperative projects on environmental goods and services to address current and future global trade-related environmental challenges.

Public Consultations and the Environment Committee

The parties are mandated to provide opportunities for public input in implementation of the environment chapter. This requires each party

---

[10] Article 20.16.
[11] Ibid.

to put in place institutional mechanisms that can allow for receipt of and consideration given to public submissions on implementation of the chapter.[12] Any public submissions on environmental issues need to be responded to by each party in a timely manner, in writing. The submissions and a party's responses are to be made available to the public, for example, by posting on an appropriate public website.

The public submissions and consultation process are subject to review of the 'environment committee' established under the chapter. The environment committee comprises of senior government representatives of each party and is responsible for overseeing the implementation of the chapter.[13] If a public submission asserts that a party is failing to effectively enforce its environmental laws, and following that party's response to the public submission, any other party may request the environment committee to discuss that submission, and assess whether the matter could benefit from cooperative activities.

At the collective level of the environment committee, public sessions are required to be held regarding issues relating to implementation of the chapter, and this is required to be open for public participation.

Provisions Relating to Private Parties/Voluntary Actions—CSR

The chapter provides that each party 'should' encourage enterprises operating within its jurisdiction to adopt voluntarily, into their policies and practices, principles of corporate social responsibility (CSR) that are related to the environment. Such provisions should be consistent with internationally recognized standards and guidelines that have been endorsed or are supported by that party.[14]

Parties also undertake to promote flexible, voluntary mechanisms, such as voluntary auditing and reporting, market-based incentives, voluntary sharing of information and expertise, and public–private partnerships, as mechanisms to complement domestic regulatory measures, and that these should be designed in a manner that avoids the creation of unnecessary barriers to trade.[15]

---

[12] Article 20.9.
[13] Article 20.19.
[14] Article 20.10.
[15] Article 20.11.

The provisions relating to private sector actions find further expression in Article 20.11(3), which provide that when private entities or non-governmental organizations develop voluntary mechanisms for the promotion of products based on their environmental qualities, they should be encouraged to adhere to aspects such as taking into account scientific and technical information, being based on relevant international standards, recommendations or guidelines, and best practices, and not treating a product less favourably on the basis of origin.

The aforementioned requirements in relation to private standards provide certain principles and frameworks in which private standards can operate. While these are worded as soft law obligations in that the parties are required to 'encourage' private sector operations to adhere to the same, they could provide the basis for TPP members questioning private standards followed by the private sector in another TPP member, if they do not adhere to these aforementioned requirements.

The approach seems to be along the lines present under the Code of Good Practice of the WTO's TBT Agreement. While the soft wording used provides the basis for questions and discussions, it does not provide a concrete forum for taking action against discriminatory private standards, or onerous requirements in such standards.

Cooperation

Parties commit to cooperate to address matters of joint or common interest, including in the areas of conservation and sustainable use of biodiversity, and transition to low emissions and resilient economies. This is expected to be achieved through dialogues, workshops, seminars and conferences.[16] The environment committee comprising of representatives of all the parties is expected to review the implementation of such cooperative frameworks.

Consultation Between Parties and Dispute Resolution

The chapter establishes a three-tier consultation process. At the first level, consultations between parties need to be conducted at the bilateral

---

[16] Article 20.12.

level to address any matter involving the operation of the environment chapter. If the consulting parties fail to resolve the issue, 'senior representative consultations' can be convened wherein any other party can also participate. If this fails to resolve the issue, the chapter provides for calling for 'ministerial consultations' from the consulting parties, for resolution of the matter. The timeline set for the three levels of consultation is 60 days, or any other timeline agreed between the parties. But it is only after the consultations are exhausted that disputes on environmental issues can be raised under the TPP.

9.3 Implications of the Environment Chapter

The most significant implication of the TPP Agreement is the enforcement of environmental obligations (both under international and domestic law), through the TPP. As explained in the introductory section, India has been opposed to the trade–environment linkage because environment is strictly a non-trade issue whose enforcement cannot be the subject matter of a trade agreement. The WTO Agreement recognizes the use of environment as an exception to trade obligations, and such environmental exceptions can be exercised within a framework of rules and disciplines that minimize the risks of protectionist use of environmental provisions.

Putting environmental obligations as a core element of a trade agreement, however, could have different implications. Instead of being the subject matter of assessment of a multilateral environmental body, a party's domestic and international environmental law obligations are sought to be implemented through the potential use of trade sanctions.

The TPP also mandates all its member countries to provide opportunities for public input in implementation of the environment chapter, including through public submissions and public sessions of the environment committee that has been established to oversee the implementation of the chapter. This implies that implementation of environmental law and decision-making would need to be opened up to public scrutiny, not only to interested parties within a territory but also to private interests across all TPP member countries. This could act as a significant pressure point on implementation of not only domestic environmental laws but also in respect of implementation of the environment chapter. The chapter allows private persons from other parties to participate in the environment committee meetings. Such a provision could lead to higher presence of non-governmental actors in questioning the country's environmental processes. Whether the underlying interest in such a process is rooted in genuine environmental concerns or protectionism will be hard to discern.

In such a scenario, any country that is confronted with TPP-type provisions on environment, would need to deliberate on the following aspects:

- Do trade agreements need to address environmental issues? Or should environmental issues be left to standalone environmental agreements?
- Will improved trade and economic liberalization lead to better environmental protection? Are trade sanctions required to achieve this?
- What is the practical implication of using environmental provisions in trade agreements? How can protectionist measures in the garb of environmental activism be eliminated?
- If environment and trade are addressed in the same agreement, is there any role for MEAs?
- If environment and trade are addressed in the same agreement, should such agreements then have more nuanced environmental provisions, encompassing differential responsibilities for developed and developing countries, and elements for technical and financial assistance?

For countries that remain outside of FTAs like the TPP, and export to the FTA parties, the key issue is whether such provisions will see any increase in use of environmental standards for differentiating between products, and thereby impact imports? In this regard, it is pertinent to note that the WTO's TBT Agreement specifically recognizes room for development of voluntary standards by both the government as well as private standardizing bodies, which can broadly be for any objective, including the environment. In other words, there is nothing today that is preventing the development of private standards for environmental concerns, and in fact private standards are implemented by some private sector entities through practices such as eco-labelling.

Furthermore, it is widely acknowledged that exporters typically adapt to standards in the importing market to maintain market access. This is likely to continue in the TPP universe as well. It is also hypothetically possible that the convergence of any standards or norms could actually result in harmonization of standards across TPP parties, and this could have spillover benefits for exporters from non-TPP parties as well.

In the event, environmental standards become barriers to market access; there is, however, a difference in terms of how government-mandated environmental standards and private environmental standards would need to be addressed.

Government-mandated Environmental Laws/Regulations/Standards that Impact Import of Products from Non-TPP Countries

Any regulation or standard that pertains to environmental aspects, such as emissions in the process and production methods of a product, would qualify as a 'technical regulation'. However, there is some difference between WTO members on the extent to which measures regarding production processes that are not embodied in the product can be used as a point for differentiating between products. In the event there is any restriction to market access in a TPP member that results from a regulation that conditions market access subject to certification of emission norms or any other environmental requirements, this needs to be considered for a possible challenge as a WTO-inconsistent norm. The limits of WTO jurisprudence will need to be tested under specific facts and circumstances so as to ensure that discriminatory regulations that have no impact on the likeness of a product cannot be maintained.

Private Environmental Standards

It has been apprehended that emphasis on 'environment' as a trade-related obligation, and the explicit encouragement that is provided to private actors to incorporate environment as a CSR obligation and use it as part of environmental audits or market-based initiatives, could provide the basis for greater use of environment as the basis for private standards. As noted earlier, exporters from any country typically adapt their products to comply with private standards.

The WTO TBT Agreement provides certain broad and basic and largely non-enforceable principles in relation to private standards. These continue to apply in respect of any standards that a TPP country may come up with on grounds of environmental protection. What the TPP Agreement appears to do is to put in place certain broad principles which could additionally act as checks on private standardizing bodies in that they are 'encouraged' to ensure that their standards are based on international standards and do not treat a product less favourably on the basis of origin.[17]

To the extent that any extensive use of common environmental standards results in product differentiation, and exclusion of imports into TPP countries from non-parties, the limits of the WTO TBT Agreement in reigning in private standards are yet to be tested. This is something that would need to be addressed as and when there is any threat emerging from any private standard. Any extensive use of private standards by entities in TPP members can also potentially be questioned as a fallout of the TPP mandate that private entities may consider private standards to 'complement' the TPP mechanism. This can possibly be questioned as an implementation of the government mandate for a specific environmental standard. To the extent that these are part of a state-mandated regulatory requirement, it should be challenged under the WTO's TBT Agreement and the limits of WTO disciplines should be tested in this regard.

References

Bhagwati, Jagdish. 1993. 'The Case for Free Trade'. *Scientific American* (November): 41–57.

Bhagwati, Jagdish N., and T.N. Srinivasan. 1996. *Trade and Environment: Does Environmental Diversity Detract from the Case for Free Trade?* In *Fair Trade and Harmonization: Economic Analysis*, edited by Jagdish N. Bhagwati and Robert E. Hudec. Cambridge, MA: MIT Press.

Daly, Herman. 1993. 'Problems with Free Trade: Neoclassical and Steady State Perspectives'. In *Trade and the Environment: Law, Economics, and Policy*, edited by Durwood Zaelke, Paul Orbuch, and Robert F. Housman. Washington, DC: Island Press.

Friedman, Joseph, Daniel A. Gerlowski, and Johnathan Silberman. 1992. 'What Attracts Foreign Multinational Corporations? Evidence from Branch Plant Location in the United States'. *Journal of Regional Science* 32 (4): 403–18.

WTO. 2004. *Trade and Environment at the WTO: Background Document*. Geneva: WTO.

WTO Secretariat. 1997, 7 November. 'Environmental Benefits of Removing Trade Restrictions and Distortions'. WT/CTE/W/67. Geneva: WTO.

---

[17] Article 20.11(3).

10

Government Procurement Provisions in the GPA

Ceding Policy Space for Uncertain Gains

Monika and Neeraj R.S.

10.1 Introduction and Overview of Implications of Accepting Obligations on Government Procurement

Under the provisions of the General Agreement on Tariffs and Trade (GATT) 1994, World Trade Organization (WTO) members are precluded from using internal taxes or other fiscal measures for granting protection to domestic production. Further, products imported into a country are required to be accorded treatment no less favourable than that accorded to like domestic products. An important exception to this non-discrimination provision relates to procurement for governmental purposes. It may be noted that the government procurement exception would not be applicable if the procured goods or services are commercially reused or used in production of goods and services for commercial resale. At the WTO, 42 countries have become parties to the Government Procurement Agreement (GPA) and voluntarily given up using this exception.

Theoretical arguments for liberalization of procurement practices have been put forth by many, including Lowinger (1976), Deardorff and Stern (1979), and Evenett and Hockman (2004). Niggli (2015) argues that nations that reform their government procurement regimes are better placed to achieve their sustainable development goals (SDGs), particularly, SDG16 (promoting peace, justice and strong institutions) and will go on to reap the development rewards that are linked with stronger institutions, better governance and faster economic growth. He ties stronger public institutions to a vast array of development objectives and asserts that the GPA is a 'powerful tool for improving governance and promoting development'. Yukins and Schnitzer (2015) consider historic evidence and suggest that accession to GPA could serve as a catalyst to undertake crucial reforms in domestic public procurement laws.

Benefits of acceding to GPA or accepting similar obligations under trade agreements as highlighted by the studies include the following: First, competition resulting from obligations under trade agreements would lead to better utilization of tax payer's money as the goods and services can be sourced from more efficient producers at lower costs; second, these obligations make available larger market access for domestic producers and an increase in exports might occur as a result of increased purchases by governments of other member countries; third, the transparency requirements reduce uncertainty for potential bidders, both domestic and foreign, which may encourage them to compete for government contracts thereby lowering the prices paid by the procuring entity; fourth, transparency requirements control 'corruption' and ensure accountability.

On the other hand, costs associated with acceding to the GPA, or adhering to non-discrimination obligations on government procurement in trade agreements, are mainly threefold. First, costs would be associated with the adverse impact on domestic industry if the reciprocal market access is large. This may be more acutely felt by small and medium enterprises (SMEs) which may not be in a position to compete with big foreign producers. Second, implementation cost of switching over from the existing procurement regime to a regime that is compliant with multilateral/bilateral obligations would arise. This would include costs for putting into place a system for supplier registration, bid challenge procedures, disclosure of tender results, etc. Third, cost associated with complying with obligations related to compiling and reporting statistics on government procurement could also arise.

Given this background, it is relevant to discuss the provisions on government procurement in the Trans-Pacific Partnership Agreement (TPP). In the second section, three questions are addressed. First, what is the size of government procurement market in some of the TPP countries, second, what is the value of procurement to which the obligations on non-discrimination apply and third, what is the extent of import penetration in the government procurement markets in some of the TPP countries. The third section discusses the provisions related to government procurement in the TPP. The final section of this chapter assesses the impact on international government procurement rules of the TPP provisions on government procurement.

10.2 Size of Government Procurement Markets in Some TPP Countries

Access to large public procurement markets and potential export gains from such increased market access is a crucial factor that motivates countries to accede to the GPA or free trade agreements (FTAs) with government procurement disciplines. This being the case, it is fundamental to first gauge the size of public procurement markets in member countries as this could be determinative while arriving at policy decisions regarding whether or not to accede to GPA and also for striking a balance while making market access commitments under the GPA.

Firstly, it is important to bear in mind that the size of a GPA member's public procurement market does not encompass the entire spectrum of goods and services procured by public bodies. While the total size of the government procurement market may be significant, this does not represent the value of procurement market that is covered by GPA. GPA covers only those procurement activities that exceed a specified value threshold and are carried out by covered entities purchasing certain listed goods and services (GPA-covered market). The procurement activity should also not have been specifically exempted in the notes contained in the Schedule of that member. With the revision of GPA and the progressive broadening of its membership, the combined size of the GPA-covered market of all the 42 GPA members was estimated at US$1.7 trillion in 2015 (WTO 2015). This represents close to 2.2 per cent of the global gross domestic product (GDP).[1] At the country level, however, there are dissimilarities in the level of commitment made by GPA members and in the share of a member's GPA-covered market in its GDP. Notifications to the WTO by TPP parties that are members to the GPA

---

[1] According to World Bank's calculation, GDP in nominal terms for 2014 was approximately US$78 trillion. At US$1.7 trillion, the GPA market constitutes 2.18 per cent of the global GDP.

Table 10.1

Comparison of public procurement markets and their share in GDP in select TPP countries

TPP and GPA Members	Procurement Agency	Total Procurement Market (Billion US$)	Above Threshold Market (Billion US$)	Procurement Market as a Share of GDP (%)
Canada (2012)			1.705	0.09
Japan (2013)	Federal	56.534	19.623	1.15
	State	11.615	No data	0.24
USA (2009)	Federal	215.052	204.140	1.49
	State	612.303	No data	4.61

Source: Statistical reports notified to the WTO Government Procurement Committee by Canada (GPA/119/Add.4, of 19/10/2015), Japan (GPA/123/Add.4, of 21/04/2015) and USA (GPA/104/Add.8 of 07/12/2015).

(Canada, Japan, United States of America [USA] and Singapore) show that the size of their GPA-covered market as a share of their GDP is relatively small (Table 10.1).

Secondly, estimates made by an impact assessment study carried out by the European Commission further distinguish the GPA-covered market from 'committed market'. The study constitutes the analytical basis for the European Commission's proposal to introduce a regulation to establish rules on the access of third countries' goods and services to the European Union's (EU) public procurement market. It shows that the public procurement market that is considered as open on the basis of de jure international commitments constitutes a small portion of the total value of GPA-covered market (Figure 10.1).

For the purpose of the impact assessment study a market was deemed as de jure 'not committed internationally' if a restriction existed at the international level either on the goods or services relevant to the market or the main purchaser. According to estimates in the study, only 25 per cent of global above threshold procurement market is accessible through the GPA- that is internationally committed (Figure 10.2).[2] This distinction between internationally committed market and GPA-covered market further reduces the size of the pie for foreign suppliers and producers.

---

[2] It is important to bear in mind that the study has extrapolated data pertaining to 13 main trading partners of the EU to represent the world data.

Figure 10.1

Internationally committed public procurement market

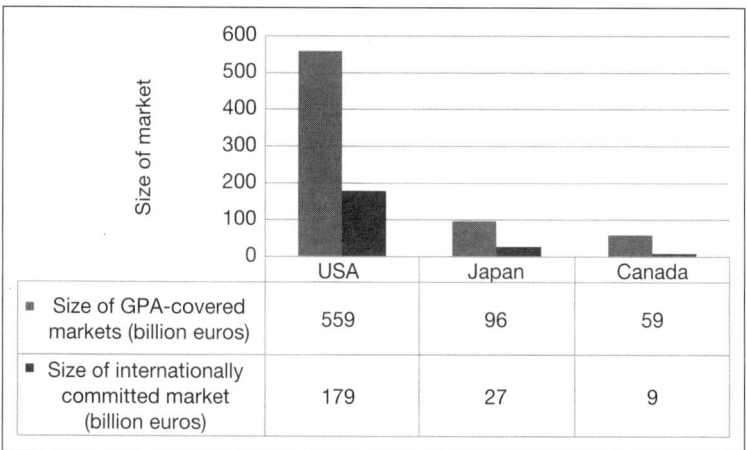

Source: European Commission (2012).

Figure 10.2

Procurement market level of openness

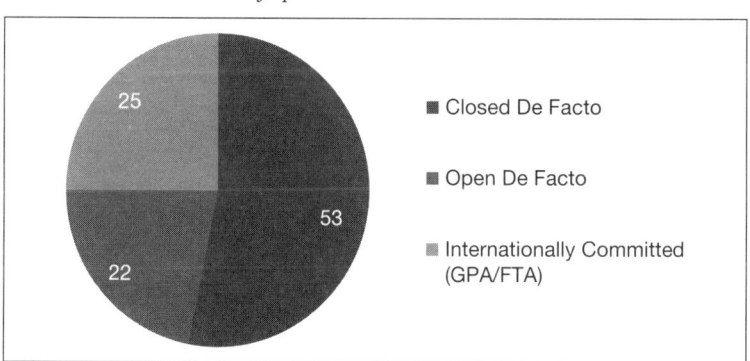

Source: European Commission (2012).

Thirdly, the de facto contestable market for a foreign supplier is often much smaller than the de jure committed market owing to national protectionist measures and implementation problems. Where a national measure—such as local content requirements, set-asides, local price preference schemes—actually prevents foreign suppliers from accessing the procurement market there is de facto closure of the market.[3] De facto closure could also occur due to implementation problems and administrative barriers. Studies show that most GPA members have actually imposed the de jure restrictions resulting in de facto closure and significantly low import penetration in public procurement markets.

The primary source of information regarding actual import penetration in public procurement markets of GPA member countries are the statistical reports submitted to the WTO by parties to the GPA. The GPA contains obligations that require members to provide information on cross-border purchases and the country of origin of the purchased goods and services.[4] Despite this obligation, Japan and Chinese Taipei are the only members that have notified information on cross-border purchases in recent years. Japan's statistical report to the GPA Committee (GPA/123/Add.4 of 21/04/2015) shows that only 1.91 per cent of Japan's total procurement is cross-border, the remaining procurements being domestically sourced.

A review of literature on import penetration ratio of public procurement markets reveals that cross-border purchases is substantially low in GPA-covered markets including in TPP countries.

A background report prepared by Ramboll Consulting Management and HTW Chur (2012) to serve as an input for an evaluation of public procurement policy by the European Commission estimated the relative level of openness of public procurement market in EU compared to that of Canada, China, Japan and the USA using data from National Accounts. It found that the penetration ratio (total public sector imports

---

[3] Where a de jure national measure (a potential restriction) results in actual market access restriction for foreign suppliers it is termed as de facto closure.

[4] Article XIX:5 of the GPA provides that 'To the extent that such information is available, each Party shall provide statistics on the country of origin of products and services purchased by its entities.'

to public sector demand[5]) of Canada (6.9%), China (6.1%), Japan (4.7%) and USA (4.6%) was lower than that of EU whose ratio was 7 per cent.[6] It should be noted that for the purpose of this study intra-EU imports was treated as public imports of the EU for arriving at the EU's penetration ratio. Nevertheless, it is striking that the import penetration ratio of China's public procurement market, which is not a GPA member, compares favourably with that of GPA members.

The Impact Assessment Working Document of European Commission[7] which followed the Ramboll study found that out of 75 per cent of the global above threshold procurement market that is de jure closed (no international commitments), 53 per cent is closed de facto on account of the imposition of domestic barriers such as offsets, set asides, price preference mechanisms, local establishment and national content requirements. The study concluded that only 22 per cent of GPA-covered market is de facto open.[8]

Messerlin (2015) calculates the share of imports in total demand for public goods and services (penetration ratio) using the World Input–Output Database (WIOD) to arrive at the true level of openness of public procurement markets. The study covers all goods and services that are procured by the public administration or its agencies (thus going beyond 'GPA covered markets') in 14 large economies for the period 1995–2011. It shows that the average import penetration ratio of public procurement markets in selected countries was 6.7 per cent in 2011 (Figure 10.3). Interestingly, the penetration ratio of some non-GPA members such as India (6.2%) and Indonesia (8%) is already higher than some GPA members such as Canada (4.3%), Japan (4.8%) and USA (4.8%).

---

[5] Public demand was defined as the final consumption expenditure by government, plus intermediate consumption by industries carrying out the procurement procedures. See Ramboll Management Consulting and HTW Chur (2012, 17).

[6] GDP-weighted average for 21 EU members where data was available.

[7] Annex 3.

[8] Annex 2, p.16.

Figure 10.3

Import penetration ratio of public procurement markets

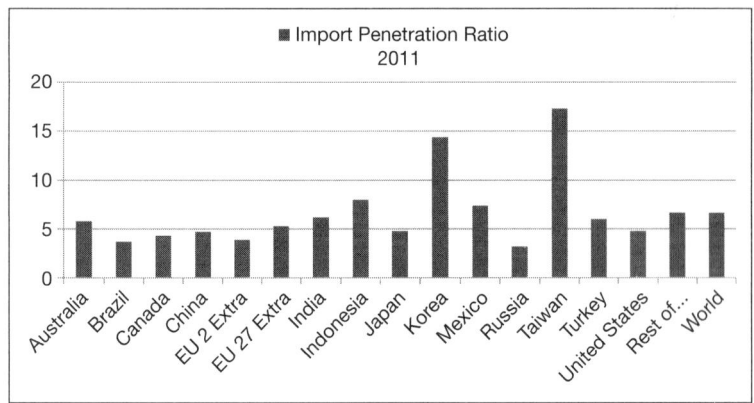

Source: Messerlin (2015).

Public procurement market that is offered by GPA members for non-discriminatory treatment is a relatively small subset of the total procurement market. Furthermore, studies show that because of statutory preferences and de facto discrimination by procuring entities, the actual export gains arising from the increased market access through GPA are limited. Strikingly, some estimates also show that the level of openness of some non-GPA members is already higher than that of GPA members such as Canada, Japan and USA. On the other hand, accession to the GPA could compromise public contracts from being used as effective policy instruments to generate jobs and spur innovation in the domestic economy. These political economy considerations of public procurement choices have warranted the exclusion of public procurement from most favoured nation (MFN) and national treatment disciplines contained in the GATT. The TPP binds its signatories to open up their procurement markets and to improve transparency in public procurement, thereby making some of these parties that are hitherto non-GPA members consider acceding to GPA by simply extending the TPP commitments to the remaining GPA parties. However, WTO members that are considering acceding to the GPA should first carry out an objective assessment of the actual export gains and the corresponding loss of policy space arising from such accession.

10.3 Analysis of Provisions on Government Procurement in the TPP

Chapter 15 of the TPP contains principles and regulations relating to government procurement. This chapter has deepened the government procurement commitments of some existing members of the WTO Agreement on Government Procurement and has introduced new disciplines for other parties of the TPP. Fundamental features of the government procurement chapter are commitments on national treatment and MFN treatment, wide coverage of covered procurement, enhanced transparency and market access requirements, exclusions to the obligations and transitional measures for developing countries.

Coverage

The obligations in the government procurement chapter apply according to the commitments undertaken by each party in Annex 15-A ('Schedule'). However, commitments undertaken in the Schedules are very extensive. Schedules largely follow negative list approach whereby each party has agreed to submit all the goods, services and construction services procured by the specified entities for application of the government procurement chapter, except those which have been specifically excluded. It is in direct contrast to the positive list approach followed by the WTO Agreement on Government Procurement. Some parties have adopted the positive list approach in their Schedules—Canada, Japan, Malaysia and Vietnam for 'services' and Singapore for both 'services' and 'construction services' have specified only the sectors to be covered by government procurement and rest of the sectors are excluded from the coverage of the government procurement chapter. As for the central level, sub-central level and other entities that are covered, each party has provided a positive list of entities in Schedules.

Thresholds

Parties have specified threshold levels in Section A, B and C of their respective Schedules. Procurement which is equal to or exceeds these threshold levels is within the purview of government procurement. All the parties except Brunei, Malaysia and Vietnam will apply the specified permanent threshold levels from the date of implementation of the TPP. Aforementioned three parties have availed the benefit of transitional measures and will implement permanent thresholds gradually over a transition period varying from 4 years to 25 years. Final permanent threshold levels are not the same for all the parties. For most parties, levels as indicated in Section 10.4 are 130,000 Special Drawing Rights (SDRs) for goods and services and 500,000 SDRs for the construction services. However, some parties, namely Chile, Malaysia, Mexico, Peru and Vietnam, have specified levels different from other parties. Japan as well has specified lower threshold of 4,500,000 SDRs as compared to 5,000,000 SDRs for construction services and 100,000 SDRs for goods and services. But this is not significant digression. On the other hand, Malaysia, Mexico and Vietnam have kept threshold levels for construction services much higher at 14,000,000 SDRs, US$10,335,931 and 8,500,000 SDRs, respectively. Malaysia's final threshold at the end of the transition period is the highest among construction services threshold applied by any TPP party. This departure may be ascribed to the special and differential treatment of developing economy of these parties. Chile (95,000 SDRs), Mexico (US$79,507) and Peru (95,000 SDRs) have much lower threshold levels for goods and services as compared to other parties. It is notable that in the context of the North American Free Trade Agreement (NAFTA), Mexico is applying NAFTA threshold levels (as amended) and not TPP thresholds. However, current value of thresholds under the NAFTA and TPP is identical for Mexico and, therefore, is not of much significance.

Special and Differential Treatment

The TPP contains certain provisions which treat developing countries more favourably than other member countries. These can be referred to as 'special and differential treatment' provisions. In the government procurement chapter these are incorporated in the form of 'transitional measures'. Article 15.5 lists kinds of transitional measures which are available to a developing country party. They are the price preference programme, offsets, phased-in addition of specific sectors or entities, threshold that is higher than party's permanent threshold and delayed implementation of any obligation. It further provides for extension of the transitional period or adoption of a new transitional measure, in the case of special circumstances. These transitional measures must not discriminate between other parties. Also, a special mandate has been imposed on the parties to give consideration to any request by a developing country party for technical cooperation and capacity building in relation to that party's implementation of its government procurement obligations. A developing country party may specify the transitional measures adopted by it in Section J of its Schedule. These measures allow a party to depart from the obligations during the transition period set out in the Schedules. Four developing country parties have availed the benefit of provision on transitional measures, namely Brunei, Malaysia, Mexico and Vietnam.

Brunei has sought to delay the application of obligations relating to domestic review (Article 15.19), notice of intended procurement (Articles 15.7.3(b), Article 15.7.1, Article 15.9.3, Article 15.14.2) and post-award information (Article 15.6.3) by a period of 3–5 years and has kept higher thresholds for 4 years. Malaysia too has deferred the application of provisions on domestic review (Article 15.19) and dispute settlement (Chapter 28) and used higher thresholds. It has further adopted offsets for a transition period of 12 years. Additionally, procurement funded by economic stimulus package for severe nationwide economic crisis will be beyond the ambit of government procurement for a period of 25 years from the date of implementation of the TPP. These measures are specially targeted for preserving interests of Bumiputera (ethnic Malays) who form majority of its population. Like Brunei and Malaysia, Vietnam too has delayed application of provisions relating to notices of intended procurement (Article 15.7.2, Article 15.7.3(g) and (h), Article 15.14.3), post-award information (Article 15.16.3(f)), domestic review and dispute settlement. It also has 25 years of transition period to comply with the provision on offsets.

Mexico has not specified any transitional measures under Section J (for developing countries). However, it has adopted few transitional provisions (Section G). It has kept procurements made by Petróleos Mexicanos (PEMEX) and Comisión Federal de Electricidad (CFE; Mexico's State Oil and Gas Company and Electricity Commission, respectively) outside the scope of the government procurement chapter for a period of 9 years and procurement of drugs that are not currently patented in Mexico or whose Mexican patents have expired for 8 years.

Offsets

The TPP Agreement mandatorily prohibits seeking, taking account, imposing or enforcing any offset at any stage of procurement (Article 15.4.6). However, as discussed above, some flexibility has been permitted to Malaysia and Vietnam in this regard. Malaysia has the flexibility to postpone its obligations under Article 15.4.6 on offsets for a period of 12 years following the date of entry into force of this Agreement (Schedule to Annex 15-A, Section J). During the transitional period of 12 years, offsets may be applied to a procurement with a value of more than Malaysian ringgit (RM) 50,000,000, conducted by the entities specified in Annex 15-A. The procuring entities may impose offsets with credit value up to 60 per cent, 40 per cent and 20 per cent equivalent to the procurement contract value until the end of the 4th year, 8th year and 12th year, respectively. Vietnam may request offsets in any form, including a price preference programme up to 40 per cent of the annual value of the total covered procurement, decreasing gradually over the period of 25 years.

Exceptions

Article 15.3 permits exclusions and exceptions to general obligations of the government procurement chapter. A party may take measures in contradiction to the provisions in interest of protecting public morals, order or safety; protecting human, animal or plant life or health; protecting intellectual property; or relating to the goods or services of a person with disabilities, of philanthropic or not-for-profit institutions, or of prison labour. However, these measures must not be arbitrary, unjustifiably discriminatory or disguised restrictions on international trade between the parties. While Article 15.3 may be used to shield the future measures taken in derogation of TPP obligations, parties have also specified certain measures and exclusions in their respective Schedules. Exceptions and exclusions mentioned in the Schedules are beyond the scope of the TPP as such. Thus, these will not be subject to examination under Article 15.3. These exceptions are created to provide policy space to member countries, particularly in areas which are of vital national interests.

Most common exceptions are exclusion of measures for the benefit of SMEs (Australia, Brunei, Canada, New Zealand, Peru, USA, and Vietnam) and procurement of defence goods and services from the scope of the government procurement chapter. A more significant exception is in favour of agricultural support programmes or food assistance schemes. Canada, Peru and USA have incorporated such exception in their Schedules. Another notable exception is the exemption of measures for the economic and social advancement of indigenous population. Developing countries as well as developed countries have utilized them. Malaysia has, in fact, secured an extensive protection for the Bumiputera agenda. It has reserved the right to grant Bumiputera status to eligible companies and provide them preference, render assistance, benefits, etc. Importantly, two kinds of measures are outlined for Bumiputeras—set aside 30 per cent of total annual value of construction services procurements above the threshold and apply price preference ranging from 1.25 per cent to 10 per cent, with higher preference to lower valued procurement.

Three categories of Bumiputera have been identified for the purpose of price preference. First, Bumiputera suppliers of goods and services that originate from any TPP country for procurement valued between RMB 0.5 million and RMB 15 million (price preference 7–2.5%), second, Bumiputera suppliers of goods and services that originate from non-party for procurement valued between RMB 0.5 million and RMB 15 million (3.5–1.25%) and third, Bumiputera manufacturers of goods for procurement (10–3%). In addition to this, Malaysia has also excluded its People's Housing Programme, rural development and poverty eradication programmes from the span of the government procurement chapter.

It is fair to conclude that even though the government procurement chapter has permitted various flexibilities, its sphere of function is considerably wide. It has maximum coverage of goods, services or construction services, most exceptions are available only during the transition period and permanent exceptions are very narrow in scope. Though, Malaysia's Bumiputera preference provision is expansive in nature, rest of the exemptions are restrictive.

10.4 Implications for the International Government Procurement Regime

The likely implications of the TPP's government procurement rules on the international procurement regime can be better analyzed in juxtaposition with the GPA. Most FTAs are significantly influenced by the GPA as a large number of FTAs either incorporate some or all of the GPA obligations or express accession to the GPA as an objective of the parties (Davies and Schefer 2016). Even where the parties establish autonomous procurement trade regimes, the content of their preferential trade agreements (PTAs) and the GPA is generally similar (Anderson et al. 2011). The TPP too has followed the similar trend. The text of Chapter 15 is based on the same principles as the GPA (non-discrimination, transparency and procedural fairness) and tracks closely the language used in the revised GPA text (Anderson et al. 2017). Article 5 of the GPA lists the non-discriminatory transitional measures, namely the price preference programme, offset, phased-in addition of specific entities or sectors, a threshold higher than its permanent threshold and delayed application of certain provisions. These transitional measures for developing countries have been included to encourage and facilitate their accession to the GPA (Grier 2016). The TPP follows the same scheme as revised GPA with regard to the offsets (10.3.4). The TPP's definition of offset is a slightly modified version of the definition of offset under the GPA. The TPP and GPA both prohibit offsets except in the form of a transition measure.

However, in the case of exceptions, the TPP goes beyond the GPA in two aspects. First, unlike the GPA it does not mention 'security interest' as a ground of horizontal exception to the government procurement provisions and second, it clearly specifies that the environmental measures necessary to protect human, animal or plant life or health constitute part of the exceptions. It must be noted that even though the TPP does not provide 'security interest' as a ground of exception per se, all the parties in their Schedules have excluded procurement of defence goods and services from the scope of the chapter. Another significant distinction is explicit obligation on TPP parties to ensure that criminal or administrative measures exist to address corruption in their government procurement and that conflicts of interest are avoided. Though the revised GPA (Article IV.4) too generally mandates that covered procurement be

Government Procurement Provisions in the GPA 273

conducted in a transparent and impartial manner that prevents corrupt practices, it does not specifically obligate establishment of criminal or administrative measures in this regard. Furthermore, the TPP as compared to the revised GPA has detailed provisions on SMEs. Article 15.21 of the TPP recognizes the contribution of SMEs to economic growth and employment. It further provides that if a party maintains preferential treatment for SMEs, eligibility criteria should be transparent and follow the rules prescribed under the article. This provision does not provide legal authority to provide preferential treatment to SMEs. Hence, the legal authority should come from derogations listed by the parties in their Schedules. Another difference is Article 15.8.5 which clarifies that conditions for participation can be shaped to promote compliance with international labour rights. Apart from a few variations between the TPP and GPA discussed above, both agreements follow the same core principles and procedures.

Another notable area of comparison is the level of thresholds and coverage committed in the Schedule to Chapter 15 of the TPP (Table 10.2). Anderson et al. (ibid.) have identified three major themes in this regard; Firstly, GPA parties (Canada, Japan, New Zealand, Singapore and USA) have not exceeded their GPA commitments with respect to both, the level of threshold and the number of entities covered. In fact, New Zealand and the USA, unlike their GPA commitments, have kept sub-central entities outside the purview of covered procurement under the TPP; Secondly, parties such as Australia, Chile, Mexico and Peru have made generous commitments. A major influencing factor for it could be that Australia is already in the process of accession to the GPA and these parties have already made government procurement commitments under existing FTAs with other TPP parties;[9] and thirdly, Malaysia, Vietnam and Brunei have made limited commitments as compared to other parties and have availed benefit of transitional measures (10.3.3).

---

[9] Australia–Japan Agreement on Economic Partnership, Australia–Chile Free Trade Agreement, Chile–Japan Strategic Economic Partnership Agreement, Japan–Mexico Economic Partnership Agreement, North American Free Trade Agreement, Peru Japan Agreement For Economic Partnership and Peru–Singapore Free Trade Agreement.

Table 10.2

Comparison of threshold levels of TPP countries with their GPA threshold levels

Party	Central Entities		Sub-central Entities		Other Entities	
	TPP	GPA	TPP	GPA	TPP	GPA
Australia	130,000	Non-member	355,000	Non-member	400,000	Non-member
	130,000		355,000		400,000	
	5,000,000		5,000,000		5,000,000	
Brunei	130,000	Non-member	None	Non-member	130,000	Non-member
	130,000				130,000	
	5,000,000				5,000,000	
Canada	130,000	130,000	355,000	355,000	355,000	355,000
	130,000	130,000	355,000	355,000	355,000	355,000
	5,000,000	5,000,000	5,000,000	5,000,000	5,000,000	5,000,000
Chile	95,000	Non-member	200,000	Non-member	220,000	Non-member
	95,000		200,000		220,000	
	5,000,000		5,000,000		5,000,000	
Japan	100,000	100,000	200,000	200,000	130,000	130,000
	100,000[a]	100,000[b]	200,000[c]	200,000[d]	130,000[e]	130,000[g]
	4,500,000	4,500,000	15,000,000	15,000,000	4,500,000[f]	4,500,000[h]
Malaysia	130,000	Non-member	None	Non-member	150,000	Non-ember
	130,000				150,000	
	14,000,000				14,000,000	
Mexico	US$79,507[i]	Non-member	None	Non-member	US$397,535	Non-member
	US$79,507				US$397,535	
	US$10,335,931				US$12,721,740	
New Zealand	130,000	130,000	None	200,000	400,000	400,000
	130,000	130,000		200,000	400,000	400,000
	5,000,000	5,000,000		5,000,000	5,000,000	5,000,000

Party	Central Entities		Sub-central Entities		Other Entities	
	TPP	GPA	TPP	GPA	TPP	GPA
Peru	95,000	Non-member	200,000	Non-member	160,000	Non-member
	95,000		200,000		160,000	
	5,000,000		5,000,000		5,000,000	
Singapore	130,000	130,000	None	None	400,000	400,000
	130,000	130,000			400,000	400,000
	5,000,000	5,000,000			5,000,000	5,000,000
USA	130,000	130,000	None	355,000	US$ 250,000	400,000
	130,000	130,000		355,000	US$ 250,000	400,000
	5,000,000	5,000,000		5,000,000	5,000,000	5,000,000
Vietnam	130,200	Non-member	None	Non-member	2,000,000	Non-member
	130,200				2,000,000	
	8,50,000				15,000,000	

Source: Schedules to Annexure 15-A of the TPP and GPA Schedules.

Notes: Values in SDR for goods, services and construction services, respectively.

a 450,000 SDRs—Architectural, engineering and other technical services.
b 450,000 SDRs—Architectural, engineering and other technical services.
c 1,500,000 SDR—Architectural, engineering and other technical services covered by Chapter 15 ('Government Procurement').
d 1,500,000 SDR—Architectural, engineering and other technical services covered by Chapter 15 ('Government Procurement').
e 450,000 SDR—Architectural, engineering and other technical services covered by Chapter 15 ('Government Procurement').
f 15,000,000 SDR—Construction Services for all other entities in Group A.
g 450,000 SDR—Architectural, engineering and other technical services covered by Chapter 15 ('Government Procurement').
h 15,000,000 SDR—Construction services for all other entities in Group B.
i US$1 = 1 SDR (as on 3 June 2016), respectively.

10.5 Conclusion

Upon analysis of the extent of import penetration in the government procurement market of some of the TPP parties and provisions of the TPP chapter on government procurement, three key conclusions can be drawn. First, as discussed in the previous section, the TPP reinforces the general trend that FTAs with government procurement rules are significantly influenced by the GPA provisions. This makes accession to the GPA easier as countries, by establishing non-discriminatory and transparent procurement regime, are brought one step closer to the GPA accession (ibid.). Nevertheless, it may not necessarily result into accession to the GPA as evident in the case of Mexico which is party to various FTAs covering government procurement, but is not even an observer at the GPA. Second, the TPP has expanded and clarified certain provisions of the GPA. These provisions may serve as blueprint for future FTAs as well as future revision of the GPA. Third, contribution of TPP towards augmenting effective market access to the international government procurement market may not be significant, since import penetration in the government procurement market continues to remain low. If India were to conform to the provisions on government procurement in the TPP, its export prospects in government procurement markets may continue to remain low. This would be on account of the low import penetration in government procurement markets in developed countries in general. On the other hand, India would lose the flexibility of using government procurement as a policy instrument for bolstering its manufacturing. Some of the existing schemes which grant preference to local producers and suppliers of electronic equipment, IT products and railway safety technology products set aside 20 per cent of the total annual purchase for SMEs, reserve specific products for mandatory purchase from SMEs and provide up to 15 per cent price preference to SMEs. These schemes would have to be discontinued. This could have adverse consequences for domestic manufacturing and would undermine the Make in India initiative.

References

Anderson, Robert D., Anna Caroline Muller, and Philippe Pelletier. 2017. 'Regional Trade Agreements and Procurement Rules: Facilitators or Hindrances?' In *The*

Internationalization of Government Procurement Regulations, edited by Aris Georgopoulos, Bernard Hockman, and Petros Mavroidos, 67–68. Oxford: Oxford University Press.

Anderson, Robert D., Anna Caroline Muller, Kodjo Osei-lah Josefita pardo de Leon, and Philippe Pelletier. 2011. 'Government Procurement Provisions in Regional Trade Agreements: A Stepping Stone Accession?' In *The WTO Regime on Government Procurement: Challenges and Reform*, edited by Sue Arrowsmith and Robert D. Anderson, 561–656, 618. Cambridge: Cambridge University Press.

Davies, Arwel, and Krista Nadakavukaren Schefer. 2016. 'Government Procurement'. In *Bilateral and Regional Trade Agreements: Commentary and Analysis*, edited by Simon Lester, Bryan Mercurio and Lorand Bartels, 318–19, Vol. 1. Cambridge: Cambridge University Press.

European Commission. 2012. 'Impact Assessment Accompanying a Proposal for a Regulation Establishing Rules on the Access of Third Countries' Goods and Services to the EU Internal Market in Public Procurement'. Commission Staff Working Document, COM 124 (Final) and SWD 58 (Final).

Evenett, Simon J., and Bernard M. Hockman. 2004. 'Government Procurement: Market Access, Transparency, and Multilateral Trade Rules'. World Bank Policy Research Working Paper 3195, Washington, DC.

Grier, Jean Heilman. 2016, December. 'Government Procurement in the WTO'. Djaghe White Paper. Retrieved 10 August 2017, from https://app.box.com/s/8byjo9re17zh1zx70fz70socpwzrqr5j

Lowinger, Thomas C. 1976. 'Discrimination in Government Procurement of Foreign Goods in the U.S. and Western Europe'. *Southern Economic Journal* 42 (3): 451–60.

Messerlin, Patrick. 2015. 'How Open are Public Procurement Markets?' European University Institute Working Paper RSCAS 2015/89, European University Institute, San Domenico di Fiesole (FI), Italy.

Niggli, Nicholas. 2015. 'Helping Nations, Businesses and People to Succeed: How Government Procurement Influences Institution Building, Good Governance, Economic Growth and Sustainable Development'. *Trade Law and Development* 7 (1): 8–20.

Ramboll Management Consulting and HTW Chur. 2012. *Cross-border Procurement Above EU Thresholds*. Copenhagen: Ramboll.

World Trade Organization (WTO). 2015. 'Government Procurement Agreement: Opening Markets and Promoting Good Governance'. GPA Brochure, WTO. Retrieved 18 July 2017, from https://www.wto.org/english/tratop_e/gproc_e/gp_gpa_e.htm

Deardorff, A.V. and R.M. Stern. 1979. 'An Economic Analysis of the Effects of the Tokyo Round of Multilateral Trade Negotiations on the United States and other Major Industrialised Countries', *MTN Studies 5*, Committee on Finance, US Senate, US Government Printing Office, Washington DC.

11
State-owned Enterprises (SOEs)
Mukesh Bhatnagar

For the first time, a free trade agreement (FTA) seeks to address comprehensively the commercial activities of state-owned enterprises (SOEs) that compete with private companies in international trade and investment. The Trans-Pacific Partnership Agreement's (TPP) Chapter 17 on SOEs contains several significant provisions which may have implications for the TPP members having SOEs. The provisions of SOEs in the TPP build on the assumption that SOEs cause distortions in markets where such enterprises receive non-commercial assistance from the governments. The provisions of the TPP on SOEs stem from concerns, as reflected in General Agreement on Tariffs and Trade (GATT) 1994, Article XVII, about the government influence, potential trade distortions and unfair competition brought by the SOEs.

11.1 GATT-WTO Provisions on STEs

Article XVII of GATT 1994 contains provisions regarding State trading enterprises (STEs). It sets out that such enterprises—in their purchases or sales involving either imports or exports—are to act in accordance with the general principles of 'non-discrimination', and that 'commercial considerations' only are to guide their decisions on imports and exports. It also instructs that members are to notify their STEs to the World Trade Organization (WTO) annually. Clarification of what is considered to be an STE, and thus notifiable, is provided in the 'WTO Understanding on the Interpretation of Article XVII'. Paragraph 1 of this text states that members shall notify the STEs in accordance with the following working definition:

> Governmental and non-governmental enterprises, including marketing boards, which have been granted exclusive or special rights or privileges, including statutory or constitutional powers, in the exercise of which they influence through their purchases or sales the level or direction of imports or exports.

Particularly important in this definition is the phrase 'in the exercise of which they influence ... the level or direction of imports or exports', as this goes to the heart of what the regulation of state trading in the WTO is aimed at—that is, the potentially distorting effects on trade of the operations of STEs. Conversely, the WTO does not seek to prohibit or even discourage the establishment or maintenance of STEs, but merely to ensure that they are not operated in a manner inconsistent with WTO principles and rules.

Under the WTO STE provision, an enterprise need not be State-owned nor need it have a monopoly position in order to be covered as an STE by Article XVII and subject to WTO rules on STEs. The important criteria are that it enjoys exclusive or special rights or privileges, and that in the exercise of these rights and privileges it influences imports or exports by its buying and selling activities. The issue of transparency of operations of STEs has been a subject matter of review in the WTO through the notification requirements. The working party setup under the Understanding on Interpretation of Article XVII of the GATT reviews the members' notifications on STEs annually.

11.2 Definition of an SOE

Under Article 17.1, the TPP text contains a definition of an SOE which has essentially the following two parts: (a) the enterprise is principally engaged in commercial activities and (b) there is direct ownership of the government in the enterprise to the extent of more than 50 per cent of share capital or ownership rights, or the government holds the power to appoint a majority of members of the board of directors. In contrast to the WTO provisions, the TPP clearly lays emphasis on ownership by the government as the criteria to treat an enterprise as an SOE. This is an important provision when viewed in the light of the Appellate Body ruling on the issue of interpretation of 'Public Body' under the Subsidies Agreement which inter alia holds that though majority ownership by the government of an entity is an important factor, it is not by itself the dispositive factor (WTO 2011).

There are exceptions from the purview of SOEs for institutions of governments which pursue public policy such as central banks, financial regulatory bodies, sovereign wealth funds and pension funds. An important exception has been carved out from the SOE provision for state enterprises and SOEs for undertaking activities for the purpose of resolution of a failing or failed financial institution or enterprise engaged in supply of financial services. This is clearly to take care of situations where failed commercial banks in a situation of financial meltdown are bailed out by government financial institutions or by other enterprises. Other exceptions include government procurement and SOEs providing goods or services exclusively to the national government for the purpose of carrying out its governmental function.

11.3 Non-discriminatory Treatment and Commercial Considerations

As per the TPP, the SOEs when engaging in commercial activities must act in accordance with commercial considerations in purchase or sale of goods or services.[1] These provisions in the TPP are similar to the STE provisions in Article XVII of the GATT. Further, as per the provisions in GATT 1994, Article XVII, STEs shall act in a manner consistent with the general principles of non-discriminatory treatment. It should be noted that a strict most favoured nation (MFN) treatment was not intended under GATT provisions, as is shown by the interpretative note to Article XVII:1, which allows an STE to charge different prices for its sales of a product in different markets, provided this is done for commercial reasons, to meet conditions of supply and demand in export markets. Also, a country's receipt of a 'tied loan' (whereby country 'A' receives a loan from country 'B' in order to buy goods from country 'B') falls in the category of 'commercial considerations'. (This too is spelled out in the interpretative note to XVII:1(b)).

---

[1] Except 'to fulfil any terms of its public service mandate that are not inconsistent with subparagraph (c) (ii) (of Article 17.4)'.

The SOEs text in Article 17.4 provides stricter rules regarding non-discrimination so as to accord MFN and national treatment to the goods or services supplied by enterprises of other TPP members as well as non-TPP members, and thereby not to discriminate. Article 17.4.1(b) creates obligations on SOEs to not discriminate in its purchase of goods or services. The text makes evident that the principle of non-discrimination is applicable both in terms of MFN and national treatment.[2] Likewise, Article 17.4.1(c) contains provisions for non-discrimination by SOEs in sale of goods or services. The condition of non-discrimination by SOEs in its commercial purchases and sales extends to SOEs dealings with the enterprises of the TPP members itself, enterprises of other TPP members and even non-TPP members. The principle of non-discrimination by SOEs also extends in respect of the enterprises that are investments of investors in the TPP members itself or investments of investors of other TPP member or even non-TPP members.[3] Thus, SOE provisions relating to non-discrimination are much deeper and cover both MFN and national treatment principles.

11.4 Non-commercial Assistance to SOEs

The provisions in the TPP on SOEs draw from the WTO Agreement on Subsidies and Countervailing Measures (ASCM) in as much as the term 'non-commercial assistance' has linkage to the term 'financial contribution' for the purpose of definition of subsidy under the ASCM. As per Article 17.1 of the chapter 'Non-commercial Assistance' means assistance to an SOE by virtue of that SOE's government ownership or control. Further, the term 'assistance' means direct transfer of funds or potential direct transfer of funds or liabilities such as (a) grant or debt forgiveness, (b) loans or loan guarantees on more favourable terms than

---

[2] Article 17.4.1(b) in its purchase of a good or service, (i) accords to a good or service supplied by an enterprise of another party treatment no less favourable than it accords to a like good or a like service supplied by enterprises 'of the party', of any other party, or of any non-party; and

[3] Article 17.4.1(b) in its purchase of a good or service, (ii) accords to a good or service supplied by an enterprise that is a covered investment in the party's territory treatment no less favourable than it accords to a like good or a like service supplied by enterprises in the relevant market in the party's territory that are investments of investors of the party, of any other party, or of any non-party.

those commercially available to the enterprise or (c) provision of equity capital which is inconsistent with the usual investment practice of private investors. The term 'assistance' also includes provision of goods or services to an SOE, other than general infrastructure, on terms more favourable than those commercially available to that enterprise. Thus, the term 'non-commercial assistance' for an SOE has been built around the provisions of the definition of subsidy under Article 1 of the ASCM.

For the purpose of the definition of a subsidy under the ASCM, there are two elements, namely, financial contribution by a government or any public body and benefit being conferred. The TPP provisions for an SOE also reflect the notion of benefit in the definition of 'assistance' under Article 17.1 such as '…B. loans, loan guarantees or other types of financing on terms more favourable than those commercially available to that enterprise'. This definition mirrors the provision relating to calculation of amount of subsidy in terms of benefit to the recipient under Article 14(b) and (c) of the ASCM. In the case of assistance to an SOE through equity capital inconsistent with the usual investment practice (including for the provision of risk capital) of private investors, which is covered under Article 17.1(a)(i)C, there is a significant departure from the corresponding provision under the ASCM under Article 14(a) as regards calculation of benefit to the recipient. Under ASCM's Article 14(a) for calculation of benefit in the case of government provision of equity capital, the investment practice of private investors in the territory of the concerned member is considered as a benchmark. However, in the SOE text in Article 17.1(a)(i)C, there is no mention of the words '…in the territory of that Member'. This may imply that for the purpose of establishing 'assistance' under the SOE provision, investment practices of private investors anywhere in the world can be a basis for comparison. It is unclear whether this is an inadvertent drafting error or a conscious ploy to expand the possibility of finding instances of 'assistance' to an SOE.

Whilst the notion of financial contribution and benefit gets reflected in the definition of 'assistance' under Article 17.1(a) under the heading 'non-commercial assistance', there is no explicit mention of specificity in the TPP text. However, the definition of phrase 'by virtue of that SOE's government ownership or control' under Article 17.1(b) under the heading 'non-commercial assistance' reflects the elements of specificity of Article 2 of the ASCM as under:

a. Para (b)(i): Access to the assistance explicitly limited to any of the member's SOEs,

b. Para (b)(ii): Assistance is predominately used by the party's SOEs,
c. Para (b)(iii): Disproportionately large amount of the assistance is for a party's SOEs,
d. Para (b)(iv): Party's SOEs are favoured through the use of its discretion in the provision of assistance.

Further footnote 5 states that account shall be taken of the extent of diversification of economic activities within the territory of the party as well as of the length of time during which the non-commercial assistance programme has been in operation.

The above elements of the definition of the phrase 'by virtue of that SOE's government ownership or control' are based on the provisions of specificity of subsidy under Article 2 of the ASCM. Thus, the non-commercial assistance to an SOE by virtue of that SOE's government ownership or control makes it implicit that the assistance is specific to the SOE by its very nature; however, it is subject to the above conditions.

11.5 Adverse Effects Caused by SOEs

Article 17.6 titled 'Non-commercial Assistance' contains the condition in respect of SOEs that in their commercial activities the SOEs, through the use of non-commercial assistance—either directly or indirectly, must not cause adverse effects to the interests of other members of the TPP. The term 'indirectly' has been explained through footnote 18 which states that indirect provision includes the situation in which a party entrusts or directs an enterprise that is not an SOE to provide non-commercial assistance. This provision resembles the definition of subsidy under Article 1 of the ASCM wherein the entrustment or direction by the government to any private body to perform certain functions can be construed as a financial contribution by the government or a public body.

Thus, SOEs receiving non-commercial assistance must not cause adverse effects to enterprises of other parties to the TPP. This can have a wider implication for those TPP members who have significant presence of SOEs engaged in commercial activities. The ambit of adverse effects caused by SOEs under the TPP is quite large and pervasive.

Articles 17.6.1 and 2 (non-commercial assistance) prohibit a party from causing adverse effects to the interests of another party through the use of non-commercial assistance, direct or indirect, to any of its SOEs.

The adverse effect that an SOE can cause in relation to goods shall be with respect to the production and sale of a good by the SOE. In relation to the supply of services, adverse effects shall be construed with respect to the supply of a service by the SOE from the territory of the party into the territory of another party. Further, in relation to supply of service adverse effect can be found to exist in the case of supply of a service in the territory of another party through an enterprise that is a covered investment in the territory of that other party or a third party. In effect, supply of services by an SOE under mode 1, that is, cross-border supply and mode 3, that is, supply of service through commercial presence in the territory of another party can cause adverse effects to the interest of another party. An important exception has been made in the TPP under Article 17.6.4 whereby a service supplied by an SOE of a party within its own territory shall be deemed to not cause adverse effects. This is a very important exclusion which keeps the services supplied by an SOE away from the accusation of causing adverse effect within its territory such as public transport, utilities such as electricity and water, telephone and telecom services, etc.

The scope of the adverse effects is further expanded under Article 17.6.2 to cover the chain of activities from one SOE to another SOE. It provides that the SOEs do not cause adverse effects to the interest of another party through the use of non-commercial assistance that the SOE may provide to any of its SOEs. This adverse effect can be in respect of production and sale of goods. In the case of services the adverse effect can be construed in a similar fashion as above, that is, in respect of cross-border supply of services or through commercial presence of an SOE in the territory of another party.

Under Article 17.6.3, the TPP text lays down that SOEs of a party present in the territory of another party shall not cause injury to a domestic industry of another party through the use of non-commercial assistance either directly or indirectly. This will cover the commercial activities of SOEs operating under the investment provisions of the TPP in the territory of another party.

11.6 What Constitutes Adverse Effects

As mentioned earlier, there are overarching obligations under Article 17.6 that SOEs shall not cause adverse effects to the interests of another party through the use of non-commercial assistance. Article 17.7 lays down constituents of 'adverse effects'. The scope of the adverse effects under Article 17.7 draws from the provisions of 'adverse effects' under Article 5 and 'serious prejudice' under Article 6 of the ASCM.

Unlike ASCM's Article 5, neither Article 17.6 nor 17.7 of the TPP expressly mention 'serious prejudice' as an adverse effect. However, the language in Article 17.7 of the TPP draws heavily from ASCM, Article 6 (serious prejudice'). Though not expressly mentioned, 'serious prejudice' within the meaning of ASCM's Article 6 has to a large extent been incorporated in the context of adverse effects caused by 'non-commercial assistance' to SOEs in Article 17.7 by incorporating provisions regarding displacement of or impediment to imports or sales of goods of another party (produced by an enterprise that is a covered investment in the territory of the party) and price undercutting by the goods produced by the SOE of a party.

Under Article 17.7.1 adverse effects may arise where the production and sale of goods by an SOE displace or impede the sales or imports of similar goods produced by enterprises of other TPP members in their territory. Thus, a loss of market share by enterprises of TPP members due to the operations of SOEs of another TPP member can be a ground for causing adverse effect under the TPP. A very significant coverage of the adverse effect provision is in respect of an SOE displacing or impeding the sales of similar goods produced by an enterprise that is a covered investment in the territory of the TPP member which implies that sales of an entity which has come into existence or is in operation as a result of the investment provisions are also sought to be protected from the commercial activities of SOEs, if the sales of SOEs displace or impede the sales of such enterprises operating under the investment provisions.

To further elaborate the provisions of adverse effects as under:

Article 17.7.1(b) provides that adverse effect may arise where non-commercial assistance to an SOE displaces or impedes:

1. Sales of a like good produced by an enterprise which is a covered investment in the territory of another party, or imports of a like good of another party, or
2. From the market of a non-party, imports of a like good of another party.
3. This provision is similar to ASCM's Article 6.3(b) which deals with 'serious prejudice'. As per an SOE text in point 2 above if the sales of an SOE displace or impede the sales of like goods of another party in the market of a non-party it may be held to cause adverse effects.

4. However, the text in point 1 above gives added cover to the sales of goods produced by enterprises that are covered investments in the territory of that party where SOEs operate.

Article 17.7.1(c) provides that adverse effect may arise where sale of goods by an SOE having received non-commercial assistance results in significant price undercutting as compared with the price of a like product of another member in the same market to which assisted goods are being imported; or in comparison with like goods produced by an enterprise that is a covered investment in the territory of the party; or significant price suppression, price depression or lost sales in the same market. Adverse effect can arise where there is a significant price undercutting by the goods sold by the SOE in the market of a non-party as compared with the price in the same market of imports of a like good of another party, or significant price suppression, price depression or lost sales in the same market.

These provisions are somewhat similar to ASCM, Article 6.3(c). However, unlike the ASCM, the TPP expressly includes the effects of price undercutting by goods sold by SOEs in the import market of the TPP parties and also in the markets of non-parties to the TPP.

Articles 17.7.1(d) and (e) contain provisions regarding adverse effects in relation to services. In the case of supply of services by SOEs receiving non-commercial assistance, 'adverse effects' may arise where the services supplied by an SOE:

- Displace or impede from the market of another party a like service supplied by a service supplier of that other party or a third party;
- Cause a significant price undercutting in the service supplied in the market of another party in comparison to service supplied by suppliers of that other party or a third party or cause significant price suppression, price depression or lost sales in the same market.

11.7 Injury

Article 17.6.3 contains an obligation that no party shall cause injury to a domestic industry of another party through the use of non-commercial assistance that it provides, either directly or indirectly, to any of its SOEs that is a covered investment in the territory of another party. The circumstances under which injury can be caused are confined to situations where the SOE receiving non-commercial assistance in respect of production and sale of a good is a covered investment in the territory of the other party; and a like good is produced and sold in the territory of the other party by the domestic industry of that other party. Therefore, an SOE receiving non-commercial assistance and which is a covered investment in the territory of another party can only be held to cause injury to the domestic industry in the territory of the other party. These provisions limit the causation of injury only in respect of SOEs operating as covered investments in the territory of another party. The term 'domestic industry' refers to the domestic producers as a whole of the like good or to those domestic producers whose collective output of the products constitutes a major proportion of the total domestic production of the like good, excluding the SOE that is a covered investment that has received the non-commercial assistance.[4]

Article 17.8 contains a reference to Article 17.6.3 and gives detailed provisions how injury will be established. The language adopted in the Article 17.8 is based on the language used in ASCM, Article 15, relating to 'injury'. The important difference is that Article 17.8 is in the context of SOEs receiving 'non-commercial assistance' and that are covered investments producing and selling goods in the territory of another party. Article 17.8.1 replicates broadly the definition of 'injury' provided in footnote 45 to Article 15 of the ASCM—'…material injury to a domestic industry, threat of material injury to a domestic industry or material retardation of the establishment of such an industry.' However, in respect of 'material retardation', the TPP Article 17 elaborates that it is understood that a domestic industry may not yet produce and sell the like good. However, in such cases, there must be evidence that a prospective domestic producer has made a substantial commitment to commence production and sales of the like good.[5] Articles 17.8.2 to 17.8.4 lay down how to arrive at a determination of injury. The language used is similar to the language of Articles 15.2 and 15.4 of the ASCM regarding determination of injury.

11.8 Remedies

Remedy against causing of 'adverse effect' can be sought by invoking provisions of Chapter 28 ('Dispute Settlement'—Consultations), upon

---

[4] Footnote 19 of Chapter 17.
[5] Footnote 20 of Chapter 17.

the failure of which an arbitral tribunal is to be constituted. Annex 17-B of the SOE chapter also contains the process for developing information concerning SOEs and designated monopolies.

11.9 Threshold of Applicability of SOE Provisions

As per Article 17.13.5, the provisions of Article 17.4 (non-discriminatory treatment and commercial considerations), Article 17.6 (non-commercial assistance), Article 17.10 (transparency) and Article 17.12 (committee on SOEs) shall not apply with respect to an SOE if in any one of the three previous consecutive fiscal years, the annual revenue derived from commercial activities of the SOE was less than a threshold amount to be calculated in accordance with Annex 17-A.

At the time of entry into force of the TPP the threshold shall be 200 million special drawing rights (SDRs). However, as an exception, these provisions shall not apply to SOEs of Brunei, Malaysia or Vietnam for 5 years from entry into force of the TPP if the annual revenue derived by an SOE from commercial activities was less than SDR 500 million.

11.10 Notification Obligation

The TPP requires the members to notify their SOEs or to make public through official website a list of SOEs within 6 months after the date of entry into force of the TPP. These transparency obligations have been staggered for Brunei, Vietnam and Malaysia who can notify their SOEs within 5 years from date of entry into force of the TPP.

11.11 Legal Enforcement

The TPP requires that members shall provide its courts with jurisdiction over civil claims against an SOE operating in its territory and which is owned by another TPP member.

11.12 Exemptions

The SOEs at the sub-central level have been exempted from the provisions relating to SOEs. Few exceptions have also been made for SOEs of Singapore which are owned or controlled by a sovereign wealth fund of Singapore or in the case of Malaysia, for few SOEs such as Permodalan Nasional Berhad and Lembaga Tabung Haji.

11.13 Conclusion

It is for the first time that an FTA has covered so extensively the commercial activities of SOEs. As the above analysis shows, the provisions in Chapter 17 of the TPP lay down very strong disciplines for the commercial activities of SOEs in their sales of goods or supply of services in the territory of another TPP country and these go well beyond the WTO provisions.

Hitherto, under the WTO ASCM, adverse effects of subsidies were seen in relation to trade in goods. Under the General Agreement on Trade in Services (GATS) disciplines on any possible trade distortive effects of subsidies are yet to be developed. However, under the TPP, the supply of services by SOEs, receiving non-commercial assistance, can be held accountable to have caused adverse effects to the interests of the service suppliers of another TPP member.

Another important feature of the TPP text is the scope of the SOEs that can be found to have caused injury to the domestic industry of another TPP member. As per Article 17.8, SOEs receiving 'non-commercial assistance' and that are covered investments producing and selling goods in the territory of another party can be found to have caused injury to the domestic industry of the other TPP member. Thus, SOEs operating under investment provisions in the territory of other TPP member can be prone to the risk of causing injury to the domestic industry of that TPP member.

The stringent provisions relating to SOEs curtail the policy space for the TPP countries where there is presence of SOEs for public policy needs in core sectors such as steel, power, fuel and fertilizers or in the case of services; there are SOEs which supply services to other TPP countries in a significant manner. The commercial activities of SOEs can be targeted for action or restraint on the pretext of causing adverse effects to the interests of enterprises of other TPP members. It can also be said that the SOE text is aimed to bring into discipline the SOEs of China in the event of China's entry into the TPP. As for non-TPP countries, these provisions should not have implications as these will impact the SOEs of TPP members. Rather, with the possible restrictions on the commercial activities of SOEs of TPP members, there can be a possibility of increased trade opportunity for enterprises of non-TPP countries.

In relation to the supply of services, adverse effects shall be construed with respect to the supply of a service by the SOE from the territory of the party into the territory of another party. Further, in relation to supply of service, adverse effect can be found to exist in the case of supply of a service in the territory of another party through an enterprise that is a covered investment in the territory of that other party or a third party. In effect, supply of services by an SOE under mode 1, that is, cross-border supply and mode 3, that is, supply of service through commercial presence in the territory of another party can cause adverse effects to the interest of another party.

A very significant coverage of the adverse effect provision is in respect of an SOE displacing or impeding the sales of similar goods produced by an enterprise that is a covered investment in the territory of the TPP member which implies that sales of an entity which has come into existence or is in operation as a result of the investment provisions are also sought to be protected from the commercial activities of SOEs, if the sales of SOEs displace or impede the sales of such enterprises operating under the investment provisions. For example, in the case of Steel Authority of India Ltd. (SAIL), which produces and sells steel products in India and abroad, if India were to be part of a future bilateral or multilateral agreement where the TPP template for SOEs was to be adopted, then there can be implications. If there are certain investments in the steel sector in India which are covered under a TPP-like template, then if SAIL's production and sale in India displace or impede the sales of such enterprise, which is a covered investment in India under a TPP-like provision, it can be argued that SAIL has caused adverse effects.

Reference

WTO. 2011. 'United States—Definitive Anti-Dumping and Countervailing Duties on China'. *Appellate Body Report* (WT/DS379/AB/R). Geneva: WTO.

12
Trade Remedies, Trade Facilitation and Regulatory Coherence under the TPP

Mukesh Bhatnagar, Monika and
R.V. Anuradha

12.1 Overview of Provisions on Trade Remedies, Trade Facilitation and Regulatory Coherence in the TPP

Most of the free trade agreements (FTAs) include provisions on bilateral safeguards, which permit a party to the FTA to impose bilateral safeguard measures in case there is a surge in imports as a result of commitments taken under the FTA. Although there are considerable similarities in procedural requirements pertaining to the investigation, in certain aspects the provisions on bilateral safeguards differ from the provisions in World Trade Organization (WTO) Agreement on Safeguards. The differences are mainly in respect of the nature of measure and the scope of products that can be covered by bilateral safeguards. The Trans-Pacific Partnership Agreement (TPP) follows the general trend of containing provisions that permit an importing country to impose safeguard measures against other parties to the Agreement, if there is a surge in imports. Further, the Agreement contains an additional policy instrument in the form of an emergency action to regulate imports of textile and clothing products if there is a surge of products in this sector resulting in serious damage, or threat thereof, to the domestic producers. In the second section, this chapter discusses details of the provisions related to emergency action on textile and clothing products. The subsequent section details the provisions of transitional safeguard measures. This is followed by a brief discussion on the provisions in the TPP related to the WTO Anti-Dumping Agreement. Implications for India of the trade remedy provisions in the TPP are discussed in Section 12.5 of this chapter.

At the WTO, the member countries have implemented the Trade Facilitation Agreement (TFA) in February 2017. This agreement seeks to enhance transparency and streamline procedures for international trade. The TPP has similar rules on trade facilitation. However, in certain respects, the TPP provisions are more prescriptive than the provisions in the TFA. Section 12.6 undertakes a brief comparison between the trade facilitation provisions in the TPP and those in the TFA and examines some of the implications for India if it were to comply with obligations contained in the TPP chapter on this issue.

The TPP contains broad disciplines on internal procedures to be followed by its signatory countries, while formulating domestic regulations. Although the stated objective of the chapter on regulatory coherence is to enhance regulatory cooperation, this is likely to result in an intrusive and onerous regime. These aspects are discussed in Sections 12.7 and 12.8 of this chapter.

12.2 Emergency Action on Textile and Clothing Products

The very fact that the TPP has a separate chapter on textiles and apparel signifies that TPP members have given due recognition to this sector and have negotiated some rules which are specific to textiles and apparel. The tariff liberalization, which will eventually result in zero tariff for TPP members, will lead to increased market access for TPP members when it comes to textiles and apparel. Article 4.3 of the TPP contains provisions for taking emergency actions if, as a result of reduction or elimination of customs duty under the TPP, the domestic industry in the importing TPP country complains of serious damage or threat of serious damage. It should be noted that the standard of injury for emergency action under the TPP is different from that under the WTO Agreement on Safeguards. Under the latter, the standard of injury is 'serious injury or threat thereof'.

The determination of serious damage can be established by the importing party by examining the effect of increased imports from the exporting party, as reflected in changes in economic variables as output, productivity, utilization of capacity, inventories, market share, exports, wages, employment, domestic prices, profits and investment. The standard for establishing serious damage seems to be loose and less stringent as compared to serious injury. There is a possibility of invocation of emergency actions by importing TPP countries on the pretext of serious damage to its textiles industry simply due to changes in economic variables, which may not necessarily be portraying serious decline in the economic parameters. Apparently, the text has been developed keeping in view the interest of the US textiles industry, so that the emergency action can be invoked. Emergency action can be taken by the government of the importing TPP member only after an investigation by the competent authorities of that government.

The transition period for taking emergency action is 5 years after the date on which the importing party eliminates duties on textiles and apparel products. In contrast, Chapter 6 on trade remedies contains the transition period for taking safeguard measures under the TPP, which is a period of only 3 years from the date of entry of the TPP (or the period up to the tariff elimination). Therefore, the emergency action that can be invoked by TPP members against the increased imports of textiles and apparel due to tariff liberalization is far easier, and such emergency actions can be taken over a longer transition period.

The emergency action will be by way of increase in the rate of customs duty to the applied rate of most favoured nation (MFN) duty. The duration of the emergency action under Article 4.3 is 2 years with a possible extension by additional 2 years. In contrast to the provisions under the 'Trade Remedies' chapter of the TPP, the provisions for applying emergency actions under the chapter on textiles and apparel seem to be more protective. Under the 'Trade Remedies' chapter, the safeguard measures on products other than textiles and apparel can be applied for 2 years which can be extended by another 1 year.

An importing party can conduct verification in respect of textiles or apparel to verify whether it is eligible for preferential tariff treatment. This also includes on-site verification. Pending verification, the importing party can suspend grant of preferential tariff treatment. This again seems to protect US interests.

12.3 Trade Remedies: Transitional Safeguard Measures

Like in most of the FTAs, Chapter 6 of the TPP contains provisions for taking transitional safeguard measures. Typically in every FTA, parties negotiate provision for taking a bilateral or transitional safeguard measure so as to impose these safeguard measures on the FTA partner, if the increased imports due to tariff liberalization under the FTA are causing or are threatening to cause serious injury to its domestic industry producing similar goods. Under the provision to take an emergency action in the 'Textiles and Apparel' chapter, the emergency measure can be taken in a situation of 'serious damage' to the domestic industry. Thus, the threshold of injury to the domestic industry for invoking safeguards measures is different and much higher under the 'Trade Remedies' chapter which will apply to products other than textiles and apparel. In keeping with the general trend in FTAs, the TPP also provides that parties can take recourse to safeguard measures permitted under Article XIX of the General Agreement on Tariffs and Trade (GATT) and the WTO Safeguards Agreement. Thus, parties' rights are not diminished in so far as taking global safeguard measures are concerned.

Transition Period

The transition period for taking transitional safeguard measures is 3 years from the date of entry of the TPP or where the period of tariff elimination is longer; the transition period shall be up to the year of tariff elimination. This apparently is a very narrow period considering the fact that any effect of tariff liberalization may be felt by the domestic industry in a year or so. It will require time to file an application for the safeguard measure and, thereafter, the authorities will need time to conduct safeguard investigation to come to a conclusion whether to impose a transitional safeguard measure. If the safeguard measure is to be applied to provide relief to the domestic industry, the duration of the measure should be reasonable enough to give the desired relief, that is, 1–2 years. However, according to Article 6.4.3, a transitional safeguard measure cannot be maintained beyond the expiration of the transition period, which is 3 years from the date of the entry of the TPP or up to the period of tariff liberalization. Thus, the transitional safeguard measures may not be an effective policy instrument to protect domestic producers from the surge in imports that might arise due to the Agreement.

Imposition of Transitional Safeguard Measures

The transitional safeguard measures can be taken only when increased imports are due to reduction or elimination of customs duty under the TPP, which cause or threaten to cause serious injury to the domestic industry of the importing party. The safeguard measure can be in the form of tariff only and cannot be in the form of tariff rate quotas or quantitative restrictions. The transition safeguard measure can be applied by either suspending the further reduction of customs duty under the TPP or by increasing the customs duty to the MFN level.

Duration of Transitional Safeguard Measures

The duration of the period for applying transitional safeguard measures is 2 years, which can be extended by 1 year, thus, a safeguard measure can be in force for maximum 3 years. But this duration may not be 3 years in reality in view of the overall 3 years transition period.

A transitional safeguard measures can be applied only once on the same goods.

Notification of Actions Relating to Imposition of Transitional Safeguard Measures

The TPP text requires obligations of notification of any proposed imposition of transitional safeguard measure including the initiation of the investigation, findings of serious injury and the decision to apply a safeguard measure.

Consultations and Right to Compensation

The provisions regarding consultations between the party applying the safeguard measure and the party on whose exports the measure is applied are similar to the WTO Safeguard Agreement. The opportunity for consultations should be given within 30 days of application of a safeguard measure. There is a provision for binding obligation for compensation to the affected party on whose exports transitional safeguard measures are applied, irrespective of the duration of the measures. The compensation should normally be mutually agreed within 30 days of the application of measures, and the compensation should be in the form of concessions that have substantially equivalent trade effects or are equivalent to the value of the additional duties expected to result from the transitional safeguard measures. In case the parties do not agree on mutual trade liberalizing compensation within 30 days, the party (parties) on whose goods the safeguard measures are applied can suspend the equivalent concessions on the party imposing such measures. The obligation to provide compensation and the right to suspend concessions shall terminate on the termination of the transitional safeguard measures.

12.4 Anti-dumping and Countervailing Duties

Parties have retained their rights and obligations under Article 6 of the GATT and Anti-dumping (AD) and SCM Agreement. Therefore, the TPP members can take anti-dumping and countervailing duty (CVD) measures in accordance with the rights and obligations under these agreements.

However, under Annex 6A, parties have agreed to the following WTO-plus provisions:

(a) To share seven days in advance information about receipt of application before initiation of AD or CVD investigations.
(b) For conducting on-site verification of AD or CVD investigation, the investigating authority will provide advance notice of 10 working days before the on-site verification. Advance notice of five days to be given for the topics to be covered during the verification and documents to be made available.
(c) After an on-site verification, a written report describing the verification is to be given, subject to protection of confidential information.
(d) Making available the public file containing non-confidential documents of every AD/CVD investigation for inspection and copying of documents.
(e) Investigating authority to provide reasons for disregarding certain information in the final determination of any AD/CVD investigation.

(f) Disclosure of essential facts before final determination by using any reasonable means to disclose essential facts, including a report summarizing the data in the record.

12.5 Implications for India

If India does not join the TPP, there may be little impact of the trade remedy and emergency action provisions on it. However, the impact may not be benign if India were to join an agreement based on the TPP template of rules. Given the past track record of developed countries, it is quite likely that they will not hesitate in seeking recourse to emergency action to addresses import surges. Thus, gains made from market access provided under the Agreement could get undermined and reversed if the United States of America (USA) were to use emergency action measures against any increase in imports of textile and clothing products from India. Conversely, if India was to liberalize tariffs on textiles and apparel, it could also use these emergency actions in accordance with the terms and conditions of the TPP.

12.6 Trade Facilitation Provisions in the TPP

Chapter 5 of the TPP covers the field of custom administration and trade facilitation. The TPP largely reaffirms the principles laid down in the WTO Agreement on trade facilitation (TFA) and has not raised the standards, barring few exceptions. Under the TFA, countries have the flexibility to implement certain obligations over a 'reasonable period of time', or 'in a time-bound manner'. In contrast, the TPP is more prescriptive, as some specific time frames have been included in respect of some of the obligations on trade facilitation in the Agreement.

On the issue of 'customs cooperation', the TPP has made provision for advance notice of any significant change in law or regulation relating to exports and imports, information sharing with respect to laws and regulations, and establishment of contact points for information and technical advice and assistance. The TFA already covers these aspects. Moreover, the TPP has referred to the TFA, because its provision for providing requested information in connection with unlawful activity related to laws and regulations governing importations is subject to party's domestic laws and relevant international agreements. However, it is to be noted that even though the TPP provisions are talking about 'encouraging cooperation' and 'endeavour', they have more weight than the WTO Agreement due to usage of 'shall'.

The scope of 'advance rulings' under TFA and the TPP is equally wide. However, TFA imposes binding requirement only on the issues of tariff classification and origin of goods. Another point of difference is that the TPP imposes maximum limit of '150 days' for issuing advance ruling, whereas TFA requires issue of rulings in a time-bound manner and has not prescribed any specific time limit. Further, the TPP requires that rulings should be in effect for at least 3 years, while TFA prescribes 'a reasonable period of time'.

The TFA is much more detailed on the subject of 'response to requests for advice or information'. In this regard, the TPP has not provided any procedure or time limit. It has simply provided a non-exhaustive list of all the topics on which advice or information can be made available.

On the topic of 'review and appeal', the TPP sets down mandatory requirement for providing access to administrative and judicial review. It also mandates a written and reasoned decision. The TFA provisions are similar in nature. However, the provision for both judicial and administrative review is optional under TFA. A member may mandate initiation of administrative review/appeal prior to judicial review/appeal. The TFA additionally specifies undue delay or delay as per the specified time limit for review/appeal as a ground for further appeal. Another TFA provision mandates that the provisions regarding review and appeal cover administrative decisions by relevant border agency other than the customs. The TPP is silent in this respect.

With respect to 'automation', the TFA encourages use of relevant international standards for importation, exportation and transit procedures. It takes into account limited resources of members and provides for periodic review of international standards subject to those limitations. The Committee on Trade Facilitation (to committee established under Article 23.1 of Trade facilitation Agreement [TFA]) is conferred with the responsibility to develop procedures and best practices on implementation of international standards. The TFA has incorporated flexibility here as well, by directing the committee that the exercise should be 'appropriate'. On the other hand, the TPP has emphasized adoption of international standards for release of goods, common standards for import and export in accordance with the World Customs Organisation Data Model and employment of electronic or automated systems for risk management and others uses. It further requires that each party should endeavour to provide facility for electronically completing standardized import and export requirements at a single entry point.

Express Shipment provisions of the TPP are more onerous as compared to the TFA. As per the TFA, procedure for expedited release of goods is mandatory only for the goods entered through air cargo facilities. Its application is discretionary for other type of cargos, whereas the TPP mandates provision of expedited release of goods without any distinction. Another notable change is that the TPP has a fixed time limit of 'six hours' from the submission of relevant documents for the release of express shipments in normal circumstances. The TFA does not provide any time limit and merely requires that goods should be released as rapidly as possible.

The TPP has reiterated TFA provisions on 'penalties'. It has added a requirement for parties to provide a fixed and finite period within which custom administration may initiate the proceedings.

The TPP has not deviated much from the TFA on the issue of 'risk management'. However, it has made the adoption and maintenance of the risk management system binding without any concessions. It has also mandated a periodic review of the system, which is not provided under the TFA.

Provisions governing 'release of goods' under the TPP are mostly similar to the TFA provisions. One major difference is that under the TFA members are encouraged to measure and publish their average release time, whereas the TPP has specified maximum time limit of '48 hours' from the arrival of goods and mandates members to implement it to the extent possible. Another point of difference is that the TPP enforces mandatory obligation to process the relevant information electronically.

With respect to the issue of 'publication', the TPP is more onerous than the TFA. It imposes mandatory obligation to designate one or more enquiry points and to make procedures of publication available online, whereas the TFA allows members flexibility in these areas by taking into account their available resources and making such obligations non-mandatory. The TPP also provides for advance publication of customs regulations and opportunity to comment on the proposed regulations to the extent possible.

On the matter of 'confidentiality', the TPP has not gone beyond the requirements specified in the TFA. Although it is silent on the procedures followed upon receiving the request for disclosure of confidential information, it allows a party to adopt or maintain procedures '…in accordance with the administration of the Party's custom laws…'.

Thus, it can be concluded that the TPP has not added any substantial discipline that is different from what is already contained in the WTO TFA. However, the TPP has specified time limits for compliance with some obligations, including release of goods for express and other shipments. Compliance with such time limits can prove to be very onerous and may require an overhaul of the customs administration.

12.7 Regulatory Coherence Key Obligations in the TPP

The general scope of Chapter 25 on regulatory coherence encompasses the use of good regulatory practices in the process of planning, designing, issuing, implementing and reviewing regulatory measures in order to facilitate achievement of domestic policy objectives and in efforts across governments to enhance regulatory cooperation in order to further those objectives and promote international trade and investment, economic growth and employment.[1]

The definition of the term 'regulatory coherence' is extremely broad, as it covers any measure of general application related to any matter covered by the TPP Agreement adopted by regulatory agencies with which compliance is mandatory.[2] The key obligations of the parties under the chapter are as follows.

There is a general obligation with regards to all regulatory measures that mandate parties to increase interagency consultation and coordination associated with processes for developing such regulatory measures. Accordingly, each party is obligated to ensure that it has processes or mechanisms to facilitate the effective interagency coordination and review of proposed covered regulatory measures. Each party should consider establishing and maintaining a national or central coordinating body for this purpose.[3]

---

[1] Article 25.2, Chapter 25 on regulatory coherence, TPP.
[2] Article 25.1, Chapter 25 on regulatory coherence, TPP.
[3] Para 1, Article 25.4, Chapter 25 on regulatory coherence, TPP.

With regard to 'covered regulatory measures', there is an additional requirement to conduct regulatory impact assessments when developing 'covered regulatory measures' that exceed a threshold of economic impact or other regulatory impact as established by that party.[4] Such a requirement leaves open some ambiguity as regards to what would constitute a 'threshold of economic impact'.

At the institutional level, the chapter establishes a committee on regulatory coherence, comprising of representatives of all the parties. The role of the committee is to consider issues associated with the implementation and operation of this chapter. The committee shall also consider identifying future priorities, including potential sectoral initiatives and cooperative activities.[5] The committee is also required to provide mechanisms for 'opportunities for interested persons' to provide inputs for regulatory coherence.[6] There is no definition of interested persons which thereby indicates the possibility of engaging non-governmental agencies and corporates in such a process.

It should be noted that the 'Dispute Settlement' chapter will not apply to the 'Regulatory Coherence' chapter.

12.8 Impact of the Chapter on Regulatory Governance

It has been observed that the TPP is not an FTA in its traditional sense, or an investment treaty, or even a PTA (Robertson 2015). It has been characterized as a new generation of document that provides a form of 'economic constitution' comprising foundational rules for the governance of cross-border trade and investment (ibid.). The chapter on regulatory coherence is the first of its kind in any FTA. It is worded broadly and, in the language of soft law, encouraging TPP members to adopt 'good regulatory practices', affirming the importance of regulatory coherence and emphasizing the need for building regulatory cooperation and capacity building between states.

It is perhaps one of the most innocuous, yet one of the most powerful chapters of the TPP in that it embodies within it the potential to direct the shape of regulations and decision-making across the TPP members,

---
[4] Article 25.5, Chapter 25 on regulatory coherence, TPP.
[5] Article 25.6, Chapter 25 on regulatory coherence, TPP.
[6] Article 25.8, Chapter 25 on regulatory coherence, TPP.

along the lines of what is seen by the USA as the right approach. This is perhaps best summarized in the assessment provided by the USTR itself:

> As in the United States, we expect these commitments to promote 'good regulatory practice' principles in the regulatory development process, including coordination among regulators, opportunities for stakeholder input, and fact-based regulatory decisions that will serve to eliminate the prospect of overlapping and inconsistent regulatory requirements or regulations being developed unfairly and without a sound basis, including so as to benefit a particular stakeholder. Nothing in the chapter will affect the U.S. or other TPP Parties' right to regulate in the public interest, *nor will anything in it require changes to U.S. regulations or U.S. regulatory procedures* (emphasis added).
>
> Governments are responsible for regulating to foster fair competition, consumer safety, environmental quality, workplace safety and many other policy goals. In the United States, the rule-making process is well developed so as to ensure transparency, impartiality, and due process....The legal and regulatory environment in countries across the Asia-Pacific is diverse. The region's governments and publics may have differing priorities and reach different conclusions on specific regulatory issues... They share a common interest, however, in developing regulations based on reliable and objective data; avoiding conflicting requirements in their own...
>
> Coherent regulatory processes—coordinated across government agencies, designed and implemented based on good regulatory practices, and with opportunities for stakeholder input—are critical to creating open, fair and predictable environments for U.S. businesses operating in Asia-Pacific markets.[7]

If India were required to comply with the obligations on regulatory coherence as contained in the TPP, then it would need to create a new institutional mechanism for designing and implementing regulatory measures. Further, it would be mandated to undertake a regulatory impact assessment analysis. In addition, the obligation to provide 'opportunities for interested persons' to give inputs for regulatory coherence may be extremely onerous, as the central coordinating body may not have

---

[7] Emphasis added by the authors; source: USTR, TPP Chapter Summary: Regulatory Governance, https://ustr.gov/sites/default/files/TPP-Chapter-Summary-Regulatory-Coherence.pdf (last visited 18 July 2017).

the resources to take into account comments that may be received from interested persons, including from other nations.

Reference

Robertson, Donald. 2015, 4 December. 'TPP: Regulatory Coherence.' Retrieved 14 July 2017, from http://www.herbertsmithfreehills.com/insights/issues/trans-pacific-partnership/regulatory-coherence

13
Conclusions and Way Forward

Abhijit Das, Shailja Singh and Harimaya Gurung

13.1 TPP and Changing Context

With President Donald Trump withdrawing the United States of America (USA) from the Trans-Pacific Partnership (hereinafter, referred to as the TPP or the Agreement), the possibility of the Agreement text, in the form as it was signed in February 2016, being implemented is rather low. This appears to be the likely scenario despite Japan's efforts to proceed with the Agreement without the USA. Notwithstanding this development, the rules on international trade and investment, as contained in the TPP, continue to remain extremely relevant. First, on certain issues, the provisions in the TPP could serve as a template for negotiations at the WTO and in free trade agreements (FTAs). Second, the TPP could be implemented in a slightly modified form but retaining most of the provisions that were agreed to in February 2016. From India's perspective, adhering to the template of rules contained in the TPP would require it to comply with the onerous obligations under the Agreement. This would result in adverse effects on at least three counts. First, the TPP style rules would require India to eliminate tariffs. In the absence of tariff protection, and on the account of other provisions in the TPP template, continued viability of India's manufacturing would come under serious question. This would severely jeopardize the 'Make in India' initiative. Second, Indian farmers could come under a persistent threat of surge in subsidized imports from developed countries, if India eliminates tariffs on agricultural products. There is the grave possibility of such developed countries continuing to provide tens of billions of subsidies to their agriculture sector. Despite this perpetual threat, a TPP style agreement would prevent the government from protecting the Indian farmers by imposing customs duty. Third, the cost of medicines would rise steeply if India agrees to the TPP template on intellectual property rights (IPRs), as it would be required to make changes in its patent laws to allow ever-greening of patents, thereby delaying entry of cheap generic medicines in the market.

The previous chapters of this book have sought to assess the likely impact on India, if it were to comply with the rules contained in the TPP, or the impact of trade diversion, if TPP is implemented (even in a modified form by signatory countries sans the USA). The key conclusions emerging from the previous chapters, along with additional observations and insights, are summarized in Section 2 of this chapter. Keeping the requirements of the evolving global scenario for international trade in mind, Section 3 of this chapter makes recommendations for India's trade policy.

13.2 Conclusions

Some of the severe adverse impacts on manufacturing and agriculture, if India complies with the TPP template, are as follows:

1. If India complies with the TPP template, it would be required to eliminate tariffs on goods, both agriculture and industrial products, in a phased manner. Based on a comprehensive unit value analysis, it would appear that India is price competitive in less than 20 per cent of the products. While a comparison of unit values across countries is beset with problems, nevertheless, the low percentage of products in which India is price competitive suggests that India may not be able to successfully face import competition under a zero duty regime. While India may have agreed to a zero duty regime on substantially all trade in its FTAs, the reality of TPP template is slightly different. Most of India's FTA partners are competitive in a narrow range of products. Consequently, India has been able to secure its interests by excluding some sensitive products from zero duty regime under its FTAs. However, extending a zero-duty tariff regime to a large number of countries with specialization in different categories of products can have significant adverse impact on domestic producers in India. To illustrate,

countries such as Australia and New Zealand, are significant exporters of agricultural products, while Japan and the USA are export powerhouses in industrial products. Vietnam has strengths in labour intensive manufacturing sectors, including apparels and leather products. Thus, these five countries, as a group, would be more price competitive than India in most of the products. Given this reality, it is extremely improbable that Indian domestic manufacturing would be in a position to survive the onslaught of competitive imports under a regime of zero import duty.

Some commentators have used the significant increase in GDP growth witnessed by the country subsequent to the economic liberalization initiated in 1991 as an argument for reposing faith in the capacity of the Indian industry to successfully face import competition, even in the face of zero customs duty. While India's GDP growth increased significantly after 1991, it is also a fact that the domestic IT hardware industry was unable to face import competition under the zero duty regime after India became a participant to the Information Technology Agreement at the WTO. In fact, most producers of IT hardware were severely adversely affected by zero duty imports. Thus, it may not be prudent to use the experience of the domestic industry in coping with 1991 economic reforms as an indicator of their continued ability to face import competition at zero duty from other countries.

2. Apart from the obligation related to eliminating tariffs, the TPP template contains a few other provisions, which would have a severe adverse impact on the manufacturing sector in India. The prohibition on imposing any restrictions on the imports of remanufactured goods could inject additional challenges for the domestic industry, as it would have to compete with similar low-priced imports. This could undermine the efforts of enhancing value addition in manufacturing in many sectors.

3. The prohibition on export duties and taxes would prevent the government from using this policy instrument for promoting domestic value addition in raw materials and establishment of downstream processing industries.

4. Overall, if India were to adhere to the TPP template, the effort of the government to increase the share of manufacturing sector in India's GDP would be undermined. Further, the Make in India initiative would be rendered meaningless.

5. The obligation in the TPP template to eliminate tariffs would have a devastating impact on India's agriculture. It is well known that the USA and Canada provide tens of billions of dollars as direct subsidy to their farmers. As the TPP template does not contain any rules on reducing the domestic farm subsidies, India's farmers would be under perpetual threat of being inundated by heavily subsidized exports from some of the developed countries. As India would be required to eliminate tariffs, if it were to adhere to the TPP template, the government would have no policy instrument to protect the livelihood of farmers in the face of challenges posed by the likely surge in subsidized imports from some of the developed countries. This would raise extremely serious questions on the continued viability of India's agriculture sector.

6. One positive aspect of the TPP is the provision allowing the USA and Japan to impose additional duty, if there is a surge in imports of certain specified products. This could provide a basis for India to argue for a similar provision at the WTO—an issue of importance for India.

7. Adhering to the TPP template in IPRs would pose challenges for India's agriculture on two grounds. First, if India enters into an agreement based on the TPP template, it would have to implement Union for the Protection of New Plant Varieties (UPOV) 1991, which is heavily biased in the favour of the rights of plant breeders. The UPOV Convention substantially deals with the rights of only one stakeholder—the breeder. There is hardly any substantial provision in the UPOV Convention which deals with the rights of the farmer or of any other stakeholder. In contrast to the UPOV Convention, India is implementing Protection of Plant Varieties and Farmers' Rights (PPVFR) Act, 2001, that seeks to balance the rights of plant breeders and farmers' rights. An important famers' right, which has been recognized under the PPVFR Act, is the right to 'save', use, 're-sow', 'exchange', 'share' or 'sell' their farm produce, including the seed of a protected variety. The PPVFR Act does not recognize the right of a breeder to prohibit stocking of seeds, that is, seed saving without the breeder's authorization. The UPOV 1991, on the other hand, establishes the rights of the plant breeders in a manner that reduces the freedom of the farmers to exchange and sell seeds among each other or to reproduce seeds (for multiplication) or use it for propagation or for stocking of seeds. India's subsistence agriculture may come

under considerable risk if the country were to join UPOV 1991. India's farmers would be forced to pay royalties for 25 years for grapevines and trees and 20 years for all other plants that meet the criteria in UPOV 1991. Further, they would be unable to reproduce or exchange seeds of the protected varieties. Consequently, millions of farmers could lose their livelihood because they may no longer be able to afford seeds, or exchange seeds.

Second, the TPP template provides for 10 years of data exclusivity protection for agrochemicals. Consequently, generic versions of those agricultural chemicals cannot be approved by the regulator for 10 years. This would provide a fresh lease of monopoly market protection to old molecules, some of which may no longer enjoy patent protection. This would raise the prices for agrochemicals. Consequently, the cost of agriculture in India would increase significantly.

8. Furthermore, on certain issues, the TPP template seems to run counter to the findings of WTO panels and Appellate Body. Five specific issues—definition of state-owned enterprises in the TPP and jurisprudence on 'public body' in the ASCM, using out-of-country benchmarks for undertaking benefit analysis under Article 14(d) of the ASCM, benefit analysis in the context of government provision of equity infusion under Article 14(a) of ASCM, 'commercial consideration' in the context of state trading enterprises in Article XVIII 1(a) and 1(b) of General Agreement on Tariffs and Trade (GATT), 1994, and 'on a commercial scale' in the context of Article 61 of the TRIPS. We need to carefully reflect on how these apparent contradictions between the WTO jurisprudence and the explicit provisions in the TPP would be addressed, if the latter is used as an inspiration for further WTO negotiations.

Services Sector: Limited Export Gains, but Serious Risk of Deregulation

9. Liberalization in the regime for the movement of natural persons, particularly to the USA, is often projected as an important channel of gains for India in the services sector. However, under the TPP template, the USA has made no commitments in this area. Hence, India is unlikely to see an increase in the movement of its professionals and skilled and semi-skilled workers to that country, even if it were to adhere to the TPP template. This should

significantly reduce the attractiveness of TPP template for India's service exporters.
10. The architecture of commitments under the services sector in the TPP template is significantly different from that under the General Agreement on Trade in Services (GATS) at the WTO. Unlike the GATS, the TPP follows a negative list approach in scheduling commitments for national treatment, most-favoured-nation treatment, market access and local presence. This implies that countries agree to take commitments for all sectors except where the exceptions have been specified in the schedule as non-conforming measures. The positive list approach under the GATS permitted countries to take commitments in those sectors and modes of supply in which there was domestic preparedness. This allowed countries to align their services commitments with national priorities. However, India may find it extremely onerous to adhere to the negative list that architecture the TPP template for commitments in services. To illustrate, the negative list approach would require India to anticipate all possible financial regulations, including future regulations applicable for financial services not yet invented, structure its domestic regime appropriately and suitably schedule its exceptions at the time of committing itself to the TPP. This is an almost impossible task. Thus, joining the TPP template would prevent India from introducing new regulations to address requirements arising from market realities.
11. The TPP template prohibits its countries from making their current regulatory measures more restrictive in the future. Thus, if India joins an agreement based on the TPP template, measures relating to licensing requirements and procedures, qualification requirements and procedures and technical standards in services cannot be made more restrictive in future, even if the imperatives of the market so demand.
12. Under the TPP template, countries do not have the flexibility to rollback any autonomous liberalization undertaken by them in future. Complying with this onerous requirement will significantly reduce the policy space for India and its ability to experiment with autonomous liberalization.
13. Certain aspects of the existing RBI policy pertaining to foreign banks are not aligned with the market access rules of the TPP template. The TPP prohibits its members from imposing any restrictions on the type of legal entity through which a financial

institution can supply a service. However, under the existing RBI requirements, foreign banks can set up business in India only through a single mode—either through a wholly owned subsidiary or by establishing branches—not both the modes.

14. Adhering to the obligations envisaged under the TPP could undermine the efforts aimed at financial stability. In order to address the risk of wholly owned subsidiaries of foreign banks and foreign bank branches from coming together and dominating the financial system in India, the RBI can impose two restrictions: (a) restriction on further entry of new foreign players in the financial services sector and (b) prior approval of the RBI for additional capital infusion by wholly owned subsidiaries. The RBI can impose these restrictions when the capital and reserves of the foreign banks in India exceed 20 per cent of the capital and reserves of the total banking system in India. Obligations under the TPP prevent its member countries from imposing such measures, even if these are aimed at ensuring financial stability in the country.
15. Certain other restrictions imposed by the RBI, including minimum capital requirements, are not in line with the obligations for financial services in the TPP template.
16. The TPP mandates opening up of legal services to foreign entities. As the Advocates Act, 1961, does not allow foreign law confirms to practice in India, suitable regulatory changes may be needed if India decides to join TPP template.
17. The TPP mandates that no party shall prohibit the resale of any public telecommunication services. The rules for resale of telecommunication services in India will need to be changed if it joins the TPP template, as India only permits resale of international private leased circuit services.

Electronic Commerce

18. The TPP prohibits countries from imposing customs duty on digital products on a permanent basis. Thus, the TPP converts the temporary moratorium on imposing customs duty on electronic transmission agreed at the WTO into a permanent moratorium. While India is a party to the temporary moratorium, adhering to a permanent moratorium would deprive the country of generating revenue from electronic transmissions in the future when a

significant volume in international trade is likely to be transacted through such means.

19. The TPP prohibits countries from imposing localization requirements. The implication of having a TPP style obligation is that firms and digital entrepreneurs relying on cloud computing and delivering Internet-based products and services cannot be mandatorily required to build physical infrastructure and data centres in every country they seek to serve. This obligation is not desirable for at least four reasons and could have an adverse impact on the development of such facilities within India.

First, given the increasing proliferation of business through cloud computing, it is possible that disputes would arise in future. Such disputes would get resolved on the basis of laws and jurisprudence applicable in the territory of location of the servers and other physical infrastructure. Thus, an aggrieved Indian firm or consumer may have to litigate in US or European Union (EU) courts (as most of the infrastructure, data centres and cloud computing computers are presently located in these countries), if it feels aggrieved by an e-commerce company or a cloud computing website. This would be extremely costly, effectively erecting barriers on access to affordable dispute resolution for consumers from non-US and non-EU territories.

Second, privacy of data stored on cloud computing facilities would be subject to the rules of the territory in which the cloud computing facilities are located. Apart from the issue of barriers to litigation in case a breach of privacy becomes known, there is another issue of concern. There is no certainty that, under the pretext of national security, the host country in which the cloud computing facilities are located will not have secret access to the data. Thus, confidential data, including government-related data that may be stored on cloud computing, may become accessible to host governments, without India becoming aware of it.

Third, prohibition on localization of computing facilities and data centre can have severe adverse implications of continued access to critical services at crucial times, particularly during wars and emergencies in international relations. This could have a huge disruptive impact not only on continued availability of services in India, which might be dependent on cloud computing and data facilities located mainly in the developed countries, but would also have extremely damaging economic impacts. To prevent this from happening, countries impose localization requirements.

Fourth, prohibiting localization may prevent cloud computing or the creation of data centres from being established within India. As global cloud computing is at a nascent stage, it may not be cost effective for the main cloud computing firms to establish these facilities in India. It is quite possible that without some degree of localization, these facilities may never get established in India. Consequently, India may fail to harness the economic benefits (employment generation, wealth creation, etc.) of an important emerging 'industry'. Instead, it may permanently become dependent on cloud computing facilities based in the developed countries.

20. Some developing countries have imposed requirements that make market access contingent on the forced transfers of technology. This has helped create a vibrant domestic e-commerce sector in some countries. However, by adhering to the TPP template, countries would be prohibited from mandating transfer of technology as a condition for providing access to the suppliers of e-commerce. It may be noted that under the existing WTO rules, governments have the policy space to impose such requirements for technology transfer in respect of services. Agreeing to an obligation that prohibits governments from imposing requirements for technology transfer would become an important constraint in India developing a vibrant domestic e-commerce sector.

21. The TPP prohibits countries from imposing restrictions on cross-border flow of information by electronic means, including personal information, when this activity is for the conduct of business. On the surface, such a provision in an agreement on electronic commerce at the WTO could facilitate the growth in exports of IT and IT enabled services (ITES) services from India, particularly to the EU. However, on the ground of protecting personal data and on privacy issues, such a provision will meet extremely strong opposition from the EU. Given the deeply entrenched position of the EU on this issue, it is extremely unlikely, if not totally impossible, that any final agreement on e-commerce will have a strong provision on cross-border data flows. India must be cognizant of the huge gap between its aspirations and what can be reasonably achieved through negotiations at the WTO on e-commerce. It should not be led down the garden path in believing that the TPP provision on cross-border data flows can be replicated at the WTO. Hence, even on the issue of most importance for India,

Conclusions and Way Forward **313**

the eventual provisions may not be commercially useful for the country. Further, a provision mandating free flow of information across borders would imply that India would give away data for free—the raw material of the digital economy. This could hamper the development of the digital economy in India.

22. The TPP requires a major supplier in the territory of its member countries to offer to public telecommunications service suppliers access to network elements on an unbundled basis on terms and conditions, and at cost-oriented rates, that are reasonable, non-discriminatory and transparent for the supply of public telecommunications services. The TPP further requires each member to ensure that any service supplier of another member is permitted to (a) provide services to individual or multiple end-users over leased or owned circuits; and (b) perform switching, signalling, processing and conversion functions. These obligations are significantly more liberal for foreign service suppliers. India would find it extremely difficult to comply with these obligations.

Intellectual Property

23. The TPP template requires countries to accede to, or ratify, some of the existing international agreements on IPR. Many of these agreements create a TRIPS-plus regime. If India were to comply with this TPP template, it would have to ratify the Singapore Treaty on Law of Trademarks, UPOV 1991, WIPO Copyright Treaty and WIPO Performance and Phonogram Treaty. Ratification of these treaties would result in significant changes in India's domestic IPR regime. If, at some stage, the TPP template gets subsumed in the Trade-Related Aspects of Intellectual Property Rights (TRIPS) then the provisions of these treaties would become enforceable under the dispute settlement mechanism of the WTO.

24. In the area of patents and undisclosed data, the TPP provisions mark a paradigm shift from TRIPS. The objective appears clearly to reduce, or eliminate, the flexibilities available under the TRIPS Agreement and to tilt the balance in the favour of IPR holders. This would result in prolonging market monopoly of pharmaceuticals and agrochemicals.

25. The TPP requires the signatory countries to make the best endeavour to harmonize the procedures for obtaining a patent in accordance with the requirements contained in the Patent Law Treaty.

The Patent Law Treaty sets down the maximum information that can be sought by a Patent office from an applicant, thereby, preventing countries from addressing any unique concerns that they may have. Complying with this obligation will prevent further negotiation on the TRIPS–CBD (CBD stands for Convention on Biological Diversity) issue at the WTO by undermining or prohibiting mandatory disclosure requirements in patent applications.

26. The TPP provisions seek to extend the market monopoly of patented medicines and delay, if not totally eliminate, the entry of generic medicines in the market. This is sought to be achieved through provisions on patents, data exclusivity, trademarks, border measures for enforcement of IPRs, standards, investment and transparency. Although some of these provisions go beyond the IPR chapter, it is relevant to discuss them here, as the impact of the provisions would be to raise the price of medicines:

   i. Provisions under the TPP lower the bar on patentability by mandating that any new use of a known substance or a new process or a new method of using a known substance would become eligible for a patent. By mandating the grant of patents for even insignificant improvements or for new uses of a known product, evergreening of existing patents is likely to become more widespread, especially for blockbuster medicines. Through this process of evergreening of patents, competition from generic pharmaceutical products would be either delayed or even blocked. Further, by adhering to the TPP template, India would be abandoning its sound policy that has helped curtail evergreening of patents.
   ii. It mandates countries to extend the patent term beyond 20 years to supposedly compensate for delays in patent offices.
   iii. It requires the signatory countries to adjust the patent term for compensating the patent owner for any unreasonable curtailment of the effective patent term that might arise as a result of delays in marketing approval. One of the ways envisaged for the adjustment to the patent term is by providing a period of additional sui generis protection.
   iv. The TPP prohibits regulatory authorities from relying on the data concerning safety and efficacy of the product/s submitted by the patent applicant while granting marketing approval to the second applicant (normally a generic medicine). The

TPP provides an initial period of data exclusivity for five years, which can be enhanced by another three years for a new indication or a new dosage form of an existing medicine. Data exclusivity protection can exist even in the absence of patent protection. During the period of data exclusivity, generic medicines would not be able to secure marketing authorization, as the regulator would be unable to rely on the data, concerning safety and efficacy of the product, submitted by the originator. As medicines cannot be sold without marketing approval, generic versions of the originator drug cannot be approved by the regulator and cannot be sold for five years. This would provide a fresh lease of monopoly market protection to old molecules, some of which may no longer enjoy patent protection.

v. Data exclusivity protection will also apply to sustained release or fixed dose combinations of molecule, paediatric dose or for developments that improve the administration of the same medicine. As small improvements in existing formulations is a continuous process, even marginal changes which satisfy the conditions for the application of data exclusivity will get protected. This will delay the entry of generics in the market.

vi. Through the provision on patent linkage, the TPP requires concerned authorities to inform patent holders before granting marketing approval to the second applicant (usually a generic medicine). This is likely to result in protracted judicial proceedings.

vii. The TPP requires countries to make best efforts to register scent marks. In order to create familiarity between a patented pharmaceutical product and the corresponding generic medicine, these are likely to have similar smell. It is apprehended that by registering scent marks, generic medicines with smell similar to the patented medicine could become liable for trademark infringement.

viii. Legitimate international trade of generic medicines could be significantly curtailed as the TPP mandates the signatory countries to suspend the release of goods with confusingly similar trademarks—a requirement that goes beyond the obligations in TRIPS.

ix. Annex 8 C to the TPP chapter on Technical Barriers to Trade (TBT) mandates the signatory countries to consider applications for marketing authorization of pharmaceutical products made in a format that is consistent with the principles of International Conference on Harmonisation of Technical Requirements for Registration of Pharmaceuticals for Human Use. World Health Organisation has commented that the technical complexities of ICH guidelines could be cumbersome for industry in developing countries to comply with. This would disadvantage the producers of generic medicines, if the format for seeking marketing authorization is based exclusively on ICH principles and applications in other formats are rejected.

x. This annex also mandates that the applicant is responsible for providing sufficient information to a signatory country for regulatory determination on a pharmaceutical product. This obligation could be used to deny marketing authorization to the producers of generic medicines by preventing them from relying on clinical trials data submitted for the originator drug even after the period of data exclusivity.

xi. The investment chapter includes IPRs in the scope of investment covered by the disciplines of that chapter. Thus, governments may be hesitant to provide marketing authorization for generic medicines, as they would be under a constant threat of being sued under investor–state dispute settlement (ISDS) for any perceived violation of obligations contained in the investment chapter of the TPP.

xii. The annex on transparency and procedural fairness for pharmaceutical products and medical devices in the TPP prescribes a cumbersome administrative mechanism that has opened a window for preventing new generic drugs from being listed as a pharmaceutical eligible for reimbursement under national health care programmes operated by different countries. Given the dozen grounds for reducing, or even eliminating, competition from generic pharmaceutical products, Joseph Stiglitz (2015) has correctly warned, 'The efforts to raise drug prices in the TPP take us in the wrong direction. The whole world may come to pay a price in the form of worse health and unnecessary deaths.'

27. The provision on patentable subject matter is an antithesis of Section 3(d) of the Indian Patents Act. If India joins an agreement adhering to the TPP template, it would have to substantially amend this provision, in order to grant patents to new forms of a known substance even if it does not result in any enhanced efficacy. This provision has proved to be effective against evergreening of patents. Amendments to bring this provision in line with the obligations under the TPP would completely erode the safeguards in Indian law against evergreening of patents.
28. The TPP mandates an increase in the term of copyright protection from existing 50–70 years beyond the life of the person concerned.
29. TPP requires that the member states implement a regime that would protect against copyright infringement in the Internet environment. This is sought to be carried out by not only making the act of accessing copyrighted material without authorization as an offense but also makes development of such technologies, their manufacture and sale to be illegal. This provision is in direct conflict with the recently amended Indian law on copyright, which provides for technology protection measures, but restricts the offense of circumvention to the final act. It clearly makes an exception for manufacture, distribution and sale of technologies that could be used for circumventing copyrighted material. These exceptions are not contained in the TPP provisions.
30. The TPP provisions on enforcement are more expansive and onerous as compared to the TRIPS provisions and remove many safeguards that are available in the TRIPS Agreement. These provisions seek to shift the onus of enforcement of private rights to the government.
31. If India becomes a party to an agreement based on the TPP template, it would be required to make extensive changes in the laws and regulations underlying its domestic IPR regime. To illustrate, the Acts that would need to be amended are Section 3(d) of the Patents Act, Section 53 of Patents Act, Section 122B of the Drugs and Cosmetics Act, 1940, and the Drugs and Cosmetics Rules, 1945, Section 11(2n) of the Customs Act, 1962, Notifications Number 51/2010, Customs (N.T., dated 30 June 2010) issued by the Department of Revenue, PPVFR Act, 2001 and Trademarks Act, 1999.

Investment

32. Although there is little empirical evidence that international investment agreements (IIAs) are significant determinants of investment flows, by adhering to rules based on the TPP, investment provisions of the agreement would impose severe restrictions on India.
33. India has signed several IIAs, some not very different from the TPP. Therefore, it can be argued that the TPP provisions will not pose a major hurdle, should India decide to join an agreement based on the TPP template in the future. Such an argument ignores the fact that the problems with the international investment regime have become more evident and understood only in the last few years. This has prompted India to review its IIAs and come out with the Indian Model BIT (BIT stands for bilateral investment treaty), which has incorporated significant improvements in the treaty text.

The provisions of India's model BIT differs significantly in several areas from the TPP text. If India becomes a part of an agreement based on the TPP template, it would result in a huge setback to its IIA reform agenda.

Standards

34. There have been many speculations and conjectures about the impact that the TPP will have on standards. Some experts have lamented that by being outside the TPP, India would miss out on the developments relating to standards. Based on a plain reading of the TPP text, much of the speculation and conjecture does not appear to have a firm basis. Further, some of the supposed impacts on standards are likely to happen autonomously and cannot be attributed to the TPP. In addition, by joining any agreement following the TPP template, it cannot be assumed that India's regulatory regime in the area of standards will automatically improve.
35. Some experts are of the view that the TPP template will result in the alignment of standards amongst signatory countries, resulting in upward harmonization of product standards. However, there does not appear to be any provision in the TPP that mandates the signatory countries to align or harmonize their standards. Hence, the question of the TPP template resulting in 'upward'

Conclusions and Way Forward 319

harmonization of standards does not arise. It is, of course, possible that developments outside the TPP could encourage countries to align their standards with each other. But such a development cannot be attributed to the TPP provisions.

36. It has been suggested that the TPP template will encompass higher-than-present standards, mainly by validating certain private standards by making reference to them or to the criteria, such as labour standards. While the TPP does make reference to certain private standards or their criteria, there is no mandatory requirement for the signatory countries to align their standards with these private standards. Further, the reference to private standards is confined to a few sectors and, in most cases, is on a non-mandatory basis.

37. It has further been speculated that the TPP template could affect the development and use of private standards, resulting in the proliferation of private standards. No doubt private standards have proliferated over time. However, even if this trend continues in future, it cannot be directly attributed to any specific mandatory provision in the TPP template.

38. It has been conjectured that the significance of private standards in commercial transactions can increase due to the TPP template. While private standards have become an important determinant of trade flows, attributing this to the TPP template appears to be without any basis in the Agreement.

39. It has been postulated that within private standards, the criteria for sustainable development and social standards will become more widespread. Of course, even without the TPP, increasingly more private standards do include criteria for sustainable development and social standards. However, it is not clear which specific provision in the TPP will make this trend more widespread.

Labour Standards: Eroding Competitiveness

40. TPP has provisions which mandate the signatory countries to effectively enforce their own labour laws. While this may appear innocuous and supposedly be for enhancing welfare of labour, the reality may be entirely different. It should be recognized that the labour provisions in the TPP are less about labour welfare and more about trade. Trade focus of these provisions is obvious from the requirement that in order to establish the violation of an

obligation, the complaining party needs to demonstrate that the other party has 'failed to adopt or maintain a statute, regulation or practice in a manner *affecting trade or investment between the Parties*' (Note 4 of Chapter 19 of the TPP Agreement). It should also be noted that as mandatory compliance with a template of rules based on TPP's provisions on labour is likely to raise the production costs in India relative to the developed countries, this would erode the price competitiveness of the manufacturing sector. As a result, not only would India's exports take a hit in the international market, even in the domestic market the local producers may be unable to face import competition in some sectors. Such an outcome would not enhance labour welfare. Further, an important study discussed in this book suggests that even if countries like China, India, Indonesia and Thailand are excluded from mega-FTAs such as the TPP, they would face severe adverse impact of the provisions on labour standards contained in mega-FTAs. Overall, there may be little gain for India if it were to comply with TPP-type rules on labour standards.

Government Procurement: Limited Gain, Considerable Pain

41. The TPP contains strong provisions aimed at providing market access to member countries in each other's government contracts. While certain time-limited flexibilities are contained in the agreement, overall, these provisions are likely to result in a significant erosion of the policy space for using government procurement to bolster domestic industrialization. On the other hand, given the extremely low import penetration in government procurement markets, it is unlikely that the TPP signatories will see any significant increase in their exports to other countries' government procurement markets.
42. By joining an agreement based on the TPP template, India will be required to discontinue some of the schemes that mandate the government to procure from domestic suppliers. This could have a significant adverse impact on the domestic manufacturing sector.

State-owned Enterprises

43. Using certain concepts contained in provisions related to state trading enterprises under GATT, 1994, and concepts contained

in the Agreement on Subsidies and Countervailing Measures (ASCM), the TPP seeks to significantly curtail the ability of governments to provide financial support to state-owned enterprises.
44. If India were to adhere to the template of the TPP rules, the government may not be able to provide financial support to some of the public sector undertakings, particularly when these enterprises may be in financial stress.

Regulatory Coherence

45. If India were to comply with the obligations on regulatory coherence as contained in the TPP, it would be required to create a new institutional mechanism for designing and implementing regulatory measures and undertake a regulatory impact assessment analysis. In addition, the requirement to provide 'opportunities for interested persons' to provide inputs for regulatory coherence may be extremely onerous.

13.3 Recommendations for India's Trade Policy and Way Forward

Having examined the trend in India's exports, its price competitiveness and inadequate trade-related physical infrastructure, compared to its main competitors, this section makes some recommendations for India's trade policy. The movement of global trade rules towards a TPP-like template provides an opportunity to reflect on the institutional changes and other domestic reforms that India needs to introduce for addressing the challenges arising from the changing global realities in the arena of international trade, including the TPP and similar other mega-trade agreements. The following suggestions are made for India's trade policy:

1. Although the share of total trade of goods and services in India's GDP has more than doubled over the past two decades, institutional mechanisms within the Department of Commerce, Government of India, for addressing challenges emerging from international trade have hardly changed. As a result, the ability of the government to anticipate changes in the external environment and assess their implications for India's trade policy has been rather limited.

Consequently, a proactive trade policy that looks forward to the future, instead of merely reacting to immediate issues on hand, appears to be missing. A successful trade policy needs to be underpinned with a strategic vision on the role of international trade in India's overall economic and strategic objectives. Such a strategic trade policy would also ensure coherence and continuity in the functioning of the Department of Commerce towards clearly defined long-term objectives. In respect of trade negotiations and trade policy, the strategic vision document could address the issues such as market access for India's exports, India's quest for natural resources, demographic changes in the developed world and their implications for India's trade policy in services, role of trade policy in India's security concerns, anticipating technology developments and assessing how India's trade policy should respond, choices in mode of international engagement—multilateralism, unilateralism or regionalism and between the various instruments of foreign policy—international cooperation, negotiation, etc. At this juncture, there is no such strategic vision document.

It is recommended that the Department of Commerce creates an inter-ministerial group supported by domain experts for preparing a strategic trade policy document that would provide broad guidance, and remain relevant, for the formulation and implementation of trade policy for the next 15–20 years. This document should be annually reviewed for making appropriate changes in the light of crucial developments that might take place at both national and international level.

2. Success in trade negotiations depends on many factors, including the adequate number of negotiators with appropriate skill sets, clarity in negotiating objectives, structured mechanism for identifying negotiating objectives, stakeholder consultations, inputs from diverse sources, support on legal and economic aspects related to negotiating issues, understanding the behavioural aspects of negotiations, institutional mechanisms for ensuring continuity despite staff turnover, appropriate communication strategy, etc. However, in respect of each of these elements, significant gaps exist, which undermine the ability of the Department of Commerce to negotiate effectively. Corrective action is required in respect of each of these elements.

3. India's success in trade negotiations depends crucially on how it is able to influence the global terms of debate on the key issues of its interest and the support India is able to garner from other countries for its negotiating position. Generally, India is

constrained on both aspects. By the time developed countries are ready to place a subject on the negotiating table, they have already conducted numerous studies on it. It is no secret that often the research undertaken by multilateral organizations strongly advocate the positive impact that negotiations on the issues of interest to the developed countries would have on developing countries. It is not a mere coincidence that most of the research emanating from these organizations supports the negotiating positions of the developed countries. Overall, through multiple channels, the developed countries are able to significantly influence the global discourse on the key issues in their favour. Barring a few exceptions, India has neither been able to effectively counter the developed countries from pursuing their trade agenda through these intergovernmental institutions nor has it been able to promote its own negotiating interests through the deliberations in some of the relevant intergovernmental organizations. This has clearly disadvantaged India in international trade negotiations. The Department of Commerce needs to create an institutional mechanism with the nodal ministries with functional responsibility for some of the key intergovernmental organizations, so that the deliberations in these organizations and their research do not prejudice India's position in international trade negotiations.

4. Policy flexibility in international trade negotiations can arise from various sources, including through a country undertaking autonomous liberalization beyond the regime mandated by the WTO and other international trade agreements. However, in order to take advantage of the autonomous liberalization, it is important that domestic reforms are undertaken in a manner that space for trade negotiations is also created. So far, the Department of Commerce has not assumed this role. To illustrate, the government is attempting direct bank transfer (DBT) for fertilizer subsidies. However, this is being undertaken without taking WTO obligations into consideration. The present approach to the DBT for fertilizer subsidies will not create any negotiating space for the government. If the DBT is undertaken in a manner that the subsidy is granted in accordance with requirement of the Green Box under the Agreement on Agriculture, then this would create a significant negotiating space for India to adopt a more aggressive position in WTO agriculture negotiations. Department of Commerce needs to closely monitor and examine initiatives being contemplated for

domestic reforms and provide detailed inputs to the concerned ministries for ensuring that the reforms create negotiating space for India at the WTO.
5. Compliance with standards and technical regulations is one of the emerging challenges confronting India's trade. Complying with varying standards in different geographical markets raises the export costs. This problem is further accentuated by the fact that the number of domestically applicable technical regulations in India is significantly lower than that prevailing in developed countries. This has two important consequences. First, in the absence of domestic standards and technical regulations, India is unable to regulate imports for protecting consumers' interests. Second, in the absence of domestic technical regulations, the additional cost incurred by Indian producers for meeting the requirements in the key foreign markets is likely to be higher.

It is a reality that the standards regime in India needs significant strengthening and upgradation from many perspectives. First, the domestic legal regime for introducing a new technical regulation is extremely time-consuming. A new regime is necessary, whereby the power to formulate new technical regulations is not confined to the Bureau of Indian Standards, but line ministries such as the Department of Telecommunications are able to formulate their own technical regulations. Second, there is a need to undertake sector-specific analysis of the gaps between applicable Indian standards/technical regulations and those prevailing in key markets, and implementing a structured programme for strengthening the capacity of domestic producers to progressively comply with higher levels of domestic standards. A blueprint for sector-specific initiatives followed by time-bound action is absolutely necessary for improving the standard compliance capacity in the country. Third, the infrastructure for standards is rather inadequate. These include the voluntary standards setting, nodal points for participation in international standard setting bodies, such as, International Organization for Standardization (ISO), International Electrotechnical Commission (IEC), Codex, WHO, etc., and private standards, accreditation of labs and inspection/certification bodies, conformity assessment inspection/certification bodies and laboratories, metrology for accuracy and reliability of measurements, counselling/training bodies. There is a need to significantly enhance the technical capacity on standards and increase the number of laboratories for testing and undertaking other compliances measures. Fourth, the Department of Commerce needs to establish a nodal institution for responding to the problems faced by Indian exports on account of standards in the key markets. Fifth, the proliferation of private labels and standards are increasingly becoming important determinants of market access. However, an overarching global mechanism needs to be agreed at an intergovernmental level in order to ensure that the private standards are not discriminatory to exports from some developing countries. Sixth, India needs to have a clear roadmap whereby the test results of its laboratories and the conformity assessment procedures get recognition from other countries. While a start has already been made on some of these issues through the various initiatives of the Department of Commerce, a comprehensive strategy for addressing challenges arising from standards needs to be formulated and implemented.

6. Turning specifically to the TPP at this juncture, the government appears to be following a cautious approach. Given the uncertain gains and that too at low levels and significantly high costs, there does not appear to be any compelling reason for India to make efforts at joining the TPP, if it is implemented even if in a modified form or agreeing to TPP type rules at the WTO.

7. If however, at some stage, the government contemplates making efforts to adhere to TPP-type rules multilaterally or bilaterally, this should be done exclusively on the basis of trade and investment concerns. If any other concern influences this decision, then it would potentially have severe adverse consequences for the Indian economy.

8. If India initiates the process to join the TPP or any agreement based on its template, this must be done only after a comprehensive, transparent and inclusive discussion between different stakeholders, including different ministries, state governments, industry associations and farmers' groups. The government must come out with a detailed document, analysing the benefits and costs of and specifying the reasons for joining such an agreement. In 2001, the Department of Commerce had started the process for extensive consultations with industry associations, farmers' groups, trade unions, political parties and research organizations before each important meeting at the WTO. This process continued till about 2007–2008, but appears to have become dormant thereafter. This needs to be revived so that the government gets inputs on trade issues from stakeholders from diverse backgrounds.

9. If India chooses not to make any effort at joining the TPP, it cannot remain complacent about trade and investment diversion. An early conclusion of the Regional Comprehensive Economic Partnership (RCEP) and Bilateral Trade and Investment Agreement with EU would go some way in mitigation the trade diversion that might arise on the account of the TPP. Of course, India's core interest in the areas of agriculture, manufacturing, IPR, etc., must not be compromised while concluding these FTA negotiations.
10. India should make a planned and structured attempt at increasing trade with other developing countries, particularly in South America and Africa. In addition, India should consider taking the leadership role in reenergising the Global System of Trade Preferences (GSTP) at the UNCTAD forum.
11. India must evolve its own standard template for FTA negotiations. This should include issues on which it has an offensive interest. These issues could include the mandatory exchange of customs information in cases of doubt about the value of the traded product, TRIPS–CBD linkage to contain biopiracy, specific obligations on its trading partners for facilitating services trade through mode 4, recognition of Ayurvedic products as medicines and not merely food supplements, market access for some geographical indication (GI) products, fast track acceptance of some Indian products as GIs in foreign markets, home country obligations in respect of investment, disciplines on export cartels, facilitating technology transfer, etc.
12. In order to mitigate the adverse impact, although limited, of remaining outside the TPP, if it is implemented, India needs to act domestically and at the international level. Within the country, efforts must be made to enhance the competitiveness of India's exports. This would require the government to make concerted efforts at addressing some of the well-known constraints relating to infrastructure that hobble manufacturing in the country.
13. If social issues, including labour standards, are included in government-mandated standards in the TPP countries, then India must not hesitate to legally challenge these measures under the WTO's dispute settlement mechanism.
14. In the area of services, India must autonomously initiate regulatory reforms for ensuring fair competition and protecting the consumer.
15. It is also important to discuss India's approach to the possible use of rules under the TPP as a template for negotiations at the

WTO. As discussed in the different chapters of this book, on most of the issues such as services, IPRs, investments, state-owned enterprises, government procurement, environment, labour, etc., adhering to the TPP template of rules would have severe adverse consequences for India. There could be an attempt by some analysts to selectively project gains for India from some of the rules contained in the TPP. To illustrate, if the requirement under the TPP that prevents countries from imposing restrictions on data flows is adhered to by India and other WTO members, then this would facilitate India's exports of IT and ITES. However, complying with other provisions on electronic commerce would severely restrict India's policy flexibilities. The point is clear: on each of the issues, India must not focus exclusively on gains from some elements contained in the TPP. Instead, the government should undertake a comprehensive assessment of the likely impact of adhering to all the elements of the TPP template of rules, before agreeing to comply with rules based on the TPP template, or even using this template as a basis for future negotiations at the WTO. It would also be in India's interest to build a coalition of developing countries that share its concerns on the new issue and firmly resist the TPP template from becoming the basis for negotiations at the WTO. This would require considerable diplomatic effort in Geneva and also in the capitals of various developing countries.

16. India joining the Asia-Pacific Economic Cooperation (APEC) has been suggested as a useful step towards India being integrated into regional trade in Southeast Asia in a better way and perhaps even joining the TPP subsequently. APEC member economies set their own timelines and goals, and undertake actions on a voluntary and non-binding basis. This should provide considerable flexibility to India in adopting and implementing the non-binding principles and guidelines in different areas of work of APEC. India could stand to benefit from access to information and institutional and human resource capacity building from various APEC initiatives. But, it should consider joining APEC only if it is confident of making progressive reforms, on a voluntary basis, in different areas of APEC initiatives.

An argument that is increasingly being articulated by a few experts is that India's membership to the APEC would be opposed by some countries who perceive India to be a reluctant liberalizer and a country that blocks consensus in trade negotiations.

According to this narrative, India must take certain initiatives to reaffirm its credentials as a trade liberalizer. This would facilitate the process of India's accession to the APEC. Initiatives suggested in this context include joining Information Technology Agreement (ITA) 2, eliminating tariffs on environmental goods, binding tariffs on all industrial products, lowering its most favoured nation (MFN) tariffs, signing the bilateral investment treaty with the USA, agreeing to negotiations on new issues at the WTO, etc. The narrative about India blocking consensus in trade negotiations is an unfair and incorrect characterization. The suggestions that India should make autonomous concessions in order to get entry into APEC does not appear to be well thought out.

On the issue of India making unilateral concessions to establish its credentials for getting APEC membership, such a move would be totally imbalanced and not advisable. As mentioned earlier, APEC is about voluntary and non-binding rules and guidelines. No doubt, membership of the APEC would be beneficial for India, but to pay an entry fee that would be legally binding appears yet another attempt at squeezing concessions from India. India must not get lured into this trap. It must make its position clear: it would be interested in APEC membership, but if the membership is contingent on it taking prior binding commitments then it may not have much interest in joining APEC.

17. Another area in which India needs to tread with considerable caution is making changes in its trade policy and investment rules with the objective of facilitating integration of Indian firms in global value chains (GVCs). A few countries have articulated the need for making suitable changes in WTO agreements for addressing the realities of GVCs. Some intergovernmental organizations, particularly the OECD, have been at the forefront of urging international cooperation to reap the full benefits of GVCs and to ensure that new strategies of firms benefit all. According to OECD et al. (2003), 'ambitious economic integration agreements that more coherently cover all dimension of market access can help countries to maximize the gains from production sharing'. In a similar vein, some analysts are of the opinion that if India does not join the TPP, it would be excluded from GVCs. Overall, the approach of some countries, intergovernmental organizsations and a few experts is that India must make changes in its trade and investment regime for making its firms attractive partners for

lead firms of GVCs. Some of the changes in the policy regime that have been suggested include reducing/eliminating tariffs, liberalising business service sectors in the key network industries such as logistics, supply chain management, ICT-related services, e-commerce, professional services, etc. and more stringent protection of IPRs.

While trade policies have an important role to play in facilitating the integration of domestic firms in GVCs, there are other equally significant determinants of GVC integration. Even if trade policy-related issues are addressed, in the absence of adequate attention to non-trade policy-related factors, it is unlikely that GVC integration will be enhanced. Efficiencies and capacities of trade-related infrastructure become extremely crucial in the GVC context. Poor trade-related infrastructure adds to the cost of GVC trade and becomes a barrier for meeting tight delivery schedules. Given the extremely thin margins for producers and suppliers in developing countries in the context of GVC trade, they may not be in a position to bear the incremental costs on account of infrastructure deficiencies. In the intense race to attract lead firms in GVCs, firms in the countries that are severely constrained by inadequate trade-related physical infrastructure and deficient trade logistics are not likely to compete successfully with firms from countries with efficient port facilities, port to hinterland connectivity and trade logistics. If the infrastructural deficiencies that afflict the manufacturing sector in India are not addressed, it is unlikely that changes in trade and investment policy regimes alone would be adequate to facilitate integration of Indian firms in GVCs.

Even if negotiations on GVC are initiated and concluded at the WTO, the outcome in itself may not be sufficient to facilitate the integration of developing countries' firms in GVCs. Trade and investment liberalization are not sufficient conditions for GVC integration. Countries, including India, need to address other relevant determinants of GVC integration, including infrastructure at ports, domestic connectivity, skill development, access to credit, etc. Trade and investment reforms, without being preceded by other domestic reforms, could have severe adverse impact on overall economic prospects of India.

18. In view of the negative consequences for India, if it adheres to an agreement based on the TPP template and the likelihood of such a template being used in future trade agreements, it is

imperative for the Indian government to develop a strategy, including developing a coalition of like-minded countries to build an effective counter to it.

This book has elaborated the challenges that countries, especially in the developing world, will face if the TPP rules become the basis for future trade regimes. Addressing and overcoming these challenges will require a higher level of preparedness and cooperation on part of developing countries, including India. The onus is on India to offer a more development oriented trade and investment integration template to the world, as an alternative to the TPP set of rules.

References

OECD, WTO and UNCTAD in September 2013 for the G-20 Leaders Summit held in Saint Petersburg (Russian Federation), September 2013. Retrieved 9 August 2017, from http://www.oecd.org/trade/G20-Global-Value-Chains-2013.pdf

Stiglitz, Joseph. 2015. 'Don't Trade Away Our Health', *New York Times*, 30 January.

About the Editors and Contributors

Editors

Abhijit Das is the Head of the Centre for WTO Studies, Indian Institute of Foreign Trade, New Delhi. He is one of the leading policy analysts in the field of international trade in India. He has been the director of the United Nations Conference on Trade and Development (UNCTAD) India Programme, a joint initiative of the Department of Commerce (Government of India) and the United Nations Conference on Trade and Development. He has participated in many multilateral and bilateral trade negotiations, including the Doha Round of trade negotiations at the WTO. He frequently comments on trade issues in the media and has jointly edited two books on the economic and legal aspects of the international trade regime.

Shailja Singh is a Legal Consultant (Assistant Professor) at the Centre for WTO Studies. She is legal advisor to the Government of India for WTO disputes and is part of India's negotiating team for the Regional Comprehensive Economic Partnership Agreement. She worked in the Advisory Centre on WTO Law, Geneva, for its Secondment Programme for Trade Lawyers in 2014. Ms Singh completed her LLB from the West Bengal National University of Juridical Sciences, India, and went on to receive an LLM from the University of Cambridge, UK.

Contributors

R.V. Anuradha is a Partner at Clarus Law Associates, which she co-founded in 2007. Her focus areas include trade law and policy, environmental law, carbon financing and climate change. She has represented India in two trade disputes at the WTO. She has been consistently recognized by the International Who's Who of Trade and Customs Lawyers and Chambers and Partners as a leading practitioner in her field.

Ms. Anuradha graduated from the National Law School of India, Bangalore University in 1995. She has Masters Degrees from the University of London and from the New York University School of Law.

Prajyna Paramita Barua is an independent consultant. She has previously worked as Research Fellow (Economics) at the Centre for WTO Studies.

Mukesh Bhatnagar is a Professor at the Centre for WTO Studies. He has 30 years of experience in international trade issues, including trade remedies and WTO dispute settlement. He has previously worked in the capacity of director, directorate general of Anti-dumping and Allied Duties, and additional director general of foreign trade, Trade Policy Division of the Department of Commerce (Government of India). He has participated in many multilateral and bilateral trade negotiations, including the Doha Round of trade negotiations at the WTO.

Pralok Gupta is an Assistant Professor (Services and Investment) at the Centre for WTO Studies. He has co-authored two books on different aspects of trade in services. He has served in the Uttar Pradesh State Civil Services and Industrial Finance Corporation of India. Dr Gupta has a PhD in economics and social sciences from Indian Institute of Management, Bangalore. He has been a faculty member in various institutions, including the Indo-German Chamber of Commerce.

Harimaya Gurung is a Research Fellow (Economics) at the Centre for WTO Studies. She received her bachelor's degree from the University of Delhi (College of Vocational Studies). She completed her postgraduation in economics from Annamalai University, Tamil Nadu.

Monika is a Research Fellow (Legal) at the Centre for WTO Studies. She completed her bachelor's degree in law from National Law University, Jodhpur.

Dilfy Ann Philip was a Research Associate (Economics) at the Centre for WTO Studies. She received her bachelor's degree in economics from the University of Delhi and her master's degree from Madras Christian College, Chennai.

Jayant Raghu Ram is a Research Fellow (Legal) at the Centre for WTO Studies. He is a 2012 law graduate from the National Law University, Jodhpur. Prior to joining the CWS, he was a Legal Consultant with the Mumbai-based Lodha Group. His areas of interests include WTO dispute settlement: trade and IPR.

Chandni Raina is a Professor at the Centre for WTO Studies. She belongs to the Indian Economic Service. She has worked in intellectual property rights during her tenure as the director of the Department of Industrial Policy and Promotion, Government of India, and is one of India's leading authorities on policy issues related to intellectual property rights. She has participated in many bilateral trade negotiations, including the Regional Comprehensive Economic Partnership Agreement negotiations.

Neeraj R.S. is a former Research Fellow (Legal) at the Centre for WTO Studies. He has a bachelor's degree in law from Gujarat National Law University. He has previously worked as a Research Assistant at the Consumer Unity and Trust Society International, Jaipur.

Index

acceptable conditions of work, 239, 240, 244
access to medicines, 156, 158, 159, 163, 168, 169, 179
aircraft repair and maintenance services, 82
airport operation services, 82
Annex-I NCMs, 78
Annex-II NCMs, 79

Bayer Corporation v. Cipla, 165
border measures, 150–51, 166, 167, 178
breeders' rights, 170, 172, 176, 177, 179

Codex Alimentarius, 221
clinical trial data, 157, 161–63
computer reservation system services, 82
conformity assessment, 217
    bodies, 218
Convention on Biological Diversity, 172
corporate social responsibility
    labour, 242
    environment, 253
cross-border trade in services, 82

data exclusivity, 156, 162–64, 178
dispute settlement
    labour, 241, 242, 244
    standards, 228
Doha Declaration on Public Health, 162, 168
domestic regulation (Article 10.8), 85
Drugs and Cosmetics Act, 1940, 160, 163, 165

emergency action on textile and clothing products, 292–93
    duration, 293
    implications, for India, 297
    standard of injury, 292–93
    transition period, 293
    verification, 293

enforcement
    labour, 239, 243
    Patent, 141–47
    SOEs, 288
    special requirement related to border measures, 144–46
    trademarks, 141–42, 144–45
environment committee, 252–56
environmental goods and services, 252
environmental laws, 251, 253, 255, 257
equivalence, 222, 230, 231
evergreening of patents
    Indonesia & Philippines: Impact of acceding to the TPP, 148, 149
    patents and undisclosed test or other data, 126–33
expropriation and compensation
    provision, analysis, 197–99
    provision *vis-à-vis* Indian IIAs, 199

farmers' rights, 307
financial services, 87
fisheries subsidies, 252
Food and Drug Authority, 160
Free Trade Agreements (FTAs)
    Central American Free Trade Agreement, 156
    Jordan–US FTA, 156
    NAFTA, 248, 250
    TRIPS-plus, 156, 167, 177

GATS, 77, 249
    annex on telecommunications, 94
GATT
    Article XX, 249
    Article XVII, 278–79, 280
    STEs, 278–79
geographical indications
    GIs—arresting the EU onslaught, 123–25

General Agreement on Trade in Services
(GATSs), 77
Genetic Use Restriction Technology
(GURT), 173
government procurement
countries, markets in, 261–66
coverage, 267
covered market as a share of GDP, 262
exceptions, 270–71
implications on international procurement regime, 272–73
offsets, 270
special and differential treatment, 268–70
threshold levels, 267–68, 274–75
government procurement of services, 83
government use of software, 147
ground handling services, 82

harmonization, 218, 221, 222
Hong Kong Ministerial, USA unable to implement decision taken at, 13

ILO Convention, 236, 237
ILO Declaration on Fundamental Principles and Rights at Work, 236, 237, 239
international investment agreements (IIAs), 184–85
IIAs and foreign investment, 185–87
Internet Service Provider, 140–41
investment
definition
provision, analysis, 187–88
provision vis-à-vis Indian IIAs, 188–89
transfers
provision, analysis, 204–5
provision vis-à-vis Indian IIAs, 205–206
public policy exceptions, 206–210
Investor–State dispute settlement (ISDS), 81, 210–13

living modified organisms, 170
local presence, 78

market access
services, 78
Marrakesh Agreement, 248
minimum standard of treatment
provision, analysis, 193–96
provision vis-à-vis Indian IIAs, 196–97
Ministerial Declaration on Trade in Information Technology Products, 20
Montreal Protocol, 247, 251
most-favoured nation treatment
investment
provision, analysis, 191–92
provision vis-à-vis Indian IIAs, 192–93
services, 78
multilateral environmental agreements, 247, 251
mutual recognition, 219, 220, 222

NAFTA, 248, 250
Nairobi Ministerial Conference, role of USA, 13
Nairobi Ministerial Declaration, 13–14
USA hostile to reaffirming the Doha mandate, 13
window for new issues, 23
national treatment
investment
provision, analysis, 189–90
provision vis-à-vis Indian IIAs, 190–191
services, 78
negative list approach, 78
new financial services, 88
Non-Conforming Measures (NCMs), 78
Non-product related PPM, 257
Novartis, 158

patents
cooperation, 119–20
general provisions
a general enhancement in norms, 116
linkage, 164, 165, 178
patents and undisclosed test or other data, 126–137

Indonesia and Philippines: Impact of Acceding to the TPP, 147
term extension, 160, 161
Patents Act, 160, 165
    Section 3(d), 159, 178
pharmaceuticals
    general provisions
        a general enhancement in norms, 116
        implications for India, 149–53
    patents and undisclosed test or other data
        substantive rule making for curtailing trips flexibilities, 126–37
positive list approach, 78
private standards, 243, 254, 256–58
    provision, analysis, 189–90
    provision *vis-à-vis* Indian IIAs, 190–91
    services, 78
performance requirements
    provision, analysis, 199–203
    provision *vis-à-vis* Indian IIAs, 203–4
Protection of Plant Varieties and Farmers' Rights Act, 2001, 169, 170, 171
    Section 1, 171
    Section 14, 170
    Section 15, 171
    Section 24, 176
    Section 29, 170
    Section 47, 176
    Section 51(1), 176

ratifications, 237
regulatory coherence, 300–302
    consultation and coordination, 300
    definition, 300
    impact assessment, regulatory, 301
    implications for India, 301–2
    threshold of economic impact, 301
rights managements information
    copyright and related rights, 138–40

sanitary and phytosanitary measures, 217, 218, 223
seed saving, 174
selling and marketing of air transport services, 82

specialty air services, 82
state-owned enterprises (SOEs)
    adverse effects caused, 283–84
        exception, 284
    adverse effects constitute, 284–86
    commercial considerations, 280–81
    definition of, 279–80
    exceptions, SOE definition, 280
    exemptions, 289
    injury, 286–87
    non-commercial assistance, 281–83
        indirectly, 283
    non-discriminatory treatment, 280–81
    notification obligation, 288
    public body, interpretation of, 279–80
    remedies, 287–88
    threshold, application of SOE provisions, 288
subsidies to services, 83

TBT Committee Decision, 218
technical regulations, 217, 219, 223, 229
technology protection measures
    copyright and related rights, 138–39, 230
TiSA and GATS annexes, 104
    new annexes in TiSA, 106
    accession of new parties to TPP, 7
    Argentina, India, Indonesia and South Africa not to renew existing BITs, 18
    Asia-Pacific Economic Cooperation, accession to TPP open to members of, 7
    accession process for non-APEC States, 8
    BATNA for the USA in Doha Round, TPP, 13
    best alternative to a negotiated agreement (BATNA), 11
    bilateral investment treaties
    implementation of TPP, quantifying impact of
        adverse impact on nonmembers, segregating sources of, 52–56
        complexities involved in modelling, 46

Index **337**

increase in costs, impact of, 54
India on, 56–57
optimistic claims based on shaky foundation, 47, 49, 51–52
Petri, Plummer and Zhai, results of, 47–51
Petri et al. model assumptions, criticism by Bertram and Terry, 51–52
Indian economy
features, 38
flexibilities contained in the TRIPS Agreement, preventing countries from making rightful use of, 15
foreign content of India's exports, 39, 41
implementation of TPP, quantifying impact of, 41
adverse impact on non-members, segregating sources of, 52–56
complexities involved in modelling, 46
declining significance of, 47
increase in costs, impact of, 54
India on, 56–57
India's exports to TPP countries, 48
Petri, Plummer and Zhai, comparing results of, 50
shaky foundations, optimistic claims based on, 47, 49, 51–52
India's exports of goods, 42–44
India's imports of services, 45
integration of India into global economy, increasing, 39, 41
significance of TPP countries in India's exports, declining, 47
India's trade policy and way forward
recommendations and suggestions made, 321–30
TPP, 321
norm entrepreneur in TPP, USA as, 21
norm life cycle, 19
Organisation for Economic Co-operation and Development, 18

pharmaceutical industry in USA, 2, 15–17
Pharmaceutical Research and Manufacturers of America
fifth among the top lobbying spenders in USA, 15
efforts for lobbying on TPP, 17
TPP and market access for goods
agricultural safeguard measures available to the USA, 61
context of food security, export restrictions in, 63–64
export duties and taxes, 62–63
IT products, trade in, 63
manufacturing and agriculture, impact on, 65–74
products of modern biotechnology, trade of, 64–65
remanufactured goods, 61–62
summary of tariff reductions, 59
tariff profile of India and TPP countries, 66
tariff concessions in, provisions on, 57–61
TPP as template for negotiations, 1
negotiating objectives as precedents for WTO, 22
TPP chapter on e-commerce, 97
TPP chapter on telecommunication services, 94
TPP chapter on temporary entry for business persons, 92
TPP's IPR Chapter
Article 18.37, 159
Article 18.51, 164
Article 51, 166, 167
Article 18.18, 168
Article 18.76, 166, 168
Article 18.48, 160
TPP's TBT Chapter, 223, 227
Article 5, 218, 223, 228
Article 2, 218
Article 6, 219
Article 8.7, 219
trade bargaining skewed, 25
trade facilitation, 297–300
advance rulings, 298
appeal, 298

automation, 298–99
confidentiality, 300
customs cooperation, 297–98
express shipment, 299
penalties, 299
publication, 299
release of goods, 299
request for advice or information, 298
review, 298
Trade in Services Agreement (TiSA), 76
trademarks
　general provisions, 118
　non-traditional trademark, 168–69
　well-known trademarks
　　focus on non-traditional trademarks and strengthening of well-known trademarks, 120–24
Trade Marks Act, 1999, 168
trade remedies, 294–97
　anti-dumping and countervailing duties, 296–97
　implications, for India, 297
　transitional safeguard measures, 294–96
　　compensation, right to, 295–96
　　consultations, 295–96
　　duration, 295
　　imposition, 295
　　notification of action, 295
　　transition period, 294
Trans-Pacific Partnership Agreement (TPP), 1, 304
　anti-dumping (AD), 296–97
　blueprint for multilateral, provisions providing
　　developing countries, be compelled to use, 25–27
　　evidence reviewing, 18–19
　　negotiating objectives as precedents for WTO, 22
　　relevance of, 19–25
　contentious provisions, 31
　contents of
　　accession of new parties to, 7–9
　　description of, 4–5
　　EIF, 6
　　ratification and entry into force of, 5, 7

countervailing duties (CVD), 296–97
dispute settlement, 228
emerge
　initial stage, 3–4
　trade liberalization under P4, rules for, 4
emergency action on textile and clothing products, 292–93
environment chapter, 250
　committee, 252–53
　consultation between parties and dispute resolution, 254–55
　cooperation, 254
　environmental goods, 252
　fisheries management and elimination of fisheries subsidies, 252
　implications of, 255–58
　Montreal Protocol, 251
　provisions relating to private parties/voluntary actions—CSR, 253–54
　public consultations, 252–53
expropriation and compensation
　provision vis-à-vis Indian IIAs, 199
　provision, analysis, 197–99
global trade and investment scenario, emerging, 9
　countries in changing economic world, 10
　implications for India, 297
　implementation in a slightly modified form, 2
　Japan pushing, 2
investment chapter, relation, 210
investment protection, 184
　IIAs and foreign investment flows, 185–87
　investment, defined, 187
　investor–state dispute settlement (ISDS) mechanism, 185
　provision, analysis, 187–88
　provision vis-à-vis Indian IIAs, 188–89
investor–state dispute settlement, 210–13
manufacturing and agriculture, assessing impact

Index **339**

export duties and taxes, prohibiting, 73
government procurement, 320
India eliminating tariffs, 65–72
intellectual property, 313–17
investment, 318
LLP, 73–74
number of products in, 67–71
regulatory coherence, 321
remanufactured goods, prohibiting restrictions on, 72–73
services sector, 308–10
standards, 319–20
state-owned enterprises, 320–21
minimum standard of treatment
provision vis-à-vis Indian IIAs, 196–97
provision, analysis, 193–96
most-favoured nation (MFN)
provision vis-à-vis Indian IIAs, 192–93
provision, analysis, 191–92
motivations and triggers behind, 9–15
BATNA for the USA in Doha Round, 11, 13
China's increased economic salience in Asia, in reaction to, 11
financial interests of Big Pharma in USA, protecting, 14–17
IIAs, 11
interest of US foreign investors, protecting, 17–18
Japan's attempts at economic integration in Asia, in response to, 11
progress in WTO, 12–14
national treatment
provision vis-à-vis Indian IIAs, 190–91
provision, analysis, 189–90
opening of market in services, 31
performance requirements
provision vis-à-vis Indian IIAs, 203–4
provision, analysis, 199–200, 203
promote the interest of the USA, 4
public policy exceptions

provision, analysis, 206–7
regulatory coherence in, 291–92
regulatory coherence key obligations in, 300–301
regulatory coherence, impact of chapter on, 301–3
resemble the existing FTA template of the USA, 4
splitting polity in signatory countries, 27–29
trade and environment, 247
environment under WTO, 248–49
proponents of, 248
trade facilitation, 291–92
trade facilitation provisions in, 297–300
trade remedies, 291–92
consultations and right to compensation, 295–96
transition period, 294
transitional safeguard measures, 295
transfers
provision, analysis, 204–205
provision vis-à-vis Indian IIAs, 209–10
type, implications of
provisions for India, 100–102
withdrawal of the USA, from, 1
Trans-Pacific Strategic Economic Partnership Agreement, 3
transparency
labour, 219, 227, 229, 241
TRIPS minus, 178
TRIPS plus
Digital Rights Management, 139–40
rights management introduction, 140

UPOV Convention, 174, 176
Article 5, 172
Article 7, 171
Article 14, 174
Article 17, 176

wages, 234, 236, 239, 240, 243
World Trade Organisation
Cancun Ministerial Conference, USA allowed the collapse of, 12

cotton subsidies, USA avoiding discussions on, 12–13
Doha Round
    BATNA for the USA in Doha Round, 11, 13
    not reflecting interests of USA, 11–14
    no meaningful progress after 2008, 13
dominance of power play, 27
Hong Kong Ministerial, USA unable to implement decision taken at, 13
Ministerial Declaration on Trade in Information Technology Products, 20
Nairobi Ministerial Conference, role of USA, 13
Nairobi Ministerial Declaration, 13–14
    USA hostile to reaffirming the Doha mandate, 13
    window for new issues, 23
TPP as template for negotiations, 1
    negotiating objectives as precedents for WTO, 22
trade bargaining skewed, 25
WTO's Government Procurement Agreement (GPA), 259
    benefits of acceding, 260
    committed market vs covered market, 262
    committed market, de jure, 262, 265
    committee, GPA, 264
    contestable market, de facto, 264
    costs of acceding, 260, 266
    cross-border purchases, 264
    de facto closure, 264, 265
    import penetration, ratio, 264–65
    openness, level, 266
    size of public procurement markets, 261
    value of public procurement markets, 261
WTO's SPS Agreement, 223, 227, 228, 229, 249, 250
    Article 5.8, 228
WTO's Subsidies Agreement (ASCM), 281–83, 285–86
WTO's TBT Agreement, 218–20, 223, 229, 231, 246, 247, 248, 254
    Article 2, 218
    Article 5, 218
    Article 6.4, 219
WTO's TRIPS Agreement, 161, 166
    Article 33, 160
    Articles 7 and 8, 162
    Article 39.3, 162, 163
    Article 51, 166